REAL ESTATE LIMITED PARTNERSHIPS, Second Edition
   by Theodore S. Lynn and Harry F. Goldberg
ESTATE PLANNING FOR REAL ESTATE INVESTMENTS
   by Charles W. McMullen
CREATIVE REAL ESTATE FINANCING: A GUIDE TO BUYING AND
SELLING HOMES IN THE 1980s
   by Garth Marston and Hugh Kelleher
SHOPPING CENTER DEVELOPMENT AND INVESTMENT
   by Mary Alice Hines

D0765687

SHOPPING CENTER DEVELOPMENT AND INVESTMENT

SHOPPING CENTER DEVELOPMENT AND INVESTMENT

M.A. HINES

C.W. King Chair of Real Estate and Finance
Washburn University
Topeka, Kansas

A RONALD PRESS PUBLICATION

JOHN WILEY & SONS

NEW YORK • CHICHESTER • BRISBANE • TORONTO • SINGAPORE

Library of Congress Cataloging in Publication Data

Hines, Mary Alice.
   Shopping center development and investment.

   (Real estate for professional practioners)
   "Ronald Press Publication."
   Includes index.
   1. Shopping centers. 2. Shopping centers—United
States. 3. Real estate investment. 4. Real estate
investment—United States. 5. Real estate development.
I. Title II. Series

HF5430.H56 1983   332.63′24   83-6540
ISBN 0-471-86851-5

Printed in the United States of America

10 9 8 7 6 5

SERIES PREFACE

Since the end of World War II, tremendous changes have taken place in the business and residential real estate fields throughout the world. This has been evidenced not only by architectural changes, exemplified by the modern shopping center, but also in the many innovative financing responses that have enabled development of new structures and complexes, such as multiuse buildings. It can be expected that real estate development will speed in new directions at an ever increasing pace to match the oncoming needs of our time. With this perspective, the Real Estate for Professional Practitioners series has been developed in response to professional needs.

As real estate professional activities have become divided into specialties, because of intensive demand for expertise at all stages, so has there developed an increasing need for extensive training and continual education for persons directly involved or dealing in business ventures requiring detailed knowledge of realty procedures.

Perhaps no field of business endeavor is more in need of a series of professional books than real estate. Working in the practical world of business and residential construction and space utilization, or at advanced levels of college training covering these areas, one is constantly aware that too little of existing creative thinking has been transcribed into viable books. Many of the books that have been written do not thoroughly enough encompass both the practical and theoretical aspects of complex subjects. Too often the drive for immediate answers has led to the overlooking of fundamental purposes and technical know-how that might lead to much more favorable results for the persons seeking knowledge

This series will be made up of books thoroughly and expertly expounding existing procedures in the many fields of real estate, but searching as well for innovative solutions to current and future problems. These books are intended to offer a compendium of each author's wide experience and knowledge to aid the seasoned professional.

The series is addressed to professionals in all walks of realty endeavor. These include business investors and developers, urban affairs specialists, attorneys, accountants, and the many others whose work involves real estate creativity and investment. Just as importantly, the series will present to advanced students in many realty fields the opportunity to review professional thinking that will help to stimulate their own thoughts on modern trends in housing and business construction.

We believe these goals can be achieved by the outstanding group of authors who will create the books in the series.

DAVID CLURMAN

PREFACE

This book was written to promote more profitable investment in shopping centers by more knowledgeable investors and developers. Prospective investors and developers may review the chief factors related to shopping center profitability. Real estate professionals—including commercial brokers, consultants, and developers—may review the dimensions of today's centers before advising their clients about specific developments and potential investments. The many professionals who may wish to use the book as a review of land development options include real estate attorneys, accountants, architects, real estate consultants, and real estate appraisers. Real estate companies and trade associations may use the book as a training manual and study guide for in-house training seminars and short courses. The book compares the specific characteristics of shopping center development and investment to other forms of real estate development and investment.

Even though the book focuses on shopping center development and investment, it also includes necessary material on shopping center finance, valuation, operation, marketing, and management. A wide assortment of current financing techniques with numerous illustrations accompany material on the shopping center development process and investment yield calculation.

The book starts with a discussion of demand and supply analysis and recent trends. This demand–supply analysis involves nationwide, regional, and local trends in new shopping center development as well as rehabilitation and renovation. The opportunities for shopping center development and investment are followed by a practical description of the shopping center development process, with emphasis on the team approach. The factors in site selection and the possible organizational structures for adequate financing of the project are described. A review of the operational characteristics of the typical center, including aspects of management and marketing, is presented, as well as the distinctive characteristics attributed to each of the principal types of center.

The last major portion of the book is devoted to the alternative forms of financing, the possible sources of domestic and international funds, and the measurement of investment yields by commonly used methods. Some observations are made about recently accepted investment yields and yield expectations from future center investment. The various sources of investment return are included for prospective investors' purposes.

Appreciation must be expressed to the many companies that provided material used in this book. A number of contributions came from courses given in 1982 and 1983 by the University of Shopping Centers, sponsored annually by the International Council of Shopping Centers and from conversations over recent years with many of the major U.S. and European shopping center developers. The book also contains appropriate and timely items from authors of articles in the leading real estate journals of the United States.

Encouragement for the compilation and completion of this book was continually given by my parents, Alberta E. and John W. Hines.

Topeka, Kansas   M.A. Hines
August 1983

CONTENTS

ONE

INVESTMENT OPPORTUNITIES IN SHOPPING CENTERS: AN INTRODUCTION

Good investment yields have been realized from shopping centers for years, even centuries. The early civilizations of Europe and the Middle East, as well as other parts of the world, had urban market centers, and people wishing to purchase or swap goods and services flocked to these centers on market day. Those who provided the facilities for such transactions first committed a minimal amount of resources. They continued to provide the facilities for the marketplace because to do so was worthwhile financially. As the centuries passed, the investors in the market facilities contributed more funds for more elaborate shopping buildings and parking facilities with more protection from the weather and interior temperature control. Today investors create many types of shopping centers in urban locations that meet numerous shopping demands. Some investors provide funds for strictly retail facilities; others provide investment funds for mixed-use facilities devoted to retailing, office space, and transient housing. These centers of commerce that integrate consumer shopping with transient housing and workplaces require even more investment capital than the smaller centers devoted entirely to retailing. Of course, some mixed-use developments are on the same investment scale as the larger regional shopping centers of five and six department stores. Admittedly, there are all sizes of mixed-use developments and all sizes of shopping centers. For that reason it is difficult to make investment comparisons.

BASIC FORCES BEHIND PROFITABLE INVESTMENT IN SHOPPING CENTERS

Inflation Protection

The profitability of a shopping center depends on the market demand for the goods and services offered by the center. The demand for the offered goods and services must increase over time in terms of consumer buying power and numbers of consumers trading at the center. This is true because most investors want increasing returns on their capital over time. The main impetus for this phenomenon is the ever-present U.S. inflation. Inflation may exist on a relatively low level, a moderate level, or a high level, but it persists. The investor in real estate, particularly the investor in the shopping center, wants inflation protection.

The Complementary Nature of the Residential, Commercial, and Transient Housing Sectors

Consumers of retail goods and services come primarily from residential sectors, particularly when the goods desired are highly perishable or fragile. Consumers approach shopping centers from their workplaces, but transportation of purchased goods is a factor. The amount of purchased goods that an employee may take back to the workplace is limited. The merchant is faced with the need for house delivery of merchandise purchased by the employee from the nearby workplace. Therefore, most shopping centers cater to customers who live nearby, drive to the center, and carry their purchases home.

The services of a shopping center may appeal more to the employee of the nearby workplace. They may purchase and consume the center restaurants' food, use their shoe and other clothing repair facilities, bank at the center and use the services of other financial institutions, and patronize car repair and service facilities, beauty and barber shop services, and laundry and dry cleaning services. As the employee leaves the office for the day, he or she may shop at the nearby center and take purchased merchandise home by his or her usual mode of transportation. Even though mass transit facilities are used by many shopping center customers in many markets, most shopping center customers drive their cars to and from the center. Many employee-customers also drive their cars to and from their workplaces.

The goods and services of a shopping center may appeal to temporary residents of hotels and motels. Some hotel and motel guests stay at the particular facility in order to shop at the center that is close by. Some hotel and motel guests attend meetings in the hostelry and plan to shop at the center nearby before they return home. Many hotel and motel guests depend on the services of the adjacent shopping center for such things as dining facilities, clothing repair and dry cleaning services, car repair and maintenance services, and financial services. The investor in a shopping center may gain in many ways from the investment in the transient housing close by. The same investor may profitably place funds in both real property investments at the same urban location.

Need for Intensive Use of Urban Land

Urban land that is appropriate for retail use is scarce and expensive. Therefore, the investor in the shopping center must make the best use of the land available. The investor must consider in today's market vertical as well as horizontal shopping centers. The investor must consider high-rise buildings that integrate parking and community facilities on the lower floors and permanent and transient housing along with office space on the upper floors. Condominium and rental buildings are both appropriate to this type of integrated development on scarce and expensive urban land.

Parking space is needed for customer shopping. Less parking space is needed per car as the average size of the personal vehicle declines and as more shoppers use mass transit facilities, but parking space remains an important factor to the shopping center. If the investor finds land reasonably priced, ground-level parking without customer charge is most desirable for drawing customers to the center. As land becomes more valuable, parking fees for customers become necessary. If the retail stores subsidize the parking of their customers, this cost to the retail store may be significant in the periodic profit and loss statement. Parking buildings require substantial investment and no return to the investor who is not directly benefiting from the retail profit margins or gross sales.

If expensive land is required for customer parking, the investor may consider complementary parking needs of nearby building occupants. Hotels and motels need parking space primarily in the evening. Office building tenants need parking space primarily during the day. The center may attract suburban shoppers principally during the day or inner city working shoppers principally in the evenings after working hours. If the center does most of its business at the close of regular business hours, it may share parking easily with nearby office buildings. If the center does most of its business during the day with suburban nonworking housewives, the nearby hotel and motel parking demand may be complementary. Two or more adjacent land uses may profitably share the same parking space.

Integration of Shopping Center Management, Marketing, and Financing

To use a Harvard Business School phrase, "synergism," or the greatest investment rewards from a shopping center, come from the increased profitability from the integration of shopping center management, marketing, and financing. As these three factors behind shopping center performance are coordinated, the investor wins. The higher the level of coordination, the greater the investment yield that results. Management is provided by the developer and the property management firm. Marketing is accomplished by the developer, the property management company, and the merchants of the center. Financing is acquired by the developer and other owners. The owners and the lenders provide the investment capital. Any mortgage debt is supplemented with equity funds.

A Reasonable Balance of Revenues and Costs

To attain reasonable investment yields, the investor must observe a balance of revenues and costs associated with the shopping center. The revenues come from the sale of goods and services to ultimate consumers. These revenues become the gross income of the individual merchants who must pay the landlord rent and cover inventory and other operating expenses. Each merchant in the profitable center must be reasonably profitable. Therefore, each merchant must attain an operating profit after the payment of inventory costs, operating expenses, and financial charges, including rent and debt service for the storeroom improvements.

As the merchant pays rent to the landlord in the form of base rent and overage payments, the landlord retains the periodic profit or cash flow after paying any lenders their basic debt service requirements as well as equity participation. The landlord must cover operating expenses as well as financial expenses from the cash flow from the tenants. After the property management firm is compensated for its many services, the landlord must attain a reasonable profit. The landlord may be a single investor or an investment group or institution. The lender deserves a reasonable yield on his or her money. The lender may be an individual, a group of individuals, or a financial institution. The lender may provide equity capital as well as debt capital.

A reasonable balance of revenues and costs must be attained to satisfy the many investment partners of the shopping center. The several investment partners in the successful shopping center may include: the land owner, the land and building sale-leaseback sources, the developer, the equity partners of the developer, each merchant who rents space in the center, the sale-leaseback or financing sources for the key tenants who finance their own structures, the key tenants who tie up equity in their own buildings, and the mortgage lenders on the fee or leasehold estates represented in the center. Each must attain a reasonable balance among his or her individual revenues and costs to assure a viable long-term profitability for the center.

The Entrepreneurial Ability of the Developer

The ability and accountability of the developer create the profitable shopping center. His or her imagination and creative ability set up the atmosphere for the creation of the attractive shopping environment. The exterior and interior architecture must conform to the market demand as must the site location and land preparation. Since a center is built for a long-run investment, the developer forecasts the future of the current retail market demand. The market studies and feasibility analyses accomplished by inside and outside consultants substantiate the developer's preconceptions of the shopping center opportunities. When the developer approaches the key tenants for lease negotiation, he or she expresses the ideas behind the creation of the center and the relevant market demand. If the key tenants see an opportunity for profits, they negotiate lease terms. With the signed letters of intent or signed leases, the developer approaches the lender for equity and debt capital. Once the lender-investor sees an opportunity for a reasonable investment yield, he or she offers the negotiated funds and their terms to the developer who proceeds to negotiate development and construction loans for forthcoming construction and development. The developer is the key individual in the creation of investment return for all the investors involved in the establishment of the new, enlarged, or rehabilitated shopping center.

OPPORTUNITIES FOR SHOPPING CENTER DEVELOPMENT

Investors seek market yields from investments from the money, capital, and real estate markets. Therefore, real estate investment has a great deal of competition. Many investors know all about money market funds, jumbo certificates of deposit, commercial paper, Treasury bills, and other investments of the short-term money market (Exhibit 1-1). The same investors and other investors know about capital market securities such as common stock, preferred stock, tax-exempt municipal bonds, corporate bonds, mortgage bonds, mortgage loan participations, and mortgage-backed securities. Investors look at and invest in real estate securities and direct ownership interests when the yields and other competitive terms are more favorable in this market (Exhibit 1-2). Foreign and domestic investors with experience in shopping center investment realize that the yields are favorable. Shopping center yields overall are competitive with the yields overall from office building, industrial building, and hotel and motel investments. On a comparative basis, apartment building yields have not been overall as high as the yields from the previously mentioned income property types. Apartment rent increases have failed to keep up with increases in operating and financial costs in many markets. Some apartment building yields of selected building have been very competitive.

In looking over the yields from particular properties within the individual income property classifications, we find that some center yields are better than others, just as the yields from particular office buildings are better than others. Overall, real properties that are income producing are matching the market yields on the majority of capital and money market securities. The investor interested in real property investment is usually looking over competing yields from other 5- to 15-year investments of the capital market. Directly competing with income-producing properties are taxable bonds and stock. Since the shopping center developer has long been aware of the competition from the bond and stock markets, the developer has not started to develop the land for a shopping center until the overall yield as well as the initial yield has been

Exhibit 1-1.   The Trend in Money and Capital Market Interest Rates (%)

Money and Capital Market Securities	1977	1978	1979	1980	1981	1982 Feb.	1983 Feb.
Money Market Securities							
Federal funds	5.54	7.94	11.20	13.36	16.38	13.86	8.47
Three-month commercial paper	5.54	7.94	10.97	12.66	15.32	13.55	8.16
Three-month finance paper directly placed	5.49	7.80	10.47	11.49	14.08	13.08	8.07
Prime bankers' acceptances, 90 days	5.59	8.11	11.04	12.78	15.32	13.59	8.16
Certificates of deposit, secondary market, three months	5.64	8.22	11.22	13.07	15.91	14.03	8.34
Eurodollar deposits, three months	6.05	8.74	11.96	14.00	16.79	15.30	9.01
U.S. Treasury bills, secondary market, three months	5.27	7.19	10.07	11.43	14.03	12.31	7.91
Capital Market Securities							
Corporate bonds, seasoned issues							
A	8.49	9.12	10.20	12.89	15.29	16.35	13.40
Baa	8.97	9.45	10.69	13.67	16.04	17.18	13.81
Conventional mortgages on new homes, primary markets							Jan.
FHLBB series	9.01	9.54	10.77	12.65	14.74	15.25	13.49
HUD series	8.95	9.68	11.15	13.95	16.52	17.30	13.44

Source: Federal Reserve Bulletin; June 1980, Table 1.35, p. A27; March 1983, Table 1.35, p. A28, and Table 1.54, p. A40; March 1982, Table 1.35, p. A27 and Table 1.54, p. A40.

aligned with comparable yields currently available from the stock and bond markets.

The Competitive Circumstances among Income-Producing Properties

As the real estate cycles continue, many markets are ready for greater residential and commercial development. Due to the recent decline in housing starts and the low level of apartment building construction, many markets in the United States indicate a demand for more housing units. Some inner city sites are selectively available, but most of the new housing construction—single- and multifamily construction—is expected to commence in the outer portion of the central city and in the suburbs. Whenever housing units are constructed in the developing areas, we have a need for retail shopping facilities. Therefore,

Exhibit 1-2. Comparison of Total Returns (%)

Asset Time Period	Nominal	Real	Standard Deviation
1951 to 1978			
Real estate*	13.92	10.25	3.83
Bonds†	3.45	(0.22)	6.65
Equities†	11.44	7.77	18.29
1968 to 1978			
Real estate*	17.97	11.27	1.51
Bonds†	6.15	(0.55)	8.81
Equities†	4.80	(1.90)	18.40

Source: John McMahan Associates, Inc., "Comparison of Total Returns, *Urban Land*, June 1981.
*John McMahan Associates, Inc. Returns are for specific composite of properties including office, shopping center, and industrial property types.
†Ibbotson, Roger, and Sinquefield, Rex, *Stocks, Bonds, Bills and Inflation*, (The Financial Analysts Research Foundation, 1977.)

as the backlog of housing demand is satisfied, these new affluent markets will need to be served by shopping centers of various types depending upon the nature of the new demand and the extent of the new markets.

We have just passed through a two- to three-year period of massive office and industrial building development and construction. The major metropolitan areas are now overbuilt as the new space comes on the market. Secondary metropolitan areas where there is economic growth may still need office space. Investment in office buildings in those markets will continue to receive market yields. But where office buildings are overbuilt, we also find that industrial buildings and warehouses are overbuilt. Millions of square feet of industrial space will be absorbed over the next four or five years, just as the millions of square feet of office building space coming on the market now will satisfy the market for four or five years. Competitive development yields can now be anticipated from retail space as the office and industrial space yields fade for a while. Their currently high vacancy rates in most major metropolitan markets reduce their cash flows and market values. As new residential space comes on the market out of the doldrums of the early 1980s, shopping center investment yields will be competitive in these new, growing, and affluent markets.

The Impact of Inflation

Inflation affects the financial and operating costs of all income-producing properties. The investor receives the highest yields where the developer and property manager control their costs. Costs must be controlled and minimized as much as possible while revenues are maximized as much as possible.

The recent attempts by the Federal Reserve to control the money supply and thereby control the increase in inflation are noteworthy. All sectors of the economy benefit from better control of inflation. A minimal amount of inflation may prompt investment, but runaway inflation discourages investment in all media.

Reasonably high shopping center investment returns are associated with stable money and capital conditions. Highly fluctuating interest rates in the money and capital markets have recently created extensive investment uncertainty. Not knowing where interest rates are going in the near future causes the individual, company, and institutional investor to hesitate before committing funds to specific investments. When uncertain conditions prevail they await indications of differential investment advantages in various investment situations. Stable money and capital markets permit continuous investment by those who have a continuous flow of investible funds in their names or under their control. Stable conditions in the market—even though interest rates may be relatively high—are preferred by investors over unstable, uncertain market conditions.

The Impact of Recession

Recessions with lowered business profits and higher-than-normal unemployment reduce investment opportunities to some extent. For example, the profitability of some income-producing properties may decline with personal and business incomes. Some investors with substantial capital find better opportunities for investment during recessions and perhaps depressions. Selected securities and real estate interests can be purchased at bargain prices. Therefore, it can be said that recession circumstances promote investment among well-to-do-constituencies. For example, institutional investors may seek good prices for real properties whose debt service is difficult to meet by the property owner with higher-than-normal building vacancies and continued high building operating costs. For example, mortgages may turn into equity as properties are foreclosed and refinanced. The acquiring investor may benefit. The current owner-investor may suffer. Recessions bring mixed results. It is particularly true when the recession is accompanied by a high level of inflation.

The Markets for Shopping Center Investment Opportunity

The current market opportunities are linked to the recent history of shopping center development. After World War II, markets for shopping centers developed in the United States and abroad. In the United States, the various retail markets have been satisfied or at least partially satisfied with the development of neighborhood, community, specialty, regional, and superregional centers. Abroad, the shopping center movement has barely begun. There are numerous reasons for the rapid expansion in the United States and the very slow expansion abroad. Among the factors are the form of government, the control of land that could be developed for shopping centers, historic consumer buying patterns, trends in disposable personal income, availability of private capital on advantageous terms, the threat of nationalization of industry and private business, and internal political discord.

U.S. Shopping Center Development over the Last 30 Years. Most of our current shopping centers have been built since the 1950s. After the end of World War II, when the servicemen came home from military posts around the world and U.S. industry converted back to domestic production from military production, we entered a period of housing construction. The credit controls, rationing programs, and full employment for military industrial production resulted in massive personal and business savings which could be used for domestic investment. Housing was needed. Developers found reasonably priced land in the outer fringes of urban areas and developed residential subdivisions. Chain stores, full-line regular-priced and discount-priced department stores, and independent retail stores followed the consumers to the areas of new housing development. At first neighborhood and community shopping centers were created; then developers in later years saw opportunities for regional centers of one or two department stores.

Regional centers were the vogue during the 1960s and early 1970s as the developers acquired sites in the midst of growing, affluent residential areas. The regional centers developed into superregional centers when very large suburban, affluent communities were permanently developed in major metropolitan areas. As the interstate highway system was completed in the 1970s and affluent people continued to build and buy in suburban areas, advantageous sites for superregional shopping centers, planned unit developments, and major mixed-use developments were acquired in the midst of the suburban affluence. At the same time, industry was moving to suburban locations which afforded more land for desired one-story mass production, assembly line manufacturing and processing systems. Warehouses were established in the suburbs near the new industrial plants and near consumer and commercial markets. Office and shopping center developers followed the same trend as the warehouse and industrial land users. Taxes were lower in the suburbs, land was cheaper, more space was available, municipal utility lines were being extended from the inner city to the suburbs, mass transit was being extended toward the suburbs, suburban school systems were better financed, and land and the proper amenities were available for executive housing.

In the early 1980s, regional and superregional centers ring and double-ring major metropolitan areas. During the 1970s, a movement began in the direction of redevelopment with private capital of downtown shopping centers. In the 1960s, the federal government through the urban renewal, community reinvestment, and block grant programs fostered downtown and inner city redevelopment with a mixture of federal government financing and private investment. With the gradual reduction in the funding of the programs of the U.S. Department of Housing and Urban Development and the demise of the HUD new towns program, we have seen government assistance with downtown and inner city redevelopment where retail enterprise is a major factor. Private capital has also turned to renovation and expansion of existing neighborhood, community, specialty, regional, and superregional centers.

In light of this major development activity of the last 30 years, new markets for shopping center development continue to appear. The new markets are arising in already developed areas and in newly developed areas of the United States (Exhibit 1-3).

To reflect this expansion pattern, the International Council of Shopping Centers, the premier shopping center development trade association, celebrated its twenty-fifth anniversary in 1982. Its membership is still growing, and it offers more services and programs for this expanded membership group. The membership is derived from the United States and abroad.

Currently Perceived Market Opportunities. Shopping center developers often split the market into primary, secondary or middle, and tertiary or other types of markets. Opportunities for development are present in all three of the markets. The primary market is associated with downtown, inner city, and suburban shopping center markets of our largest metropolitan areas. The middle market or secondary market is associated with less densely populated urban areas. The tertiary or other type of market is associated with small markets of smaller urban areas, perhaps in essentially rural areas, or local urban settings of neighborhood market dimensions.

Many developers and investors specialize in primary market development or middle market development. For example, Paul Broadhead and Associates of Meridian, Mississippi and Dallas, Texas concentrate on middle market development on a regional scale. Some shopping center developers and investors concentrate on strip centers that serve smaller market areas. A developer who tends to fit this pattern is the Carl Storey Company of Nashville. The developer may specialize in strip centers of 50,000 square feet or less. The Davis Company, a diversified real estate company of Houston, tends to fit this pattern. The development company may specialize in strip centers of up to 300,000 square feet of gross leasable area. The Mitchell Company of Mobile, Alabama fits this shopping center development pattern even though the company is a diversified development firm. Other developers are less specialized and develop any type of center with sufficiently profitable dimensions. That type of developer may build a discount center or renovate and convert an existing center into a discount center. This type of developer may also be involved in downtown redevelopment, suburban regional and superregional center construction or expansion, and mixed-use development. Melvin Simon and Associates of Indianapolis, Indiana fits this diversified pattern. The diversified developer may operate nationwide; the specializing developer may also operate nationwide. For example, the Edward J. DeBartolo Corporation of Youngstown, Ohio tends to specialize in regional and superregional centers on a nationwide basis. The Aronov Development Company and Jim Wilson & Associates of Montgomery, Alabama tend to specialize in regional and superregional centers on a regional scale only.

Some shopping center developers serve a local area; most major developers with sizable work forces seek sites on a regional basis or on a national basis. If the particular region of the country has ample development potential, that developer need go no further. Major developers with large staffs often work in any growing, affluent part of the country. Branch offices in existing centers or mixed-use developments supplement the facilities of the headquarters office. Computer information systems often link the many company offices.

OPPORTUNITIES FOR THE REDEVELOPMENT AND EXPANSION OF EXISTING SHOPPING CENTERS

As foreign and domestic investors seek outlets for their capital that promise ample overall yields and inflation protection, they perceive investment opportunities in existing centers as well as proposed shopping centers. In many ways, existing centers are better investments for conservative investors. The term "conservative investor" often is rightly applied to both foreign and domestic investors.

Attractions of the Existing Center

The existing shopping center has a track record. Nothing beats current and recent past sales figures for projection of future sales from retail units. The current operating statement and capital improvement schedule show what the shopping center at the particular site can produce under established conditions. The investor can observe operating conditions of the center and each of its current and past tenants. The investor can play the "what if" game. What if the management plan were altered? Would the net operating income increase or decrease? What if the tenant in Storeroom 3 were replaced by the tenant who wishes to move into that space? How much would the storeroom and center profits increase? What if the current tenant were given more space? What financial impact would result? What if the current tenant were to redecorate? What if all the tenants were given less storeroom space than previously allocated? Would their sales per square foot increase? Would the overage payments to the lender and investor increase? If reduced space were allocated each tenant as leases came up for renewal, would the additional tenants put into the center increase the overall square foot sales figures? Would the increased sales result in higher before- and after-tax cash flows and increased percentage or overage rents? Would the landlord and lender be rewarded by more equity participation with the rise in net operating income and cash flows? The operating history of the center would go a long way toward answering the foregoing questions. A proposed center at a particular site affords only conjecture about

Exhibit 1-3. Summary of 1981 New Shopping Center Locations*

State	Opened in 1981		Under Construction		Planned		Total 1981 Listings	
	Centers	GLA†	Centers	GLA†	Centers	GLA†	Centers	GLA†
Alabama	7	739,607	5	502,060	3	2,754,972	15	3,996,639
Alaska	—	—	—	—	—	—	—	—
Arizona	12	1,480,621	4	1,642,160	—	—	16	3,122,781
Arkansas	2	314,440	3	659,000	—	—	5	973,440
California	47	7,408,941	38	4,273,578	14	2,003,850	99	13,686,369
Colorado	1	166,000	7	2,792,646	3	635,480	11	3,594,126
Connecticut	3	350,000	3	238,000	3	347,500	9	935,500
Delaware	—	—	1	250,000	—	—	1	250,000
Florida	37	5,074,170	26	3,946,119	5	5,286,836	68	14,307,125
Georgia	3	965,000	4	1,213,730	1	309,000	8	2,487,730
Hawaii	1	55,000	—	—	—	—	1	55,000
Idaho	3	1,275,250	—	—	—	—	3	1,275,250
Illinois	14	2,993,717	1	131,000	3	435,000	18	3,559,717
Indiana	6	1,329,723	1	350,000	—	—	7	1,679,723
Iowa	2	150,000	—	—	1	150,000	3	300,000
Kansas	5	1,379,800	2	320,000	3	604,000	10	2,303,800
Kentucky	6	1,012,101	9	1,875,154	4	1,138,000	19	4,025,255
Louisiana	7	921,746	8	993,068	2	722,000	17	2,636,814
Maine	—	—	—	—	—	—	—	—
Maryland/DC	8	1,026,240	3	328,000	1	1,600,000	12	2,954,240
Massachusetts	6	980,268	1	100,000	1	250,000	8	1,330,268
Michigan	4	656,546	3	149,000	2	619,000	9	1,424,546
Minnesota	—	—	5	658,000	—	—	5	658,000
Mississippi	9	882,939	—	—	1	1,000,000	10	1,882,939
Missouri	9	1,109,250	2	565,000	3	1,590,000	14	3,264,250
Montana	—	—	—	—	—	—	—	—

State	No.	GLA	No.	GLA	No.	GLA	Total No.	Total GLA
Nebraska	3	245,800	1	120,000	4	427,000	8	792,800
Nevada	3	535,000	—	—	1	900,000	4	1,435,000
New Hampshire	5	845,000	3	1,234,000	—	—	8	2,079,000
New Jersey	1	6,860	3	483,000	3	1,761,350	7	2,251,210
New Mexico	3	1,535,342	3	241,750	—	—	6	1,777,092
New York	11	1,507,500	1	240,000	8	5,095,000	20	6,842,500
North Carolina	7	442,750	3	296,000	5	1,495,790	15	2,234,540
North Dakota	1	190,000	—	—	1	250,000	2	440,000
Ohio	11	2,129,000	2	183,500	3	2,188,120	16	4,500,620
Oklahoma	4	479,805	—	—	—	—	4	479,805
Oregon	—	—	3	510,997	—	—	3	510,997
Pennsylvania	14	2,128,100	6	1,995,000	10	4,309,000	30	8,432,100
Rhode Island	—	—	—	—	1	300,000	1	300,000
South Carolina	5	588,813	2	102,000	2	272,758	9	963,571
South Dakota	—	—	—	—	—	—	—	—
Tennessee	13	2,098,999	5	510,000	6	3,170,208	24	5,779,207
Texas	34	11,301,555	19	3,919,603	12	5,530,897	65	20,752,055
Utah	2	777,192	2	213,018	—	—	4	990,210
Vermont	—	—	—	—	—	—	—	—
Virginia	8	4,297,848	5	1,144,000	2	1,188,000	15	6,629,848
Washington	9	2,342,200	1	85,000	1	634,000	11	3,061,200
West Virginia	1	1,083,155	—	—	—	—	1	1,083,155
Wisconsin	2	1,100,000	4	784,000	2	569,000	8	2,453,000
Wyoming	2	759,000	1	215,000	—	—	3	974,000

Source: "Expansions, Renovations Pick Up Pace of Center Activity," Shopping Center World, 11:1 January, 1982, p. 129. Copyright 1982 Communication Channels, Inc., 6285 Barfield Road, Atlanta, GA 30328.

*This table represents only those U.S. projects listed during 1981 in the "New Shopping Center Locations" columns of Shopping Center World. The centers listed in that section have been tabulated by state in three categories: (1) those which opened during 1981; (2) those still under construction at the end of the year; and (3) those that were planned to be completed sometime after 1981. This table is by no means a total accounting of all the shopping centers which opened during the year or which are now planned; it is simply a summary of SCW's "New Locations" monthly department. While this tabulation does not represent all of the building activity which went on during 1981, the editors of the magazine feel it does point to some current trends in shopping center development.

†Gross leasable area, in square footage.

sales possibilities at that site. The existing center has a sales, taxable profit, and cash flow history that is observable in "black and white."

Growth in Mature, Densely Populated Higher-Income Markets

Due to the rapid growth of the various types of centers, many existing centers are located in mature, densely populated markets. Many of these markets have benefited from the rise of personal and business income over recent years. The increase in population and buying power of the established market may call for more goods and services from the existing center. The signal that this phenomenon has occurred is the unusually high sales per square foot of gross leasable area of the existing center. As average sales per square foot for the center exceed the magic number of $200 and are propelled toward $300 and $400 a square foot, the investor has an indication that more capital investment is needed for expansion of the goods and services offerings of the existing center.

The investment in larger shopping facilities in this existing center depends on the sales forecast. Will the customer group retain their current buying habits? Will their personal and business income continue to increase? Will the market continue to seek the same general quality and quantity of the center's goods and services? Will current and proposed competitive centers draw a major portion of this clientele away? Have transportation facilities altered so that customers are encouraged or discouraged in their travel to the center? Is the center offering the correct quality and quantity of goods and services for future sales? Are more consumers moving into the area? Are the living and working conditions of the market area conducive to further population and buying power growth? Are other developers building, expanding, and renovating additional residential, commercial, and industrial structures in the market area? Will this investor's capital be combined theoretically with the investments of others in the further development of this mature and densely populated market?

It is generally recognized that neighborhoods go through cycles of growth. When the neighborhood is newly formed, new development is in vogue. The neighborhood will later reach its maturity and then start to decline in property values and business activity. Many neighborhoods then reach a revitalization stage where neighborhood growth again occurs. Property values and business activity reach a new peak. This new peak in neighborhood development may be followed by another period of investor apathy and stable or declining market conditions.

As the developer or source of funds, equity or debt, considers further investment in a residential, commercial, industrial, or institutional neighborhood, that investor must be assured of the current place of the neighborhood in the neighborhood economic cycle. If the neighborhood is currently in a slight slump in business activity, the investor may get a good price for the investment venture and see greater profits and cash flows as the neighborhood develops upward in business activity. If the neighborhood is currently showing stable economic values, a reasonable amount of capital may be placed in the particular land and structures. The stability of market conditions lends itself to investment for the future. The investor can forecast increased growth from this stable economic base.

Some spectacular examples of recent investment in existing shopping centers may come from the Galleria mixed-use center of Houston; Water Tower Place in Chicago; and Lenox Square Shopping Center in Atlanta. Increased infusions of capital appear justified by the investors even though interest rates have recently reached new peaks and lending terms are relatively stringent (Exhibit 1-4). The investors have seen opportunities for higher yields from higher loan rates, shorter terms, and greater equity participation.

Exhibit 1-4. 1981 Upgrading of Existing Shopping Centers[*]

	Expansion		Remodeled/ Renovated		1981 Totals	
State	Centers	GLA[†]	Centers	GLA[†]	Centers	GLA[†]
Alabama	—	—	1	60,294	1	60,294
Alaska	1	175,000	—	—	1	175,000
Arizona	—	—	1	80,000	1	80,000
California	18	1,655,850	8	2,449,985	26	4,105,835
Colorado	4	159,746	—	—	4	159,746
Connecticut	—	—	1	668,000	1	668,000
Florida	7	981,250	1	1,105,000	8	2,086,250
Georgia	1	235,000	—	—	1	235,000
Hawaii	—	—	1	1,500,000	1	1,500,000
Idaho	1	102,000	—	—	1	102,000
Illinois	5	706,000	4	1,802,540	9	2,508,540
Indiana	2	806,000	—	—	2	806,000
Iowa	1	305,000	—	—	1	305,000
Kansas	1	12,000	—	—	1	12,000
Louisiana	2	70,000	1	588,000	3	658,000
Maine	1	45,600	1	100,000	2	145,600
Maryland/DC	—	—	1	220,000	1	220,000
Massachusetts	—	—	5	1,967,215	5	1,967,215
Michigan	4	316,000	—	—	4	316,000
Minnesota	2	47,000	—	—	2	47,000
Mississippi	1	55,600	—	—	1	55,600
Missouri	6	679,000	—	—	6	679,000
Montana	1	60,000	—	—	1	60,000
New Jersey	1	5,800	2	1,460,000	3	1,465,800
New Mexico	1	39,500	1	19,700	2	59,200
New York	4	330,000	2	389,539	6	719,539
North Carolina	1	22,000	—	—	1	22,000
Ohio	1	125,000	3	2,494,074	4	2,619,074

(Continued)

Exhibit 1-4. *(Continued)*

State	Expansion		Remodeled/ Renovated		1981 Totals	
	Centers	GLA[†]	Centers	GLA[†]	Centers	GLA[†]
Oklahoma	1	51,000	—	—	1	51,000
Pennsylvania	9	1,084,845	1	80,000	10	1,164,845
South Carolina	1	123,000	—	—	1	123,000
South Dakota	—	—	1	525,000	1	525,000
Tennessee	1	72,000	—	—	1	72,000
Texas	5	1,317,320	2	132,279	7	1,449,599
Utah	1	730,000	—	—	1	730,000
Virginia	1	45,000	—	—	1	45,000
Washington	4	406,000	1	414,085	5	820,085
Wisconsin	1	195,000	—	—	1	195,000
U.S. totals	89	10,957,511	38	16,055,711	127	27,013,222

Source: "Expansions, Renovations Pick Up Pace of Center Activity," *Shopping Center World*, 11:1, January 1982, p. 130. Copyright 1982 Communications Channels, Inc., 6285 Barfield Road, Atlanta, Ga. 30328.
*During the past year, 127 U.S. projects involving the upgrading of existing shopping centers were listed in SCW's "New Shopping Center Locations" columns. Of those, 89 involved expansion (either opened during 1981, under way or planned) amounting to just under 11 million square feet; 38 projects involved remodeling or other renovation work adding up to some 16 million square feet, a major indication that many older shopping centers are "face-lifting" and recycling space.
†Gross leasable area, in square feet.

Leverage the Original Construction and Land Costs

Existing centers that are performing well today were built with less expensive capital and at lower land and building costs. If more funds are invested to gain even greater sales, profit, and cash flow results, the new, higher-priced funds are joining the original, lower-priced funds to gain a leverage effect. The weighted average cost of earlier funds and present funds is relatively reasonable. The return on this weighted cost is better than the future returns on higher-cost funds for an entirely new center. The customer attraction or potential may be just as good from the refurbished and expanded center as from a totally new center at a site that is not as favorably located. If a totally new center can be constructed today at a significantly better location, the new investment on shorter terms at relatively high rates may be justified. The additional investment in an existing center versus investment in a totally new center involves a comparable financial analysis based on sales and cash flow predictions under both circumstances.

TWO

REGIONAL EXPANSION AND SHOPPING CENTER INVESTMENT

Emerging markets for new and expanded retailing complexes are linked to regional expansion. Trends in regional expansion are important to shopping center development. Regional expansion is one of the favorable conditions for increased shopping center investment. New shopping center markets are also found in regions that are not expanding rapidly. These regions may have profit opportunities for the investors that even exceed the profit opportunities to be gained from the rapidly expanding regions of the country. But, at this point, let us concentrate on shopping center investment opportunities in the expanding regions of the United States.

THE REGIONS OF CONTINUED, RAPID GROWTH IN POPULATION AND INCOME

In recent times, the Southeast, the Southwest, California, and the Mountain States have been growing rapidly in terms of population and personal and business incomes. The populous areas of the Northeast and Midwest, particularly the major urban areas, have been losing population and businesses to the growth regions.

The Northeast has been losing population because of industry relocation in the growth areas, high taxation, extreme winter weather, and increased crime rates. Increases in property values and building rents in many places have outrun growth in business and personal incomes. For example, the increase in Manhattan real estate values has come from the scarcity of desired space, the prevalence of massive sources of funds for real estate investment in Manhattan, and the need for headquarters office space in Manhattan by U.S. and foreign private and public organizations. The Northeast keeps gaining population because of job opportunities and normal population increases. The massive welfare and crime problems are counteracted by the presence of unusual concentrations of high- and upper-middle-income residents in the Northeast, not just Manhattan. The older urban centers of the Northeast represent massive amounts of investible funds. Much of the growth of the expanding regions is propelled by the investible funds from the Northeast and Midwest that seek profit opportunities beyond their regional boundaries. Many of the investment sources including the major financial institutions are located in the Northeast and Midwest.

The Midwest has been losing population because of economic and winter weather conditions. The Northeast and the Midwest have had unusually extreme winter weather conditions for a number of years. Many residents have decided not to tolerate the snow drifts and ice any more and have been attracted by job opportunities in the West and especially the Southwest. More and more retired persons with sufficient financial resources have been moving to the regions with warmer climates year-round.

The extended recession of the late 1970s and early 1980s has reduced employment in the Northeast and the Midwest. The auto companies and the many related industries and "parasite" companies have laid off large numbers of employees on temporary and permanent bases. Of course, the auto industry has not been the only industry to feel the financial impact of the continued recession with inflation. Most of the basic industries are housed in the Northeast and the Midwest, as are many of the financial and operating headquarters of major U.S. companies. Many of these companies merely have plants, subsidiaries, warehouses, and district and divisional offices in the southern and western growth areas.

A period of prosperity with controlled inflation would probably prompt further growth in the Northeast and the Midwest as well as in the South and the West. Increased business profits and increased employment would mean higher personal incomes and greater economic growth in all areas of the country including the so-called "economically stagnant" Northeast and Midwest. Growth of the U.S. economy would stimulate investment in all regions of the United States.

THE GROWTH OF THE SOUTHEAST REGION

Florida continues to be the state of greatest economic growth of the Southeast region. The climate is conducive to part-time or full-time retirement housing. The climate also attracts tourism and condominium development. The natural resources and the space available inland encourage commercial and industrial development by U.S. and foreign investors. The part- and full-time residential communities on both coasts, inland, and in the Florida Keys must be served by retailing and wholesaling enterprises. Therefore, the growing residential population has prompted heavy commercial development including massive shopping center investment. The funds for the real estate investment have come from foreign and domestic sources.

Much of the real estate growth of the Southeast has been attributed to foreign investment. Actually, the majority of the invested funds in real estate has come from U.S. sources—institutional, corporate, syndicate, and personal. However, some of the so-called "U.S. sources" have hidden foreign capital that has been pooled with U.S. capital in money and capital funds managed by North American institutions and investment advisors.

Foreign investors from all over the world are represented in Florida. Research shows, though, that most of the foreign investment comes from Central American, Caribbean, and South American countries and from Europe. A small percentage comes from the Middle East and from the Far East.

Part of the growth in shopping center investment in Florida has come from the foreign investment activity. Centers in the southern portions of Florida in particular have felt the influx of foreign capital. Foreigners from Central America, South America, and Western Europe have deposited funds in south Florida banks and have invested in U.S. bank and industrial corporation stock and business assets. They have also invested in residential properties and shopping centers of various dimensions. Much of the investment in Florida is tied to foreign investor need for capital security; often they are fleeing from socialist political regimes where nationalization of business and industry threatens. Many foreigners find the living conditions of Florida similar to or better than those of their native habitats.

The enactment of numerous environmental protection laws which has come as a result of Florida's economic growth gives the shopping center developer and investor problems. Florida residents have encouraged their state legislators to pass unusually stringent environmental regulations and rules. Almost any kind of land development project prompts the need for thorough environmental impact reports to state and federal environmental agencies who dispense the necessary licenses and permits with their approval of the proposed projects. Some Florida municipal governments have passed ordinances which control urban growth. Sewer moratoriums prove to be one of the devices for controlled growth which affect shopping center development. Emission control standards affect plans for shopping centers intended to serve customers who drive to and park at the shopping center site. Developers must consider water control standards, as rain water that flows from shopping center parking lots can create pools of standing water in nearby residential areas. Water drainage and pollution standards must be met. Some of these environmental protection controls exist in every area of the country. Some additional controls have been enacted by the Florida legislature for their state's protection.

Georgia's growth has been centered in Atlanta and a few urban areas such as Savannah. The corridor through Georgia along the freeway linking the North with Florida has seen considerable economic growth. Otherwise, the development in Georgia has been rather gradual and on a localized basis around industrial complexes such as the textile mills of west central Georgia. Atlanta is continuing to develop as a prime center of commerce, banking, retailing, and wholesaling for the Southeast. The major commitment to the Hartsfield International Airport indicates Georgia's and Atlanta's expectations for further economic growth in the region. Large merchandise marts are located in the Atlanta central business district.

The Carolinas have made a concerted effort to attract business and industry to previously undeveloped areas. Centers for applied and theoretical research are located near office complexes and industrial plants where a lot of research and development is going on. These centers of business in the Research Triangle area near Chapel Hill, North Carolina prompt community development for affluent professional people with supportive middle-income personnel. Growing residential and business populations with these characteristics appeal to shopping center developers.

The states of Alabama and Mississippi have also seen recent growth. The urban centers of Birmingham, Mobile, Montgomery, and Jackson have been the locations for the expansion of financial services, district and divisional office development, industrial development related to the generous supply of energy sources, and the subsequent increase in retailing and wholesaling services. Mississippi and Alabama are still relatively unexploited by business and industry. Further economic development with additional domestic and foreign investment in business and industry will prompt greater shopping center development in growing residential and commercial areas within and outside the major metropolitan areas.

THE GROWTH OF THE SOUTHWEST REGION

Room remains for expansion in the moderate climates of the Southwest. The dry, warm winters of Arizona continue to attract "snowbirds" (winter residents from the North) and permanent residents. Major companies have relocated in the area to capture the benefits of the region. Company employment attracts permanent residents to the area. Resort facilities attract tourists while planned retirement communities attract the elderly on a permanent basis.

The state of Texas continues to display rapid economic growth. The mild year-round climate attracts relocating companies, households, and families who are employed by new and existing Texas companies. The political climate of Texas tends to favor economic growth. For example, it is said that there are no zoning ordinances governing the future land development of the city of Houston. The forces of supply and demand are permitted to determine the land use design of that major city. Hundreds—perhaps thousands—of people migrate to the cities of Houston and Dallas every day. Residential and commercial development accompanies the massive migration from other parts of the United States.

The oil fields of Texas and Oklahoma and the companies auxiliary to the oil business fuel the expansion of this portion of the Southwest. Reports show that most of the millions of new square footage of office buildings in downtown Houston are occupied by oil and oil-related businesses. The growth of Oklahoma City is partially attributed to the growth of the oil business. Even part of the economic growth of Dallas is associated with the oil industry. As long as oil and oil by-product prices are relatively high and new domestic oil sources are scarce, this oil-based economic growth should persist. Since fall, 1981 worldwide oil prices have generally declined due to decelerated use of gasoline and other oil-based products, but petroleum prices per barrel and oil company profits still remain relatively high because of the continuing scarcity of oil in locations worldwide.

As profitable companies with large labor forces and financially secure retirees are attracted to the Southwest, including the attractive states of New Mexico, Texas, and Arizona, land developers will find suitable sites for shopping centers in markets of growing populations with rising disposable incomes. Domestic and foreign investors and developers have increasingly been drawn to the Southwest real estate market. We should note that many Canadian and French land developers have been particularly attracted to the Southwest. Investors from all over the world have sought real estate investment opportunities in this area.

Shopping center development involving all types and configurations has been part of the Southwest investment movement. The multilevel, multi-building facility called the Houston Galleria has recently been expanded by the Gerald Hines Interests. Another Galleria with similar luxury hotels and office buildings with approximately 500,000 square feet of retail space on approximately four levels has been created by the Gerald Hines Interests in Dallas. The retail anchors are Marshall Field & Company, headquartered in Chicago, and Saks Fifth Avenue of New York. In addition to these extravagant retail-hotel-office centers, many neighborhood, community, and specialty centers serve smaller markets close to residential and commercial areas.

THREE

THE GENERAL ATTRACTIONS OF SHOPPING CENTER INVESTMENT

In an era of high gasoline costs, with consumers willing to purchase a variety of durable and nondurable goods and services for their businesses and households, the shopping center has become a vital factor in the lives of Americans. These planned complexes of retail stores and service units within easy walking or driving distance of many consumers may provide a wide variety of convenience, shopping, and specialty goods and services. The various types of planned retail complexes—shopping centers—are often characterized as neighborhood, community, regional, superregional, and specialty centers. The investment characteristics of each of these center types tend to be similar, but differences of risk and return in general do exist among the various types. These differences are covered later.

THE REWARDS OF SHOPPING CENTER INVESTMENT

Psychological and financial rewards exist for the investor. If the investor places debt or equity money in a local center, that investor may drive by, walk through, view the customer crowds, and admire the architecture of the center. The psychological enjoyment and satisfaction are unmeasurable. Without the expected financial rewards, though this psychological reward is tarnished. The return on investment in the center must surpass the investor's possible yields on alternative investments or the satisfaction in the investment is short-lived.

The shopping center investor is an owner or lender or perhaps both at one time. The lender expects a return in the form of fixed or variable interest on the mortgage amount, and perhaps some form of equity participation. The lender may finance the center on the basis of a convertible mortgage; that is, the mortgage may be converted into equity or ownership at the exercise of the prearranged option to convert. Until the mortgage debt is converted to an equity position in the center, the original owners meet the obligations of the mortgage debt. The equity participation, otherwise, may take the form of creditor participation in:

Cash flow before taxes
Gross revenues collected from the tenants
Net operating income

In periods of high money costs, inflation, and substantial investible funds in the hands of lenders, the lenders may become equity partners as well as creditors of center owners. Regardless of the financial background of the equity investor in the center, reasonable return is expected on the investment. The yield on the investment usually comes from several possible sources:

Periodic cash flow
Tax-free proceeds from refinancing
Equity buildup through mortgage repayment
Capital appreciation
Tax shelter
Hedges against inflation

Periodic Cash Flow

When the cash operating expenses (fixed, variable, and repair and maintenance), estimated vacancy allowance and bad debt loss, and debt service payments are subtracted from the total gross income, the cash flow before taxes is realized. The periodic cash flow received by the investor may vary because of fluctuations in tenant overage rents, operating expenses, debt service payments, and other factors. Percentage or overage rents depend on the gross revenues or net incomes of tenants. For instance, merchandising and selling risks are associated with each tenant of the center; therefore, the rents received by the landlord vary. When the mortgage lenders participate in the good fortunes of the center in the form of various types of equity participation, these fluctuating debt service payments influence the residual cash flow payments before taxes to the equity investors. Federal income tax payments vary according to the tax-deductible expenses of the center. If returns to creditors increase from increased equity participation sums, then the tax burden will possibly decline. If the variable returns to the creditors decline, the tax burden of the equity investors may increase. Therefore, the cash flow to equity after taxes is subject to fluctuation.

Tax-Free Proceeds from Refinancing

When a center is refinanced, there is an opportunity for investor receipt of tax-free proceeds. For example, if the existing mortgage on the center has a balance of $15,000,000, the owner may refinance the center when lender terms are perceived to be advantageous. The refinancing at perhaps a lower interest rate may increase the mortgage balance to $20,000,000. In essence, the Internal Revenue Service considers the new cash gained by the landlord, the $5,000,000, to be tax free. This is one form of yield to the owner.

The refinancing may be accomplished to prepare the center for sale. The owner may wish to pocket the tax-free refinancing proceeds and still increase the leverage for the prospective owner, which may be an attractive selling feature. The return on equity for the new owner may be increased with the higher amount of debt now placed on the property. For this favorable situation to exist, generally the cost of the new debt must be less than the overall return on the property; that is, net operating income to total investment should exceed the effective cost of the debt as a percentage of the total new funds borrowed.

Equity Buildup through Mortgage Repayment

Mortgage financing usually forces the center owner, the mortgagor, to save. As the debt service on a mortgage is paid, this payment usually covers the interest income to the mortgage plus the return of principal. Admittedly, many shopping center loans require interest only for a short, early period of the mortgage term or for the total period of the mortgage, and a balloon payment at the maturity of the mortgage. If the debt service involves principal repayment, the owner accumulates equity in the property through this forced repayment of principal.

Capital Appreciation

In this inflationary era, we expect property values to increase over time. This is only a common expectation and may not occur. The value of a property such as a shopping center may increase over time, depending on the location, the consumer buying power, customer acceptance of the center, interest rates, and relative operating costs and revenues. The appreciation or depreciation in value may also stem from investor interest in the type of income-producing property. If there is great investor demand for center ownership, the value of the center usually climbs with the active bidding for the ownership, as occurred in 1979 and 1980. If investor demand subsides, the values tend to fall to normal or even subnormal levels.

More favorable financing of one center may cause its value to exceed the value of another similar center with less favorable financing. This occurs because the capitalization rate for the center valuation is lower for the center with the more favorable financing. (Derivation of capitalization rates and their use is discussed in Chapter 11).

How do you know what the capital appreciation actually is? Merely subtract the purchase price from the sale price. It has been possible to gain an annual compound rate of growth in the center value from 10 to 15 percent in recent years.

Tax Shelter

Depreciation is the key factor in the tax shelter derived from the ownership of income-producing property. As of 1982, the owner of a shopping center may use the following methods of depreciation accounting: (1) 175% declining balance, and (2) straight-line methods. If the 175% declining balance method is used, all depreciation expense taken for tax purposes is subject to recapture at the sale of the nonresidential property. Most real estate investors view the depreciation expense as a noncash expense even though they realize that real property requires monies for renovation and repairs over time to keep the property operating at its full potential.

Depreciation, considered as a noncash expense, gives the taxpayer-owner tax relief. For example, if the center generates a net operating income of $500,000, mortgage interest payable amounts to $200,000, and depreciation expense is calculated for tax purposes to be $350,000, the property will generate a tax loss that operating period.

Net operating income	$500,000
Less: mortgage interest expense	$200,000
Balance before depreciation expense	$300,000
Less: depreciation expense	$350,000
Taxable income or (loss)	($ 50,000)

If the center owner or ownership entity falls into a 45 percent overall tax bracket, a tax savings of $22,500 will result ($50,000 × 0.45 = $22,500). In this case, the $300,000 of otherwise taxable income is sheltered by the noncash depreciation expense from federal income taxation. Even if the depreciation expense has been only $250,000, the otherwise taxable income of $300,000 would have been reduced to $50,000.

Balance before depreciation expense	$300,000
Less: depreciation expense	250,000
Taxable income	$ 50,000

Instead of paying 45 percent of $300,000, or $135,000, to Uncle Sam, the taxpayer-owner pays only 45 percent of $50,000 or $22,500. The depreciation allowance tends to reduce the necessary payment of federal income taxes according to the current tax law.

Tax Shelter and Developers. If a developer is working only for a fee and does not hold an ownership interest in the center, that developer may have a high tax position with few large tax-deductible items each year. He or she is looking for compensation in terms of tax shelter. When the developer holds an ownership position in the center, the tax shelter opportunities from the center may be very important to the developer or very insignificant. The importance of the tax shelter opportunities depends upon the developer's tax position in light of the tax shelter opportunities from the ownership of other depreciable properties. That developer may have need for little additional tax shelter since the other real property holdings have already reduced the developer's tax status to a low level. If depreciation deductions are made, only straight-line depreciation methods may be useful even though accelerated methods may be available for use. If this developer has partners who need large amounts of tax shelter, the accelerated depreciation methods which are available for the property owner-ship may be used to compensate the other owners. The developer in this situation may want principally cash flow from the project while the individual partners may want various amounts of tax shelter depending upon their indi-vidual and personal tax positions.

If the owners form a general or limited partnership, the depreciation deduc-tions for the property may flow through to the individual partners. The same thing is true if the ownership is syndicated in a form of partnership arrange-ment. If the partners form a joint venture for this single property development and investment, those partners may receive distributions of depreciation de-ductions.

If a corporation holds the ownership of the center, though, only the corpora-tion itself may benefit from the tax shelter offered by the noncash depreciation deductions. The depreciation cannot flow through to the individual owners of the corporation. The tax shelter aspects of the corporation would have more significance if the business entity is a personal holding company made of officers who are family members.

If the developer is a foreign-based owner, the tax shelter opportunities of the center and their usefulness depend on the taxation of the developer by the foreign government. Generally foreign investments in U.S. shopping centers are structured legally so that their periodic incomes and often capital gains are not subject to U.S. federal income taxation.

Tax Shelter and Investors. If the investor or investment company is domiciled in a foreign country, the tax shelter benefits of the shopping center may be of no interest to the investor, regardless of the investor's primary line of business.

The investor may be a financial institution which is not subject to income taxation at home or abroad. For example, U.S. qualified pension funds are not subject to federal income taxation; therefore, tax shelters are of no interest. Real estate investment trusts which conform to the special Internal Revenue

Service tax regulations also are tax exempt. Only their cash distributions to their holders of shares of beneficial interest are taxable as part of the overall taxable income of these stockholders. If the cash distribution is a return of capital, it is not taxable.

Some of the American financial institutions which invest in shopping centers are subject to lower than normal corporate taxation. After U.S. life insurance companies of deduct all the eligible reserves for contingent losses, they are not subject to as heavy a tax burden as regular American corporations are. Even commercial banks and thrift institutions—savings and loan associations and mutual savings banks—which are subject to federal income taxation experience a lighter tax burden than regular industrial corporations because they, too, may deduct reserves for possible future loan and security losses.

The investor, on the other hand, may benefit enormously from the tax shelter possibilities of shopping center ownership. Individual owners and partners who are subject to high levels of tax payments find great benefit in the depreciation potential of the high depreciable base of the shopping center buildings and other site improvements. Found in this group are the physicians, architects, accountants, celebrities from the sports world, entertainers, and other self-employed persons with high incomes.

Hedge against Inflation

The current shopping center lease terms help protect the landlord from erosion of investment returns from inflation. When inflation, as represented by the Consumer Price Index, ranges from 9 to 12 percent per year, the landlord particularly is aware of the need for inflation protection of the property returns. Therefore, many shopping center landlords today prefer relatively short-term indexed net leases that have percentage rent clauses. The competition permits many landlords to build most of these characteristics into new store leases. The retailers who have signed center leases in the last few years have become familiar with these inflation-protection agreements. The landlords have recently started to pass on to the tenants all operating expenses possible and future increases in operating expenses in the form of net leases. Inflation protection comes primarily from the percentage lease clauses and the indexation of the basic square footage rents.

The Impact of Net Leases. The landlord passes on to the tenant either (1) all of the landlord's historical operating expenses for the center, or (2) only that part of the expense which has been incurred by the landlord since the lease was signed. In the latter instance, the landlord continues to pay the operating expense amount that existed when the lease was signed.

These are the kinds of operating expenses that are passed on to the tenant:

Hazard insurance for the real property
Heating, ventilating, and air conditioning costs for common areas

Electricity and other fuel costs associated with the exterior and interior of the center

Property *ad valorem* taxes

Merchants association costs or marketing fund and advertising costs

Common area maintenance costs

Since the tenants today agree to pay many of the costs historically paid by the landlord, the center owner now experiences a much lower operating ratio based on effective gross income or total gross income than was experienced in earlier years. (The operating ratio is the portion of gross income or effective gross income which is consumed by operating expenses.)

The Impact of Percentage Leases. When the tenant grosses revenues over an established dollar amount, the percentage clause of the lease goes into effect. The landlord usually participates in a portion of the gross revenues over this base amount. For example, the percentage lease may call for landlord participation in 5 percent of the gross revenues of the tenant over $600,000 per year. If the tenant generates $750,000 that year, or $250 gross income per square foot in a 3,000-square-foot store, the tenant will pay the landlord overage rent of $7,500 − ($750,000 − $600,000) × 0.05 − for that year.

Because the merchandise and services are priced higher by the tenants as inflation occurs, the landlord participates in the profitability of the tenant, which comes partially from the general price inflation. Of course, part of the gross revenues over the base amount is attributable to the superior merchandising skills of the tenant, the strategic location of the center, and the acceptance of the total merchant attraction of the center by the consumers in the trading area. The percentage participation of the landlord usually remains nominal; the tenant reaps most of the reward that comes in the form of sales beyond the base gross revenue amount. The percentage rents are inflation protection for the landlord because the owner is already charging the tenant a fixed or indexed amount of dollars per square foot of net leasable area of the store.

The Impact of Indexed Square Footage Leases. The basic rent of the lease may be a fixed amount per square foot of net or gross leasable store area. Most lease charges are established on the net leasable area rather than gross leasable area. Many older leases still have fixed rental charges per square foot; newer leases often have indexed charges.

The index used for the adjustment of the square footage charge to the current level of general inflation is usually the Consumer Price Index estimated and published by the Bureau of Labor Statistics of the U.S. Department of Commerce. The landlord and tenant could agree to the use of any index, widely published or not. Most parties tend to agree to use widely published indexes calculated, maintained, and standardized by the federal government.

If the index has changed significantly between the beginning of the lease period and the end of that lease period, that change is reflected by a change in the square footage rental charge per year. Therefore, the new lease period opens with a space charge per square foot the same as, lower than, or higher than that for the prior lease period. For instance, if the index has increased 10 percent over the last lease period, the new base rent for the next lease period would be increased 10 percent by the landlord. Therefore, the forthcoming monthly rental payments would rise by 10 percent for the entire lease period (often a year for the index adjustments). The adjustments based on the chosen index could be made at the end of every month, quarter, six months, or year. Today most of the index adjustments take place at the start of a new year where rental payments are made in advance on a monthly basis.

The Overall Picture of the Inflation Hedge. Indexed net percentage leases tend to give the landlord the best inflation protection in real estate today. This protection depends on the overall success of the center and the profitability of the center's merchants. In recessionary periods some tenants tend to suffer as consumers cut back their purchases in some areas. In recent recessions with inflation in the United States, consumers have continued to spend their decreasing real incomes on consumer nondurable and durable goods. Consumer spending has moderated the deeper recessionary tendencies of the economy. Industrial investment and production is usually subject to management control so that plans are held back until higher profit conditions prevail. Our economists are finding that consumer investment and spending during recent recessions may continue on a relatively high level in contrast to the actions taken in the industrial and wholesale sectors of the economy. Expansionary economic periods are, of course, the profit-generating periods for the shopping centers since consumer spending reaches unusually high levels.

The inflation protection of the new forms of leases also depends on the energy crisis and its management. Obviously, indexed, net, percentage leases offer no inflation protection unless the consumers in the normal trading area patronize the center. The higher fuel costs tend to restrict the trading area radius of a regional center, for example. However, because of higher fuel costs, regional centers may become the central business districts for communities within a larger metropolitan area. The older central business district may suffer more than the regional centers in suburban residential areas.

THE RISKS OF SHOPPING CENTER INVESTMENT

The investor faces risks in all three of the well-identified phases of shopping center development and investment. These phases of development are often labeled: (1) the planning and construction phase, (2) the operating phase, and (3) the termination or sale phase of the development.

The Planning and Construction Phase

The critical factors in the planning and construction phase include obtaining the best location at the intersection of major highways, the selection of the most advantageous method of financing the land, the correct evaluation of the spendable income and competition in the target market, and the judgment for the future about the best manner of raising capital. Once the bids are let for the construction of the permanent improvements, the developer-investor must assess the possibilities of cost overruns and the accuracy of the cost estimates in light of weather conditions for construction, the stability of labor conditions, and the general nature of the surface and subsurface site conditions. If zoning does not currently fit the development plans, what costs will be encountered in obtaining zoning changes or variances from the city government? What costs will be encountered and what time will be taken for the submission of the required environmental impact studies and their subsequent changes in order to acquire the necessary construction permits and operating licenses from the federal, state, and local environmental regulation agencies? How long will it take to lease up the center adequately so that construction and permanent lenders and investors can be approached for necessary funds? How long will it take to reach the 75- and 90-percent-leased-up stages?

The Operating Phase

The risks of the operating phase include the selling period required before overage payments are received from the percentage leases, the strength of the consumer attraction generated by the center, and the efficiency and capability of the onsite and supervisory management. The forecasted revenues and expenses may materialize along different patterns than expected. Is a recession over the horizon going to affect cash flows and profitability? Will the market support the expected revenues or will the previously established competing centers continue to strongly draw the local clientele?

The Termination or Sale Phase

Will the owner recognize the best time to sell in order to receive the highest overall yield for the property? Will a buyer or purchaser-organization be located easily without much time passing and without exorbitant costs of search? Will adequate financing be available to the new investor or will the current owner have to finance the sale? What will be the competitive investment climate for this type of center at the time of the desired sale?

The owner seeks the highest capital gain from the center when the sale is made because long-term capital gains taxation has been more favorable in recent years than ordinary taxation of income. The owner speculates on the capital gain to be realized on the sale. Not all properties benefit from strong growth in value over time. Will tax changes in the future mean greater taxation of long-term capital gains than at the present? Will the tax forecasts for the future sale be measurably different from actual taxation?

The investor concludes that shopping centers have substantial risk associated with them. According to a financial adage, assumption of high levels of risk should be compensated by high possible earnings levels. In past years in shopping center development, the developer who has assumed significant levels of risk in establishing a viable retail complex has often received higher than normal rewards for the risk assumption. As centers of the future are developed with substantial amounts of risk capital from nondeveloper sources, the developer may assume only part of the development risk and may receive less compensation. In other words, a joint venture partner may assume more of the entrepreneurial risk than has occurred in recent years.

CONSTANTLY CHANGING INVESTMENT CONDITIONS

The opportunities for profitable shopping center development and investment change over time. The changes in the shopping center outlook come from many sources. As economic conditions change, the demand for shopping center goods and services changes. Investors in income properties may favor shopping centers over all other forms of income properties, or they may place shopping centers further down their list of possible income property investments. The changes in investment preferences occur whether the investor is domestically based or has a foreign domicile. Equity investors may prefer shopping center development and investment over all other forms of income property investments, but these investors are usually concerned with the availability of sufficient loanable funds on the right terms from lenders at the time of their equity investment or they may shy away from the shopping center investment area. Even though many centers are being financed with increasing amounts of equity capital, the developers are still relying on substantial amounts of borrowed capital for land development, construction, and long-term investment. The profitable opportunities are related to the size of the center, the mix of tenants, the sources of capital, and the investor demand for the type of center.

THE RISK AND RETURNS FROM THE VARIOUS TYPES OF CENTERS

The smaller the shopping center, the lower the cost of construction and the more development opportunity there is for the local construction and real estate development firm. The development and construction loans may be obtained at the local bank that examines the credit standing of the developer, perhaps a local firm. A few acres can be found in an advantageous location. The landowner may become a partner in the development or, with a little negotiation, sell or lease the necessary land to the local developer. If the developer-builder does not live in the same town, he or she may live and have an office in an adjacent urban area. The smaller center may entail a small-scale development and construction operation.

　　The smaller center usually costs less to construct on a square footage basis. The local developer may use nonunion labor to keep costs down and still control the quality of construction. The value of the center will depend primarily on the local investor demand for such an income property, the forecasted increase in sales, the forecasted overage payments for the developer, lender, and investors, and the tenant demand for space in the center. The capitalization rate for the property valuation techniques will also reflect the current costs of equity and mortgage monies locally.

While the smaller center may take months to develop and build, the larger center takes *years*. Land acquisition and center leasing and financing of the larger center may go on for years before construction can even begin. The construction of the various improvements may take many months or perhaps extend through a couple of years. The preleasing that underlies permanent financing may take months that may extend into years. For the development of the regional or superregional center, the cooperative construction agreements and the reciprocal easements take substantial time of multiple attorneys.

A small, local real estate development firm may wish to diversify into smaller centers, but may not wish to tie up significant resources and assume the risk of major centers. On the other hand, the large domestic or foreign real estate development firm may wish to diversify its businesses and its invesments by engaging in large center operations. This type of firm may seek large development opportunities with limited or no involvement in neighborhood, community, or specialty centers.

Local investors such as high-tax-bracket physicians, architects, accountants, real estate brokers, and other such business and professional people may prefer investment in neighborhood, community, or specialty centers. They can drive past them and point to them with pride. They can watch the construction and operation. The profitability of the smaller centers depends partially on the forecasted growth in sales from the primary and secondary trading areas which are located in the area. To gain increasing overage payments for the participation of the investor, lender, and developer, the transactions of the center should be forecasted to increase, the price levels of the goods and services may be forecasted to increase with inflation, more residents and workers should be forecasted for the trading area, and the location should be convenient and continually advertised. Most of the tenants of the smaller center should be local for the profitability of the developer and investors, but the neighborhood and community centers require enough regional and national chain tenants to satisfy the risk and financial requirements of the mortgage lender. If the mortgage terms and supply of money are appropriate, the developer and investors can generate enough cash flow over time that they may not wish to sell their investment for long periods. In many urban areas, small centers are such attractive investments that the developers and investors hold their centers indefinitely. They like their operating results and/or the capital appreciation that they perceive as time passes.

If lenders prefer large real estate investments for their portfolios and those of their clients, more money on better terms may be available at a given time for the larger centers. The lenders may perceive less risk and greater return from the larger centers that may be occupied primarily by mall chain stores and major department stores. The investor or lender may prefer financing the mall of a major center to financing the total small neighborhood or community center.

The specialty center may appeal to investors who reside locally who prefer assumption of higher risk that may result in higher investment returns. The specialty centers may contain no chain stores at all. The investor and lender may have no security from the good credit rating and investment holding power and merchandising and advertising prowess of a chain holding company behind their specialty center investment.

If the larger center has a desirable mix of tenants that attracts customers from a wide and expanding trading area and supports a well-negotiated set of leases and mortgages, the investor may view the center as an extraordinary inflation hedge. The center may even be viewed as a good tax shelter with good capital appreciation potential. If these conditions exist, the investor demand for such a center may result in high multiples of gross income for valuation and purchase price negotiation. Based on market conditions, the capitalization rate may therefore be unusually low and the gross income multiplier unusually high. Such a center may attract primarily equity capital from domestic and foreign sources. This type of center may be first on the investor's list of desirable real property investments.

FOUR

LEGAL FORMS OF BUSINESS ORGANIZATION FOR SHOPPING CENTER INVESTMENT

The laws of the country in which the shopping center investor is domiciled determine the types of legal organization for investment available for use. The various forms of organization offer tax, legal, and financial benefits. The objectives of the shopping center investor should be facilitated by the chosen form of business organization. The attributes of the chosen legal organization should work for the investor and not against the plans and goals of that investor. In the United States, a substantial body of law surrounds the following commonly used legal forms of business organization:

Proprietorship
Partnership
   General partnership
   Limited partnership
   Joint venture
   Syndicate
Corporation
Trust
   Real estate investment trust
   Business trust
   Personal trust

Other joint ownership vehicles are the condominium, the cooperative, the joint tenancy, the tenancy in common, the tenancy by the entirety, and community property. These are legal variations of the general partnership. Let us review a few of the basic legal, financial, and tax attractions of these investment forms.

THE PROPRIETORSHIP

The sole proprietorship is legally called *ownership in severalty*. The single owner of the real property takes full legal, tax, and financial liability for the investment. The funds committed to the shopping center investment are limited to the individual's sources of funds, equity, and debt. The net taxable income from the real property is merged with the net taxable income of the investor from all other sources and the investor's normal tax rates are applied. Unless the mortgages on the real property contain exculpatory clauses, the investor assumes the full legal liability for the mortgage debt if the net income from the property is not sufficient to cover the mortgage debt service requirements.

THE PARTNERSHIP

The partnership form of joint ownership involves two or more persons or investment entities. The general partnership assumes that all partners have equal legal and financial responsibility for the debts of the income property. The contributions of the partners may be unequal and the partnership agreement may specify unequal profit, cash flow, and depreciation distributions depending upon their respective equity contributions. The general partnership may be formed under a joint tenancy, a tenancy in common, a tenancy by the entirety, or a community property relationship. The joint tenancy, the tenancy by the entirety, and the community property form offer survivorship rights to the original investors. When one investor of the group dies, the surviving investors assume the total undivided interest including that originally held by the deceased partner. The tenancy by the entirety and the community property forms are uniquely designed only for married couples. The tenancy in common form of partnership organization does not offer survivorship rights for the surviving joint owners at the death of a co-owner. The share of the undivided interest that accrues to the deceased partner may be inherited by heirs and assigns. In order for a co-owner to sell or otherwise transfer his or her interest to another outside person, the undivided interest of the joint tenancy, the tenancy in common, the tenancy by the entirety, and the community property forms must be partitioned by the courts.

The net income of the partnership is not taxed. When the individual partners receive their partnership distributions, they pay federal and state income taxes on the total of their taxable income from all sources. The general partners retain full legal and financial liability for the obligations of the partnership whether the form of organization is a general or a limited partnership. Each general partner has a right to manage the affairs of the general or limited partnership. Limited partners of the limited partnership do not retain any management rights. In return, their financial liability is limited to their capital contributions in most instances. The partnership legal liability rests with the general partners. To reduce its legal liability, a general partner may incorporate. A limited partner could incorporate but has little reasons for such an action.

Fund raising of the partnership depends on the resources of the individual partners and their credit capacity. The partnership agreement must be revised if more partners join the venture or if the original partners leave. Additional partners could bring more funds to the venture; more real estate could be purchased or existing real property could be expanded.

The Joint Venture

This form of business investment organization represents a special type of partnership. The tenancy in common legal arrangement may be used if the joint venture partners are individuals who wish survivorship rights. Often the partners are corporations, partnerships themselves, and financial institutions under various types of charters. Some financial institutions are chartered as corporations, for example, commercial banks. Others are mutual forms of organizations and may legally be called business associations rather than corporations. When a real estate investment trust is a joint venture partner, it represents a special type of tax-exempt business trust.

The joint venture organization is usually reserved for a single real estate venture which involves several forms of business expertise and several forms of financing for the long-run success of the project. The project is often a large-scale shopping center, office complex, or mixed-use planned development. Combined into the single partnership will be a developer and the associated development company, an architect and the associated company, a local commercial bank, an intermediate-term source of funds such as a life insurance company, and a long-term source of funds such as a pension fund or real estate equity fund. Each contributes a particular expertise or type of capital for the project.

The distributions from the joint venture to the individual parties to the joint venture are taxable when received by the parties. The joint venture or partnership is not subject to income taxation as a form of partnership. The legal liability of each of the partners is usually limited by its essential form of business organization. The partner acting as the general or managing partner of the joint venture retains any forms of legal and financial liability for the total venture.

Real Estate Syndicate

The ownership of real property is syndicated among a number of investors. The manager of the real estate syndicate, the general partner, sells limited partnership or syndicate shares to investors within the state in which the real properties are located in a private offering or to investors located anywhere in a public offering. If the syndicate manager has not yet selected the appropriate properties or the properties are not disclosed, the manager is offering a blind pool investment. If the prospective property purchases are described in the offering, the syndication involves a defined property offering. State laws cover private syndication offerings to a limited number of persons residing within the state's boundaries. If the number of syndicate members exceeds the state legal limit, the syndication is regulated by the U.S. Securities and Exchange Commission as a public offering.

Where private real estate placements are oriented toward tax shelter and capital appreciation, the public offerings is less tax oriented. The required capital contributions of the private placement are payable over a period of years; the public fund is usually funded at the initial investment. Most of the syndicate managers prefer investment in existing properties with good track records; some, though, enter into property development or establish good relationships with developers in order to buy quality properties after their completion. Some of the funds borrow against the equity that they have accumulated from syndicate members; other funds are strictly equity funds. Some funds offer only one pool at a time; offerings may include several invesment opportunities with varying types of properties and various investment objectives. The typical public fund raises $30 to $60 million in equity over a six to eighteen month period.* The private fund may raise less money over the same period. The public funds may be better known and advertised, and the offering information may be circulated more widely. The investment decisions are made by the syndicate manager, the fund sponsor or the fund's affiliates. Public offerings are subject to stringent disclosure regulations of the Securities and Exchange Commission as well as the state securities authorities; private offerings are subject only to the regulations of the state securities authorities and the state blue-sky laws.

THE CORPORATION

The corporation is a business entity with an indefinite life which is directed by a board of directors and managed on a daily basis by a management or officer group. Its net income is taxed by federal and state income tax authorities. When the stockholders receive dividends and the creditors receive their interest, the income forms are taxable at the recipients' ordinary income tax rates. Therefore, many generalize that the corporation is subject to "double taxation." This contrasts with the "single taxation" exacted from partnerships of the various types.

---

*Jarchow, Stephen P., "Real Estate Syndications: Structure of Public Real Estate Offerings," *Real Estate Review*, Vol. 11, No. 4, Winter 1982, p. 17.

The owners of the corporation assets, the stockholders, have limited financial liability. They may lose only their contributed capital. Until the stockholder takes an active role in the management of the corporate business, the stockholder has limited legal liability. The corporation, unlike the proprietorship and the partnership, has unlimited means of raising capital. The articles of incorporation may permit fund-raising by numerous means. Several types of stock may be offered; several types and varieties of debt instruments may be offered to raise borrowed capital.

The corporate form of organization may not be used for shopping center investment since cash flow generated by the center may not flow through untaxed at the corporate level to the individual owners. Depreciation may also flow through to the individual owners in the partnership form, but not the corporate form. The partnership entity may offer tax shelter advantages to the partner where the corporate entity may not. Under other conditions, the corporate form may be used for shopping center investment due to its limited legal and financial liability characteristics. Because of these valuable characteristics, the development company may be incorporated to be shielded from the many risks associated with land development.

THE TRUST

The trust is an association of asset owners who are not subject to income taxation on asset earnings until cash distributions from the trust are received by the owners. A board of trustees holds the title to the real property owned and managed by the trust. An advisory group or board manages the properties on a day-by-day basis. The owners are called *shareholders of beneficial interests*. Each owner has a beneficial interest in the earnings of the trust assets. The best known types of trusts that may deal in real estate are the real estate investment trust, the business trust, and the personal trust. The real estate investment trust is a public investment entity that is tax exempt if its management group abides by the regulations imposed on the REIT by the Internal Revenue Code, first amended in 1960 to create the REIT and then revised in recent years as REIT financial exigencies arose. The business trust is an association of investors in shares of beneficial interest in real estate, stocks, bonds, and other assets held in title by the board of trustees. Their shares and debt securities are usually not publicly traded on the national stock exchanges. The personal trust may hold title to real estate along with stock and bonds. It may be created at the death of an individual in order to give financial security to those surviving family members or may be created as a living trust by a living person who wishes portfolio management to benefit the financial status to the beneficiary. The person who creates the personal trust may specify real estate investment by the trustee, or he or she may not limit the trust investments to non-real estate investments such as stock and bonds.

THE COMMERCIAL CONDOMINIUM

Several users of space of a single commercial building may individually own their space under a condominium form of joint ownership. This form of joint ownership of real property may be the wave of the future for shopping center development and investment.* The financing of many major centers is already componentized for practical financing purposes.

Each condominium owner has bought appropriate space from the condominium developer. The developer has finished the construction of the building to the specifications listed in the condominium sales agreement. The finished building contains individually owned units and common areas which are maintained by the contributions of unit owners and managed by condominium owners' associations and the professional property management company. The common areas normally consist of the landscaped space on the site outside the building, the parking lots, sidewalks, retaining walls, the building's common lobby, hallways, elevators, storage rooms, utility equipment and maintenance rooms, public rest rooms, and cleaning supply closets. The unit owner is responsible for the interior maintenance and finished interior construction. This unit area is generally defined as the airspace from the unfinished base flooring to the drop ceilings of the airspace and from the interior of the hall corridor walls to the interior of the exterior walls. The airspace between the drop ceiling and the concrete slab for the condominium unit above is often declared common area so that maintenance and expansion of utility service may take place unimpeded. When units are resold, the utility service requirements may be different for the new owner-occupant. The property manager and the maintenance personnel should have access to this common area for needed changes in unit utility services within periods outside of normal business hours and on a basis that does not interrupt the normal functioning of the adjacent units.

The condominium space is financed by the unit occupant. The user of the unit may purchase the condominium space for all cash or may finance the purchase and then rent the unit to the business operating in the space. A market rent may be established by the owner for the business occupying the space or an above-market rent may be charged if the business can afford the additional tax-deductible expense so that the owner may receive a reasonable return from the real estate ownership.

The condominium owners may wish to expand or contract their space as time passes. Therefore, the condominium agreement may specify that the condominium owner who wishes to sell all or a part of the condominium space first must offer the space to the other owners of the building for a period of

*Conroy, John T., Jr., "Commercial Condominiums: Wave of the Future?," *Real Estate Perspectives*, Vol. 3, No. 3, 1981, pp. 8–13.

perhaps 10 days before listing the condominium space for sale to the public. Other owners in the building may wish to purchase additional space. This provision gives them an opportunity to do so. If an owner perceives the need for more building space in the future, that condominium owner may purchase more space at the outset than is currently needed in order to be prepared for future expansion. The surplus space may be rented to other businesses on relatively short lease terms until the owner needs the space. Ownership of this surplus space also extends the real estate investment of the original owner. A good yield may be obtained from the surplus space.

In the future, many chain stores on individual pads or within the mall buildings may be asked to purchase their own condominium airspace and develop their own premises. The reciprocal easement and operating agreements between the condominium and rental space users will continue to tie the operations of the overall center together to the benefit of all the center merchants and the owners.

THE COMMERCIAL COOPERATIVE

Since the cooperative form of ownership has worked well for residential development in major cities, this form of joint ownership of building space may reach the shopping center. A development company erects the building to be occupied by the joint owners of airspace. A proprietary lease is legally placed on all the airspace. Values are assigned to each confined and described airspace. Master mortgages placed on the building by the development corporation permanently finance the total building and its land. The prospective unit owner assumes the portion of the master mortgages assigned to the particular airspace, the assigned portion of the common area maintenance expense per month, and the apportioned *ad valorem* taxes and building insurance for the airspace. The new unit owner purchases the equity value of the space and agrees to abide by the rules and regulations of the building owners' association. The equity value may be purchased with all cash or financed with the airspace agreement or easement as collateral for the commercial loan.

As componentized financing of shopping centers continues, the condominium and cooperative forms of financing and joint ownership may be considered thoroughly. The attributes of these residentially successful joint ownership forms may be very appropriate to shopping center development and permanent financing.

FIVE

DEVELOPMENT OF SHOPPING CENTERS

The magnetic appeal of the planned and coordinated cluster of retail stores called the shopping center has generated high profits for the developer and the investor. The razzle-dazzle of the colored spotlights, the glamorous mannequins in the display windows, the blare of music from the record shops, and the tempting foods and beverages of the restaurants and supermarkets have attracted throngs of customers. The developer has created the magnetic features of the retail center and, along with the outside investors, has profited from his or her entrepreneurial endeavors. The investors of equity and debt capital have gained financial rewards along with the developer as lease payments have been made by the tenants from their increasing storeroom revenues.

THE EVOLUTION OF THE SHOPPING CENTER

The shopping center probably had its roots in the retail bazaars, farmers' markets, and flea markets of the oldest civilizations and cultures of the world. Even before the advent of money, the barter system for the transfer of goods and services was carried on in the central marketplace. Here the sellers congregated to compete for the buyers' attention. These marketplaces were the forerunners of the current integrated retail developments planned, financed, constructed, leased, coordinated, and managed by a single developer or development group for the financial benefit of the ultimate consumer, the developer, the lenders, the equity contributors, and other business entities.

The modern shopping center in its many forms continues to thrive because so many parties benefit from its facilities and conveniences. The city and regional planner is pleased that the retail consumer is pleased with the coordinated grouping of retail stores, while the bright lights shining day and night, the traffic congestion, the noise, and the environmental pollution are confined to one general area. Quiet residential areas nearby may be isolated from commercial encroachment. Industrial areas may be free of retail establishments which attract unwanted cars where delivery trucks must come and go. The hazards of industrial areas do not despoil the environment for profitable retail trade. The ultimate consumer can go to one retail location and find a number of needed goods and services instead of spending time and burning gasoline driving all over an urban area. The city may assign special zoning ordinances to this area; property tax regulations may apply especially to this complex of retail units as separated from residential and industrial areas; extra provisions for utility services may benefit many retail units in the center; mass transit facilities may link this heavily used retail area with other significant areas of residential and commercial land use. Police and fire protection may serve a number of retail units congregated at the site, and the extra traffic controls and street widening for customer traffic benefit a large number of retail units at the site and their numerous customers. When competing merchants are located at one site, each tends to benefit from the increased customer traffic. Many shopping centers house competing tenants. The customer who seeks a wide variety will be attracted to this center.

The consolidated retail center requires a large sum of investment capital, usually from lenders as well as equity investors. Most investors wish to reduce their financial risks as much as they can while increasing their yields. Coordinated, integrated retail centers that attract high volumes of prospective customers reduce the financial risk of the investor. The investor observes more chance for stable and increasing tenant sales receipts, timely lease payments, ample overage lease payments based on the increasing gross or net income of the tenants, and a longer economic or profitable life for the retail complex. Investment risks may be reduced while increasing current and future yields may be predicted.

RISING PERSONAL INCOMES AND POPULATION

The population of the United States continues to increase steadily. The increase is occurring mainly in the minority sectors: the Cuban refugees, Mexican immigrants, Vietnamese refugees, and the native black community. These groups tend to swell the urban areas, and so do migrants from rural and semirural areas. As the economy and the industrial and commercial base of the United States expand, the American household tends to be represented by two adult workers employed outside the home. Household personal income, therefore, has tended to rise while per capita income has recently stabilized.

Households are tending to be smaller for several reasons. The birth rate of the United States has declined over the years, the divorce rate has risen, marriages are occurring at later ages than formerly, the death rate has decreased, life expectancy has risen, and higher personal incomes have contributed to the formation of separate households by members of the same family who once lived together in a single household.

The two-worker household usually maintains two or more automobiles. Each worker usually drives to work in a separate car. Mass transit facilities reach only certain areas of any major urban area. Even when mass transit facilities and services are available and handy, the relatively affluent worker may prefer his or her own transportation at a higher cost but with more flexibility of travel time. These multiple-automobile households may easily drive to nearby shopping centers. Only the high cost of gasoline and car upkeep and relatively high car prices may tend to restrict the driving to workplaces, community facilities, and shopping centers. The cars now being manufactured by foreign and domestic companies, therefore, have tended to conserve gasoline consumption and be smaller in size, horsepower, and overall weight. One by-product is the reduction in parking space per car at shopping centers. The same size parking lot may serve more cars today.

THE ONE-STOP SHOPPING CENTER

One-stop shopping is appealing to all segments of the population. As the shopping center developer promotes this concept, so does the local financial institution. The consolidated and coordinated medical center also appeals to the potential users on this basis. "All medical specialties housed under one roof," the ads may say. In the case of shopping centers, one-stop shopping may apply to convenience goods and services offered by a neighborhood shopping center or to the full line of convenience, shopping, and specialty goods and services offered by a central business district or other superregional center in the suburbs of a major city. The customer may take care of more shopping needs in one trip than would be possible if the retail goods and services were offered at many diverse locations within an urban area. The two-worker household tends to be particularly appreciative of the shopping convenience because of limited shopping time. Many consumers wish to restrict shopping time and keep more time available for entertainment and pursuit of hobbies and other leisure time activities. On the other hand, many consumers treat the shopping center trip as entertainment and a leisure time activity in itself. Therefore, the developer, investors, and tenants provide an atmosphere which will encourage leisure time use of the center, offering mall exhibits, fashion shows, musical performances, entertainment and sports celebrity appearances, art shows, antique shows, boat and camping exhibits, and other management- and tenant-sponsored activities.

In a time of expensive urban parking, the free parking of shopping centers and its proximity to the tenant storeroom are very appealing to the economical consumer. The parking facilities close to older retail stores tend to be expensive and small. Few cars can be accommodated in the provided lot, and the entrances and exits to the lot or parking building may be hazardous and inconvenient.

When the potential customer does not have the time or inclination to drive or ride the public buses or trains to the central business district, the shopping center is the convenient alternative. Several shopping centers in the near vicinity may serve the majority of the needs of this customer. The neighborhood, community, regional, and specialty shopping centers may be located within reasonable driving distance of the potential consumer.

The high costs of city growth promote the encouragement by the city of the shopping center. The infrastructure for a single consolidated retail center costs less for the city and its taxpayers than the extension of utility lines and services to isolated locations scattered around an urban area. Street planning and maintenance as well as traffic control may be less costly for a single center than for retail units scattered through a large area. Police and fire protection may be focused on a single location rather than spread widely. Less encroachments on residential and industrial space may occur with controlled retail locations, planned and coordinated by a single development and investment group.

DEVELOPMENT AND INVESTMENT CHARACTERISTICS
OF THE VARIOUS TYPES OF CENTERS

Five types of shopping centers have been identified by the real estate industry: (1) neighborhood, (2) community, (3) regional, (4) superregional, and (5) specialty. Each of these has its own development and investment characteristics. There are profit opportunities associated with each type, but each has its own risk-return characteristics. The various types of centers may be identified in terms of the chief anchor store types, the store mix, customer driving time, the type of goods and services, and the general location.

Neighborhood Center

When a person wants something for his or her personal use, an item which is frequently purchased by brand name or not, that person will probably go to the closest source. The closest shopping center offering that item or service, such as cigarettes, bread, or milk, will probably be classified as a neighborhood or convenience shopping center. Persons living close by may walk or drive to the center. The regular customers will live or work within five minutes' driving time or less. The few stores—perhaps six to eight storerooms in total—occupying the center will be anchored by a supermarket and drugstore.

Only a few acres of land may be consumed by the center store buildings, customer parking spaces, employee parking spaces, truck loading docks, and rear access driveways. A single developer will probably house the few storerooms under one roof where a covered walkway will link the storerooms. Few neighborhood centers have weather-controlled covered malls connecting the few stores.

This type of small urban complex may be located anywhere in an urban area—downtown near high-rise apartment and office buildings, in central city areas adjacent to heavily populated residential districts, and in suburban areas near residential and office areas. The small center can be fit into corner locations and along main arteries where local residents and workers can move in and out of the complex quickly and easily. City planners often zone commercial land adjacent to residential areas for such small retail centers. The appropriately zoned land may act as a buffer to separate residential areas from heavily traveled thoroughfares, major office developments, and industrial areas. The land is an area of transition between quiet residential and noisy and polluted industrial areas.

Community Center

The retail complex anchored by a supermarket and a discount junior department store or regular variety store and surrounded by several other smaller tenants which draws customers from a 10- to 15-minute driving radius may be classified as a community shopping center. Convenience and shopping goods and services are usually offered by the 10 to 15 storeroom tenants. Even though some of the center's goods and services will be purchased on an immediate, convenience basis, some of the goods and services will be purchased after comparison shopping by the potential consumers. The ultimate consumers will make shopping comparisons with respect to these goods and services on the basis of price, quality, credit programs available, credit costs, color, brand, and expected performance. For these reasons, apparel, card and stationery, shoe, and florist shops may supplement the supermarket, drugstore, and discount or regular variety store.

Since this type of center consumes more land than a neighborhood shopping center and appeals to a wider customer radius, there are fewer community centers than neighborhood centers. There are similarities with regard to location, though; the developer may locate the center in the central business district near large residential complexes, in any central city area near major residential populations, and in the suburbs where the center is surrounded by residential buildings of all kinds: single-family, two-family, garden, and high-rise apartment buildings.

The developer or development group will have to find properly zoned land totaling several acres for the building housing 10 to 15 storerooms plus customer and employee parking. Corner locations are sought for their customer driving convenience and for the advertising value of visibility from two or more main thoroughfares. Fast-food and movie chains may desire auxiliary space adjacent to the community center since the customer traffic in and out of the center is sizable.

Regional Center

The retail complex planned and developed by a single development entity which attracts customers to convenience, shopping, and specialty goods and services from a 15- to 20-minute driving radius is often labeled a regional shopping center. Several acres must be acquired for the 30 to 50 tenants and the necessary parking space for delivery trucks, customer cars, and employee cars. Satellite buildings for commercial bank branches, supermarkets, movie houses, fast-food outlets, office buildings, motels, discount department stores, and tire, battery and accessory buildings of the major department stores of the center are usually a part of the developer's plans for the urban area. The retail complex, often with a weather-controlled mall connecting the many store-rooms, contains at least one major department store associated with a corporate retail chain. A second department store integrated into the center may be a discount department store such as a K-Mart store.

Since the regional center requires many acres of prime commercial land, usually at the intersection of two or more major highways or freeways, relatively few of them are built in any major urban area. Most of the new regional centers with one or two full-line department stores are located in the outlying suburbs where large, appropriately zoned parcels of land exist. Some retail centers of smaller urban areas which lie in the central business district may be called regional shopping centers. This retail center—perhaps recently renovated by a developer—may draw customers from a wide area, perhaps a 25- to 30-minute driving radius. Admittedly, the regional center described by the central business district retailing complex is usually financed by several owners and tenants on independent bases. Most regional centers developed and controlled by a single developer, in contrast, are located in the suburbs.

Superregional Center

When a regional shopping center contains three or more full-line department stores, that center is usually classified as superregional. This center of 100 or more storerooms usually is built with a weather-controlled covered mall and is located in the central business district or in a newer outlying suburban area at the intersection of at least two major highways. The ultimate consumer may select from convenience, shopping, and specialty goods and services which are offered by stores in the integrated retail complex or in the numerous retail stores which surround this major shopping center. The single development company often acquires the many acres for the shopping center along with acres of surrounding land which is leased or sold to complementary commercial businesses for extra profit and land use control. The superregional center may be developed in phases as the major department stores gradually build and occupy their premises.

The wide range of goods and services are sold by a variety of retail units that are primarily chain store units. The participation of the high-credit chain stores reduces the financial risk to the developer when the center is financed. The many tenants may be housed in a single- or multilevel center with integrated parking buildings and uncovered ground-level parking lots. This center with its multiple full-line department stores will attract customers from a wide radius. The primary trading area has a 30- to 45-minute driving time. The secondary and tertiary trading areas may pull customers from an even greater driving distance.

Specialty Center

The specialty center concentrates on specialty goods and services rather than on convenience and shopping goods and services. The ultimate consumer will drive considerable distances to acquire the goods and services that are offered by the specialty center merchants.

This type of center may be a collection of boutiques and small specialty restaurants with no chain store anchor tenant. Goods and services at this type of top-of-the-line pricing center may offer for sale such goods and services as assorted candles, lingerie, stationery, lamps, picture framing, ice cream, Mexican food, French cuisine, T-shirt printing, camera equipment, personal photography service, a delicatessen, or a rental-and-sale picture gallery.

Another type of currently popular specialty center is the discount center. Primarily discount outlets are assembled under the single roof. These centers have often been inspired by successful flea markets in the area. Recession and depression fear and negative psychology may also lend the atmosphere for the development of such a center. Consumers may wish to preserve their financial resources by patronizing several discount retailers who are located as a coordinated merchandising group under one roof. During the recession conditions of the late 1970s and early 1980s, many discount centers of various sizes popped up to serve the waiting, well-defined clientele. Many textile manufacturers are represented among the soft-goods merchandisers of these centers.

CURRENT DEVELOPMENT TRENDS

Recently the vast majority of centers that have been constructed have contained 300,000 or less square feet of gross leasable area Exhibit 5-1. More regional and superregional centers were built in 1976, 1977, 1980, and 1981 than in 1978 or 1979. Developers find good sites for the smaller neighborhood and community centers every year.

We have not yet specified the range in square footage of the gross leasable area of each of the center classifications. Classifications on the basis of GLA is difficult. The data of Exhibit 5-1 might be used. A note might be added that a specialty center might range from 50,000 to 300,000 GLA. One of the most successful shopping center developers recently used another classification scheme for centers. His ranges for GLA for each of the center types are

Exhibit 5-1. Size Distribution of New Centers*

	Percent of Total Centers in Sample					
GLA Size Class (square feet)	1976	1977	1978	1979	1980	1981
Up to 100,000	55.8	56.9	55.9	58.9	39.5	49.6
100,001–300,000	30.7	31.4	36.2	34.3	48.1	40.2
300,001–600,000	6.1	4.3	3.3	4.1	7.5	5.1
Over 600,000	7.3	7.4	4.6	2.7	4.9	5.1

Source: Sussman, Albert, "Sussman: Centers' Place in Retailing Scheme Is Firmly Entrenched,"
Shopping Center World, Vol. 11, No. 1, January 1982, p. 81. Copyright 1982 Communications
Channels, Inc., 6285 Barfield Road, Atlanta, GA 30328.
*Based on survey of developments by International Council of Shopping Centers members.

indicated in Exhibit 5-2. The reader can decide for himself or herself what
dimensions are usually associated with the five center classifications.

Due to economies of scale for the large developer, it is becoming more
frequent that the developer acquires sizable parcels that are appropriate for
mixed-use projects. The shopping center becomes one of the several land uses
of the project. The other uses are usually compatible with shopping center use.
For example, Trammell Crow Development Company and the Trammel Crow
family are currently constructing an Atlanta Galleria as a part of an office
building-hotel complex in northwest Atlanta across the road from the superregional shopping center of 1.2 million square feet called Cumberland Mall.
The five office buildings and luxury hotel planned for the 70-plus-acre tract are
complementary to the specialty shopping center that will have no major full-
line department store. The owners of the project will benefit from the profitability of the project as a whole and from the individual buildings devoted to
their particular land use. The Gallerias of Houston and Dallas are similar
mixed-use configurations. Water Tower Place in the Chicago Loop integrates a
multilevel vertical center into a super-block also containing two major department store buildings, the Ritz Carleton Hotel, office space, and underground
parking.

Land and energy conservation have become more important as land and

**Exhibit 5-2. One Method of Classifying Centers in Terms
of the Range in Gross Leasable Area**

Type of Center	Range of Gross Leasable Area (square feet)
Neighborhood shopping center	20,000–40,000
Community shopping center	40,000–200,000
Regional shopping center	200,000–1,000,000
Superregional shopping center	1,000,000–2,000,000
Specialty shopping center	50,000–300,000

energy costs have risen rapidly in commercial areas. Parking spaces may be smaller for the smaller vehicles; therefore, the parking lot may be smaller for the same customer vehicular volume. Since energy costs are higher for more storeroom space, merchants have agreed to smaller storeroom space as rents and construction costs have gone up with inflation. Now parking lots *and* shopping center buildings are getting smaller. Energy conservation systems based on the latest cost savings ideas are incorporated in the initial and renovated center designs. The exterior and interior designs and equipment are influenced by the energy conservation systems.

THE DEVELOPMENT PROCESS

There is a process that the developer follows in creating the finished shopping center. The process starts with such questions as whether the project should involve only a shopping center or a mixed-use development with a shopping center as only one of the elements. The developer goes on to determine the general characteristics needed for a site. Then a site must be selected. The end point of the process may be the grand opening of the center with all tenants in place, or it may be the sale of the center upon its completion or after years of operation.

Single-Use versus Mixed-Use Development

Many developers have the opportunity, the personnel, and the financial capacity to develop large mixed-use projects. The various land uses of a single project may reinforce the profitability of the other land uses. For example, in one super-block mixed-use development near Embarcadero Drive and the waterfront in San Francisco, the high-rise apartment and office buildings provide part of the market for the shopping center that is incorporated into the super-block development. In Kansas City, the hotel and office space of Crown Center and the restaurant space of the renovated adjacent railroad station that is an integral part of the development feed a market to the retailers of the shopping center of Crown Center.

Some developers may have the opportunity, personnel, and financial capability for developing mixed-use projects but prefer to commit themselves only to a shopping center when the site is appropriate only for single-use development. Other developers do not have the capacity to develop mixed-use projects regardless of the site possibilities and characteristics. For example, small tracts for shopping centers have been developed near the University of Chicago and Huntingdon College of Montgomery, Alabama as specialty centers. The tracts of land and the market in the affluent residential areas do not permit multi-use large-scale development regardless of the capability of the development organization.

The option for single or multiple land use exists with respect to some large tracts for some developers. The question must then be asked: What is the highest and best use for the site? Once the feasibility study determines the highest and best use, the developer must still decide what the company's role will be in the development. The land may be sold off or leased so that others may participate in the development of the total area. To guarantee the completion of a coordinated development, the group of developers and investors may form a joint venture or other business arrangement. The legal forms for joint ownership and development of real property have already been mentioned. Additional comments about organization forms will be made in the financing section.

Site Characteristics

The site for a center must exhibit certain characteristics. The location must be appropriate for retail sales. The developer knows that certain utilities must be available at the site. There must be access to the site in terms of usual mode of customer transportation. There must be sufficient buying power in the possession of prospective customers. These prospective customers must be able to view the center buildings and signs for eventual advertising purposes. The site must be large enough for the planned development. The soil must have absorptive qualities to meet percolation tests for the prospective septic tank system. Otherwise, city sewerage lines must be brought into the site for building hookup. The soil must partially absorb water runoff from the parking lots and other improved land; storm sewers may absorb the remaining heavy water flows. The site must be drained properly. The surface soils must exhibit load-bearing qualities. The weight of the land improvements, particularly multi-level malls and department store buildings, must be supported by foundations that are appropriate for the soil and subsurface conditions. Other necessary site conditions will be covered later.

The Importance of Location

It is said that the three principal determinants of the good center are "location, location, and location." All other considerations, it is said, are of considerably lesser importance. Therefore, the developer must struggle against the competition to gain control of the well-located shopping center site. As real estate development proceeds, all developers of centers are looking for new locations. Several developers who work in a large area of the country or nationwide may view the same site as a key location. Out of the active competition will come the winning developer.

Land Availability at the Right Location

Very few sites are usually available at the right locations for a shopping center, particularly a regional or superregional center. Superregional centers in suburban areas usually require a major tract at the intersection of two interstate highways or freeways in major metropolitan areas. Accessibility and easy line of sight for the many potential customers are required for the major marketing center. The same thing is true for regional centers. Accessibility and visual approach to the center are also required for community and neighborhood centers, but the required customer clientele for smaller center profitability is far less than for the major centers.

The improved or unimproved land must be located in the heart of expanding population and buying power. The investor's yield requirements over time require increasing customer sales from the day of center opening. Most investor yield requirements may be reached only if the center sales increase and the center's property value increases over time. Therefore, the area around a new shopping center site may be established and densely populated, but the developer will receive adequate financing if that area's buying power and relevant population is increasing. Such growth requirements may be more easily obtained from new suburban sites where real estate growth is exemplified.

The right site may be vacant, but essentially unavailable to the developer. The owner must be ready to lease or sell the site to the developer on negotiated terms. Land transfer may be restricted by estate settlement agreements. The attorney representing the estate may not have the power or authority to even lease the land. The land owners may wish to defer the payment of capital gains taxes and may not wish to sell the site that the developer wishes. The income from a ground lease may or may not be attractive to the institutional or family land owner. The family may be subject to a relatively high state and federal income tax rate and may prefer no additional annual income; the land may be held for future generations who will be given the right to decide how the land will be improved. If a state or federal government agency owns the land, that agency may or may not have a financial motivation to sell or lease the desired site.

In some cases, the community wishes to restrain future land development and may have a scheduled plan for utility service expansion. Sewer moratoriums, for example, have become common in such places as communities in Florida, suburban areas surrounding Washington, D.C., suburban areas north of Manhattan in the lower Hudson Valley area, and the bedroom communities to the north across the bay from San Francisco. Expansion of water sources has been a development problem in Arizona.

Land Competition in the Urban Area

Since the right location is the key factor, the developer may find this location is a number of places in the urban area. The key location may be (1) downtown in the central business district, (2) in other commercial centers in the inner city outside the central business district, and (3) in suburban areas. After considering this land competition, the developer may see only one site that is appropriate for the proposed center. Sites that are available but less appropriate may be observed at the same time in the same urban market area. If the prime site is not available for purchase or lease, several developers may compete for the site of secondary location. The customer drawing power of this alternative site may be adequate for continued developer interest.

Major developers such as the Rouse Company of the Baltimore area have recently concentrated on center development in the central business districts or nearby commercial areas in the major, older cities of the country. They have perceived new sites in these central, densely developed areas that are subject to redevelopment with significant retail space. The competition for these sites may have been less intense, but these developers perceive growing, affluent markets in such downtown areas. In recent years retailing centers have been developed, therefore, on the waterfront of downtown Baltimore, Battery Park of Manhattan, and Faneuil Square of Boston. The Navy Pier of the Chicago Loop is subject to redevelopment at any time according to the retail press.

Utility Service Needed at the Site

The site for the center must be served by natural gas and electric lines. A source of water under the right pressure must be provided at the site. Existing sanitary and storm sewer lines must be extended into the site for hookup to the building plumbing and drainage systems. Phone service may be provided by the same cluster of cables as the electric service. These lines are usually buried under ground as much as possible. If appliance departments and stores are to display their television sets adequately, cable television service may need to be at the site. Cable hookups at the right places in the appropriate storerooms and buildings may be established during construction. If the utility service is not available from the local communities, the developer must provide the service on an independent basis. It is possible that it may be feasible for the developer to maintain a separate sewerage system or water treatment plant. Electricity may be generated by an independent system and sold by the development company to the various tenants. Drainage into local creeks and rivers may be permitted by the health department and environmental protection agencies.

Transportation Access and Traffic Control

Prospective customers must be able to get to the center with minimal delay and driving frustration. Access to the center must be easy and unobstructed. The right-of-ways must be wide enough; enough driving lanes must be provided; and freeway ramps must be long enough to accommodate normal traffic conditions.

Most planners actually anticipate peak hour traffic volume during the heaviest retail buying seasons, if the shopping center is the only land use being considered. If the center is located in a mixed-use area, the peak traffic volume may be associated with several land uses. The transportation system for the area usually accounts for near-peak traffic volume for the area, not normal or peak traffic conditions. In like manner, parking lot design and total space usually revolve around near-peak parking conditions. The parking lot and transportation planners know that the peak shopping period is Christmas. Other peak periods arise before Easter, at Thanksgiving, and before school opens in the fall. Land owners tie up costly commercial land if they want to accommodate the single peak shopping day of the year. The rest of the days of the peak buying seasons will not require that much land for parking and traffic control.

Traffic planners usually avoid stoplights and give preference to ramps where traffic may flow continuously from freeways into the area of the center. The path of the center should not cut through existing heavy traffic. Another access method should be devised to circumvent the patterns of heavy traffic that already exist. Bridges over existing thoroughfares are sometimes devised to handle the regional shopping center that comes primarily from interstate systems or freeways. Stoplights may have to be used to permit cross traffic movement. When stoplights are employed, the ramps for the waiting vehicles must have sufficient lanes and be long enough to accommodate the waiting vehicles without obstructing normal traffic flow on the original transportation artery, such as the freeway or main street. For example, the multi-lane exit ramps from freeways may need to be a half mile long or more.

Large, easily read signs should aid the traffic flow into the center toward convenient parking spaces in ground-level or parking building lots. The city or county government may provide for the desired traffic systems and signs. The developer may contribute toward the changes needed.

Since the developer benefits directly from the changes in the street systems, the city may appreciate the financial contribution of the owners of the development. For example, to accommodate the needs of the center, the curb cuts and medians that direct traffic flow may need to be changed, and additional lanes for existing streets and highways, new stoplight systems, and new exit and entrance ramps may be called for. All of these transportation system changes are costly. The developer realizes, of course, that the community benefits from the provision of needed and desired goods and services at a convenient community location. The local and state governments receive greater property, sales, and income tax payments as a result of the center completion and operation.

Ecology and Environmental Impact Studies

Since the formation of the U.S. Environmental Protection Agency in 1969, many environmental protection agencies have been created on the state level of government. Any developer who engages in a real estate project of regional or wider dimensions, who acquires funds from federally regulated financial institutions, or who receives any federal subsidies or monies is regulated by the federal environmental protection agencies. The state agencies regulate the development of larger real estate projects within the individual state boundaries.

The Extent of Governmental Environmental Regulation. Sizable real estate projects are regulated by numerous state environmental protection agencies. Separate state agencies or a single state agency with several subsidiary units usually controls air pollution, water pollution, and solid waste disposal. Other agencies found in many states are:

Land use control agency
Power plant siting agency
Coastal resources agency
Noise control agency
Pesticide control agency
Radiation monitoring agency
Hazardous waste control agency
Occupational safety and health agency

These agencies review and approve real estate project plans. They issue construction and operating permits and licenses. They generally enforce state regulations passed by state legislatures which apply to the particular real estate project. Shopping center developers have been scrutinized closely for excessive indirect sources of pollution. The developer's shopping center tends to attract heavy customer vehicular traffic. If the center is successful, this will result. The exhaust fumes from customer vehicles traveling to the single site of consolidated retail units in the form of a shopping center may cause concentrated air pollution. Water drainage problems may develop if not anticipated by the developer. The water runs off the parking lot expanse, which does not have absorptive qualities, into adjacent residential and commercial areas. The center may overload the original neighborhood water treatment facilities and energy sources. Plans can be made by the developer to correct these environmental problems before they get a chance to occur.

As the developer plans the center, the environmental impact studies must be prepared so that the necessary construction and operating permits and licenses from each of the relevant federal and state agencies can be acquired. The acquisition of permits and licenses may take some time *after* time is consumed by the preparation of the necessary environmental impact studies. The financing is contingent upon the acquisition of the proper permits and licenses so that construction may start.

The Impact of Private Ecology Organizations and Groups. Very vocal in some areas are private ecology organizations who seek to preserve the environment. These private groups can impede the progress of the developer of a shopping center, particularly a regional or superregional center which can have significant ecological impact. If the developer anticipates the usual objections of the private groups, ecological studies may be prepared during the center's planning stage so that the objections can be met promptly. The developer may engage in a community and public relations campaign through the local media to alleviate the threat to development progress.

The General Content of the Ecological and Environmental Impact Studies. The regulatory agency usually wants a description of the center being developed. The summary of the development plans should be followed by a description of the environment before the commencement of construction. The federal and state regulators then wish to know what impact the center will have upon the environment. What impact will the center have on the land form? Noise? Water quality? Air quality? What impact will the center have on natural systems such as the landscape, the vegetation, and the wildlife? What impact will there be on the open space system including the park and recreation systems of the community, region, and state? What impact will the center have on the historical and scientific resources of the area? Will the center impact on other environmental features of the area and region?

The developer, with the aid perhaps of assistants or consultants, will need to analyze any adverse environmental effects caused by the center which cannot be avoided. What alternative measures can be taken by the developer to minimize these adverse environmental effects? What measures does the developer plan to take to maximize the relationship between local, short-term uses of the land and the enhancement of long-term productivity of the land? Will irreversible changes occur when the center is completed and in operation? Will the center induce further growth in the area or region? What kind of growth?

After the regulatory agency reviews the developer's summary of the ecological and environmental impact of the proposed center, the regulatory agency may or may not issue construction and operating permits and licenses for the development. The developer may need to make changes in plans to gain the permits and licenses in order to proceed with the project.

Key Elements in Site Selection

Before plans for the center can move forward, the site must be selected and put under developer control. The key elements in the site selection process are:

Population in the trading area and its trend
Population demographics and their trends
Traffic count
Access to the property
Driving time to the site
Visibility
Competition in the trading area
Size and shape of the site
Site conditions
Ecology of the site and potential sources of pollution

Most of these factors have been considered, but let us consider a few additional factors related to the key elements of site selection. The population of the metropolitan and regional trading areas is usually broken down into the populations of the one-mile, two-mile, and five-mile trading radii of the center. The trends in the population sectors are noted. Successful development usually requires "up trends" or expected future increases in the majority of the trading area sectors. The trading area demographics should agree with the proposed type of shopping center. (The term "demographics" refers to population characteristics such as age distribution, ethnic group concentration, income distribution, predominating life styles, religious preferences, racial composition, and educational levels of achievement.)

The traffic counts for the portion of the roadways adjacent to the center are important, but the type of traffic is even more important. There must be easy visual observation of the retail offerings. The more motorists that are aware of the shopping center location, the more heavily the center will be patronized. The traffic analyst should note the volume of the traffic at various times of day over the various days of the year. Traffic congestion will probably occur at specific times of the day. What causes the traffic congestion? What is the destination of the traveller who passes the shopping center site? What are the demographic characteristics of the drivers and their passengers? The ultimate question is: Will the usual traffic benefit the proposed shopping center?

The site must be accessible to the potential customers. Will the current road system suffice for the potential traffic generated by the center? Will changes be needed? Will an arterial road around the outer edge of the center be necessary to control the customer traffic and truck deliveries?

The driving time to the shopping center is strategically important. How many people with how much buying power live within three minutes' driving time? Five minutes' driving time? Ten minutes' driving time? Longer driving times will concern regional and superregional center developers. How many of the potential patrons from each of the radii will shop at the center? What should the center developer expect as a share of the market from the market potential that exists?

Since the center should be visible to the prospective customer, it should not be built too high on a hill or in an extremely low place. Trees and other obstructions should not prevent the driver and passengers in a vehicle on an adjacent interstate freeway from seeing the shopping center. Some of the vegetation may need to be removed with the permission of the landlord. A location in a high or low spot may be detrimental during the winter, when ice and snow create hazardous driving conditions on steep inclines. A low place will attract water flows from the thawing of winter ice and snow. High locations will probably provide their own drainage, which may or may not create problems on adjacent land, but low places will need substantial drainage facilities. If the center is being built in a location with a high water table such as in Florida, drainage becomes a major problem.

The competition in the trading area must be noted and analyzed for its impact on the proposed center. There may or may not be direct competition for the proposed investment. The proposed center may be complementary to the existing retailing. Even if direct competition exists, the proposed development may offer superior goods and services, better parking, better access, better and more attractive design, better center management, and better merchandising in a new, totally planned, weather-controlled facility. A superior share of the market may be attained with this winning combination. Then again, the existing competition should not be underestimated. The potential customers of the trading area may be very loyal to the merchants they have patronized for years. The shopping patterns may have become entrenched; habitual shopping routines may have developed and may not easily be broken.

The size of the tract must, at a minimum, accommodate the center buildings and the necessary parking lots. The developer may prefer a tract that is much larger than that needed for the center so that profits may be generated from the sale or lease of appreciating adjacent land. Part of the developer's profit comes often from the sale or lease of outparcels that are not necessary to the center itself.

The outparcels must be located in appropriate places. They also must have accessibility and visibility and be improved with all necessary utility systems. The size and shape of the outparcels must be conducive to lease by outside tenants and developers. Usually the concern for the eventual profitability of the outparcels leads to their integration into the overall planning for the center development. The outparcels may promise a substantial portion of the total profit for the developer.

The shopping center site itself must be the appropriate shape. The surface soil conditions must be appropriate for the development, but the immediate subsurface conditions must permit the digging of foundations. Rock ledges or stone deposits immediately underground will cause foundation problems. Shifting sand in many layers beneath the surface will also promote problems, but of a different kind. In sandy areas, concrete caissons may have to encase foundation materials and retaining walls may have to be constructed to hold back the soft matter until the foundations are completed and the building construction above ground started. In commercial districts of major metropolitan areas, the foundation work may involve many underground cables, utility lines, subway tunnels, truck delivery streets and tunnels, and other such complicated underground systems.

The ecology of the site may be permanently or temporarily disturbed. Often demolition and construction vehicles and crews destroy the original landscaping and vegetation of the site. The environmentalists and others worry about the displacement of the birds and other creatures who originally inhabited the site.

On the other hand, when residential buildings are demolished to make way for the shopping center, some will question the displacement of people. The developer may have to aid the original building tenants in finding substitute residential space in order to quiet public clamor. Displacement of lower income people without developer assistance can prompt negative press very easily.

Techniques for Rating Sites for Subsequent Selection

The developer uses informal and, at times, formal means for rating sites before making the final site selection. The informal method of site selection may involve giving 60 percent of the valuation to the nature of the trading area of the site, 30 percent of the value to the neighboring tenants or nearby competition, and 10 percent of the valuation to the site characteristics. Each possible site is analyzed by these weighted criteria.

Formal site rating systems have been developed. One of these systems, a composite index system for better shopping center site selection, was summarized in the January 1982 issue of *Shopping Center World*. The weighted rating system takes into account:

Population	Age of mall
Income per household	General condition of mall
Other demographic variables	General area conditions near mall
Size of mall	Pedestrian traffic count
Mall sales per square foot	Industry competition in the mall
Competitive malls within six miles	Mall anchors
Location of our store	Opinion of the person completing the form
Size of our store	National chain consensus
Store frontage	Other (Exhibit 5-3)

Site Acquisition

The best site for the proposed center is selected. In case this site cannot be acquired, the next best site is also selected. The selections are made from the trading area that has the greatest potential for the new center. The developer then proceeds to acquire the best site.

In many instances the developer will select the same site for the center that competing developers will select. This is particularly true if the center is to be a regional or superregional center. In a major urban area only one or two sites at any time may be considered by regional or superregional center developers. Other locations are definitely inferior. So the competition among the developers ensues. Who will gain control of the site?

Gaining control of the site may involve several people. A local commercial broker may represent the developer. The developer may not wish to disclose his or her identity or intentions for the development of the site. The developer's attorney or leasing staff may negotiate for the parcels without disclosing the buyer's identity. The site may have to be acquired or leased in small parcels. All of the small parcels will have to be leased or purchased before the site may be developed. If the individual landowners learn the identity and the intentions of the developer, they may hold up the acquisition by refusing to lease or sell or they may negotiate for an extremely high sale price or lease terms. They may figure that the developer foresees a whopping big profit from the investment and they should get their share now!

Composite Index Form

Name of mall:

Address of mall:

Total Composite Number: _____
Developer:

1. Population
   Add 1 point for each 50,000 people
   living within 6 miles of mall. _____

   Add an extra 2 points if trade area
   of mall is greater than 10 miles. _____

2. Income per household _____
Under $15,000	1
15,000 - 20,000	2
20,001 - 25,000	3
25,001 - 30,000	4
Above $30,000	5

3. Other Demographic Variables
   Add or deduct up to 6 points depending
   upon whether the other demographic
   factors are favorable. _____

4. Size of mall _____
   Add 1 point for each 100,000 feet
   of G.L.A. over 350,000 square feet.

5. Mall Sales Per Square Foot _____
Below $100	1
100 - 125	2
125 - 150	3
150 - 175	4
Above $176	5

6. Competitive Malls Within 6 Miles
   Subtract 1 point for each mall over
   400,000 square feet within 6 miles _____

   Subtract 1 point for each larger mall
   within 6 miles. _____

7. Location of our store _____
Center third of mall	5
Second third of mall	3
Last third of mall	1½
Entrance corridor	½
Secondary corridors	–2

8. Size of our store _____
   Add 1 point for each 10% of space beyond
   our minimum requirements (maximum of 4
   points).

9. Store Frontage _____
   Add ½ point for each 20% of store
   frontage beyond our minimum requirements (maximum of 2 points).

10. Age of Mall _____
1 - 3 years old	1
4 - 6 years old	2
Over 7 years old	3

11. General Condition of Mall _____
Mall is attractive	2
Mall is unattractive	–2
Mall has been expanded within last 2 years	2

    Mall vacancies
    Deduct 1 point for each 10,000 square
    feet vacant in mall (maximum of –4 points)

    Deduct 2 more points if there are any
    vacancies within 100 feet of proposed
    space.

12. General Area Conditions Near Mall _____
Major highway access within 1 mile	2
Busy retail area	2

13. Pedestrian Traffic Count _____
    Add up to 3 points depending upon
    the amount of traffic in the mall.

14. Industry Competition In The Mall _____
    Deduct 2 points depending upon the
    amount of competition in the mall.

15. Mall Anchors _____
    For each of the following, add the #
    of points following each type of score:
Mass merchandiser	1½
Popular dept. store	1½
High fashion dept. store	1
Discount dept. store	¾
Theater	½
Other tenant over 30,000 sq. ft.	½

16. Opinion of the person completing form
    who has visited proposed site. _____
    Add 1 to 5 points.

17. National Chain Consensus

Name of Chain	Below Average −3	Average 3	Above Average 4	Excellent 5

(Contact 6 national chains in the mall and average their
responses)

OTHER: _____
_____
_____
_____
_____

Exhibit 5-3. Composite Index Form for Better Shopping Center Site Selection

Source: Solomon, Noal S., "Composite Index Form Can Help Chains Select Better Sites," *Shopping Center World*, 11:1, January 1982, p. 157. Copyright 1982 Communication Channels, Inc., 6285 Barfield Road, Atlanta, GA 30328.

The land may be owned or controlled by a single party. That may make the land acquisition or lease easier for the prospective developer. It may not prove easier if the owner has his or her own ideas for future development or if he or she wishes to hold the large tract until another developer offers an even higher price. The single landowner may be a real estate broker, an institutional investor, a farmer who normally cultivates the land or grazes cattle on the land, or a land speculator. If the landowner is a real estate broker, the land may have been acquired through a tax-deferred real property exchange. If the landowner is a sophisticated real estate person, the negotiations between the developer and that owner may be relatively brief and to the point. They may both see the potential in the proposed income property and merely have to agree upon mutually beneficial lease or sale terms. Each of the sophisticated negotiators bargains on the basis of his or her current tax, legal, and financial requirements. Once the terms of control are approved by both parties, their respective attorneys draw up the necessary documents and record the financial instruments and other contracts at the courthouse, parish house, or town hall where the real property is located.

Acquisition Methods

There are three methods that are commonly used in acquiring the control of a proposed shopping center site. They are:

Land purchase
Joint venture with the landowner
Ground lease

Each of the methods is associated with certain financial benefits and detractions. Tax considerations on the part of the seller-lessor and the buyer-lessee are part of these financial attractions. The property owner may or may not have a need for cash and may or may not have a need for tax shelter. The developer may be short of cash in terms of the total development or may have ample financial resources so that all options are valid alternatives. The developer may or may not need tax shelter. The development company may face a high income tax incidence in the current and future years, or the company may have sufficient tax shields to maintain a low income tax profile.

The Option Contract. Once the agreement is reached, an option may be taken. An option gives the developer time to negotiate for the rezoning of the land, if this is needed, and time to acquire the necessary environmental protection agency licenses and permits. The developer also has time to negotiate for acceptable financing. If the land cannot be rezoned so that the center development may take place or if the environmental licenses and permits are not forthcoming even after extended negotiations with the agencies, the land would be worthless to the developer. The necessary funds may or may not be available from investors and lenders on the appropriate terms. The developer would let the option lapse or sell the option to another developer of a permissible land use before the option terminates. In the meantime, the landowner would receive the option consideration or fee for withholding the land from the market. This option consideration may be nominal or it may involve several thousands of dollars when the agreed-upon price of the land or lease is substantial. The option consideration or fee may be applicable to the purchase price if the option is exercised. Otherwise, it may be forfeited through the terms of the option agreement. The option contains all of the terms of the negotiated agreement and permits the developer to exercise or renew the option or let it lapse. The agreement may permit the developer to sell the option before its termination date. By its termination date, the option buyer may wish to exercise the option on its original terms. A sample option to purchase real estate may be viewed in Exhibit 5-4.

Exhibit 5-4. Option to Purchase Real Estate

NORTH CAROLINA

OPTION TO PURCHASE REAL ESTATE

COUNTY

FOR AND IN CONSIDERATION of the sum of FIVE THOUSAND DOLLARS ($5,000.00) to them in hand paid, the receipt of which is hereby acknowledged, the undersigned,   , his wife,   and his wife,   , (hereinafter sometimes collectively called "Optionor") do hereby grant unto W.A. Heath, Jr., his heirs, successors and assigns, (hereinafter sometimes called "Optionee"), the right and option to purchase that certain piece of property (hereinafter called the "Option Tract") located on the west side of U.S. Highway #   bypass and south of the intersection of   Road, and being approximately twenty (20) acres in size, and shown more particularly as outlined in green on Exhibit "A" attached hereto, and initialled by all parties, and by this reference made a part hereof.

The parties hereto covenant and agree that the option granted herein is subject to the following terms and conditions:

1. The option is granted and may be exercised any time within the period commencing with the date of execution of this instrument and ending at 12:00 midnight on the date which is one hundred eighty (180) days from the date of execution of this instrument. Notice of the Optionee's intention to exercise such option shall be given in writing to the Optionor on or before the time of expiration of the original option term or its authorized extension if such extension right has been exercised, and such notice shall be deemed sufficient when deposited in the United States mail, addressed as directed in Paragraph 3, and sent by certified mail, return receipt requested.

2. The term of this option may be extended for one additional period of one hundred eighty (180) days upon payment of an additional Six Thousand Dollars ($6,000.00) to Optionor. Notice of Optionee's intent to extend and payment of said sum shall be made to the Optionor in writing on or before the time of expiration of the original term and such notice shall be deemed sufficient when deposited in the United States mail, addressed as directed in Paragraph 3, and sent by certified mail, return receipt requested.

(Continued)

Exhibit 5-4. *(Continued)*

3.   Notice of election to purchase or extend this option as authorized shall be sent to Optionor, care of

4.   In the event the Optionee elects to exercise this option, the Optionor shall, within thirty (30) days following receipt of notice to that effect, convey the Option Tract to the Optionee by delivery of a General Warranty Deed free and clear of all liens and encumbrances but subject to all existing rights-of-way of record for public roads, streets or highways, upon payment of the specified purchase price. The exact date of closing shall be mutually agreed upon by the parties, but shall not be later than thirty (30) days after notice of intent to purchase hereunder. Closing shall take place in the offices of Optionor's attorneys absent mutual agreement among the parties to hold the closing elsewhere.

5.   The total purchase price to be paid by the Optionee to the Optionor as consideration for the conveyance of the Option Tract (upon exercise of the option by the Optionee) shall be Six Hundred Fifty Thousand Dollars ($650,000.00), to be divided among Optionors in such manner as they shall then direct. The purchase price shall be paid in full in cash at closing.

6.   Notwithstanding the foregoing, Optionee shall have the right, privilege and option, at his election, but within the same option period and subject to all other terms and provisions of this option, to purchase a smaller tract (hereinafter called the "Alternative Option Tract") being a fifteen (15) acre portion of the Option Tract, and shown more particularly as outlined in red on Exhibit "A" attached hereto. If Optionee elects to purchase the Alternative Option Tract, the total purchase price to be paid by Optionee to Optionor for the conveyance of the Alternative Option Tract (upon exercise of the option by the Optionee) shall be Five Hundred Twenty-Five Thousand Dollars ($525,000.00), to be divided among Optionors in such manner as they shall direct at closing. The purchase price shall be paid in full in cash at closing.

7.   In the event Optionee exercises the option to purchase either the Option Tract or the Alternative Option Tract, Optionor shall convey to Optionee at closing the following easements:

A.   A twenty (20) foot wide permanent easement for the installation and maintenance of a sewer line, said easement to be located as shown by the orange broken line on Exhibit "B" attached hereto. The westerly most boundary of said easement shall be the westerly most boundary of the Optionor's property as shown on said Exhibit "B" and the easterly most boundary of said easement shall be a line parallel with the westerly most line and twenty (20) feet distant therefrom. Optionee, at his sole expense, shall provide a survey description of said easement to Optionor at least five (5) days prior to closing. If Optionee does install a sewer line within said easement, Optionee shall have the right to grant said easement to the City of   or the appropriate authority therein with jurisdiction over sewer lines, and Optionor covenants and agrees to join in such conveyance if requested by Optionee to do so. Optionee shall pay all costs and expenses of installing and maintaining said sewer line. In addition to the sewer easement, Optionor covenants and agrees to grant Optionee such temporary construction easements as may be reasonably necessary to enable Optionee to install said sewer line. If Optionee has not installed a sewer line within said easement by the date which is three (3) years from the date of closing, then said easement shall terminate and Optionee shall have no further right, title or interest in same.

Exhibit 5-4. *(Continued)*

B.   A fifty (50) foot wide permanent, non-exclusive easement for the construction and maintenance of an access road to the Option Tract or the Alternative Option Tract along the westerly boundary of U.S.   Bypass, said easement being as shown outlined in blue on Exhibit "A" attached hereto. Optionee, at his sole expense, shall provide a survey description of said easement to Optionor at least five (5) days prior to closing. If Optionee has not installed an access road within said easement by the date which is three (3) years from the date of closing, then said easement shall terminate and Optionee shall have no further right, title or interest in same. If Optionee constructs said access road, same shall be available for use by all parties to this instrument and their successors and assigns. Optionee shall construct and maintain said access road at his sole cost and expense. If Optionee constructs said access road, Optionee shall have the right to dedicate same to the State Transportation Commission, and Optionor shall join in such dedication and convey any necessary right-of-way to the State Highway Commission.

C.   Notwithstanding the foregoing, in the event, after closing and within the time limited above, Optionee exercises his right to use either or both easements granted above, Optionee will, during the course of construction, be fully responsible for all such activities, and shall hold Optionor harmless from any claims, damages or rights of action arising out of his activities in the construction or use of said easements, and will restore and replace the soil over the sewer easement and/or the soil surrounding the access road easement to substantially the same condition as before the exercise of his easement rights.

8.   All monies paid for this option, or subsequent extension thereof, shall be credited against the purchase price; but if said option is not exercised within the period above set out or if the purchase is not consummated within thirty (30) days following notice of exercise of the option to purchase for any reason other than default by the Optionor, then all sums paid hereunder shall be retained by Optionor as the purchase price of this option and thereafter Optionee shall have no further rights under this option.

9.   In the event said property is purchased under the terms of this option, property taxes for the year in which said option is exercised shall be prorated between the parties as of the date of closing. It shall be the Optionor's obligation to pay for State transfer taxes on the warranty deed and the cost of preparing the deed. Optionee certifies that it has dealt direct with Optionor, and that no commissions or fees are involved.

10.   In the event Optionee exercises this option, or its extension,   shall have the right without charge at any time within ninety (90) days after the closing of said purchase to remove his dwelling and improvements and any or all of his personal property from the premises; but in the event any part or all of said dwelling (and personal property) is not removed within said ninety-day period, then said unremoved property shall be deemed abandoned by him and shall become the property of the Optionee.   shall have the right to occupy said dwelling free of rent for said ninety-day period.

11.   The Optionee, or its agent, shall have the right during the term of this option, or its extension, to enter upon the Option Tract at any time for the purposes of making an examination of the property and a survey or surveys thereof. Optionee shall be fully responsible for all such activities and shall hold Optionor harmless from any claims,

Exhibit 5-4. *(Continued)*

damages or rights of action arising out of its activities on or about the land in question. If soil drillings are made on the property due care shall be taken in order that no damage will occur to the dwelling, to the existing septic tank system, to the well, to the immediate area around the dwelling, to the existing entrance and driveway into and out of the dwelling so as to insure free access to public   Road. In the event Optionee elects not to purchase hereunder it shall replace the soil in substantially the same condition as before the tests.

12.   This option shall be assignable by the Optionee at its discretion.

13.   The Optionor makes no representations and does not guarantee any access to the lands in question, except for the access right-of-way specified in Paragraph 7.B above.

14.   In the event Optionee desires to place evidence of this option of record, it is agreed that a memorandum shall be executed and recorded, rather than this original option.

IN TESTIMONY WHEREOF, Optionors and Optionee have hereunto set their hands and seals to this contract in duplicate originals, this the _____ day of _____, 1980.

OPTIONOR:

_____(SEAL)

_____(SEAL)

_____(SEAL)

_____(SEAL)

OPTIONEE

_____(SEAL)

STATE OF NORTH CAROLINA
COUNTY OF _____

I, _____, a Notary Public in and for said County and State, do hereby certify that   and wife   personally appeared before me this day and acknowledged the due execution of the foregoing instrument.

WITNESS my hand and notarial seal, this _____ day of _____, 19___.

_____
Notary Public

Exhibit 5-4. *(Continued)*

My Commission Expires:

_____

(NOTARIAL SEAL)

STATE OF NORTH CAROLINA
COUNTY OF _____

   I, _____, a Notary Public in and for said County and State, do hereby certify that   and wife   personally appeared before me this day and acknowledged the due execution of the foregoing instrument.
   WITNESS my hand and notarial seal, this _____ day of _____, 19_____.

                                 _____

                                            Notary Public

My Commission Expires:

_____

(NOTARIAL SEAL)

STATE OF NORTH CAROLINA
COUNTY OF MECKLENBURG

   I, _____, a Notary Public in and for said County and State, do hereby certify that W.A. HEATH, JR. personally appeared before me this day and acknowledged the due execution of the foregoing instrument.
   WITNESS my hand and notarial seal, this _____ day of _____, 19_____.

                                   _____

                                            Notary Public

My Commission Expires:

_____

Source: Faison Associates, Charlotte, NC, October 21, 1982.

Land Purchase. The land may be purchased in one lump sum or in installments. The purchase contract sets forth (1) the earnest money paid by the purchaser, (2) the assumptions of any existing loans or mortgages, and (3) the nature of lump sum payment or promissory note that establishes installment payments with interest (Exhibit 5-5, Offer to Purchase and Contract). The conditions

Exhibit 5-5.   Offer to Purchase and Contract

OFFER TO PURCHASE AND CONTRACT

.... , as Buyer, hereby agrees
to purchase and .... , as Seller,
hereby agrees to sell and convey, all of that plot, piece or parcel of land described below, together with all improvements located thereon and such personal
property as is listed below (the real and personal property are collectively referred to as "the Property"), in accordance with the Standard Provisions on the
REVERSE SIDE HEREOF and upon the following terms and conditions:

1. REAL PROPERTY: Located in the City of .... , County of
.... , State of North Carolina, being known as and more particularly
described as:

Street Address ....

Legal Description ....
....

2. PERSONAL PROPERTY: ....

3. PURCHASE PRICE: The purchase price is $ .... and shall be paid as follows:

(a) $ _____ , in earnest money paid by .... ,
(cash; bank, certified, or personal check) with the delivery of this contract, to be held in escrow by _____
_____ , as agent, until the sale is closed, at which time it will be
credited to Buyer, or until this agreement is otherwise terminated and it is disbursed in accordance with the Standard
Provisions on the REVERSE SIDE HEREOF.

(b) $ _____ , by assumption of the unpaid principal balance and all obligations of Seller on the existing loan secured by a deed of trust on the
Property;

(c) $ _____ , by a promissory note secured by a purchase money deed of trust on the Property with interest prior to default at the rate of
_____ % per annum, payable by _____ payments of $ _____ commencing on _____ . Prepayment rights, if
any, shall be: _____
_____

Assumption or transfer rights, if any, shall be: _____
_____

(d) $ _____ , the balance of the purchase price in cash at closing;

4. CONDITIONS: (State N A in each blank paragraph 4 (a) and 4 (b) that is not a condition to this contract)

(a) The Buyer must be able to obtain a firm commitment effective through the date of closing for a ....
loan in the principal amount of $ .... for a term of .... year(s), at an interest rate not to exceed .... % prior
to .... Buyer agrees to use his best efforts to secure such commitment and to advise Seller immediately upon
his receipt of the lender's decision. Mortgage loan discount points not to exceed .... % of the loan shall be paid by
_____ , and loan closing cost shall be paid by _____ . (b) The Buyer must be able to assume the unpaid principal balance of
the existing loan described in paragraph 3(b) above for the remainder of the loan term, at an interest rate not to exceed .... % fixed or ....
If such assumption requires the lender's approval, approval must be granted prior to .... Buyer agrees to advise Seller
immediately upon his receipt of the lender's decision. In addition to any reasonable transfer fee (see STANDARD PROVISION No. 2), mortgage loan
assumption and/or discount points not to exceed $ .... shall be paid as follows: ....
....

(c) There must be no restrictions, easement, zoning or other governmental regulation that would prevent the reasonable use of the real property for
.... purposes.

5. ASSESSMENTS: Seller warrants that there are no encumbrances or special assessments, either pending or confirmed, for sidewalk, paving, water,
sewer or other improvements on or adjoining the Property, except as follows: ....
....

(Insert "none" or the identification of any such assessments, if any; the agreement for payment or proration of any assessments indicated is to be set forth in
paragraph 6 below.)

6. OTHER PROVISIONS AND CONDITIONS:

(a) All of the Standard Provisions on the REVERSE SIDE HEREOF are understood and shall apply to this instrument, except the following numbered
Standard Provisions shall be deleted: ....
(If none are to be deleted, state 'None" in this blank)

(If additional space is needed, the bottom of the reverse side of this page may be used)

7. CLOSING: All parties agree to execute any and all documents and papers necessary in connection with closing and transfer of title on or before
.... , at a place designated by ....
Deed is to be made to ....

8. POSSESSION: Possession shall be delivered .... ; in the event that Buyer has agreed
that possession is not delivered at closing, then Seller agrees to pay to Buyer the sum of .... per day
to and including the date that possession is to be delivered as above set forth.

9. COUNTERPARTS: This Offer shall become a binding contract when signed by both Buyer and Seller and is executed in ....
.... counterparts with an executed counterpart being retained by each party hereto.
Date of Offer: ....   Date of Acceptance: ....

.... (SEAL)   .... (SEAL)
(Buyer)   Seller (Owner)

.... (SEAL)   .... (SEAL)
(Buyer)   Seller (Owner)

....
Agent/Firm   Agent/Firm

I hereby acknowledge receipt of the earnest money herein set forth in accordance with the terms hereof.

....
Date   Agent/Firm

                                                                 By: _____

This Standard Form has been approved jointly by: The North Carolina Bar Association and The North
Carolina Association of Realtors®, Inc.

N.C. Bar Assoc. Form No. 2° 1979, Revised 1982

Exhibit 5-5. *(Continued)*

STANDARD PROVISIONS

1. EARNEST MONEY: In the event this offer is not accepted, or in the event that any of the conditions hereto are not satisfied, or in the event of a breach of this contract by Seller, then the earnest money shall be returned to Buyer, but such return shall not affect any other remedies available to Buyer for such breach. In the event this offer is accepted and Buyer breaches this contract, then the earnest money shall be forfeited, but such forfeiture shall not affect any other remedies available to Seller for such breach.

2. LOAN ASSUMED: In the event a loan is assumed as part of the payment of the purchase price, then all payments due from Seller thereon must be current at closing, and the principal balance assumed shall be computed as of the date of closing. The amounts shown for the assumption balance and cash at closing shall be adjusted as appropriate at closing to reflect the final computations. Unless Buyer has otherwise specifically agreed in writing, the existing loan must be assumable without acceleration of the amount secured or any change in the original terms of the note and deed of trust and without imposition of any charge, fee or cost to Buyer other than a reasonable transfer fee or similar charge not to exceed $175.00. The escrow account, if any, shall be purchased by Buyer.

3. PROMISSORY NOTE AND DEED OF TRUST: In the event a promissory note secured by a deed of trust is given by Buyer to Seller as part of the payment of the purchase price, the promissory note and deed of trust shall be in the form of and contain the provisions of the promissory note and deed of trust forms approved by the N.C. Bar Association as Forms 4 and 5, as modified in paragraph 3(c) on the reverse side.

4. PRORATIONS AND ADJUSTMENTS: Unless otherwise provided, the following items shall be prorated and adjusted between the parties or paid at closing:

(a) Ad valorem taxes on real property shall be prorated on a calendar year basis to the date of closing.

(b) Ad valorem taxes on personal property for the entire year shall be paid by Seller.

(c) All late listing penalties, if any, shall be paid by Seller.

(d) Rents, if any, for the Property shall be prorated to the date of closing.

(e) Accrued, but unpaid, interest and other charges to Seller, if any, shall be computed to the date of closing and paid by Seller; interest and other charges prepaid by Seller shall be credited to Seller at closing and paid by Buyer. (Other charges may include FHA mortgage insurance premiums, private mortgage insurance premiums and Homeowner's Association dues.)

5. FIRE OR OTHER CASUALTY: The risk of loss or damage by fire or other casualty prior to closing shall be upon Seller.

6. CONDITIONS:

(a) The Property must be in substantially the same condition at closing as on the date of this offer, reasonable wear and tear excepted.

(b) All deeds of trust, liens and other charges against the Property, not assumed by Buyer, must be paid and cancelled by Seller prior to or at closing.

(c) Title must be delivered at closing by general warranty deed and must be fee simple marketable title, free of all encumbrances except ad valorem taxes for the current year (prorated to date of closing), utility easements and unviolated restrictive covenants that do not materially affect the value of Property and such other encumbrances as may be assumed or specifically approved by Buyer. The subject Property must have legal access to a public right of way.

(d) If a portion of the purchase price for the Property is being paid by assumption of an existing loan and if the lender requires its approval for the assumption, then the approval of the Lender, after diligent application therefore by Buyer, is a condition of this contract.

7. NEW LOAN: Buyer shall be responsible for all charges made to Buyer with respect to any new loan obtained by Buyer and Seller shall have no obligation to pay any discount fee or other charge in connection therewith unless specifically set forth in this contract.

8. UTILITIES: Unless otherwise stated herein, the electrical, plumbing, heating and cooling systems and built-in appliances, if any, shall be in good working order at closing. Buyer has the option to have the same inspected by a reputable inspector or contractor at Buyer's expense, but such inspections must be completed in sufficient time before closing so as to

permit repairs, if any, to be completed by closing. If any repairs are necessary, Seller shall have the option of (a) completing them, (b) providing for their completion, or (c) refusing to complete them. If Seller elects not to complete the repairs, then Buyer shall have to option of (a) accepting the Property in its present condition, or (b) terminating the contract, in which case the earnest money shall be refunded. Closing shall constitute acceptance of the electrical, plumbing, heating and cooling systems and built-in appliances in their existing condition unless provision is otherwise made in writing pursuant to this paragraph. [RECOMMENDATION: Buyer should have any inspections made prior to incurring expenses for closing.]

9. TERMITES, ETC.: Unless otherwise stated herein, Seller shall provide at Seller's expense a report from a licensed pest control operator on a standard form in accordance with the regulations of the North Carolina Structural Pest Control Committee, stating that there was no visible evidence of wood-destroying insects and that no visible damage therefrom was observed, or, if new construction, a new construction termite bond. All extermination required shall be paid for by Seller and completed prior to closing, unless otherwise agreed upon in writing by the parties. If any structural repairs are necessary, Seller shall have the option of (a) paying for them, or (b) refusing to pay for them. If Seller elects not to pay for such structural repairs, then Buyer shall have the option of (a) accepting the Property in its present condition, or (b) terminating the contract, in which latter case the earnest money shall be refunded. The inspection and report described in this paragraph may not reveal either structural damage or damage caused by agents or organisms other than termites and wood-destroying insects.

10. LABOR OR MATERIAL: Seller shall furnish at closing an affidavit and indemnification agreement in form satisfactory to Buyer showing that all labor or materials, if any, furnished to the Property within 120 days prior to the date of closing have been paid and agreeing to indemnify Buyer against all loss from any cause or claim arising therefrom.

11. FUEL OIL: Buyer agrees to purchase from Seller the fuel oil, if any, situated in a tank on the premises for the prevailing rate per gallon with the cost of measurement thereof, if any, being borne by Seller.

12. CLOSING EXPENSES: Seller shall pay for the preparation of a deed and for the revenue stamps required by law. Buyer shall pay for recording the deed and for preparation and recording of all instruments required to secure the balance of the purchase price unpaid at closing.

13. EVIDENCE OF TITLE: Seller agrees to exercise his efforts to deliver to Buyer as soon as reasonably possible after the acceptance of this offer, copies of all title information in possession of or available to Seller, including but not limited to: title insurance policies, attorney's opinions on title, surveys, covenants, deeds, notes and deeds of trust and easements relating to the real and personal property described above.

14. ASSIGNMENTS: This contract may not be assigned without the written agreement of all parties, but if the same is assigned by agreement, then the same shall be binding on the Assignee and his heirs.

15. PARTIES: This contract shall be binding and shall inure to the benefit of the parties and their heirs, successors and assigns. The Provisions herein contained with respect to promissory notes and deeds of trust shall be binding upon and shall inure to the benefit of all parties to the same as well as subsequent owners of the Property and the said notes and deeds of trust. As used herein, words in the singular include the plural and the masculine includes the feminine and neuter genders, as appropriate.

16. SURVIVAL: Any provisions herein contained which by its nature and effect if required to be observed, kept or performed after the closing shall survive the closing and remain binding upon and for the benefit of the parties hereto until fully observed, kept or performed.

17. ENTIRE AGREEMENT: Buyer acknowledges that he has inspected the above described property. This contract contains the entire agreement of the parties and there are no representation, inducements, or other provisions other than those expressed in writing. All changes, additions or deletions hereto must be in writing and signed by all parties. Nothing herein contained shall alter any agreement between a REALTOR and the Seller as contained in any listing contract or other agreement between them.

(CONTINUATION OF OTHER CONDITIONS FROM REVERSE SIDE, IF APPLICABLE)

that must be satisfied before the sale is final may involve (1) acquisition of the stated loan on the stated terms, (2) the receipt of mortgage loan discount points by the lender, (3) negotiated allocation of the payment of the various closing costs between the buyer and the seller, and (4) evidence that there are no restrictions such as zoning ordinances that would preclude the development of the site as a shopping center. The prospective buyer usually makes the offer through the real estate broker who represents the seller. If the seller wishes to accept the terms of the offer, the seller, the seller's spouse, and other owners sign the purchase contract as legal evidence of their approval of the offer.

If immediate payment in total takes place, the buyer makes all the funds immediately payable to the seller. A small part of the closing costs, such as prepaid interest, is immediate tax-deductible expense for the developer for income tax purposes. The seller must pay any capital gains taxes on the sale. If at least one payment toward the purchase price is made in a tax year other than the year of sale, the seller may defer income taxes on the possible capital gain by paying a proportional amount of the capital gains tax in the tax year in which the installment payment was received.

The developer could acquire the desired property through a swap for other property of the buyer. The exchange might be tax free, depending on its nature, except for any transfer of boot. If unlike property such as cash or notes is traded as a part of the exchange to equalize values, this boot is normally subject to taxation.

If an installment contract is negotiated with the seller, that contract may be either a purchase money mortgage with a standard down payment or a land contract with a nominal front-end payment. Under purchase money mortgage financing, the seller transfers the title to the land to the buyer and receives installment payments over time. Under land contract financing, the buyer makes a nominal down payment and has the right of possession of the land until the installment payments are completely paid to the seller. At the completion of the land contract payments, the seller is obligated to transfer to the buyer the title to the property.

Ground Lease. The seller may agree to lease the land to the developer for an extended time period. Then the lease may be subject to renewal. If renewal of the lease is desired, negotiations would take place between the landowner, the lessor, and the lessee, the developer. The ground lease usually provides use of the land under stipulated conditions in exchange for periodic lease payments. The lessee may be obligated to make the given improvements to the land within a specified time period. When the lease term ends, the provision for the ownership of the leasehold improvements is stated. If no provisions are made, the leasehold improvements revert to the landowner. The lease contract may permit the ground lessee to purchase the ground lessor's interest in the buildings by payment of the appraised value of the leasehold improvements at the end of the lease or for some other sum. For Internal Revenue Service purposes, the ground lease should not closely resemble a mortgage loan agreement with only nominal payment for the leasehold improvements at the lease termination date. Otherwise, the Internal Revenue Service will disallow the full tax deductibility of the total lease payments by the lessee during the term of the lease.

The negotiated lease terms usually permit the landowner to receive a reasonable yield on the investment. That yield to the ground lessor may come in the form of periodic fixed or escalating lease payments plus ground lessor participation in the gross or net income of the lessee who constructed the income property. The lessee receives income from the shopping center tenants. This income may be subject to ground lessor participation. As an alternative, the net operating income of the center owner may be subject to ground lessor participation.

The ground lessor may subordinate his or her land ownership to the leasehold lender if the center developer finances the center improvements with a leasehold mortgage. If the ground lessor subordinates the land ownership, a higher rate of yield may be negotiated from the center developer-lessee to compensate for the possible loss of land ownership if the developer-lessee defaults on the leasehold mortgage contract. Most leasehold lenders want the best collateral they can get for their loans. They generally prefer the added security of the subordinated landowner's interest so that the mortgage rests on the collateral of the land as well as the building and site improvements.

Joint Venture. The joint venture, a type of joint ownership agreement, is commonly employed as a form of business organization for shopping center development, operation, and financing. The landowner may be asked to contribute the land as a joint venture partner in the proposed shopping center development. As a joint venture partner, the landowner would expect to recapture the capital invested in the venture in terms of the land and to receive a yield on that contribution as well as a portion of the net operating receipts and sale proceeds from the center.

Cash Flow Considerations

The funds expended for site acquisition are part of the front-end or planning costs of the development. These costs may be part of the developer's overall contribution to the project. This expenditure may be short-lived, though, for the developer may turn around and sell the purchased land to an investor and lease it back. The cash invested by the developer is thus freed for other uses. The developer commonly wishes to reduce his or her investment in any one project so that several development projects may be engaged in at the same time. For this reason, most developers wish to use other people's money by way of sale-leasebacks, componentized development, or mortgage financing. Even the institutional partnership in which the institution provides the construction, development, and permanent financing is palatable to the developer as long as the price is right. The developer's return often is substantial, but does not depend on the permanent investment of substantial funds in the center.

Preliminary Engineering and Project Layout

After the site is acquired or leased, the development organization moves forward to finalize the engineering and project layout. The engineering work relates to site preparation and development. Approved plans lead to acquisition of required permits and licenses and to coordinated development toward the target opening date. With the proper engineering and preliminary planning, the operation of the completed center will result in profits for all parties involved.

Engineering Work

The developer's cost engineers and outside architects draw up the various plans for construction. The buildings are placed on the site with due regard to the topography, drainage, customer visibility, chain store preferences, and highway access. The preferences of the preleased major department or other chain stores will determine the relative location of the various premises on the site. Within the mall buildings, preliminary and then permanent partitioning will be determined according to the preferences of the chain and independent retail stores that lease space in the center. Usually individual retail stores by line of business have definite preferences for their locations in the mall with relation to outside customer entranceways, department store mall entrances, center court position, and compatibility with other mall retail businesses. The engineering work of store layout within the building layout must take many leasing considerations and preferences into account.

The local government—city, county, parish, or town—will have to approve the many detailed construction plans for the center. Building codes and zoning ordinances apply to the overall development. The local government is concerned with storm and sanitary sewer systems, water drainage, utility service, and roadway systems. They are also concerned with air, water, and noise pollution. The emissions from the automobiles, trucks, buses, and other gasoline-powered vehicles that visit the center will generally pollute the air in the neighborhood. The extra traffic must be controlled or neighboring residents and building occupants will complain of the measurable increase in traffic congestion. Therefore, before the city or county issues building permits, occupancy permits, and electrical, plumbing, and environmental protection licenses and permits, they must approve the site development and construction plans. The city or county will probably maintain a building inspection department, a department of health, and a environmental protection agency. The environmental protection agencies may operate on the state government level, though, instead of the local government level. Their approval of the engineering plans is still required before construction and development may proceed.

The lenders providing funds for the center and the utility companies must approve the engineering plans. The lenders must be assured that the necessary governmental approvals are obtained before they will commit their money.

The utility companies must know what services are needed; they must schedule the extension of their services to coincide with the needs of the project; and the parties providing the utility services must be assured of payment for their costs. The city or county must finance the extension of the storm and sanitary sewer lines. The power company must finance the extension of natural gas and electric lines into the site from the closest existing sources of power. The phone and the cable television companies must finance the extension of their lines into the project. Fire and police protection must extend to the center or the insurance companies will not underwrite the risks associated with the possible destruction of the center premises. This protection may involve the construction and financing of nearby fire and police stations. The developer often provides on-site private police protection to guarantee customer security and safety in the parking lots, the center mall, and the center storerooms. The developer often contributes to the financing of the utility line extension, highway and street changes, and other such local government expenses as well.

Certain preliminary tests are required before final engineering plans may be made. Water pressure tests may be needed. The sprinkler systems designed for the center may have to undergo tests to be sure that they are adequate for center building and tenant protection. Soil tests must be made to ascertain percolation, load-bearing, and other necessary qualities. Once roof designs are tentatively drawn up, roof tests may be needed to see if they will withstand the climatic conditions of the area. Compaction tests may be needed before foundation plans may be finalized. The tentatively selected concrete may have to undergo tests related to the time of curing in the given environmental conditions and the strength and durability for the construction purposes. After the necessary tests, precast concrete components may be used for the exterior walls of the center to reduce the initial costs of construction and the future costs of exterior wall maintenance. Precast concrete may also provide architectural beauty to the modern exterior of the center. Various textures and designs may be simulated in the precast concrete parts. The mechanical equipment tentatively suggested for the center must be tested to see if the capability of the equipment fits the long-term needs of the center. The heating, ventilating, and air conditioning systems for centers are particularly under scrutiny as power bills have soared. Center managers and developers seek the lowest cost systems commensurate with efficient and adequate operation. Enclosed malls must have stable climatic conditions inside the center no matter what the weather outside the mall. The capability and efficiency of escalators and elevators must be tested to assure the proper performance.

Building Design and Building Codes

Center designs include strip, L-shaped, U-shaped, air-conditioned "sidewalker," open mall, and enclosed mall. The strip design with parking in front, on the side, and behind is most often used for neighborhood centers that incorporate only a few stores. The largest store, usually the supermarket or grocery, is usually located on the end so that parking spaces on three sides may accommodate the customer volume. The L-shaped center may accommodate two key tenants, one at the end of each extension. These key tenants of the neighborhood or community center may be supermarkets, drugstores, and variety stores. In recent years, the air-conditioned "sidewalker" is seldom used. If it is, the merchant combination may describe a neighborhood or a community center. When storerooms and retail buildings are placed around a focal point such as a center court, fountain, or major intersection of several walkways, this center configuration may be an open or an enclosed mall. If a roof ties the buildings and storerooms together so that the customer may enjoy climate control, we may view an enclosed mall. Whether the outside weather fluctuates drastically with the seasons or not, enclosed malls are preferred for regional, superregional, and specialty centers. The roof systems may employ natural lighting from skylights, artificial lighting from indirect lighting systems, or a combination of the two. In northern climates, heating is very important in the winter and air conditioning very important in the summer; in southern climates, varying amounts of air conditioning for coolness may be important all year 'round.

The shopping center today may encompass any number of levels. The majority still have either one or two levels. Larger superregional centers tend toward two or more levels since a large mixture of shopping and specialty stores is accommodated under the umbrella of the roofing system. Specialty malls in congested areas of major cities often consume space on several levels. Urban Development and Investment, the real estate subsidiary of Aetna Life and Casualty Company, has put up successful multilevel centers in major cities. Water Tower Place in Chicago is one of their best examples. The Rouse Company's mall in the center of Philadelphia is also an outstanding example of multi-level mall construction of the early 1980s.

The multilevel enclosed mall has complicated engineering and merchandising opportunities and problems. Several multilevel transportation systems for customers must be employed for comparison shopping. Grouping of tenants to assure relatively even customer drawing power in the various corridors and mall locations must be engineered. The merchandising of the center is more complicated because a greater variety of tenants may be located in these unusually large multilevel malls. The multilevel mall need not necessarily involve substantial square footage of retail space, but usually does. The greater construction costs associated with high-rise buildings and elaborate customer transportation systems may be met by more rent volume from more merchants in the larger complex.

In contrast to the multilevel centers of recent years, we observe the expansion of existing suburban centers where additional land is available or can be acquired at a reasonable cost. Major department stores are finding attractive new sites in existing suburban centers. Therefore, many superregional centers are adding new department and specialty stores. Some of the additions are being attached to existing centers so that the single roof system encompasses the old and new retail space. Many of the additions are independent store locations at existing suburban retail locations. The independent store locations, perhaps connected by covered walkways to existing stores and malls, provide more parking closer to the entranceways of these new, major retail units. Expanding existing centers under a central roof system may give parking problems. Expensive parking buildings may be required. At this point, most suburban shopping center developers resist the temptation to charge for parking. Part of their competitive retail attraction is free parking in easily located, nearby parking spaces.

The center design must conform to building code requirements. The building code requirements vary between single level and multilevel centers. The construction materials must achieve specified fire ratings. The codes affect plans for egress; construction dimensions for corridors, passageways, and stairs; and the provisions for the handicapped customers. There are usually code specifications that affect mall widths and ceiling clearances including the space around kiosks. Fire walls may be needed between tenant storerooms. There are mechanical, electrical, and other such codes that have a bearing on the energy systems of the center. The building codes may have a bearing on the plans for food malls or courts, kiosk locations, kiosk sizes, public toilet facilities, service and utility areas, and theme or specialty areas of the large center. The developer has to plan the tenant mix, storeroom size, building layouts, and storeroom layouts in light of the building code requirements.

Permit and Insurance Requirements

Before construction may start, certain permits must usually be acquired from the proper agencies. A few of these commonly needed permits are:

Driveway permit for the roadway surrounding the center on the developer's site
Grading permit
Sedimentation permit
Encroachment permit
Building permit
Zoning permit

Insurance coverage is needed according to lender and government requirements even as construction and development take place. Builders risk insurance is needed for the construction risks that involve real and personal property damage and bodily injury. The developer and lender usually require performance bonds from the contractor so that the construction will be finished even if the contractor or subcontractors run into unforeseen problems such as bankruptcy. Surety bonds may be required for those handling sums of money in the development process and in the operation of the center.

Final Plans

The final engineering of the development must incorporate the needs of all parties involved. The developer, the lenders, and the other investors must approve these plans. The major department stores are important entities to satisfy; they may be major investors in the center. The institutional lender may provide the majority of the funds for the project. Other parties to be satisfied with the final plans before construction commences are:

City manager or president of the city commission
Chief building inspector
Local planning board
Regional planning board, if it is involved in the development
Zoning board
Power companies
Telephone company
Cable television company
Health department
Fire marshal
City street and engineering department

The final development plans must incorporate the eventual needs of the outparcels as well as the center if the developer plans to sell off or lease auxiliary parcels. The neighborhood will benefit from the landscaping plans that will shield residential areas from the negative aspects of the commercial area. Trees and fences may give the neighboring residential areas their needed privacy and serenity.

THE DEVELOPMENT TEAM

The development of a shopping center is not a "one man show." One person rarely possesses the many, varied types of expertise. Even if one did, he or she would have to perform several functions at the same time. Therefore, a team of experts from various fields is formed to produce a profitable shopping center within a scheduled time period. Since time means money, a reasonable time schedule should be set for the development of the project, and all members of the team must be engaged in their various functions to meet the schedule requirements. These experts are actually functioning during the planning and operating stages of the development. They may leave the scene as soon as the construction is complete or later in the operating stage. By the third stage of the development, the termination stage, only the owners, lenders, and attorneys may be actively functioning as the project team.

What types of expertise are needed for successful center development? Legal, marketing, financing, architectural, construction, accounting, management, investment, and consulting expertise are usually needed. The consulting expertise lies in the areas of market analysis, feasibility analysis, site planning, environmental protection analysis and report writing, and mortgage brokerage. The various consultants in their specialized areas complement the work of the active members of the development team. The team usually includes:

Developer
Leasing agent
Attorney
Architect
General contractor
Lenders
Advertising professionals
Knowledgeable principals, investors
Certified public accountants

The development company may include all members of this team except for the principals and the lenders, or the team may be a joint cooperative venture involving many different companies and business interests. Some developers retain flexibility by employing very small permanent staffs. Outside expertise is a must. Other developers exemplify a "development machine," a large organization of many skilled individuals. The owner or president of the large development company must constantly find work for these numerous skilled development people and must also meet a large permanent payroll. Some developers feel that size sometimes means slow movement, and speed is associated with maximum profitability for an organization. When the real estate cycle continues to run its course and recessions roll around after periods of economic and real estate prosperity, it is difficult for some large developers to meet their payrolls during the slow periods.

The development company is sometimes a subsidiary or division of a larger corporate holding company. Fluctuating development conditions may be counterbalanced by property insurance, property management, real estate brokerage, real estate appraising, mortgage lending, and other subsidiary operations. Several functional operations may be combined under the holding company to stabilize cash flows and profits through all phases of the real estate and economic cycle.

The lenders and the investment principals associated with the center are team members from the planning stage through the termination stage of the center development. After the permanent or standby permanent loan commitment is obtained, the construction lender starts advancing money as construction takes place. When the construction lender is repaid at the end of construction when the center tenants occupy their designated storerooms and buildings, the permanent lender takes a more active, supervisory role in the operations of the center. Any refinancing, new financing, expansion, or renovation of the center interests the permanent lender and the original equity investors who wish to approve the developer's plans. They wish to protect their financing positions as the center generates profits.

SIX

CASH FLOW, FEASIBILITY, AND PRO FORMA ANALYSIS

Before an investor places any money in an asset or a real estate project, he or she wants to see the financial picture in its many and varied aspects. The real estate investor often invests money for an extended time period. The real estate operator, on the other hand, visualizes a short-term position where profits are generated by purchase and immediate sale at a profit. Let us take the longer-term position that most shopping center investors take. Several years will probably pass after the completed development or purchase of the existing property before the investor sells an asset.

The longer-term financial position involves cash outflows and cash inflows as well as accrued and prepaid revenues and expenses for tax purposes and periodic disclosure to owners. If the investors in the center are stockholders of a public corporation that is listed on a stock exchange, several financial statements will have to be prepared and sent to the list of current stockholders every quarter and annually. Regardless of the investment organizational form, the investors will want to receive periodic reports showing the status of their invested funds and the risks being assumed. The periodic statements that are familiar to many stockholders are:

Profit and loss statement
Balance sheet
Net worth statement
Sources and uses of funds (cash)

The profit and loss statement shows the level of profitability at the end of the particular operating period. The real estate company may, like any other industrial corporation, show a taxable profit or loss by the end of the operating period. The profit and loss statement shows the operating position at the stated period in time. The balance sheet shows the level of the assets, liabilities, and net worth as of a stated point in time. The profit and loss position is usually incorporated into the balance sheet in the net worth section where net income after taxes and dividend distribution are added to the previous net worth balance. The net worth statement shows the changes in net worth and the common and preferred stock accounts over the preceding period that is usually one year. The sources and uses of funds or cash show the major company changes that involved substantial inflows and outflows of funds or cash. Many shopping center developers incorporate the sources and uses of cash statement into the regular set of financial statements that are drawn by the center accountants.

CASH FLOW AND PROFIT ANALYSIS

The investor, the manager, and the lender each want to know immediately the cash flow and profit status of the investment. Full sets of financial statements may be formally available every month, every quarter, or only once a year. A continuous accounting system makes available needed reports at any time. Many of the larger center developers are computerized to maintain the up-to-the-minute financial position. Noncomputerized but efficiently maintained accounting and bookkeeping systems may serve the same purpose.

Whether the center is owned by an industrial corporation or a full-service real estate company, cash flow and profit analysis are important for different reasons. Most industrial corporations that are publicly held report their financial progress to the investment and general business community in terms of earnings per share diluted and undiluted, price earnings ratio, and current stock price. The investment community that focuses on stock and bond trading is generally not interested in cash flow per share diluted and undiluted. This is related to the conversion into stock of convertible debentures that are often issued by industrial corporations and real estate investment trusts to raise money. "Diluted earnings per share" takes into account the number of shares that would be outstanding if the debentures were converted into stock. The total possible stock holdings are divided into total earnings for stockholders that period. Cash flow per share of stock may not be figured for public distribution.

To the real estate investor, cash flow is the basic denominator of profit. The taxable income figure is only important in investment return analysis to the extent of the needed payment of income taxes or the benefits of tax savings from the tax loss. The yield measurements in real estate are based on cash flow.

The differences between cash flow and taxable income or profit can be summarized. Taxable income or loss is the difference between operating revenues and operating expenses for tax purposes. Expenses that are deductible for income tax purposes include local *ad valorem* tax payments, mortgage interest, and depreciation expense. Cash flow, on the other hand, is the difference between cash operating revenues and cash operating expenses. Depreciation expense for income tax purposes is not recognized as a cash operating expense. Very few real estate owners use the depreciation allowance as it is set aside for federal income tax accounting to renovate and repair the real estate.

The cash flow analysis usually focuses on cash flow after taxes and after-tax cash proceeds from the ultimate sale of the property. Specially designed forms are available for cash flow analysis for several consecutive years. At the end of the contemplated holding period and on the last sheet of the form analysis, the analyst may calculate the tax payments that lead to the after-tax cash proceeds from the sale (Exhibit 6-1, Cash Flow Analysis). Taxable income is shown on line 14; cash flow before taxes on line 19; and cash flow after taxes on line 22. On line 33 to the right, the analyst may see the estimated cash proceeds after taxes from the property sale.

FEASIBILITY ANALYSIS

Before a center is built, expanded, or renovated, the prospective investor usually wants to see a feasibility analysis. This analysis will establish the economic or noneconomic feasibility of the proposed project. After the costs, revenues, and expenses are estimated and placed into a pro forma analysis setting, the prospective investor observes whether a reasonable return on investment may be achieved. If a reasonable return may be achieved, the prospective investor may wish to improve the potential yield. The question then is: What revenues and expenses could be changed separately or jointly so that the yield could be substantially improved? Actually this question may be raised whether the feasibility analysis shows an uneconomic yield or a reasonable yield from the initial analysis. Through subsequent reexaminations of the estimated cost, revenue, and expense structure, any initial return might be enhanced. When sophisticated calculators, accounting equipment, or computer systems are used, we often call the subsequent feasibility runs and changes of certain accounts sensitivity analysis. The analyst hopes to see how investment return changes with the change of individual components of the financial layout.

In advance of the feasibility analysis, a market study is usually commissioned from an outside source or generated by the party wishing the analysis. The market study prior to the investment or development becomes an integral part of the financial analysis. Construction costs, sales and lease revenues, and operating expenses of all kinds are closely related to the market conditions and existing and proposed competition. From the market, the amounts for each of the accounts of the investment feasibility study may be estimated. The market competition shows the necessary level of construction costs, such as the amount

Cash Flow Analysis

Date _____

Name _____ Purpose _____

Mortgage Data

Encumbrances	Beginning Balance	Remaining Term	Number of Payments Per Year	Interest Rate	Payment	Annual Debt Service	Remarks
1 1st Mortgage							
2 2nd Mortgage							
3 3rd Mortgage							

	Year: *11*	Year: *12*	Year: *13*	Year: *14*	Year: *15*	Year:
4 Investment Amount/Base						
5 1st Mortgage EOY						
6 2nd Mortgage EOY						
7 3rd Mortgage EOY						
8 Total (Lines 5, 6, 7)						
9 Principal Reduction						

Ownership Analysis of Property Income: **Taxable Income**

10 Gross Operating Income					
11 – Operating Expenses					
12 Net Operating Income	24 725	24 725	24 725	24 725	24 725
13 – Non-Operating Expense					
14 – Interest					
15 – Depreciation					
16 Real Est. Taxable Income	(3 621)	(3 138)	(2 604)	(2 015)	(1 363)

Cash Flows

17 Net Operating Income	24 725	24 725	24 725	24 725	24 725
18 – Annual Debt Service	19 628	19 628	19 628	19 628	19 628
19 – Funded Reserves					
20 – Capital Additions					
21 Cash Flow before Taxes	5 097	5 097	5 097	5 097	5 097
22 – Tax Liability on Real Est.	(1 448)	(1 255)	(1 042)	(800)	(545)
23 Cash Flow after Taxes	6 545	6 352	6 139	5 903	5 642

Analysis of Sale Proceeds   Year:

Adjusted Basis			Excess Depreciation			Tax Liability on Sale		
24 Original Basis	260 000		Total Depr.	200 000		Excess Recapture Tax		
25 + Capital Improvements			S/L Depr.	200 000		Capital Gain Tax 20%	43 800	
26 + Costs of Sale			Excess Depr.			Capital Gain Tax		
27 Sub-Total			Excess Depr. C.O.			Tax Pref. Items Tax		
28 – Depreciation			**Gain**			Tax Liability on Sale		
29 – Partial Sales			Sale Price	300 000		**Sale Proceeds**		
30 AB at Sale			– AB	60 000		Sale Price	300 000	
31			Gain	219 000		– Costs of Sale	21 000	
32			– Excess	– 0 –		– Mortgage	123 772	
33			Capital Gain	219 000		Proceeds before Taxes	155 228	
34						– Tax Liability on Sale	43 800	
35						Proceeds after Taxes	111 428	

The statements and figures presented herein, while not guaranteed, are secured from sources we believe authoritative.

Prepared by _____

Exhibit 6-1. Cash Flow Analysis

Source: Copyright Realtors National Marketing Institute of the National Association of Realtors 1983. All Rights Reserved. Reprinted with permission of the Copyright Proprietor.

of land that must be acquired for parking space per 1,000 square feet of gross leasable area. It also shows the rent structure and the coincident vacancy rates. The market study shows the possible level of operating costs, where expenses may be reduced, and how expenses may be passed on to the center tenants. The rate of absorption of the completed storerooms of the center may be estimated from the rates of absorption of competing malls. Market studies are considered in more detail later in the book.

PRO FORMA ANALYSIS

The developer, the lender, and the investor want to see pro forma statements that come out of the feasibility analysis and subsequent analysis after the decision to proceed with the development or investment has been made. The pro forma statements showing summaries of development costs, rents over the anticipated holding period, and cash flow statements for the first and

Exhibit 6-2. Form for Pro Forma Development Cost Analysis.

Cost of land
   Land cost
      Nonrefundable option   _____
      Other nonrefundables   _____

Total land cost   _____

   Land selloffs

      Lot 1   _____
      Lot 2   _____
      Lot 3   _____
      Lot 4   _____

Total land sales   _____

Net land cost   _____

Financing charges
   Construction loan brokerage   _____
   Construction loan interest   _____
   Permanent loan brokerage   _____
   Permanent loan standby fee   _____

Total financing charges   _____

Construction costs
   Basic contract   _____

Exhibit 6-2. *(Continued)*

Optional addition to contract at
  request of landlord   _____
Extras to contract required through
  leasing   _____
Extras to contract through errors   _____
Extras to contract through city codes   _____

Total construction cost   _____

Leasing costs
  Leasing broker fee   _____
  Office expense   _____
  Cost of leasing tools   _____
  Travel expenses   _____
  Other   _____

Total leasing costs   _____

Other charges
  Legal fees   _____
  Recording costs   _____
  Engineering and soil testing   _____
  Mall and sidewalk furniture   _____
  Landscaping   _____
  Preopening   _____
  Architect's fees   _____
  Architect's travel and inspection   _____
  Appraisal fee   _____
  Signs   _____
  Advertising   _____
  Taxes   _____
  Insurance   _____

Total other charges   _____

Total cost of project   _____

Sources of income

  First mortgage loan   _____
  Refund of standby fee   _____
  Rental income before closing of
    permanent loan   _____
  Other sources of income   _____

Total income   _____

Cash requirements   _____

subsequent years are often based on the refinements of the much earlier feasibility analysis. Exhibit 6-2 is a form for pro forma development cost analysis. Exhibit 6-3 is a suggested form for pro forma operating analysis. Exhibits 6-4, 6-5, and 6-6 illustrate pro forma statements for the proposed community shopping center encompassing 15 acres and 163,500 square feet of gross buildable area. The prospective investor may go on to calculate expected investment yields from this estimated financial data. Investment yield determination is considered in a later section of the book.

Exhibit 6-3. Form for Pro Forma Operating Analysis

Income
  Minimum rents, first 12-month
    period $_____
  Estimate of percentage
    income _____%   _____
  Miscellaneous income
    (public telephones
    rides, etc.)   _____
  Common area income   _____

Total income   _____

Expenses
  Taxes   _____per sq. ft._____
  Insurance   _____per sq. ft._____
  Real estate commission_____%   _____
  Common area   _____per sq. ft._____
  Promotion   _____per sq. ft._____
  Legal and auditing   _____per sq. ft._____
  Miscellaneous   _____per sq. ft._____
  Vacancy   _____%   _____
  Reserve for replacement
    and maintenance   _____per sq. ft._____

Total expenses $_____

Cash available for debt service $_____

Debt service
  _____@_____% for_____years $_____
  _____constant

Cash throwoff $_____

Exhibit 6-4.   Pro Forma Analysis of Development Cost

COMMUNITY SHOPPING CENTER
15 ACRES
163,500 SQUARE-FOOT GROSS BUILDABLE AREA

Land

15 acres × $3/sq. ft.		$1,960,200	
Tax reserve		20,000	
Total land			$1,980,200

Improvements

Market	35,000 sq. ft. × $30/sq. ft.	$1,050,000	
Drug	25,000 sq. ft.	Ground Lease	
Discount	30,000 sq. ft. × $28/sq. ft.	840,000	
Shops	53,000 sq. ft. × $29/sq. ft.	1,537,000	
Pads			
Fast food	3,500 sq. ft.	Ground Lease	
Bank	8,000 sq. ft. × $70/sq. ft.	560,000	
Savings & loan	4,000 sq. ft. × $70/sq. ft.	280,000	
Coffee shop	5,000 sq. ft. × $80/sq. ft.	400,000	
On and off sites	653,400 sq. ft. × $2.25./sq. ft.	1,470,150	
Total improvements			$6,137,150

Indirects

Architectural and engineering			
Building	128,000 sq. ft. × $1.10/sq. ft.	$ 140,080	
Site	653,000 sq. ft. × 6¢/sq. ft.	39,180	
Legal		35,000	
Commissions		275,000	
Overhead and contingencies		500,000	
Points (construction loan)		80,000	

Interim interest

Land	$1,980,200 × 20% × 1 year	$ 396,040	
Improvements	$7,206,410 × 20% × 1 year × 50%	720,641	
Total indirects			$ 2,185,941
Subtotal			10,303,291

Less

Pro data reimbursements for			
On and off site improvements			
Drug		$ 220,500	
Fast food		67,620	
			$ (288,120)
Total development cost			$10,015,171

Source: Handout of a small center financing session of the 1982 University of Shopping Centers, Atlanta, Georgia. Moderator: William K. Krauch, Hahn Devcorp., El Segundo, California.

Exhibit 6-5. Income Projection

Tenant	1	2	3	4	5	6	7	8	9	10
Market										
Minimum Rent (1.25)	$ 276,500	$ 276,500	$ 276,500	$ 276,500	$ 276,500	$ 276,500	$ 276,500	$ 276,500	$ 276,500	$ 276,500
% Rent										2,400
Drug										
Minimum Rent (.075)	40,000	40,000	40,000	40,000	40,000	48,000	48,000	48,000	48,000	48,000
% Rent					1,000			3,500	10,000	16,000
Discount										
Minimum Rent (3.0)	187,500	187,500	187,500	187,500	187,500	206,000	206,000	206,000	206,000	206,000
% Rent		6,900	22,452	39,240	57,387	58,500	79,600	86,000	93,000	100,440
Shops										
Minimum Rent	636,000	652,000	669,000	733,125	751,125	771,131	846,258	867,842	880,206	967,932
% Rent						1,000	1,500	2,000	2,500	3,000
Fast Food										
Minimum Rent	35,000	35,000	35,000	35,000	35,000	45,000	45,000	45,000	45,000	45,000
% Rent								1,000	1,500	2,000
Bank										
Minimum Rent	168,000	168,000	168,000	193,200	193,200	193,200	222,180	222,180	222,180	255,070
Savings & Loan										
Minimum Rent	84,000	87,000	90,000	103,500	103,500	103,500	119,025	119,025	119,025	136,879
Coffee Shop										
Minimum Rent	100,000	100,000	105,000	105,000	110,000	110,000	116,000	116,000	121,000	121,000
% Rent				8,400	12,000	13,000	27,000	38,000	45,000	57,000
Total	$1,527,000	$1,552,900	$1,593,452	$1,721,465	$1,767,212	$1,825,831	$1,987,063	$2,031,047	$2,069,911	$2,248,221

Source: Handout of a small center financing session of the 1982 University of Shopping Centers, Atlanta, Georgia. Moderator: William K. Krauch, Hahn Devcorp., El Segundo, California.

84

Exhibit 6-6.   Pro Forma Net Income Statement

COMMUNITY SHOPPING CENTER
15 ACRES
163,500 SQUARE FOOT GROSS BUILDABLE AREA

Income

Market	35,000 sq. ft. × $7.90/sq. ft.	$ 276,500	
Drug	25,000 sq. ft. (Ground Lease)	40,000	
Discount	30,000 sq. ft. × $6.25/sq. ft.	187,500	
Shops	53,000 sq. ft. × $12/sq. ft	636,000	
Pads			
Fast food	3,500 sq. ft. (Ground Lease)	35,000	
Bank	8,000 sq. ft. × $21/sq. ft.	168,000	
Savings & Loan	4,000 sq. ft. × $21/sq. ft.	84,000	
Coffee shop	5,000 sq. ft. × $20/sq. ft.	100,000	
Total			$1,527,000

Expenses

Management	$1,527,000 × 3%	$ 46,000	
Vacancy	636,000 × 5%	32,000	
Maintenance Reserves	118,000 sq. ft. × 6¢/sq. ft.	7,000	
Merchants association		5,000	
Miscellaneous		5,000	
Total			$ (95,000)
Net income			$1,432,000

Source: Handout of a small center financing session of the 1982 University of Shopping Centers, Atlanta, Georgia. Moderator: William K. Krauch, Hahn Devcorp., El Segundo, California.

SEVEN

THE CONSTRUCTION PROCESS

The construction of a shopping center is accomplished through the coordinated efforts of a team of construction specialists. The developer and his or her construction department must select the right architect and the right general contractor for the project. Many developers employ their own permanent staff of construction assistants. They form a permanent construction control and management mechanism for the ongoing construction jobs of the developer. The work of the outside architect and general contractor is coordinated with the work of the developer's construction department. Construction contracts must be drawn up and signed by the developer, architect, and general contractor. Once the architect and general contractor are selected, detailed plans must be prepared and decisions must be made about site utilization, general center positioning, storeroom layout, and construction methods and materials. The general contractor usually puts the construction work out for bids by eligible subcontractors. Construction costs must be estimated taking normal problems of construction into account. Pro forma cost analysis must be determined, and cost control systems must be instituted.

SELECTING AN ARCHITECT

The architect for the project will become a very important part of the development team. Once the architectural contract is negotiated, the architect will earn his fee through initial and revised renderings and plans for the detailed components of the proposed center. Usually the following architectural plans must be furnished by the architects:

Preliminary plot plan
Site plan
Grading plan with the topographic survey superimposed
Retaining wall plan, if a retaining wall is needed
Soil and erosion control grading plan
Storm drainage plan
Plumbing site plan
Offsite septic tank and tile fields, if necessary
Site plumbing detail
Domestic water plan
Site detailings such as signing, parking stalls, catch basin detail, and man-
    hole detail
Site lighting plan
Landscape plan
Typical tree planting detail

The architect should be experienced in shopping center work. The architect's staff should be capable of performing the necessary work in a skillful manner so that it can be accomplished on the previously established timetable of the developer. While the architect and his or her staff should have sufficient imagination for the development of an attractive and functional center that will generate the forecasted sales, the architect and his or her associates must be conscious of cost. The developer and his or her construction department establish a cost budget within whose bounds the architect must work. After the architect satisfies the developer and his or her construction department, the individual tenants must be satisfied with the basic designs for their assigned storerooms. Therefore, the architect must be able to communicate with the developer and the tenants. The architect must also work with the general contractor in this team effort to complete a center within the scheduled time.

The contract between the architect and the developer must be negotiated and drawn up for signature. If the architect works for individual tenants on completion of their interior work, their individual contracts must be negotiated and signed.

THE APPLICATION FOR CONTRACTOR PAYMENT

As the general contractor completes a recognized phase of the construction or works to the end of a designated time period, the contractor applies for payment in terms of a construction loan advance from the construction lender or the lender's representative. The party advancing the construction funds as a representative of the construction lender may be a local title company. When the requisition for funds is made, the architect as a representative of the developer must certify the completion of the stated work and the application of the described labor and materials. The architect works as an on-the-job inspector for the developer as he or she certifies the completion of work that will be paid for from the particular construction loan advance. Once the work has been completed, the general contractor is obligated to pay his or her subcontractors their deserved amounts. Often the construction lender advances the requested amount with a 5- to 15-percent holdback so that the general contractor and his or her subcontractors and their employees will be prompted to meet the time and work schedule set by the developer, the developer's construction department, and his architect.

CHANGE ORDERS

Most large construction projects require change orders from the original construction plans and specifications as construction work moves ahead. Sometimes the amount of a certain stock on hand in warehouses dictates the need for timely material change so the the construction time schedule may be maintained. Different construction methods and techniques may be used as the contractor and his or her subcontractors see the need for revision. The architect must certify and approve the change orders before they are submitted to the construction lender. Usually the construction lender must approve substantial changes from the agreed construction plans before additional loan advances will be made by the lender or the local representative.

SELECTING A GENERAL CONTRACTOR

The selection of the general contractor has a significant bearing on the total cost of the proposed construction project. In order to assess the possible costs for the center, the developer and his construction department may put the final architectural plans out for bid. Within a rather short period of time, cost estimates may be received from a number of general contractors. The developer must first weed out from the bids those from general contractors who do not have the necessary experience in shopping center construction, a sufficient and skilled work force, and/or financial and bonding capacity to complete the proposed work. The selected contractor is expected to maintain internal construction controls and a workable cost accounting system. The developer must select from the eligible contractors the best bid and negotiate a construction contract.

THE CONSTRUCTION CONTRACT

The contract between the developer and the general contractor may take several forms, but the most common forms are the lump sum and the cost plus contracts. The American Institute of Architects has established standard forms for these two commonly used agreements.

THE APPLICATION FOR CONTRACTOR PAYMENT AND CHANGE ORDERS

The general contractor processes the application for contractor payment as work proceeds and labor is employed and materials used. The architect usually must certify that the payment is due for each of the items enumerated by the contractor. The signatures of both the developer's architect and the developer's general contractor are usually required by the construction lender and the local representative who may be processing the loan advance. Change orders that must be requested by the contractor as work continues are processed through the architect in a similar manner.

THE SELECTION OF THE FACADE AND CONSTRUCTION MATERIALS

The facade must be selected on the basis of customer attraction, original cost, and maintenance cost. The customer looks for new and exciting retail environments when a purchase decision is imminent. The exterior of the center must attract favorable attention of the prospective purchaser. Centers with competing goods and services should appear less attractive to this ultimate consumer. Many shoppers seek individual and family entertainment by "going to the mall." The up-to-date design of the facade should blend with the interior design and the tenant merchandising to give entertainment to the purchaser while goods and services are being selected for purchase.

Since construction costs of materials and labor have increased significantly in recent years, the developer must be very cost-conscious in selecting the materials for the facade. He or she may select local building materials which tend to be less costly due to decreased shipping charges. In some areas, such as the Deep South, bricks are manufactured rather economically from the natural red clay. Many builders use bricks for all kinds of exterior coverings. In contrast, in southern Indiana where limestone is quarried and tends to be economical, many builders use limestone for exterior coverings of all kinds of private and public buildings. In most areas of the country, precast concrete and aluminum are used extensively for facades of public and private buildings. There is little upkeep associated with brick, limestone, and precast concrete facades.

The building materials selected for the center must satisfy to the greatest extent the developer, the major tenants, and the mall tenants. The mall and the major tenant premises must be coordinated in their building materials as well as architecturally. The developer's architect and construction department must seek to please many parties involved in the shopping center development. An architect's rendering of a 100,000-square-foot center in Columbus, Georgia is shown in Exhibit 7-1.

Exhibit 7-1.   Buena Vista Plaza
Source: Jim Wilson & Associates, Shopping Center Development, P.O. Box 4480, Montgomery, AL 36195.

In general, the building materials for the interior and exterior are selected on the basis of:

Cost
Useful life
Speed of installation
Cost of installation
Maintenance requirements
Construction procedures

CONSTRUCTION PROBLEMS

Center construction problems are seemingly endless, but a few specific areas should be mentioned at this point. The construction must adhere to the building code requirements and zoning ordinances. The construction plans for the tenant space improvement must be drawn up and approved in contract form just as the developer's construction plans must be formulated and approved. The actual construction of the center must be coordinated so that all parties to the construction may perform their jobs efficiently and economically and the deadline for completed construction must be met. As a special development problem, the parking space and individual space requirements must match the customer needs of the proposed center. Parking requirements change with time, the market for passenger automobiles, shopping patterns, and mass transit use.

Building Code Requirements and Zoning Ordinances

City engineers and building code administrators determine the building codes for specific types of buildings including shopping centers. The architect and contractor must be familiar with these local code requirements. The preliminary plans must take the code requirements into account, and the actual construction must adhere to the same requirements. The architect and the general contractor must work with the appropriate city and county officials to resolve all difficulties and misinterpretations that arise over the development time. The developer or the developer's representative must be available to discuss problems as they arise to help prevent delays in approval of needed changes.

As the developer has preliminary site plans and market studies drawn up, he or she must be assured that the land is appropriately zoned. The characteristics of the city or county zoning ordinance that fits the particular zoning designation applied to the land must be known by the architect and the developer. The zoning requirements usually specify the land coverage ratio for the building improvements, building height restrictions, open space requirements, parking ratios, setbacks from site boundary lines, and so on. Drainage requirements may exist. At the same time, the architect and builder must recognize and account for the easements on the land. They cannot be violated.

Construction of the Tenant Space

The tenants of the center must complete the construction of their premises after the developer has provided the outer shell of the space. (The developer may agree that the department store or other key tenants build their own premises with their own construction crews and other personnel.) The developer's contractor must view the preliminary plans of each tenant and plan for each of these tenant construction jobs. The tenant must be encouraged to finalize the plans with the approval of the persons in authority with the tenant company according to the development time schedule so that the total center opening may occur on a planned date.

The developer may give the lessee an allowance for the costs of the finished interior. Generally the developer recoups this money through additional base rent and overage rent requirements over the period of the tenant lease. In other cases, the tenant pays the total cost of interior storeroom improvement with no allowance from the developer.

Coordination of the Actual Construction

Several construction crews must perform their jobs at different times in different sections of the center site. The land must be graded; drain tiles must be laid;

utility lines must be laid; adjacent street and highway changes must be made; and preliminary roadways on the site must be paved. Construction vehicles going to and from their various site destinations tend to demolish the preliminary roadway surfaces, so final paving must be done after the heavy construction vehicles leave the construction job. Construction vehicles and materials must be stored on the site; the contractor and subcontractors often maintain temporary offices for construction management from one-site vehicles. These construction vehicles, their construction equipment, and building materials awaiting use must be secured from theft and vandalism. Developer security systems must be provided early in the development and must be maintained through the eventual sale of the center by the developer, perhaps several years later.

Continual job supervision is provided through continual site visits by the developer and his or her company representatives, by the architect and the architect's associates, by the lender and the lender's local representatives, by the key tenants and their area representatives, and by other parties concerned with the timely completion of the center.

Parking Accomodations

Construction requirements associated with any kind of building may change over time. Because the average size of customer car has diminished since the energy crisis of the mid-1970s, the amount of center land that must be devoted to parking has decreased. The smaller foreign cars do not take the same amount of parking space that the earlier American cars did. The developer, therefore, may accomodate more customer traffic with the same amount of parking space.

Previous shopping center industry standards called for 5.5 car spaces per 1,000 square feet of gross leasable area. The results of a recent study of the Urban Land Institute with funding from the International Council of Shopping Centers recommended the following ratios for adequate parking for a typical center:

1. 4.0 spaces per 1,000 square feet of gross leasable area for centers having a GLA of 25,000 to 400,000 square feet
2. An average of 4.5 spaces per 1,000 square feet of GLA for centers having a GLA of between 400,000 and 600,000 square feet
3. 5.0 spaces per 1,000 square feet of GLA for centers having GLAs of over 600,000 square feet with some possible downward adjustment of the parking index for centers over 1.2 million square feet of GLA

The reasons given by the Urban Land Institute study for the lower ratios included (1) a greater tendency by shoppers to avoid centers at peak hours, (2) intensified center competition, (c) an increase in car pooling and mass transit use, and (d) the fact that customers make fewer trips to centers than they previously did.*

COST ANALYSIS

The development company, the architect, and the builder must constantly update their cost estimates in order to continue to build profitable centers at economical costs. The developer's construction department keeps cost histories from previous jobs and keeps cost analyses on current construction jobs. The architect and the builder must keep up on the newest construction methods, efficient cost controls, and sources of economically priced quality building materials and skilled and unskilled labor. Generally, a builder thinks in terms of overall costs and labor and materials required as well as subcontractor costs and services. The cost analysis may revolve around the following general categories:

Foundation systems
Structural systems
Roof framing systems
Drainage of the site
Lighting of the site
Paving methods
Energy sources
Utility sources

As an estimate of the proposed center is determined, the cost analysis will probably cover the land cost, the sale of surplus land, financing charges, construction costs, leasing costs, other front-end soft costs, and present sources of funds. The "bottom line" of the cost analysis indicates the amount of cash required to finance the project totally (Exhibit 7-2).

COST CONTROL

The developer and the general contractor must control the costs of the development. Any type of accounting system is appropriate as long as it accomplishes the job. Budgets are set for the numerous cost accounts. Then a continual accounting for current and accumulated expenditures against total budget amounts must be rendered by the cost accounting system. A computerized accounting system is shown in Exhibit 7-3. The budgeted sum for each general account is first shown. Then the current expenditure for the account and the

---

*"Lower Parking Ratios Are Recommended," *Shopping Centers Today* (New York: International Council of Shopping Centers, June 1981), pp. 1 and 2.

Exhibit 7-2. Sample Cost Analysis Form

Cost of land
  Land cost
    Nonrefundable option   _____
    Other nonrefundables   _____

Total land cost   _____

  Land selloffs
    Lot 1   _____
    Lot 2   _____
    Lot 3   _____
    Lot 4   _____

Total land sales   _____

Net land cost   _____

Financing charges
  Construction loan brokerage   _____
  Construction loan interest   _____
  Permanent loan brokerage   _____
  Permanent loan standby fee   _____

Total financing charges   _____

Construction costs
  Basic contract   _____
  Optional addition to contract at
    request of landlord   _____
  Extras to contract required through
    leasing   _____
  Extras to contract through errors _____
  Extras to contract through city codes _____

Total construction cost   _____

Leasing costs
  Leasing broker fee   _____
  Office expense   _____
  Cost of leasing tools   _____
  Travel expenses   _____
  Other   _____

Total leasing costs   _____

Other charges
  Legal fees   _____

Exhibit 7-2. *(Continued)*

Recording costs	_____
Engineering and soil testing	_____
Mall and sidewalk furniture	_____
Landscaping	_____
Preopening	_____
Architect's fees	_____
Architect's travel and inspection	_____
Appraisal fee	_____
Signs	_____
Advertising	_____
Taxes	_____
Insurance	_____

Total other charges   _____

Total cost of project   _____

Sources of income	
First mortgage loan	_____
Refund of standby fee	_____
Rental income before closing of	
permanent loan	_____
Other sources of income	_____

Total income   _____

Cash requirements   _____

accumulated expenditures are shown. Finally, the project's total estimated cost is shown. An even more detailed cost distribution system is employed in Exhibit 7-4. The developer and the general contractor may see from the continual cost distribution analysis which detailed account expenditures are running under and over the budgeted amounts.

THE COST OF BUILDING A SHOPPING CENTER

From several sources of data, one might conclude that a center will cost from $27 a square foot of gross leasable area up to double that amount, as a general rule. Generally, the smaller the center, the lower the cost per square foot of GLA. The larger the center and the more complicated the construction, of course, the higher the cost. The larger regional and superregional centers may cost $50 to $70 a square foot of GLA. A vertical center built now in the crowded central business district of a major city would probably cost more than $70 a

Exhibit 7-3. Cost Distribution System

				Schedule Completion Date—7/25/8X Projected Completion Date—8/30/8X			Month of Report—10/30/8X Run Date—9/30/8X	
ID No.	Description	Original Budget	Cost This Month	Percent Complete	Cost to Date	Final Projected Cost	Projected Cost Over/Under Budget
010	Legal Fees	26,020.00	774.02	21.65	5,635.46	26,017.82	2.18−
020	Insurance	4,900.00	2,465.00	50.31	2,465.00	4,899.62	.38−
030	Construction Interest	110,000.00	1,231.20	2.17	3,614.19	166,552.53	56,552.53
040	Survey	11,250.00	830.00	12.88	1,532.50	11,898.29	648.29
050	Soil Test	10,000.00	.00	24.84	2,483.75	9,998.99	1.01−
055	Development Fees	36,200.00	3,337.62	81.05	29,339.77	36,199.59	.41−
060	Engineering Fees	18,700.00	.00	82.44	15,223.48	18,466.13	233.87−
070	Architectural Fees	26,000.00	5,000.00	77.40	20,113.53	25,986.47	13.53−
090	Clearing & Grubbing	10,000.00	600.00	100.00	6,000.00	6,000.00	4,000.00−
100	Grading	166,550.00	43,173.25	74.92	80,648.25	107,645.82	58,904.18−
110	Strm Drnage & Rest. Pond	55,000.00	47,088.00	60.49	47,088.00	77,844.27	22,844.27
120	Sanitary Sewer	20,000.00	9,759.87	100.00	9,759.87	9,759.87	10,240.13−
130	Water Lines	25,000.00	3,180.00	97.00	10,195.00	10,510.30	14,489.70−
160	Curbs & Walks	7,500.00	.00	.00	.00	7,500.00	.00
180	Landscaping	35,000.00	14,250.00	40.71	14,250.00	35,003.68	3.68
190	Site Lighting & Distribution	30,000.00	.00	11.71	.00	26,487.00	3,513.00−
200	Paving	100,000.00	27,011.25	26.13	27,011.25	103,372.56	3,372.56
210	Striping	3,000.00	.00	.00	.00	3,000.00	.00
250	General Contract	1,138,800.00	42,815.00	4.10	42,815.00	1,067,705.73	71,094.27−

Exhibit 7-3. *(Continued)*

Project Accounting Procedures
Cost Report No. 3
Date of Report—9/30/8X

Location—

Acct. No.	Description	Budget (if applicable)	Net Change This Month	Balance to Date
1001	Cash Account	.00	2,622.33	3,268.85
1310	Prepaid Taxes, Insurance	.00	3,331.82–	.00
1621	Legal	.00	.00	723.52
1630	Partnership Agreement Wor	.00	.00	7,919.07
1650	Proposed Construction	.00	.00	13,425.74
2100	Loan-William Jennings	.00	198,000.00–	264,502.14–
2101	Loan-Sylvia Schmidt	.00	.00	16,623.01–
2150	N/P-Construction Loan	.00	.00	127,000.00–
	Total Project	.00	198,709.49	382,787.97–

Recap of Cash from Other Sources

ID No.				
	Total Cash from Other Sources	.00	.00	.00

97

Exhibit 7-4. Budget by Account Number

Budget Menu: 5

Run Date 8-/01/11

CO/PRJ Account	Description	Budget	Committed	Most-Commit	Forecast	Over/Under	Chg-This-Mo	Spent-T-D
53 135 0100	Backcharge to Gen Contract							
53 135 0101	Backcharge to Elect Contr							
53 135 0102	Backcharge to HVAC Contra							
53 135 0103	Backcharge to Site Contra							
53 135 0105	Proj Sign-Leasing & Const							
53 135 0106	Legal Lease Expense	7,520	7,520		7,520			910
53 135 0107	Legal Loan Expense	4,000	4,000		4,000			
53 135 0108	Legal Organizational Ex							
53 135 0110	Legal Fees HF-12K Hp-2.5K	14,500	14,500		14,500			4,725
53 135 0111	Property Taxes Dur Const							5,885
53 135 0112	Zoning Permit Fees	50	27		27	23–	23–	27
53 135 0113	Building Permit Fees							
53 135 0114	Sign Permit Fees							
53 135 0115	Insurance-Builders Risk	1,483	1,439		1,439	44–	44–	
53 135 0116	Insurance-Title	3,417	3,417		3,417			2,465
53 135 0117	Performance Bnd-Developer							
53 135 0118	Performance Bnd-Gen Cont							
53 135 0119	Performance Bnd-Site Cont							
53 135 0120	Construction Interest	110,000	110,000		110,000			3,614
53 135 0121	Bank Charges	200	200		200			114
53 135 0122	Non Refundable Loan Fees							
53 135 0123	Refundable Loan Fees							
53 135 0125	Survey-Property	1,200	243	957	1,200			63
53 135 0126	Survey-Topographical	1,500	40	1,460	1,500			220
53 135 0127	Survey-Physical-Fndation	550		550	550			650
53 135 0128	Survey-Phys Final-Ln Clos	2,000		2,000	2,000			

Account	Description						
53 135 0129	Survey-Layout Dur Construc	6,000	1,250	4,750	6,000		600
53 135 0130	Soil Test-Preliminary						
53 135 0131	Soil Test-Borings, Invest, Rpts	2,500	2,500		2,500		2,484
53 135 0132	Soil Test Quality Control	7,500		7,500	7,500		
53 135 0135	Telephone	200		200	200		
53 135 0136	Blueprints	2,150	2,148	2	2,150		544
53 135 0137	Postage	200		200	200		
53 135 0138	Courier Service-Bus						
53 135 0139	Courier Service-Air	200	200		200		67
53 135 0140	Coureir Service-Car						
53 135 0141	Office Supplies	200	10	190	200		10
53 135 0142	Drafting Supplies	200		200	200		
53 135 0143	Copying						
53 135 0150	Eng Serv-Const Mgt	10,000	10,000		10,000		10,000
53 135 0151	Eng Serv-Electrical-Bldg	4,500	4,500		4,500		3,673
53 135 0152	Eng Serv-Electrical Site	700	636		636	64	350
53 135 0153	Eng Serv-Plumbing-Bldg	2,300	2,130		2,130	170–	

foot. The land cost of the center city would add a large cost dimension to the overall cost of the center. Suburban land costs may be high, but usually nothing like the extraordinarily high costs of central business district land. Foundation costs of high-rise centers are higher than the foundation costs of one- and two-story centers.

EIGHT

LEASING BUILDING SPACE AND LAND

Most space of a shopping center is leased from its owner by the occupying tenant. To begin with, the land under the center is often leased from the original or subsequent owners. Land sale-leasebacks are often arranged so that significant sums of money are not tied up in the land ownership by the developer. The developer and other investors usually own the store buildings including the mall buildings. When the major department stores arrange for the financing of their individual store buildings, often institutional investors purchase the completed department store buildings and lease them back to the department store operating companies. Then the developer and other investors will continue to own the mall and other buildings of the center after they lease or sell the department store land—sometimes called the "pad"—to the builder/owner. Of course, many department stores lease or purchase land for satellite auto service centers, also.

It is usually accurate to say that a shopping center represents componentized ownership. The land may be owned by certain investors and leased to the development company. The buildings may be constructed on leased or purchased land. Various institutions and other types of investors may own each of the department store buildings and lease them to the store operating companies. The developer may end up owning very little property or may own total or partial interests in the mall buildings and the outparcels. The outparcels, the auxiliary space around the center that is subject to development, may be sold or leased to operating companies such as fast-food franchisers and oil companies.

THE GENERAL RENT REQUIREMENT

The owner of the property that is subject to tenant lease must consider the costs of that property ownership. They may include:

    Mortgage debt service
    Ground rent
    Other financial payments
    Operating costs
    Normal overhead and profit

The rents built into the lease contracts must amply cover the owner's costs of property ownership. In addition, the property owner may wish to hedge against inflation with participation in the tenants' sales over a base amount, with indexed base rents, and tenant assumption of all operating costs normally attributed to the owner.

THE IMPORTANCE OF INITIAL MARKET STUDIES

From a study of the competition and the market needs, the proposed tenant mix and the general nature of the contemplated leases may be determined. The existing and proposed centers whose locations and retail offerings will compete with those of the proposed center must be thoroughly analyzed in the market studies. Of course, the prospective investor may be considering the purchase of an existing center rather than the development of a new center. The study of the competition is still vitally important. Who are the key tenants of the competitive centers? What is the general tenant mix of each of the competing centers? What kind of lease agreements prevail at the competitive centers? What do their lease agreements portend for the proposed center investment?

What does the market need in light of the competition? What lines of business should be added to satisfy the consumer need? Where do market opportunities exist by price level, brand name, quality of merchandise, and quality of service? From the answers to these and similar questions, we must determine the most advantageous tenant mix. The merchants within the tenant mix generally agree to certain types of leases; therefore, we can generally determine what our center will gross in rents. Competitive lease terms determine the base rents. From expected sales per square foot of each of the merchants of the tenant mix, we can estimate the overage rents that may be paid. Therefore, we can estimate from competitive conditions what our total lease revenue will be. Once we have estimated our operating and financial expenses in pro forma statement analysis, we may determine through sensitivity analysis what our possible return on equity investment will be.

LEASING TOOLS

To attract the tenants we want, we must generate the information and exhibits necessary to entice them. The necessary information must be cast into forms that will prompt productive presentations for major tenants. Once the major tenants sign letters of intent to lease or lease agreements themselves, the other national and local chain stores and the independent local stores will be tempted to join the group without too much additional sales effort from the developer and his or her staff.

The major tenants (including the major department stores) usually want to see certain items of information about the proposed investment location. These items include:

Plot plan
Aerial photographs
Traffic map or study
Traffic counts
Demographic information about the trading area
Retail sales information including trends

The presentation made by the developer and his or her staff before the major chain store leasing executives may include the above plus:

Complete information about the proposed development or the expansion of the existing center
Competition in the trading area
Growth information, that is, population and buying power
Highway information
Market history
Rendering of the project

This same information is generally presented to prospective investors and lenders so that they may see the proposed investment plans, the long-term financial security that is promised, and the potential financial rewards for the proposed investment funds.

THE GROUND LEASE VERSUS THE STOREROOM OR BUILDING LEASE

Shopping center space of all types is subject to lease. The land may be leased to a single party, or it may be leased in parcels to more than one party. The same thing is true about the land improvements. All land improvements of the center may be owned by a single party, or various building components may be owned by various parties. The prospective tenant negotiates lease terms with the owner of the desired space. In some cases, the owner of the building and/or land sells the real property to another party and leases that space back.

The ground lease of the center may involve individual, syndicated, or institutional owners of the land. The developer may be the leasing party. In Exhibit 8-1, we note that the developer controls the land in the middle of the site of Anytown Mall. The developer may own or lease that land. Parcel A is controlled by Department Store A while Parcel C is controlled by Department Store C. The control may be ownership or ground lease control.

The ground lease amounts to release of rights of possession held by the owner to the lessee and a promise to pay rent over the specified time period at the specified intervals on the specified ground lease terms to the owner, the lessor, by the lessee. The owner usually asks the tenant to pay all ownership costs related to the land such as *ad valorem* taxes and any forms of needed liability insurance. A desired financial return to the owner is built into the lease payments. The owner may or may not subordinate his or her ownership interest to the leasehold mortgage lender if the lessee seeks mortgage financing for the development of the site. If the landowner subordinates to the leasehold lender's legal and financial position, the landowner will probably exact a higher invest-ment return through the periodic lease payments.

Roadway access, utility, drainage, and other easements may be accepted in the lease as necessary conditions for the profitable operation of the shopping center. Exhibit 8-1 shows a permanent access easement that goes completely

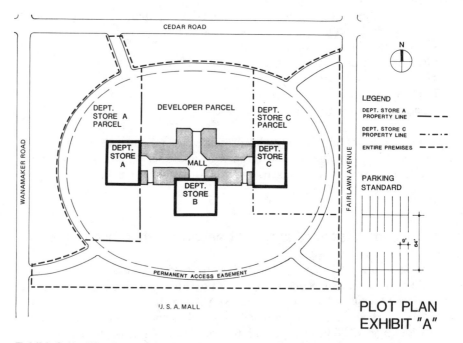

Exhibit 8-1. Plot Plan with Multiple Parcels of Land and an Access Easement

around the center. Reciprocal easement agreements are usually required for the cooperative use of the land by the various ownership and leasing partners to the project.* Parking space, for example, is maintained by the center management for the joint use of all tenants, owners, customers, and other individuals visiting the center. Through reciprocal easement agreements, the parties to the shopping center operation agree to use the entire parking lot cooperatively and jointly without partitioning of the lot for the use of specified parties. The easements benefit all parties, so the deeds and leases related to the center all contain clauses pledging adherence to the easement conditions and rights.

The ground or building lease agreement may require lease payment of part of the gross receipts acquired from the operation of the land improvements as one form of rental payment. That type of lease agreement is common to storeroom leases. Most basic lease terms apply to ground leases as well as building and storeroom leases. Other clauses may have special application to the type of property being leased.

LEASE TERMS

Shopping center leases negotiated between the developer and the retail merchant usually contain clauses dealing with the following subjects:

Term of the lease

Starting and ending lease dates

Rent payments due

Percentage rent conditions

Indexed base rent conditions

Site plan related to the retail space

Reciprocal easement agreements

Operational rules and regulations and default clause

Construction, maintenance, and repairs of the land improvements

Expansion provisions

Provisions for subsequent destruction and loss through the exercise of eminent domain

Sales reporting

Record keeping

Developer/owner right to audit retailer books

Tax payment

Insurance coverage and premium payment

Common area maintenance responsibility and expense assumption

Storeroom use and restrictions

Assignment and subletting

Financing contingency conditions

Promotion and advertising, including the grand opening and merchants' association or promotional fund

The term of the lease should be stated in terms of the total period of time starting and ending on a specific date. The statement of the time of day of the

---

*The reader may wish to explore the recent International Council of Shopping Centers monographs on reciprocal easement agreements written by Francis Gunning, executive vice president and general counsel for the Teachers Insurance and Annuity Association, New York.

starting and ending dates will also avoid misinterpretation. For example, noon or midnight in a specific time zone could be stated as the lease starting or ending time. The rent payments should be stated in terms of amount, periodic date due, and the address and name of the agent or institution to be paid that established amount. To follow up the lease provisions, a reminder of the required rent payments may be sent to the new tenant in memorandum form (Exhibit 8-2). The percentage rent and indexed base rent provisions should be clearly spelled out.

Exhibit 8-2.   Rent Payment Reminder Sent to New Tenant by the Center Manager

Date:

To:

Gentlemen:

It is with great pleasure that we take this opportunity to welcome you as a Tenant of The Mall. We hope that we will be able to work together in the future to make The Mall one of the finest and most productive shopping centers.

Your rental payments are due as follows:

Annual minimum rent $_____

Monthly installments	$_____
Estimated monthly common area	$_____
Estimated monthly real estate taxes	$_____
Total monthly rent	$_____

Your first month prorated rent is: $_____

Please note: Your monthly rental payments are due and payable on or before the first day of each and every month. No further invoices will be sent. Please insure that your monthly rental payments in the amount of $_____ will be made promptly when due.

Very truly yours,

General Manager

Source: Marketing Department, Cousins Properties Incorporated, 300 Interstate North, Atlanta, GA 30339.

The percentage rent may be established as a net percentage of the annual gross sales volume above a set amount of the tenant from the storeroom in the mall, or the percentage rent may be based on a set percentage of an amount above a changing base amount of annual gross storeroom sales. The base amount may change with an index such as the Consumer Price Index. As a result of tenant-developer negotiations, a ceiling may be established for the developer's participation in the gross sales of the tenant.

The base storeroom rent may change as a selected index changes. The selected index will probably be maintained by a government agency which is controlled in no way by retail interests. The base rent per square foot of gross leasable area may start at $8, for example, and increase over time with the increase of the Consumer Price Index. The index selected may best reflect, in the judgment of the developer and owner, the level of inflation during the time of the lease. At the end of the sales year, the percentage of change in the index is noted. This rate of inflation is applied to the rent level of the previous period. The increased rent is due periodically during the coming year. The Consumer Price Index has fluctuated on an upward trend over the past nine years (Exhibit 8-3, The Consumer Price Index Based on All Items and Its Changes over Time).

At this point in shopping center development, most storeroom leases do not contain indexed base rent clauses, but office building leases often do. This method of owner inflation hedging may be adopted by shopping center owners and developers in the near future. Office building tenants have accepted the reality of and need for such indexed base rents for the owner's financial protection.

The lease establishes the physical boundaries of the store building location, its potential expansion dimensions, and the parking space available to the tenant, the tenant's employees, customers, and other visitors to the storeroom

Exhibit 8-3. The Consumer Price Index Based on All Items and Its Changes over Time.

Year	Consumer Price Index Based on All Items	Annual Percent of Change
1981	272.4	8.9%
1980	246.8	12.4
1979	217.4	13.3
1978	195.4	9.0
1977	181.5	6.8
1976	170.5	4.8
1975	161.2	7.0
1974	147.7	12.2
1973	133.1	8.8

Source: Economic Report of the President, 97th Congress, 2nd Session, House Document No. 97–123, February 1982.

or retail building. Usually reciprocal easement agreements provide for the joint use of the adjacent mall space, walkways linking the mall to the parking lots or buildings, and the parking lots. If the pad is being leased from the developer and the other owners by the major department store, the site dimensions, easements, and improvement restrictions such as height and ground coverage are fully described. (See the sample percentage, indexed lease agreement and the accompanying exhibits which are located in Exhibit 8-7).

The lease clauses usually call for monthly and annual sales reporting. The monthly statement often requires the current month's gross sales along with the year-to-date gross sales (Exhibit 8-4). A form may be given the new tenant for the monthly reporting of the required data (Exhibit 8-5). At the end of the sales year, a form may be sent the tenant as a reminder that the percentage rent is due by an established date following year-end based on the annual gross sales generated in the particular storeroom. Using the tenant data, the management may periodically let the merchants know how sales in each line of business of the mall are doing (Exhibit 8-6).

In order to encourage efficient and accurate sales reporting, the developer usually requires under the lease that the tenant keep adequate records for appropriate sales and expense accounting and that the tenant's books or accounts be subject to owner and center manager auditing at any time during usual business hours.

Exhibit 8-4.   Memorandum from the Center Bookkeeper to the Tenant Requesting Monthly and Year-to-Date Sales Figures for the Tenant Space

Date:

To:

Gentlemen:

Pursuant to Article _____, Section _____, of your lease, a written monthly statement showing gross sales; monthly, and year-to-date, is due _____ days after the close of each month.

For your convenience, attached are twelve monthly gross sales statements, which should be filled out monthly and submitted to the Mall General Offices _____ days after the close of each month.

Very truly yours,

Bookkeeper

Source: Marketing Department, Cousins Properties Incorporated, 300 Interstate North, Atlanta, GA 30339.

Exhibit 8-5. Monthly Sales Statement

Store Reporting _____

Sales Reported _____

Month Reported for _____

Year-to-date Sales _____

Authorized Signature _____

Please return this statement to any mall on or before the 10th of each month.

Source: Marketing Department, Cousins Properties Incorporated, 300 Interstate North, Atlanta, GA 30339.

Exhibit 8-6. Memorandum Regarding Comparative Sales Performance by Business Category for the Shopping Center

Date:

To: Store Managers and Home Offices

From: General Manager

Gentlemen:

We have done an evaluation, by category, of the performance at The Mall for the period beginning _____ and ending _____.

I am sure you will find it interesting to compare your performance to that of the appropriate, individual category as well as the entire Shopping Center.

Categories	Production P.S.F.
Restaurants	$_____
Jewelry	$_____
Perishables	$_____
Shoe Stores	$_____
Specialty Shops	$_____
Services	$_____
Home Furnishings	$_____

(Continued)

Exhibit 8-6. *(Continued)*

Categories	Production P.S.F.
Apparel	$_____
Gifts, Cards, Books, etc.	$_____
Entire Shopping Center	$_____
How well did you compare?	

Source: Marketing Department, Cousins Properties Incorporated, 300 Interstate North, Atlanta, GA 30339.

Most shopping center leases are net rather than gross leases. The net lease calls for tenant assumption of most or all the owners' expenses related to property taxes, insurance premiums, and common area maintenance expense that are assigned or allocated to the tenant space. The landlord may assume financial responsibility for the initial level of property taxes, insurance premiums, and common area maintenance expense. Expenses beyond that level may then be allocated on various bases to the mall tenants. The provisions for the payment of the operating expenses are found in clauses in each storeroom lease.

Since the center owner decides upon the optimum tenant mix for the future profitable operation of the center, the retail offerings of the individual tenants are restricted to maintain the optimum and unduplicated offerings from the center as a whole. If the storeroom operator were unrestricted, the individual tenants might change their offerings of goods and services and upset the profitable balance of the center's merchandising attraction. (Later in this chapter, the optimum tenant mix for the various types of centers will be covered in some detail.) The current tenants in the center are restricted usually from establishing competitive retail units within the same trading area either while they do business in the center or a specified number of years after they leave the center premises. The landlord gains market control to some extent over certain popular lines of merchandise in this manner. Of course, the landlord cannot control competitive offerings in the trading area from merchants not located in the landlord's center. Unreasonable restrictions on tenant offerings are not permitted by the federal antitrust laws such as the Robinson-Patman Act and its amendments.

Through the lease, the lessee is subject to the general operational rules and regulations of the center. These rules and regulations pertain to such factors as hours open for business, days open for business during the year, employee parking, rubbish control, in-store and storefront signing, noise levels, and common area use. If the operating rules and regulations as well as other lease terms are violated, the lease may be terminated due to default or violation of lease terms. Specific conditions for default and lease termination should be spelled out in the lease.

The tenant is charged with the improvement of the storeroom or building shell after the developer has constructed the foundation, outer walls, and roofs over the center buildings. These lease terms show the agreement between the owner and tenant regarding the responsibility for construction, maintenance, and repairs of the land improvements inhabited by the lessee. The lessee may wish to contract with the developer's construction company for the storeroom improvement. If this is the case, the lease must detail the necessity for scheduled preparation of storeroom design and construction specifications. The payment for the interior construction and equipment must be negotiated between the development-construction company and the tenant. In many cases, the base rent reflects an allowance for storeroom interior preparation. The periodic lease payments may be higher than usual as a form of periodic payment for the interior improvements to the landlord, or the allowance may reflect landlord payment for some or all of the individual tenant's interior improvements so that the developer may entice the prospective lessee to sign a lease for center space. Sometimes, in addition, the landlord agrees to buy the retail company's lease to its maturity at another location in order to get a signed lease from the prospective tenant. As an alternative, the landlord may merely meet the periodic lease payments of the tenant at the other location until the maturity of the existing lease. The maintenance and repairs to the interior of the storeroom shell are usually the financial responsibility of the lessee. Any expansion of the lessee's storeroom is usually the financial responsibility of the lessee, also, not the landlord.

Sometimes part or all of the center is destroyed by fire, tornado, hurricane, or other disaster. On some occasions, parties exercising the power of eminent domain for the pursuit of a publicly approved community project acquire land and/or buildings of the center. It often amounts to partial land and/or building acquisition on an involuntary basis from the center owners. The landlord usually negotiates into the lease clauses which do not permit cancellation of the lease due to decrease in real property holdings of the center. Many national chain stores wish cancellation rights if any part of their store building or overall parking lot is taken by condemning authorities or weather conditions. The landlord and the mortgage lenders usually want to guard against such opportunities for cancellation of vitally important major financial leases of the center.

The landlord and tenant must negotiate the assignment and subletting agreement. The tenant may wish unrestricted subleasing rights. The landlord and the mortgage lenders usually want restricted subleasing and only landlord-approved assignment rights. The landlord and the mortgage lenders usually want the privilege of releasing the storeroom to totally approved new tenants who meet the credit and merchandising standards that prevail for the center at the time of the tenant replacement. If the landlord permits tenant subletting, the original lessee remains financially and legally responsible for the replacement lessee's adherence to all the terms of the original lease agreements. Under these subleasing circumstances, the original tenant remains fully accountable under the lease. The original tenant, therefore, may prefer to negotiate for unrestricted lease assignment in case the tenant wishes to vacate the storeroom space for various possible reasons during the term of the lease.

Shopping centers are usually financed on the strength of the major tenant leases. The mortgage lenders and equity investors will want to negotiate noncancellation clauses except on extremely valid terms which are enumerated in the lease. In the case of mortgage default and foreclosure, the lenders will want lease assignment so that they may take title to the center, continue to receive the required lease payments, and pay necessary operating costs from these funds. The mortgage lender may have to take the place of the original developer-owner in the case of loan default and foreclosure.

The retail offerings and the individual retail operators of the center must be advertised frequently and effectively if the center is to thrive as projected. The grand opening at the completion of the initial construction and at the completion of major expansion programs must be planned and financed. The advertising and promotion of a center has three potential sources of financing: (1) the landlord or center management, (2) the tenant or local operating companies, and (3) retail holding companies who have established subsidiary units in the center. Generally the landlord negotiates for advertising and promotional funds from the lessee through the lease. The advertising and promotional funds may be attached to the local retail operating unit in terms of a percentage of the year's total sales, but the monies may come from the local retail unit or from the advertising and promotional budgets of the holding companies. If the tenant is an independent store, of course, the advertising and promotional funds come strictly from that local organization. Most shopping center tenants are chain stores on a local, regional, or national basis. In many instances, cooperative advertising allowances are given the center merchant by the retail holding company or by various manufacturers and distributors of goods and services. The cooperative advertising becomes part of the tenant's contribution to the overall marketing effort of the center. The sample percentage, indexed lease agreement of Exhibit 8-7 indicates the wording of typical lease clauses.

PREPARATION OF LEASE CARDS OR COMPUTER FILES

The terms of each tenant lease must be organized for continual reference by the center manager, marketing director, accountants, and other center personnel. The terms of the particular lease should be abstracted for easy reference. The lease card may be used (Exhibit 8-8). Many shopping center developers and owners maintain computer systems with access and output terminals at individual shopping center sites. Computer records may be continually updated so that information on current lease terms for the tenant may be readily viewed.

THE GENERAL LEASING PLAN: TENANT MIX

Tenant mix has two aspects: (1) the balance between national and local chains and independent stores, and (2) the balance among the various storeroom classifications. Over 80 percent of the gross leasable area of superregional centers is occupied by national chain store units. Another 15 percent of the superregional GLA is occupied by local chain stores. The national chain stores represented a little less of the GLA of regional centers while local chain stores represented a little more of the GLA of these centers. Independent stores, therefore, represent 10 percent or less of regional shopping centers, according to 1981 Urban Land Institute data.* These chain stores represent about 90 percent of the sales of the regional and superregional centers, but they pay a little less of the total rent and total charges on a proportional basis. In like manner, the independent stores pay 13 to 17 percent of the total rent and total charges.

Most of the space of superregional and regional centers is devoted to general merchandise units including major department stores. In the mall buildings alone, about a quarter of the gross leasable area is devoted to clothing stores and about 15 percent of the GLA to general merchandise stores. Another 15 to 20 percent of the GLA is devoted to food and food services. Many other types of stores offering convenience, shopping, and specialty goods and services make up the rest of the GLA of the superregional and regional centers.

In contrast, community centers devote about one-third of their space to general merchandise stores, and neighborhood centers devote about the same amount of their space of food and food service stores. General merchandise stores comprise less than 10 percent of the GLA of the neighborhood center (see Exhibit 8-9, Composition by Tenant Classification Group of Community and Neighborhood Shopping Centers). Food and food service sales make up two-thirds of the sales of neighborhood centers, but only 40 percent of the sales of community centers. One-fourth of the sales of community centers come from general merchandise stores.

TENANT LEASE DIFFERENCES

Since leases have many negotiated provisions, lease terms differ among tenants on many bases. Even between regions and between new and old centers, there exist many lease differences (see Exhibit 8-10, Rent Rate Comparison). Percentage lease terms for chain stores differ over time and by store category (Exhibit 8-11, National Percentage Lease Ranges for Selected Store Catego-

---

* "Tenants by Operational Type," *Dollars & Cents of Shopping Centers*, Urban Land Institute, 1981, Table 8F–1, p. 299.

Exhibit 8-7. Lease Agreement

THIS LEASE AGREEMENT, made as of the _____ day of _____,
_____, by and between _____   _____, a
_____ partnership with its principal office in Charlotte, North Carolina,
whose general partner authorized to execute leases is   of Mecklenburg County,
North Carolina, (hereinafter called "Landlord"), and _____,
_____ (hereinafter called "Tenant");

W I T N E S S E T H:

The parties hereto agree for themselves, their successors and assigns, as follows:

1.*Premises.*   Landlord hereby leases to Tenant, the Tenant hereby accepts and
rents from Landlord, that certain store space (hereinafter called "Demised Premises"),
containing approximately _____ square feet, shown outlined in red on the site
plan attached hereto as Exhibit A and made a part hereof and situated in the shopping
center known as _____ _____ (hereinafter
called "Shopping Center") erected or to be erected on the tract of land described in
Exhibit B attached hereto and made a part hereof, together with the non-exclusive right
to use all of the parking areas, driveways, entrance ways, footwalks and other common
facilities furnished from time to time in the shopping center by Landlord, all subject to
such reasonable and uniform rules and regulations as may be prescribed by Landlord
from time to time.

TO HAVE AND TO HOLD the said Demised Premises and appurtenances upon
the terms and conditions hereinafter set forth.

2. *Term.*   The term of this lease shall be for a period of _____
(_____) years, commencing on the "Rental Commencement Date" (as hereinafter
defined in Paragraph 3a) and terminating on the last day of the twelfth (12th) full
calendar month of the _____ (_____) lease year thereafter.

3. *Rental.* Tenant shall pay to Landlord for the use and occupancy of the
Demised Premises and appurtenances thereto rental as hereinafter provided:

(a) *Guaranteed minimum rental.*   Guaranteed minimum rental at the rate of
_____ Dollars ($_____) per
year, payable in equal monthly installments of _____
_____ Dollars ($_____) in advance on or before the first day of
each and every calendar month beginning on the "Rental Commencement Date" (as
hereinafter defined) and continuing throughout the term of this lease.   As used
herein, the Rental Commencement Date is defined as the earlier of either:

(i)   the _____ (_____) day after Landlord has delivered the
demised premises to Tenant,
or
(ii) The date on which Tenant shall open the demised premises for business.

If such date is not the first day of a calendar month, the guaranteed minimum
rental from the Rental Commencement Date to the end of the calendar month in which
said date occurs shall be prorated per diem and paid on the Rental Commencement
Date.

(b) *Percentage rental.*   An additional sum as percentage rental equal to
_____ percent (_____%) of the amount by which Tenant's gross sales in the
Demised Premises for each lease year exceed the sum of _____
_____ Dollars

114

Exhibit 8-7. *(Continued)*

($_____) hereinafter called "Percentage Rent Base"); provided, however, that for the first lease year and the last lease year, the percentage rent shall be computed on the excess of Tenant's sales over a per diem, prorated portion of the Percentage Rent Base.

Such percentage rental shall be payable on each calendar year or part thereof during the term of this lease within thirty (30) days after the end of such calendar year and within thirty (30) days after the termination of this lease; and, upon each such payment date Tenant shall furnish to Landlord a statement duly certified by an officer of Tenant showing in complete detail the gross sales made during the immediately preceding calendar year or part thereof. Tenant shall also furnish to Landlord at the end of every calendar quarter during the term of this lease such a statement showing the total amount of gross sales made during such calendar quarter.

(c) *Definition of "Gross Sales".* As used herein the term Gross Sales means all sales, both cash and charge, of merchandise and services made in or from the Demised Premises, including telephone sales and orders taken in or from the Demised Premises although such orders may be filled elsewhere, less refunds and allowances to the customer, but not including any sales, use or excise tax upon such merchandise or services if such tax is separately stated and separately charged to the customer. A sale upon installment or credit shall be treated as a sale for the full price in the month during which such sale is made, regardless of when or whether Tenant shall receive payment therefor.

(d) *Records and audit.* Tenant shall keep at the Demised Premises or at its general office complete and accurate books of account and records in accordance with accepted accounting practices with respect to all business conducted in the Demised Premises; and Landlord shall have the right at any reasonable time to examine such books and records (including all tax returns) or have them audited at Landlord's expense, except that if any such examination or audit discloses a deficiency of more than three percent (3%) in any annual statement of gross sales theretofore furnished by Tenant to Landlord, then Tenant shall pay the reasonable cost of such examination or audit. If any examination or audit by Landlord shall disclose any deficiency in any payment of additional rental, Tenant shall immediately pay such deficiency with interest at the rate of six percent (6%) per annum from the date on which such payment should have been made.

Landlord agrees that any financial information relating to Tenant's business received by it has been disclosed in confidence and shall not be disclosed to any third party without Tenant's express written consent. However, such information may be disclosed in a court action to recover additional rent or to the Landlord's mortgage lenders.

(e) *Payment of rental.* All rental payments provided herein shall be made to Landlord at its principal office at until notice to the contrary is given by Landlord.

4. *Improvements and Delivery of Demised Premises.* Tenant hereby acknowledges that it has examined the Demised Premises, that same are acceptable for the use for which Tenant intends to occupy the Demised Premises, and that Tenant is leasing the Demised Premises "AS IS". Landlord shall have no obligation to make any improvements to the Demised Premises prior to Tenant's occupancy of same.

5. *Taxes.* Landlord covenants and agrees to pay promptly all taxes and assessments of every kind or nature which are now or may hereafter be imposed or assessed upon the Demised Premises, except as otherwise expressly provided in this Lease Agreement. Landlord shall not be required to pay any taxes or assessments of any

Exhibit 8-7. *(Continued)*

nature imposed or assessed upon fixtures, equipment, merchandise or other property installed in the Demised Premises or brought thereon by Tenant or any other person, but such shall be the obligation of the Tenant, and Tenant agrees that it will promptly pay all such taxes or assessments as the same become due.

In addition, Tenant shall pay to Landlord its pro rata share of the annual ad valorem real property taxes attributable to the Demised Premises in each calendar year. For the purpose of this provision, the ad valorem real property taxes attributable to the Demised Premises shall be that portion of the total of such taxes on the Shopping Center as the number of square feet in the Demised Premises as specified in Paragraph 1 hereinabove bears to the total number of square feet of store space leased to all tenants in the Shopping Center. Landlord shall annually compute and notify Tenant of the amount due hereunder, and Tenant shall pay such amount within twenty (20) days after such notice.

6. *Insurance.* Landlord will maintain and pay for adequate fire insurance, with extended coverage, on the Demised Premises. Tenant agrees to pay its pro rata share of Landlord's premium costs using the same ratio provided in Paragraph 5 hereof. In addition, Tenant will provide and pay for all insurance on its own contents in the Demised Premises. Landlord and Tenant hereby waive the right of subrogation against the other as a result of loss or damage to the property (personal and real) of Landlord and Tenant.

7. *Use of Demised Premises.* Tenant shall use the Demised Premises only for

_____

_____ . Tenant shall comply with all laws, ordinances, orders or regulations of any lawful authority having jurisdiction over the demised premises or the adjacent public streets including without limitation making at its own expense all alterations to the Demised Premises required by any such authority; and Tenant shall not do any act or follow any practice in or about the Demised Premises which shall constitute a nuisance or detract from or impair the reputation of the Shopping Center. Without limiting the generality of the foregoing, Tenant shall make such arrangements for the storage and disposition of all garbage and refuse as may be reasonably required by Landlord from time to time and shall at all times keep the Demised Premises and all adjoining entry ways, sidewalks and delivery areas in a neat and orderly condition and clean and free from rubbish, dirt, snow and ice, and shall not cause any noxious, disturbing or offensive odors, fumes or gases, or any smoke, dust, steam or vapors, or any loud or disturbing noise or vibrations to originate in or be emitted from the Demised Premises.

Tenant shall continuously during the term of this lease keep the entire Demised Premises occupied and open for business during the same hours as the majority of the stores operating in the Shopping Center (except Tenant shall not be required to open on Sunday); and Tenant shall in all respects conduct its business in the Demised Premises in a diligent and dignified manner and exert its best efforts to generate a maximum volume of gross sales. During the term of this lease Tenants shall not, directly or in- directly, engage in any business within _____ (_____) miles of Tenant's store space in competition with any business being conducted in said store space; provided, however, that this provision shall not prohibit Tenant from continuing to conduct any business being conducted by Tenant on the date of this Lease Agreement, and provided further, if Tenant violates this restriction, the gross sales of such

Exhibit 8-7. *(Continued)*

business shall be treated as additional gross sales of Tenant hereunder and shall be used in computing percentage rental hereunder in accordance with Article 3 hereof.

8. *Landlord's Covenant to Maintain.* Landlord will, at its own expense, keep and maintain in good order and repair during the full term of this lease the exterior and principal structural portions of the buildings and other improvements constituting the Shopping Center; provided, however, that Landlord will not be responsible for or required to make, and Tenant will make, any repairs which may have been occasioned or necessitated by the negligence of Tenant, its agents, employees or invitees.

9. *Tenant's Covenant to Maintain.* Tenant will, at its own expense, keep and maintain in good order and repair during the full term of this lease all other parts of the Demised Premises, including without limitation, the entire interior and all window glass, plate glass, plumbing, wiring, electrical systems and heating and air conditioning systems; and Tenant will, at the end of the term of this lease, deliver the Demised Premises to the Landlord in as good condition as they were when received by it, excepting only normal wear and tear repairs required to be made by Landlord and loss by fire or other casualty.

10. *Common Facilities.* Landlord shall at all times during the term of this lease maintain in good condition and repair the parking areas, mall, driveways and footwalks in the Shopping Center. All common facilities in the Shopping Center shall at all times be subject to the exclusive control and management of Landlord; and Landlord shall have the right from time to time to change the area, level, location and arrangement of the common facilities, to restrict parking by tenants and their employees to employee parking areas, and to make all rules and regulations and do such other things from time to time as in Landlord's discretion may be necessary regarding said facilities.

11. *Damage or Destruction by Casualty.* If the Demised Premises are damaged or destroyed during the term of this lease by fire or other casualty covered by an ordinary fire insurance policy with extended coverage, Tenant shall give immediate written notice thereof to Landlord, and Landlord will reconstruct the Demised Premises or repair such damage as promptly as practicable, and Tenant shall meanwhile be entitled to an abatement of rental to the extent of the loss of use suffered by it; provided, however, that if the Demised Premises shall be damaged or destroyed by casualty to the extent of fifty percent (50%) or more of their replacement value, Landlord shall thereupon have an option to terminate this lease.

12. *Utilities.* During the term of this lease, Tenant shall provide and pay for all lights, heat, water, janitor service and other utilities required by it in the use of the Demised Premises.

13. *Signs, Advertising and Selling Activities.* Tenant may install such signs on the Demised Premises as may be approved by Landlord and as shall not damage or impair the attractiveness of the Shopping Center; provided, however, that the care and maintenance of such signs shall be the sole responsibility of Tenant. Tenant shall not (a) paste or otherwise affix any banners, posters or other advertising material to any outside display window or wall in the Shopping Center or in any other manner display any merchandise or advertising media closer than twelve (12) inches to the interior side of any such display window; (b) maintain or display any vending machines, show cases, coin-operated devices or other selling devices, or any merchandise or property of any nature whatsoever in any mall areas, parking lot or other common facilities or on the outside of any store building in the Shopping Center; or (c) permit, allow or cause to be

Exhibit 8-7. *(Continued)*

used in or about the Shopping Center any phonographs, radios, public address system, sound production or reproduction devices, mechanical or moving display devices, motion picture, television devices, excessively bright lights, changing, flashing, flickering or moving lights or lighting devices, or any similar advertising media or devices, the effect of which shall be visible or audible from the exterior of any store space.

14. *Indemnity.* Tenant covenants and agrees that it will defend, indemnify, protect and save harmless the Landlord from the claims of all persons arising from or out of the use or occupancy of the Demised Premises by or under Tenant or Tenant's agents, employees or invitees. Tenant shall carry public liability insurance naming Landlord as an insured and having a minimum coverage of $500,000 for injuries to one person and $5,000,000 for injuries to more than one person, in one accident, and $100,000 property damage coverage; and Tenant shall, upon demand, furnish Landlord with a copy or a certificate of such insurance.

15. *Fixtures and Personal Property.* Any trade fixtures, equipment and other personal property installed in or attached to the Demised Premises by or at the expense of Tenant shall remain the property of Tenant, and Tenant shall have the right at any time, provided it is not then in default hereunder, to remove any and all of such fixtures, provided, however, that in such event Tenant shall restore the Demised Premises to substantially the same condition in which they were at the time Tenant took possession, ordinary wear and tear and Landlord's covenant to maintain excepted.

16. *Landlord's Entry.* The Landlord shall have the right to enter upon the Demised Premises at all reasonable times during the term of this lease for the purposes of inspection, maintenance, repair and alteration and to show the same to prospective tenants or purchasers.

17. *Assigning, Mortgaging, Subletting.* Tenant agrees not to assign, sublet, mortgage, pledge or encumber this Lease Agreement in whole or in part, or sublet the whole or any part of the Demised Premises, or permit the use of the whole or any part of the Demised Premises by any licensee or concessionaire, except to the extent such use is not restricted by Paragraph 7, without first obtaining the written consent of Landlord. Tenant agrees that, in the event of any such assignment, subletting, licensing or granting of a concession, made with the written consent of Landlord as aforesaid, Tenant will nevertheless remain primarily liable for the performance of all the terms, conditions and covenants of this Lease Agreement.

18. *Default.* If the tenant shall continue in default in the payment of any rental or other sum of money becoming due hereunder for a period of ten (10) days after notice of such default has been given to Tenant, or if either party hereto shall default in the performance of any other of the terms, conditions or covenants contained in this lease to be observed or performed by it and the party in default does not remedy such default within thirty (30) days after written notice thereof or, if such default cannot be remedied in such period, does not within such thirty (30) days commence such act or acts as shall be necessary to remedy the default and shall not complete such act or acts promptly, or if the Tenant shall become bankrupt or insolvent, or file any debtor proceedings, or file in any court pursuant to any statute, either of the United States or of any State a petition in bankruptcy or insolvency or for reorganization, or file or have filed against it a petition for the appointment of a receiver or trustee for all or substantially all of the assests of the Tenant and such appointment shall not be vacated or set aside within fifteen (15) days from the date of such appointment, or if the Tenant makes an assignment for the benefit

Exhibit 8-7. *(Continued)*

of creditors, or petitions for or enters into an arrangement, or if the Tenant shall vacate, fail to operate in or abandon the Demised Premises or any substantial part thereof or suffer the lease to be taken under any writ of execution and such writ is not vacated or set aside within fifteen (15) days, then in any such event the party not in default shall have the right to terminate and cancel this Lease Agreement; provided, however, that Tenant shall not have the right to terminate and cancel this Lease Agreement unless and until it shall have given written notice, by registered or certified mail, of the default by the Landlord to the holder of holders of any mortgage or deed of trust covering the Demised Premises and shall have given said holder or holders a reasonable opportunity to cure such default, including time to get possession of the premises by an expeditious trustee's sale or foreclosure action, if this should be necessary to effect such cure; and if the Tenant is the party in default the Landlord, without excluding other rights or remedies that it may have, shall have the immediate right of re-entry and may remove all persons and property from the Demised Premises and dispose of such property as it sees fit, all without resort to legal process and without being deemed guilty of trespass, or becoming liable for any loss or damage which may be occasioned thereby. If the Landlord should elect to re-enter as herein provided, or should it take possession pursuant to legal proceedings, it may either terminate this Lease Agreement or it may from time to time without terminating this Lease Agreement, make such alterations and repairs as may be necessary in order to relet the Demised Premises, and relet the Demised Premises for such term and at such rentals and upon such other terms and conditions as the Landlord may deem advisable. No such re-entry or taking possession of the Demised Premises by the Landlord shall be construed as an election to terminate this lease unless a written notice of such intention be given by the Landlord to the Tenant at the time of such re-entry; but, notwithstanding any such re-entry and reletting without termination, the Landlord may at any time thereafter elect to terminate this lease for such previous breach. In the event of any termination by Landlord, whether before or after reentry, Landlord may recover from Tenant damages incurred by reason of such breach, including the cost of recovering the Demised Premises and the difference in value between the rental which would be payable by the Tenant hereunder for the remainder of the term and the reasonable rental value of the Demised Premises for the remainder of the term.

19. *Remedies Cumulative – Nonwaiver.* No remedy herein or otherwise conferred upon or reserved to Landlord or Tenant shall be considered exclusive of any other remedy, but the same shall be distinct, separate and cumulative and shall be in addition to every other remedy given hereunder, or now or hereafter existing at law or in equity or by statute, and every power and remedy given by this lease to Landlord or Tenant may be exercised from time to time as often as occasion may arise, or as may be deemed expedient. No delay or omission of Landlord or Tenant to exercise any right or power arising from any default on the part of the other shall impair any such right or power, or shall be construed to be a waiver of any such default or an acquiescence thereto.

20. *Eminent Domain.* If any substantial part of the Demised Premises or more than thirty percent (30%) of the total Shopping Center is taken under the power of eminent domain (including any conveyance made in lieu thereof), and such taking shall in the reasonable judgment of Tenant make the operation of Tenant's business on the Demised Premises impractical, then Tenant shall have the right to terminate this lease by giving Landlord written notice of such termination within thirty (30) days after such

Exhibit 8-7. *(Continued)*

taking; and if Tenant does not so elect to terminate this lease, Landlord at its own expense will repair and restore the Demised Premises to a tenantable condition, and the rental to be paid by Tenant hereunder shall be proportionately and equitably reduced.

21. *Advertising.* In each year during the term of this lease Tenant shall spend not less than one-half of one percent (½%) of its gross sales (as hereinabove defined) in advertising its business in the Demised Premises on radio or television or in newspapers or other media approved by Landlord. Within thirty (30) days after the end of every calendar year during the term of this lease Tenant shall furnish to Landlord, together with the statement required by Paragraph 3(b) hereinabove, a further statement certified by an officer of Tenant showing the amounts spent by Tenant on advertising as required by the provisions of this paragraph.

22. *Notices.* All notices provided for in this Lease Agreement shall be in writing and shall be deemed to be given when sent by prepaid registered or certified mail to the parties as follows:

to the Landlord in care of

to the Tenant at _____

_____

_____

Either party may, from time to time, by notice as hereinabove provided, designate a different address to which notices to it shall be sent.

23. *Holding Over.* If Tenant remains in possession of the Demised Premises or any part thereof after the expiration of the term of this lease with Landlord's acquiescence and without any written agreement of the parties, Tenant shall be only a tenant at will, and there shall be no renewal of this lease or exercise of an option by operation of law.

24. *Subordination.* Tenant will, upon request by Landlord, acquiesced in by the holder of any loan secured by a deed of trust on the Shopping Center, subject and subordinate all or any of its rights under this Lease Agreement to any and all mortgages and deeds of trust now existing or hereafter placed on the property of which the Demised Premises are a part; provided, however, that Tenant will not be disturbed in the use or enjoyment of the Demised Premises so long as it is not in default hereunder. Tenant agrees that this Lease Agreement shall remain in full force and effect notwithstanding any default or foreclosure under any such mortgage or deed of trust and that it will attorn to the mortgagee, trustee or beneficiary of such mortgage or deed of trust, and their successors or assigns, and to the purchaser or assignee under any such foreclosure. Tenant will, upon request by Landlord, execute and deliver to Landlord, or to any other person designated by Landlord, any instrument or instruments required to give effect to the provisions of this Article.

25. *Transfer of Landlord's Interest.* In the event of the sale, assignment or transfer by Landlord of its interest in the Shopping Center or in this lease (other than a collateral assignment to secure a debt of Landlord) to a successor in interest who expressly assumes the obligations of Landlord hereunder, Landlord shall thereupon be released or discharged from all of its covenants and obligations hereunder, except such obligations as shall have accrued prior to any such sale, assignment or transfer; and Tenant agrees to look solely to such successor in interest of Landlord for performance of such obligations. Any securities given by Tenant to Landlord to secure performance of Tenant's obligations hereunder may be assigned and transferred by Landlord to such

Exhibit 8-7. *(Continued)*

successor in interest of Landlord; and, upon acknowledgment by such successor of receipt of such security and its express assumption of the obligation to account to Tenant for such security in accorance with the terms of this lease, Landlord shall thereby be discharged of any further obligation relating thereto. Landlord's assignment of the lease or of any or all of its rights herein shall in no manner affect Tenant's obligations hereunder. Tenant shall thereafter attorn and look to such assignee, as Landlord, provided Tenant has first received written notice of such assignment of Landlord's interest.

26. *Warranty.* Landlord warrants that it has full right and authority to lease the Demised Premises upon the terms and conditions herein set forth and that Tenant shall peacefully and quietly hold and enjoy the Demised Premises for the full term hereof so long as it does not default in the performance of any of its covenants hereunder.

27. *Short Term Lease.* Upon the commencement of the term of this lease, the parties hereto shall execute a memorandum or short form lease agreement, in recordable form, specifying the commencement and termination dates of the term hereof and including any such other provisions hereof as either party may desire to incorporate therein.

28. *Estoppel Certificate.* Within ten (10) days after request therefor by Landlord or any mortgagee or trustee under a mortgage or deed of trust covering the Demised Premises, or if, upon any sale, assignment or other transfer of the Demised Prem- ises by Landlord, an estoppel certificate shall be required from Tenant, Tenant shall deliver in recordable form a statement to any proposed mortgagee or other transferee, or to Landlord, certifying any facts that are then true with respect to this Lease Agreement, including without limitation (if such be the case) that this Lease Agreement is in full force and effect, that Tenant is in possession, that Tenant has commenced the payment of rent, and that there are no defenses or offsets to the Lease Agreement claimed by Tenant.

29. *Common Area Maintenance.* In addition to the rental payable as provided hereinabove, Tenant shall pay to Landlord, Tenant's pro rata share of common area maintenance during the term hereof, using the same ratio as provided in Paragraph 5 hereof and payable in equal monthly installments, with the rental as provided in Paragraph 3 hereinabove. Landlord shall bill Tenant for such costs as a separate charge in advance on the first day of each calendar month in an amount estimated by Landlord. The initial estimated cost per square foot of floor area of the Demised Premises shall be set by Landlord at least _____ (_____) days prior to the Tenant opening for business in the Shopping Center.

Within sixty (60) days after the end of each calendar year, Landlord will furnish to Tenant a statement showing in reasonable detail the amount of Landlord's costs for such services for the preceding calendar year and monthly payments for the ensuing calendar year shall be estimated accordingly.

30. *Nature and Extent of Agreement.* This instrument contains the complete agreement of the parties regarding the terms and conditions of the lease of the Demised Premises, and there are no oral or written conditions, terms, understandings or other agreements pertaining thereto which have not been incorporated herein. This instrument creates only the relationship of landlord and tenant between the parties hereto as to the Demised Premises; and nothing herein shall in any way be construed to impose upon either party hereto any obligations or restrictions not herein expressly set forth.

31. *Binding Effect.* This Lease Agreement shall be binding upon and shall inure to the benefit of the parties hereto and their respective successors and assigns.

32. *Merchant's Association.* In the event a Merchant's Association is established

Exhibit 8-7. *(Continued)*

for the Shopping Center, Tenant agrees that it will join and maintain membership in the said Merchant's Association and will pay such dues and assessments as are set by a majority vote of the members of the Merchant's Association. Tenant shall also comply with such other by-laws, rules and regulations as may be adopted, from time to time by the said Association.

33. *Landlord's Lien.* As further security for the full and complete performance by Tenant of all of the terms and conditions by it to be performed hereunder, Tenant does hereby grant and convey unto Landlord, and Landlord shall have during the full term hereof, a first lien upon any and all fixtures, equipment, merchandise and other personal property installed or stored in, attached to or used in the Demised Premises by or at the expense of Tenant; and Tenant hereby covenants and agrees, upon demand by Landlord to execute and deliver to Landlord such security instruments as Landlord may reasonably require to perfect such liens.

34. *Cost-of-Living Adjustment.* At the end of every ＿＿＿＿＿＿ (＿＿) complete calendar ＿＿＿＿＿ during the term of this lease, the ＿＿＿＿＿＿ ＿＿＿＿＿＿＿＿＿＿＿＿＿＿＿＿ ＿＿＿＿＿＿＿＿＿＿＿＿＿ payable hereunder shall be increased in proportion to the change in the cost-of-living between the commencement date of the term hereof and the ending date of said ＿＿＿＿＿ ＿＿ (＿＿) ＿＿＿＿＿ period. The cost-of-living on each such date shall be measured by the Consumer Price Index–Urban Wage Earners & Clerical Workers, U.S. City Average, All Items (1967 = 100) published on the date nearest to each such date by the Bureau of Labor Statistics or, if such index shall not then be in use, by the index most nearly comparable thereto.

IN WITNESS WHEREOF, the parties hereto have executed this Lease Agreement under seal as of the day and year first above written.

LANDLORD:

＿＿＿＿＿＿＿＿＿＿＿＿＿＿＿＿

By: ＿＿＿＿＿＿＿＿＿＿(SEAL)
,General Partner

TENANT:

Attest:

＿＿＿＿＿＿＿＿＿＿＿＿＿＿＿＿

＿＿＿＿＿＿＿＿＿＿＿＿＿＿＿＿＿＿＿＿ By: ＿＿＿＿＿＿＿＿＿＿(SEAL)
Secretary ＿＿＿＿＿ President

(CORPORATE SEAL)

STATE OF NORTH CAROLINA
COUNT OF MECKLENBURG

I, _____, a Notary Public in and for said County and State, do hereby certify that general partner of _____ _____, personally appeared before me this day and acknowledged the due execution of the foregoing instrument.

WITNESS my hand and notarial seal, this _____ day of _____, _____.

_____
Notary Public

My Commission Expires:

_____

(NOTARIAL SEAL)

STATE OF _____
COUNTY OF _____

This _____ day of _____, _____, personally came before me _____, who, being by me duly sworn, says that he is the _____ President of _____ and that the seal affixed to the foregoing instrument in writing is the corporate seal of the company, and that said writing was signed and sealed by him, in behalf of said corporation, by its authority duly given. And the said _____ acknowledged the said writing to be the act and deed of said corporation.

_____
Notary Public

My Commission Expires:

_____

(NOTARIAL SEAL)

IN WITNESS WHEREOF, the parties hereto have executed this Lease Agreement under seal as of the day and year first above written.

LANDLORD:

_____

By: _____ (SEAL)
,General Partner

123

TENANT:

_____

By: _____ (SEAL)

STATE OF NORTH CAROLINA
COUNT OF MECKLENBURG

    I, _____, a Notary Public in and for said County and Starte, do hereby certify that general partner of _____ _____ personally appeared before me this day and acknowledged the due execution of the foregoing instrument.
    WITNESS my hand and notarial seal, this _____ day of _____, _____.

_____
                          Notary Public

My Commission Expires:

_____

(NOTARIAL SEAL)

STATE OF _____
COUNTY OF _____

    I, _____, a Notary Public in and for said County and State, do hereby certify that _____ _____ personally appeared before me this day and acknowledged the due execution of the foregoing instrument.
    WITNESS my hand and notarial seal this _____ day of _____, _____.

_____
                          Notary Public

My Commission Expires:

_____

(NOTARIAL SEAL)

ries). Candy stores may have percentage lease terms between 6 and 10 percent while the percentage lease terms for discount stores over 75,000 square feet in size may range from 1 to 2.5 percent. There is a great deal of difference in percentage lease terms among the retail stores that operate in shopping centers.

What are the basic reasons for the lease differences? Here are a few:

Amount of space used
Merchandise turnover
Merchandise profitability
Customer drawing power
Advertising budgets

Generally, the greater the customer drawing power and the higher the store's advertising budget, the lower the base and percentage rent terms. As the retailer occupies less space and realizes higher merchandise turnover with relatively high markups, the percentage terms and base rents go up per square foot of GLA. Merchants with slower moving inventories that require a lot of space with relatively high markups usually pay lower base and percentage rents. An example of the latter case is the furniture store in the mall. An example of the retailer with little space, high turnover, and high markup is perhaps the hosiery or candy shop. A retailer with great drawing power and a large advertising budget is the national chain department store such as Federated Department Stores, Associated Dry Goods, Sears Roebuck, or J. C. Penney.

Retail stores in a shopping center generate widely differing sales per square foot. A merchant may generate $90 a square foot of GLA a year or may generate double that amount per square foot per year. Patterns tend to be established for each category of retail store that is located in a center. Some recent sales data for a regional center may be found in computerized reporting form in the section on shopping center management and operation. Management must periodically receive merchant sales data, and the data must be compiled in readily accessible and readable management reports.

NEGOTIATING LEASE TERMS WITH THE VARIOUS TYPES OF TENANTS

Since the mortgage financing of the center is based on the percentage of key national chain store tenants, the negotiations with these tenants must be early in the development picture. The developer may even go to a major national department store chain and inquire about the sites where they would prefer new stores. From this starting point the developer may take a tentative commitment from the department store chain and negotiate for the site that the retail company prefers. The rest of the major tenant negotiations will hinge on the needs of the one key tenant. If that key tenant happens to be Sears

EXHIBIT A
(Site plan to be inserted here)

EXHIBIT B
(Legal description to be inserted here)

EXHIBIT C
(Plans and specifications, if any,to be inserted here)
(only to be attached if Alternate B was used for Paragraph 4)

Source: Henry J. Faison Associates, 122 East Stonewall, Charlotte, NC 28202.

Exhibit 8-8.   Lease Card Information

The following information is compiled and then transferred onto index cards for filing.

Tenant Name _____

D/B/A _____

Address _____

Lease Dated _____   Lease Year End _____

Date Opened _____   Term of Lease _____

Square Footage _____   Dimensions _____

Options _____   Lease Termintion Date _____

Minimum Rent _____   P.S.F. _____   Annual _____Monthly

M.R. Adj. _____   P.S.F. _____   Annual _____Monthly

M.R. Adj. _____   P.S.F. _____   Annual _____Monthly

Adjustment dates _____

Percentage Rent_____ % over $ _____Minimum Gross Volume

Percentage Rent Adjustments _____

Exhibit 8-8. *(Continued)*

Sales Reported Monthly in _____ Days, Quarterly in _____ Days, Annually in _____ Days. Certified: CPA Officer of Tenant Corporation?

Percentage Rent Payable: Monthly, Quarterly, Annually, or When MGV Reached?

Real Estate Taxes _____

Common Area _____

Security Deposit _____

Security Deposit Returnable Tenant (Date) _____

Repairs Responsibility _____

Insurance Requirements _____

Radius Restriction _____

Default of Lease _____ per Year, _____ Days to Cure

Preopening Contribution $_____ Promotion Fund $_____

Adjustable in Promotion Fund _____

Circular Participation Requirement _____

Use Clause _____

_____

_____

HVAC Contract Required _____

Riders: Number Description

_____ _____

_____ _____

_____ _____

_____ _____

_____ _____

_____ _____

Source: Marketing Department, Cousins Properties Incorporated, 300 Interstate North, Atlanta, GA 30339.

Exhibit 8-9.   Composition by Tenant Classification Group of Community and Neighborhood Shopping Centers

	Community Center		Neighborhood Center	
Tenant Classification	Percent GLA	Percent Sales	Percent GLA	Percent Sales
General merchandise	35.4	25.6	6.6	3.6
Food	14.9	34.3	27.8	57.9
Food services	4.7	4.5	8.6	6.5
Clothing	7.4	7.1	5.3	5.1
Shoes	2.0	1.8	1.1	0.8
Home furnishings	2.5	1.4	2.2	0.8
Home appliances/music	1.8	1.8	2.0	1.2
Building materials/garden	2.2	1.6	3.1	1.3
Automotive supplies/service station	2.1	1.2	2.4	1.1
Hobby/special interest	2.2	1.9	2.6	1.8
Gifts/specialty	2.1	1.5	2.6	1.7
Jewelry and cosmetics	0.8	1.5	0.6	0.7
Liquor	0.6	0.4	1.5	2.0
Drugs	4.6	5.9	9.3	9.9
Other retail	2.8	1.6	3.5	1.5
Personal services	2.5	1.1	5.4	2.1
Recreation/community	3.3	0.8	3.4	0.7
Financial	3.0	5.4	4.3	0.1
Offices (other than financial)	2.1	0.2	3.2	0.7
Other	3.0	0.4	4.5	0.5
Total	100.0	100.0	100.0	100.0

Source: "Shopping Center Composition by Tenant Classification," *Dollars & Cents of Shopping Centers*, Urban Land Institute, 1981, Section D, Tables 8D–3 and 4, p. 296.

Roebuck, the other "majors" will tend to go along with the Sears "reading of the market" at the preferred site. Of course, today Sears' development group has the capacity to develop their own centers as well as work with outside developers in leasing or buying sites at shopping centers developed by other firms.

Major presentations may have to be made to key tenants during the beginning phase of the development. Other major tenants, after receiving development prospectuses in the mail for preliminary scrutiny, may ask a few strategic questions over the phone about a trading area, the site, and other factors and decide immediately about participation in the proposed project. Major chain stores are accustomed to many new store openings and many lease negotiations per year. Their sophistication may lead to early response about interest in a location at the proposed center. Local or regional chain stores may also give fast decisions about proposed center locations. Then again, since their lease terms tend to be less attractive in comparison with the major national department store lease terms, their responses may be slower to the sales advances of the developer and his or her sales staff.

Exhibit 8-10.   Rent Rate Comparison*

Region	New Regionals[†] (Range)	Old Regionals[‡] (Range)[§]
East Coast (New England, New York, New Jersey, Pennsylvania, Ohio, Maryland)	$13–$19 (average in middle of range)	$13–$19 (average from $14–$15)
Southeast (Virginia, North Carolina, South Carolina, Georgia, Florida)	$13–$19 (average in middle of range)	$13–$19 (average from $14–$15)
Southwest (Texas, New Mexico, Arizona, Oklahoma)	$15–$20 (average in broad middle of range)	$15–$20 (average in narrow middle of range)
West Coast (California, Oregon)	$17–$21	$15
Northwest (Idaho, Washington, Montana)	$13–$17	$14–$15
Mountain States (Wyoming, Nevada, Utah, Colorado)	$12–$15	$13–$14

Source: "Rent Rate Comparison," *Shopping Center World*, Vol. 11, No. 1, January 1982, p.180. Copyright 1982 Communication Channels, Inc., 6285 Barfield Road, Atlanta, GA 30328.
*Information supplied by Shopping Center Marketing Division, Coldwell Banker.
[†]"New Regionals" are new regional shopping centers and malls or recently rehabbed regionals (renovations, expansions, additions, etc.)
[‡]"Old Regionals" are regional shopping centers or malls which have had no recent renovation, expansion or "fix-up" work
[§]Rent rate range from low to high, dollars per square foot

The independent stores may not occupy the majority of the center space, but they may contribute from their base and percentage rents a sizable portion of the developer's profits. Their presence is vital to the developer. The independent store managers tend to be less sophisticated in lease negotiations since they engage in such negotiations less often than the major chain stores. These stores tend to realize their merchandising and financial value to the center developer, and negotiations may be more protracted and require more patience and perserverance from the developer. The credit standing of the local independent merchant may not be ascertained as readily as the credit standing of the major chain store. Public financial data is available for the large chain stores for their long operating histories. The local independent stores may have short or relatively long operating and financial business histories. They may have no reason to issue public financial statements. Their principal source of borrowed funds may be the local commercial bank.

CONTINUING LEASE ANALYSIS AND ENFORCEMENT

Once the lease is signed, it must be enforced by center management and the owner. Rents must be collected. If any base rents or overage payments are overdue, overdue notices must be issued to the merchant. Form notices may be

Exhibit 8-11. National Percentage Lease Ranges for Selected Store Categories

Store Category	1950	1960	1970	1976	1980
Art shops	8–10	6–10	6–10	6–10	6–10
Auto accessories stores	4–8	2–5	3–5	3–6	3–6
Barber shops	10–12	8–10	6–10	5–10	6–10
Beauty shops	10–15	8–10	6–12	5–10	6–10
Book and stationery stores	8–11	5–11	4–10	5–8	5–8
Candy stores	8–12	5–8	6–10	6–12	6–10
Department stores	3–4	2–3	1.5–4	1.5–3.5	1.5–3
Discount stores (over 75,000 sq. ft.)	NA*	1–2.5	1–2	1–2.5	1–2.5
Discount stores (under 75,000 sq. ft.)	NA	NA	NA	1–4	1–3
Drugstores—independent	6–8	3–6	3–8	2.5–6	3–6
Drugstores—chain	3–6	2.5–4.5	2.5–5	2.5–5	1–5
Drugstores—prescription (medical buildings)	8–12	5–10	5–10	5–10	5–10
Electrical appliance stores	4–7	2.5–5	3–6	3–6	3–6
Fabric (yard goods) stores	NA	NA	4–6	4–6	4–7
Florists	8–10	6–10	6–10	6–10	6–12
Furniture stores	4–8	3–7	3–8	3–6	3–7
Gas stations (cents per gallon sold)	1–1.5¢	1–1.5¢	1–2¢	1–2¢	1–2¢
Gift shops	7–9	5–9	6–10	6–10	6–10
Supermarkets	0–1.5	0.75–1.5	0.5–2.25	1–2	1–2
Convenience food stores	NA	NA	NA	2–3.5	1–4
Hardware stores	5–8	3–6	3.5–6	4–6	3–6
Hosiery and knit goods stores	6–8	6–8	6–10	6–10	6–10
Jewelry stores	8–10	3–8	4–10	4–10	5–10
Luggage/leather goods stores	7–10	5–9	5–10	5–10	6–8
Liquor and wine stores	6–8	3–8	4–6	2–6	3–8
Men's clothing stores	6–8	4–8	4–8	4–8	4–7
Men's furnishings (haberdashery) stores	6–10	5–10	4–10	5–8	5–8
Motion picture theaters	14–25	8–18	8–15	7–15	7–15
Radio, TV, and hi-fi stores	NA	NA	4–8	3–8	3–7
Record shops	NA	5–7	5–7	5–7	5–8
Restaurants	6–10	5–7	3–8	5–9	5–10
Restaurants—liquor	6–8	6–8	4–10	6–10	5–10
Sporting goods stores	6–8	5–8	4–8	3.5–8	4–8
Women's ready-to-wear stores—chain	5–8	2.5–6	4–8	3–6	4–8
Women's ready-to-wear stores—independent	7–9	4–8	4–10	4–8	5–10
Women's furnishings/accessories stores	NA	4–10	5–10	5–8	5–8
Women's shoe stores	6–8	4–7	5–8	5–7	5–8

Source: Schloss, Nathan, "How Inflation-Proof Are Those Retail Percentage Leases?" *Real Estate Review,* Vol. 11, No.3, 1981, p.100.
*NA = not available.

used to make the overdue rent collection more efficient and more impersonal in the early stages of the collection effort (Exhibit 8-12). The form notice may be used as a forerunner to a personal interview or contact of the storeroom operator by the center manager.

Sales histories must be maintained. These histories alongside standardized regional or national sales averages per square foot may indicate at strategic times whether a tenant should be replaced or whether the tenant's sales justify expansion of the storeroom space. Good sales histories are valuable management tools. The good lease requires the continual reporting of sales for various purposes.

USE OF COMMERCIAL BROKERS TO LEASE SPACE

The development company personnel and the center management work diligently to lease and re-lease the center space. Sometimes they are assisted in the leasing effort by commercial brokers who represent clients who fit the requirements for vacant center space. These clients must meet the financial and merchandising requirements for the typical lease extended for the particular storeroom space. Their line of business must blend with the desired tenant mix. If the client is suitable for the space and signs the negotiated lease, a sales commission is payable to the commercial broker who located this tenant. The commission is often based on a percent of the total lease payments over the term of the lease. The brokerage commission percentage often ranges from 5 to 10 percent of the total future lease payments of the tenant.

Exhibit 8-12.   Overdue Rent Collection Letter

Date:

To:

Past Due Notice

Gentlemen:

It has come to our attention that we have not as yet received your rent payment for the month of _____ in the amount of $_____

_____.

Please remit on or before (date)* _____.

Very truly yours,

Bookkeeper

Source: Cousins Properties Incorporated, 300 Interstate North, Atlanta, GA 30339.
*Give seven days from date of notice. Call on the third day after sending of notice for promised date of payment.

NINE

SHOPPING CENTER OPERATION AND MANAGEMENT

Property management may be defined as the art or science of operating, dealing with, or otherwise handling land or the improvements which are held for rent or for the production of income in such a manner as to produce for the owners, within the limitations of applicable law and responsibility to the community, a maximum of economic return over the period of management. This area of business applies to the management of income properties, such as shopping centers, vacant land, and owner-occupied properties regardless of the financial and legal arrangements of the investor organization. Even though we are concerned chiefly with the management of shopping centers, we know that the real estate owner, including the center owner, expects the professional property manager to (1) optimize the return from the productive resources of the property; (2) extend the productive life of the building; and (3) preserve and enhance the capital value of the center. To accomplish these objectives, the principal functions of the property manager become (1) merchandising the space to obtain a maximum gross income; (2) reducing operating and maintenance costs to attain maximum net income; (3) reducing the financing costs of the owner; and (4) adapting the center to environmental and market changes over time.

As the center manager acts for the owner in the principal-agent relationship, the manager owes the employer loyalty and is bound to exercise care, diligence, and skill in carrying out the functions and duties required by the terms of the management contract. As an agent for the center owner, the manager must periodically inspect the premises, arrange for the necessary repairs, release vacant space promptly, assure compliance with local ordinances, and account for the owner's revenues and expenses. The manager must also notify the employer of all legal notices served by tenants, any rent delinquency, "lease jumping" by a tenant, offers of purchase, and notices of ordinance violations. Since the manager is obligated to keep proper accounts of all income and expense related to property management, the owner has a right at any time to scrutinize the records for the center. The records should indicate the owner's investment, the owner's tax liabilities, tax payments in the name of the owner, and necessary information to indicate the owner's return on investment for the accounting periods. The manager's funds should not be commingled with the funds of the principal, the center owner.

THE OBLIGATIONS OF THE MANAGEMENT CONTRACT

The center management staff may be a part of the overall development organization, or the management company may be a company apart from the development company. The management company may be an outside company that is totally independent of the developer. This is usually not the case. The management company may be a subsidiary of a real estate brokerage firm that is a partner in the development of the center. Often the management group is merely a subsidiary or a staff department of the development company. The institutional investor/lender may staff the management function of the center with one of their management subsidiaries.

If a formal management contract is negotiated for the independent management company, the contract terms should cover the following strategic items:

Exclusive agency agreement
Terms of renewal and termination
Renting and lease negotiations
Periodic statements to the owner
Separation of owner and manager funds
Bonding of employees
The property manager's authority with respect to:
    Repairs and remodeling
    Management of employees
    Management of service contracts
The limitation of agent liability by the center owner
Owner payment to the management agent for services rendered

Even though the management staff is part of the development company, these same items are strategic to the management of the center by the individuals concerned. The employment agreement between the management employee and the center owner should cover these working relationships for the well-being of both parties.

THE PROPERTY MANAGEMENT PLAN

A professional property manager considers the requirements and responsibilities and contemplates a plan of action for the coming report period. The plan of action covers the many management areas including the following:

> The physical plant including capital improvements and maintenance program
> The management organization and assigned responsibilities
> The market to be served
> The competition
> Sales management
> The marketing plan for the center and its tenants overall
> Tenant mix and lease management
> The operating budget, cash control, and owner reporting

As each of these areas of shopping center operation is managed, the professional manager incorporates into the plan of action for the time period a method of notification of changes and shifts in the market and the operating accounts that take place. Some center managers call this a "tracking" program. The manager needs a signaling system so that important market and financial changes will be noticed in time for management corrective or remedial action. For example, cost control systems may be based on the following items:

> The budget set for the expense or income item for the period
> The expense or income of the current period
> The accumulated expense or income of this fiscal budget year

In a similar manner, a sales volume tracking system could note each month:

> The current monthly sales for the storeroom
> The accumulated sales this fiscal period for the storeroom
> Sales for the storeroom last year this month

Such cost and revenue control systems let the perceptive manager-analyst know whether market and sales shifts are taking place. Potential problems or marketing opportunities may be recognized early enough so that changes in the management, marketing, and promotional programs may be made in advance of significant market and sales changes.

Management of the Physical Plant

The management of the physical plant entails full description and records maintenance of the existing physical facilities, the operating systems, the original contractors and subcontractors, and the contractors on maintenance agreements. This management area also involves identification of needed capital improvements and major maintenance jobs. Property taxes need to be paid, and appropriate insurance coverage needs to be maintained. The operating rules and regulations for the center must be enforced.

Description of the Current Premises and the Original and Maintenance Contractors

The center manager needs to keep a record of the characteristics of the physical plant and the operating systems. The site plans and the building layouts in the original and subsequently revised forms should be retained in an accessible place. Sample descriptions of the physical plant, site, center layout, and operating building systems of the Hickory Hollow Regional Shopping Center of Nashville, Tennessee may be observed in Exhibits 9-1 through 9-7.

Capital Improvements and Major Maintenance

As time passes, the center will probably need capital improvements and major maintenance. Example of major improvements would be major refurbishing of the mall and an attached parking garage building. Examples of major maintenance would include parking lot resurfacing and striping and preventative maintenance of the escalators, elevators, and central air-conditioning system.

The air-conditioned mall may have been very attractive as it was furnished when the center opened several years ago. Today the mall appearance and furnishings may be very outdated. New plantings, new ceiling treatment, new skylights, new lighting fixtures, new customer seating arrangements, ramps for wheelchair use, and new flooring may be needed to spruce up the center to attract more customers. To remain competitive, the center owner must continually adapt to the competitive marketplace.

When the customer volume for the center reaches such a point that ground-level parking around the center becomes inadequate, the building of parking garages integrated into the center on the various shopping levels may become a necessity, not just a pleasant addition. Customers are not willing to walk beyond a reasonable distance from their cars to the mall entranceway. Normal shopper traffic may cause shopper parking resistance as cars must be parked farther and farther from the mall entranceways. Normal parking conditions—not holiday peak customer traffic conditions—should be considered in the decision to build parking garages. Such major expenditure normally could not be justified for the peak buying periods of the year, such as Christmas, Thanksgiving, and Easter. The construction of integrated parking buildings becomes feasible when dense urban settlement surrounds the center so that more land for ground-level parking cannot be acquired at a reasonable cost.

Professional and amateur thieves inhabit the shopping center premises today. Mall customers have long been threatened by thievery; today theft under many conditions at a shopping center seems even more prevalent.

Exhibit 9-1.   Fact Sheet

FACT SHEET: A REGIONAL SHOPPING CENTER
AND COMMERCIAL DEVELOPMENT

Hickory Hollow Mall and the Courtyard at Hickory Hollow

Nashville, Tennessee

October 30, 1980

The Hickory Hollow Regional Shopping Center is an enclosed mall center currently containing three major department stores with 134 supporting shops along the Mall. Phase II, opening in August 1982, will add J. C. Penney and approximately 24 supporting shops. The Courtyard at Hickory Hollow is an adjacent community center with a free-standing triple theater and 20 shops. The Mall and The Courtyard are integral parts of the larger Hickory Hollow project which includes associated retail, commercial, office, apartment and hotel development. The project is owned by Hickory Hollow Associates, a Joint Venture composed of Intereal Company, a subsidiary of NLT Corporation and Hickory Hollow Mall, Inc., a subsidiary of Cousins Properties Incorporated.

Building area:	Existing mall GLA	
	Cain Sloan (Allied)	117,000 sq. ft.
	Castner-Knott (Mercantile)	142,000 sq. ft.
	Sears	168,000 sq. ft.
	Mall shops	276,000 sq. ft.
	Subtotal existing GLA	703,000 sq. ft.
	Phase II expansion (opening August, 1982)	
	J. C. Penney	150,000 sq. ft.
	Mall shops	50,000 sq. ft.
	Subtotal phase II GLA	200,000 sq. ft.
	The Courtyard at Hickory Hollow	
	Consolidated Theaters	15,000 sq. ft.
	Shops	40,000 sq. ft.
	Subtotal Courtyard GLA	55,000 sq. ft.
	Total GLA	958,000 sq. ft.
Acreage:	The Hickory Hollow Development totals 324 acres of which approximately 79 acres is used for the mall and 6 acres for the community center. The remainder is being developed into apartments and other commercial developments.	
Location:	The shopping center is on the northeast corner of Bell Road and Hickory Hollow Parkway, approximately 0.5 miles from I-24. It is approximately 12 miles from downtown Nashville and is in Davidson County, Tennessee.	
Access:	Access is provided by two interstate interchanges, I-24/Bell Road interchange and I-24/Hickory Hollow Parkway, 3/4 of a mile south of Bell Road, as well as from Bell Road east and west.	

Exhibit 9-1. *(Continued)*

Mall parking:	5,060

Project schedule:	Mall and two department
	   stores opened September 13, 1978
	Third Major Opened February 28, 1979
	The Courtyard at Hickory
	   Hollow Opened October 1, 1979
	J. C. Penney and
	   mall shops to open August, 1982

Developer/manager/leasing agent:	Retail Planning Division Cousins Properties Incorporated 300 Interstate North Atlanta, Georgia 30339 (404) 955-0000
Architects:	Cooper, Carry & Associates 1819 Peachtree Road, N. E. Atlanta, Georgia 30309 (404) 352-2660
Mailing address:	Hickory Hollow Mall 5252 Hickory Hollow Parkway Antioch, Tennessee 37013 (615) 331-3500
Engineers:	Barge, Waggoner, Sumner & Cannon, Inc. 404 James Robertson Parkway Nashville, Tennessee 37219 (615) 254-1501
Development team:	R. Kent Rose Vice President/Development Director James A. Rumph Vice President/Construction Manager Nancy Reynolds Tenant Coordinator Retail Planning Division Cousins Properties Incorporated 300 Interstate North Atlanta, Georgia 30339 (404) 955-0000

Source: Cousins Properties Incorporated, 300 Interstate North, Atlanta, GA 30339.

Exhibit 9-2. Outline of the Factors Included in the Physical Plant Description

I. Hickory Hollow Mall physical plant general description
   a. Building
   b. Parking area

II. HVAC system
   a. Chillers
   b. Condenser
   c. Condensing dumps
   d. Chilled water pumps
   e. Cooling towers
   f. Electric duct heaters
   g. Air handling units
   h. Fans
   i. Honeywell numatic controls

III. Electrical system
   a. Lighting
   b. Circuit breaker panels
   c. Transformers
   d. Sound system
   e. Telephones
   f. Controls
      1. Sprinkler
      2. Pools
      3. Smoke alarm

IV. Floor to floor transport system
   a. Escalators
   b. Passenger elevator
   c. Freight elevators
   d. Customer service stairways

V. Landscaping
   a. Interior
   b. Exterior

VI. Roof
   a. Three-ply built-up roof, slick finish

VII. Floor
   a. Fired quarry tile 4 × 8 and 8 × 8 unglazed
   b. Sealed with Hydrozo water-repellent sealer
   c. Fire floor corridors sealed concrete

Source: Cousins Properties Incorporated, 300 Interstate North, Atlanta, GA 30339.

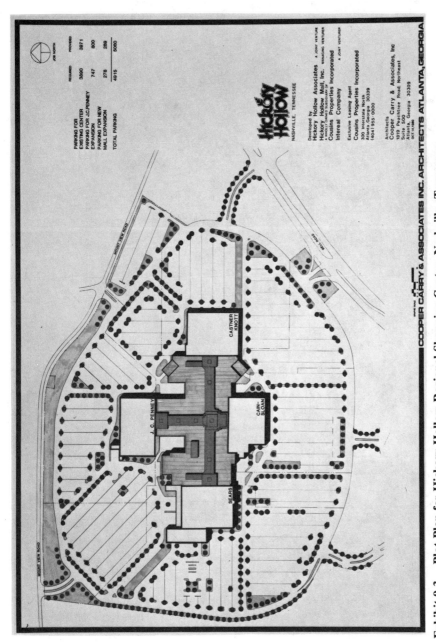

Exhibit 9-3. Plot Plan for Hickory Hollow Regional Shopping Center, Nashville, Tennessee

Source: Cousins Properties Incorporated, 300 Interstate North, Atlanta, GA 30339.

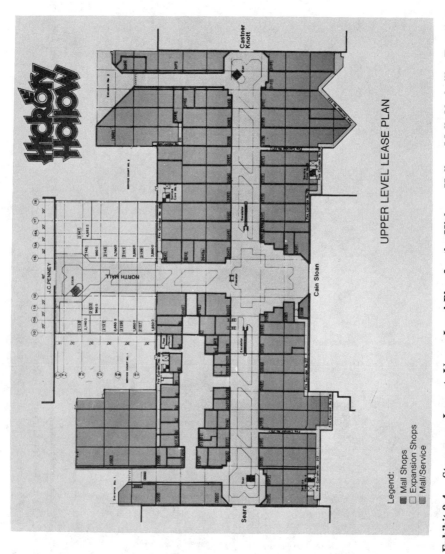

Exhibit 9-4. Storeroom Layout, Upper Level Plan for the Hickory Hollow Mall, Nashville, Tennessee

Source: Cousins Properties Incorporated, 300 Interstate North, Atlanta, GA 30339.

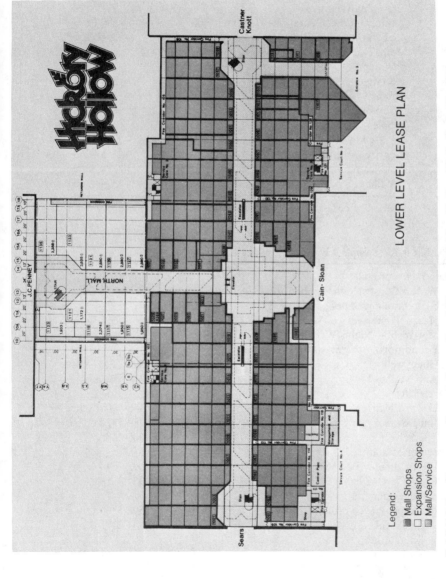

Exhibit 9-5. Storeroom Layout, Lower Level Plan for Hickory Hollow Mall, Nashville, Tennessee

Source: Cousins Properties Incorporated, 300 Interstate North, Atlanta, GA 30339.

Exhibit 9-6. Sample List of Emergency (24-hour) Numbers

Police	911
Information	579-6111
Florida Highway Patrol	325-3606
Information	325-3602
Fire Department	911
Information (Operations Headquarters)	596-8600
Ambulance—Fire Rescue	374-3131
Metro/Dade Water and Sewage	
Water	665-7471
Sewage	324-6454
Wrecker Service	
Southwest Wrecker Service	858-1816
Peoples Gas Systems	893-2522
Florida Power and Light Company	374-5365
Security Control Center	358-2268
American International Adjustment Company, Inc.	374-3360
William Bridgen, Claims Representative	374-3360

Source: Faison Associates, 122 East Stonewall, Charlotte, NC 28202.

Exhibit 9-7. Sample List of Emergency Contacts

Contractor of mall	
Witters Construction Company (Present Contractor)	887-9471 Office
Air-conditioning/chiller	
Hazen Trane Service Agency	667-5661 Office
Mel Webb—Nights/Weekends	
Air-conditioning thermostat control	
Honeywell	592-8140 Office
Ann Mathews	
Electrical	
Lowry Electric	448-4905 Office
Jim Lowry	989-7822 or 661-2782
Ted Schneider	665-2488
Elevator/escalator	
Westinghouse Elevator	592-1640 Office
Herb Clark—Nights/Weekends	374-3718
Emergency generators	
Pantropic Power Products	592-5360 Office
Nights/Weekends	444-7171
Fire extinguisher	
City Fire Equipment, Inc.	261-1241/2 Office
Glass breakage	
Tropical Glass	757-0651 Office
Gene Lomando	
Mall automatic doors	
Southern Automatic Doors	

Exhibit 9-7.   *(Continued)*

Jerry Perente	1-473-9449
Openings South	
Mike Beck	1-404-993-2785
Mall sound system	
Melody, Inc.—Muzak	591-9905 Office
Radios	
Motorola Communications & Electronics, Inc.	
Louis Ziegler	592-4480 Office
Roof leaks	
Zack Roofing Company	592-5950 Office
Western Waterproofing	624-5481 Office
Mark Albright	
Security control center computer	
Robert Shaw	652-1133 Office
Rob Sterr	
Nights/Weekends	652-1133
Sprinkler/mechanical/plumbing	
Fred McGilvary, Inc.	592-5910 Office
Nights/Weekends—Answering Machine	592-5910
Sweeping service	
Admiral Pavement Sweeping, Inc.	661-0071 Office
Telephone service	
Southern Bell	883-2366 Office
Repair Service	611
Universal Communication System	1-800-336-9650 Office
In-House (Hotel)	374-0000 Ext. 360
Time clocks	
Dimep Time System Corporation	649-4100 Office
Trash compactors	
United Sanitations	324-6100 Office
Gil Reisman	
In-house service	
Locksmith service	
Steve Kamzic, Security Department	371-6664 or Beeper 125
Sewage/grease/traps	
A Roto Matic	821-8220 Office

Therefore, the center owners must design better security systems for parking lots, the center mall, and other common areas. The tenants are normally in a position to control theft within their own storerooms and buildings. Security guards and systems within and outside the center are needed in today's market. As major electronic systems and lockable door screens are added for greater safety of store personnel, customers, and merchandise, major capital improvements are added to the center expenditures.

Innovations in energy conservation have recently been introduced. As a result, many existing malls need more insulation, more efficient heating and cooling systems, and individual metering of the air-conditioned spaces of the center. As utility rates and overall costs go up with inflation, the tenants may prefer less storeroom space for their merchandising, inventory storage, and company offices. Less total space that is individually metered takes less all-season air conditioning. Energy conservation has been one of the chief causes for the general reduction in storeroom and center building space in recent years. (The other major reason is the overall rise in construction and development costs. Building materials and labor and financial costs have risen along with inflation.)

As any property ages, major maintenance becomes important. Parking lots must be resurfaced, then they must be restriped and any partially destroyed concrete car bumpers replaced, if their usefulness continues. Since many shopping center buildings have flat built-up roofs, the drains in the roof must be checked periodically to be ready for the next "goose drenching" downpour of rain. Major maintenance contracts are usually maintained on the center of mall escalators and side-wall elevator systems. Preventative maintenance may cost less than equipment repair after it eventually fails in an emergency situation. Customer trauma and expensive and time-consuming lawsuits may be averted. Sales volume may not be lost from center close-down if all equipment and operating systems are kept in continual working condition through preventative maintenance.

Economic Justification for Capital Improvements and Major Maintenance

Return-on-investment analysis may be used to justify major expenditures economically with respect to an existing, operating center. First the need for the capital improvement or other major expenditure must be described. The cost must be estimated from interviews with equipment and labor suppliers. The time for the initiation and completion of the proposed project may be determined. The source of funds and their cost may be found. Once the outlays and the inflows in terms of reducing costs or increasing revenues are determined, the return on investment may be arithmetically established. The rate of return on investment is the discount rate which equates the needed expenditures at present and over time with the decreased costs or increased revenues at present and in the near future. The capital budgeting study may also show the increased costs or reduced revenues if the project is not instituted on the proposed time schedule with the proposed capital outlays.

PROPERTY TAXES

Every year—perhaps twice a year even—property taxes must be paid on the center. The tax assessor sets a value on the property. The manager looks over the assessment to see if the amount is reasonable. If the assessed value does not seem reasonable in light of the assessments on other similar shopping centers, the manager consults with the owners about protesting the level of the assessed value before the board of property tax equalization or other such appellate body. If the assessed value appears reasonable, the owner and manager may expect to receive an *ad valorem* tax bill for the amount determined by applying the appropriate tax rate to the assessed valuation. Many states derive the assessed valuation from a percentage of the fair market value of the real property; other states set the fair market value equal to the assessed valuation. The single annual property tax payment may be due in the fall of the year. Otherwise, semiannual tax payments may be required so that the tax collector receives the annual *ad valorem* tax amount due from the property in two installments.

INSURANCE COVERAGE

Hazard and liability insurance coverages are needed for the center. The hazard insurance policy with extended coverage should cover vandalism, theft, tornadoes, fire, and other such calamities caused by weather conditions. Flood insurance may be obtained through a private insurance carrier or through the National Flood Insurance program if the center lies in a designated flood-prone zone. The flood insurance premium is partially subsidized through the federal insurance program. Plate glass insurance coverage is needed when the center owner is responsible for large glass display windows and cases.

Both the storeroom tenants and the owners need to keep the center appropriately insured. Generally the owners are responsible for the outer building shells and the mall space while the tenants are responsible for the building storeroom interiors and their inventories of merchandise. Lease agreements usually require that each tenant is covered by appropriate storeroom and inventory insurance. The manager's recording system must show a continuous record of paid or unpaid tenant insurance premiums. Insurance paid by the tenant that protects the center premises must be payable jointly to the tenant and the owner in case of insured disaster. Some owners require each tenant to be covered by income insurance so that the storeroom lease payments may be made if a disaster occurs.

ENFORCEMENT OF RULES AND REGULATIONS

The manager, in cooperation with the tenants, establishes operating rules and regulations for the center. The responsibility for the enforcement of these rules and regulations lies with the manager. Monitoring the adherence to the center operating requirements is a continuous job for the manager, the owners' representative in the center. The areas of rules and regulations for the center include:

Store opening and closing times for customer sales
Center opening and closing times for public admission
Truck delivery schedules for the loading docks
Employee and tenant parking
Supervision of storeroom and center management employees
Holidays celebrated by the closing of the center
Storeroom line of business restriction
Required tenant advertising and promotional expenditure
Contributions to the mall marketing fund
Attendance at mall management meetings

Other financial and legal restrictions are directly related to the various clauses in each lease. The lease cards of the manager's files must note the special terms of each lease.

THE MANAGEMENT ORGANIZATION AND ASSIGNED RESPONSIBILITIES

To accomplish the many facets of center management and operation, an organizational chart may be drawn up to show the various officers of the management staff or company and their chief areas of responsibility. The property manager may have a number of assistants to cover such narrower management areas as record keeping, marketing, landscaping, maintenance, and security. Such an organizational chart has been designed for the Hickory Hollow Mall (Exhibit 9-8). This organizational chart may not fit the personnel of any other center, but it is a management tool for the center for which it was designed.

Job descriptions may be drawn up for each of the individuals and functional positions indicated on the organizational chart. The job description will aid in informing employees of the extent of their responsibilities. Prospective employees may make job decisions based on uniform job descriptions, such as the one for a maintenance supervisor in Exhibit 9-9. When salary increases and bonuses are considered by the employer, the job performance of the individual may be compared to the job description.

THE MARKET TO BE SERVED

Before a developer spends time and money on site acquisition and architectural plans for a center, the market for the proposed center with its unique tenant mix must be determined. The market dimensions pivot around the potential customers within certain driving time zones and their buying power. A driving

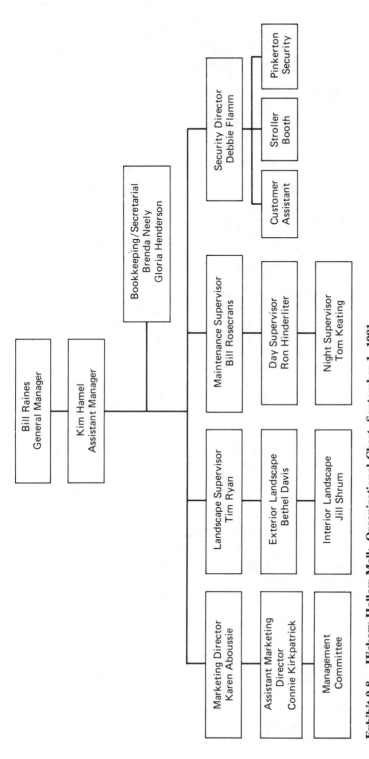

Exhibit 9-8. Hickory Hollow Mall: Organizational Chart, September 1, 1981

Source: Cousins Properties Incorporated, 300 Interstate North, Atlanta, GA 30339.

Exhibit 9-9.   Sample Job Description for a Maintenance Supervisor

1. To supervise maintenance person (day and night shift):

    This involves checking on:
    1. Punctuality
    2. Work performance
    3. Appearance
    4. Cooperation
2. To oversee all contracted work
    1. Lot cleaning
    2. Landscaping; interior and exterior
    3. HVAC checks and temperature control
    4. Stripping, electrical, plumbing, etc. when in progress
3. To be responsible for monthly reports:
    1. Work schedules
    2. Work duties updated and revisions
    3. Monthly checklist and quarterly checklists
    4. To include tenant grease trap condition
4. To work along with and help whenever possible the Merchants Association.
5. To revise, update and experiment with energy conservation, etc.
6. To keep the mall manager and where appropriate, the marketing director, abreast of current happenings
7. To perform primary seeking of and screening of new employees and terminations when necessary along with the mall manager for those who do not work out.
8. To be available 24 hours a day or have mall manager aware of my whereabouts
9. To be on hand for emergency situations (hurricanes, etc.)
10. To be responsible for keeping mall clean and all maintenance items and preventive maintenance items under control, either through myself or another employee (s).

Source: Cousins Properties Incorporated, 300 Interstate North, Atlanta, GA 30339.

time of 5 minutes may describe the primary market for the neighborhood center; a 10-minute driving time may describe the primary market for the community center. The primary market for regional centers will often be 25 to 30 minutes. Superregional centers will attract customers in the primary market from an even greater driving time radius—perhaps 40 to 45 minutes. Then the secondary market will extend even further in driving time from the center location. Some developers consider the furthest market reach and will consider briefly the tertiary market. The primary market determines the annual "bread and butter" trade of the center.

Since driving time is difficult to measure, some developers use radii in miles instead. For example, in Exhibit 9-10, the trading area population of the Lincolnton, North Carolina retail center is estimated at over 47,000. The economic base or the industrial base for Lincolnton, the county seat of Lincoln County, is shown in Exhibit 9-11.

The market for a shopping center changes with time. Some dimensions may increase; at the same time, other market dimensions may decrease. For exam-

Exhibit 9-10.   1980 Trade Area Population, Lincolnton Retail Center

Lincoln County		
Northbrook	60%	2,187
Howards Creek	100%	4,156
Lincolnton	100%	18,971
Ironton	100%	9,061
Catawba Springs	50%	3,326
		37,701—89% of county
Catawba County		
Jacobs Fork	40%	1,100
Newton	25%	6,080
Caldwell	50%	2,373
Mountain Creek	10%	352
		9,905—9% of county
1980 Total		47,606

Trade Area—1980

	E.B.I. ($000)
Lincoln County	$ 298,502
Catawba County	788,101
	$1,086,603

Source: Faison Associates, 122 East Stonewall, Charlotte, NC 28202.
Note: Lincoln County population increased 30% from 1970 to 1980.
During the same period Catawba County population increased 15.3%

ple, the total population, the number of households, the number of persons in the average household, and the median income per household for the trading area may be expected to increase (Exhibit 9-12). At the same time, the population of the trading area under the age of 20 may be expected to decrease. The number of households with income less than $14,999 per year may also be expected to decrease. All of these future expectations may result in a favorable impact on the center's financial success.

THE COMPETITION

Before the developer seriously considers a site for a new center or before an investor sinks a substantial amount of funds in preliminary investment exploration, the party looks at the current and forecast competition for the subject development. A survey of the current competitors may result in a map with numbered competing sites and a short report giving the name, address, total gross leasable area, principal tenants, and number of stores of each.

Exhibit 9-11.   Economic Base for Lincolnton, North Carolina

Lincolnton is the county seat of Lincoln County in west central North Carolina. The city is the focal point of the trade area and is served by Highways 321, 27 and 150.

Lincolnton has enjoyed a strong diversifying economy. The major employers are:

Company	Approximate Employees
Burris Industries—furniture	450
Edmos Corporation—textiles	325
Mochican Mills—textiles	900
J. P. Stevens—textiles	850
Homespun Hosiery—textiles	300
Cochrane Furniture—furniture	500
Leslie Fay—textiles	300
Vermont American—hardware, tools	300
The Timken Company	700

The city of Lincolnton–Lincoln County Government, Lincoln County Hospital, Duke Power and Lincolnton–Lincoln County Educational System are all major employers with each having well over 100 employees.

Lincolnton serves a trade area of over 47,000.

Source: Faison Associates, 122 East Stonewall, Charlotte, NC 28202.

On the same map or a different one, the sites of announced centers should be pinpointed. Another short report should give the proposed total gross leasable area, principal tenants, and number of stores proposed for each. City building permits may aid the search for future competitors. Newspaper company clipping files may disclose publicized development plans for each of the centers. The competing developers may make preliminary information available through their public relations department. Local lenders and lender representatives may disclose information about proposed development that would directly compete with the proposed center development or investment. Exhibits 9-13 and 9-14 show a written summary of the current and future competition for the Omni International Miami retail center.

SALES MANAGEMENT

The profitability of the center and individual tenants depends on the sales volume generated. Each tenant keeps track of its revenues and expenses. The center landlord and management agent do likewise. Usually the management staff calls for monthly and annual sales statements as required in each lease agreement. Within a specific number of days after the end of the lease year, the required statement is due in the office of the center manager (Exhibit 9-15). A form may be issued by the manager to each tenant for his or her reporting of monthly and annual sales and overage payments (Exhibit 9-16). Management

Exhibit 9-12. Changes Expected in the Market Profile, 1981 and 1986

Category	1981	1986	Percent Change
Size			
Population	842,269	889,299	+ 5.6%
Households	288,438	304,073	+ 5.4%
People/household	2.9	2.9	—
Race			
White	83 %	83 %	+ 5.6%
Black	16	16	+ 5.3
Other	*	*	+ 3.2
Age			
Under 14	22 %	23 %	+ 8.3%
14–17	7	6	− 12.9
18–20	5	5	− 10.2
21–29	16	16	+ 5.9
30–39	15	16	+ 16.1
40–49	11	12	+ 10.0
50–64	14	13	+ 1.3
65 and over	10	9	+ 5.6
Median Age	30.0	30.0	
Household income			
Under $10,000	20 %	8 %	− 59.6%
$10,000–$14,999	19	11	− 37.8
$15,000–$24,999	38	39	+ 7.2
$25,000–$49,999	16	27	+ 74.9
$50,000 and over	7	15	+144.2
Median income	$17,895	$22,949	

Exhibit 9-13. Major Existing Shopping Areas That Compete with Omni International Miami, Listed in Order of Competitive Impact

Retail Area	Square Feet	Principal Tenants	Stores
Downtown Miami	3,000,000	Sears, Jefferson, Burdines	752
Lincoln Road	1,000,000	Burdines, Woolworth	180
163rd St. Shopping Center	1,100,000	Burdines, Jordan Marsh, J.C. Penney, Woolworth	76
Miracle Mile	1,200,000	Sears, J Byrons, Woolworth	170
Dadeland Mall	1,135,000	Jordan Marsh, J.C. Penney, Burdines	133
Bal Harbour Shops	309,000	Saks Fifth Avenue, Gucci, Neiman Marcus	44
Mayfair	85,000	Specialty (no department stores)	44
Midway Mall	700,000	Jefferson, Woolco	66

Exhibit 9-13. *(Continued)*

Retail Area	Square Feet	Principal Tenants	Stores
The Falls	165,000	Specialty (no department stores)	63
Westland Mall	820,000	Sears, J.C. Penney, Burdines	97
Palm Springs Mall	1,000,000	J Byrons, Jefferson, Zayres	145
Cutler Ridge Mall	900,000	Sears, Burdines, Luri, Jordan Marsh	91
Northside Shopping Center	565,000	Sears, J Byrons	75

Source: Cousins Properties Incorporated, 300 Interstate North, Atlanta, GA 30339.

Exhibit 9-14. Major Planned Shopping Areas and Major Existing Shopping Areas with Announced Plans of Immediate Expansions That Compete with International Omni Miami Center

Retail Area	Square Feet	Principal Tenants

Major Planned Shopping Areas (completion by 1982)

Retail Area	Square Feet	Principal Tenants
Miami International Mall	1,200,000	J.C. Penney, Lord & Taylor, Burdines, Jordan Marsh, Sears
Aventura Mall	under 1,000,000	Sears, J.C. Penney, Lord & Taylor

Major Existing Shopping Areas with Announced Plans of Immediate Expansions

Downtown Miami. Extensive projects under construction will add office, retail, hotel, commercial, and convention facilities. In addition, many buildings are being turned into mini vertical retail malls. No major department stores planned.

163rd St. Shopping Center. A complete face-lift to enclose Miami's oldest shopping center is scheduled. No announced plans to replace the form Richards location. Many stores are on month leases.

Dadeland Mall. Saks Fifth Avenue and Lord and Taylor have both announced scheduled locations at Miami's most successful suburban mall. Owned by Equitable Life, managed by Mall Management.

Bal Harbour Shops. Lying north of Miami Beach this most exclusive top-of-the-line mall is planning expansion of eight additional stores on a second level with the possibility of more square footage added to the Saks store. Further expansion is slated across Collins Street that divides the mall with the hotel row.

Midway Mall. This mall managed by the Breder Corporation has a vacant Richards location. Management is actively looking for a tenant.

The Falls. This specialty center with a close competitive proximity to Dadeland continues to search for a department store tenant and a luxury hotel. No definite commitments to date. Courtelis Company management.

Cutler Ridge Mall. The expansion of Miami's southernmost regional center is faster than the population growth.

Source: Cousins Properties Incorporated, 300 Interstate North, Atlanta, GA 30339.

Exhibit 9-15. Draft of Letter Requesting Annual Certified Sales Plus a Check for Any Overage Rent Payment That Is Due

Date

Name of Tenant
Tenant Address

Gentlemen:

The lease year for your store at Any Mall ended (date) _____.

According to the lease, an Annual Statement of Gross Sales, certified by a Certified Public Accountant, is due _____ days after the close of each lease year.

Please fill in and return the attached statement with a check for any overage rent due, on or before (date) _____.

Very truly yours,

Bookkeeper

Exhibit 9-16. Sample Annual Certified Statement of Gross Sales

We hereby certify that the annual sales, as defined in the lease for the _____ store at Any Mall, for the lease year ending January 31, 1981 are as follows:

February	1980	_____
March	1980	_____
April	1980	_____
May	1980	_____
June	1980	_____
July	1980	_____
August	1980	_____
September	1980	_____
October	1980	_____
November	1980	_____

Exhibit 9-16. *(Continued)*

December	1980	_____
January	1981	_____
Total		_____

Signature: _____ Date: _____
                    (CPA)

Signature: _____ Date: _____
                    (Tenant)

This statement is due no later than (date) _____

must keep track of the amounts received each month from each tenant for (1) base rent, (2) overage or percentage rent, (3) payment toward common area maintenance expense, (4) payment toward apportioned real estate taxes, (5) payment of apportioned utility expense, (6) payment toward center promotional fund, and (7) other miscellaneous payments. A weekly delinquency list may be maintained per month that tends to give center management closer control (Exhibit 9-17). For each tenant, percentage rents per month must be calculated. The same file form per tenant may disclose the percentage rent computations and the delinquent amounts (Exhibit 9-18).

Once the monthly sales reports are rendered to the center manager by each lessee, overall sales reports may be compiled. This record keeping may be done by hand, by accounting machine, by key punch card, or by computer terminal direct access. Continuous computerized systems normally give the center owners and managers the best continuous operating information. Periodically sales analysis reports are prepared that indicate:

Current month sales per storeroom, this year, last year, % change
Year-to-date sales per storeroom, this year, last year, % change
Sales per square foot of leased area, annual and current projected annual volume, breakeven point, current accumulation
Projected percentage rent (Exhibit 9-19)

This sales report shows the trend in sales by storeroom tenant, type of merchandise or service, and overall for the center. The computerized sample report of Exhibit 9-19 shows only two years of comparison figures plus accumulated total over several years. Other management reports may give longer-term annual and monthly sales trends per storeroom tenant. Such reports aid overall center sales and tenant storeroom management. As the management views areas of high profitability and areas displaying sales problems, these periodic

Exhibit 9-17.   Sample Weekly Delinquency List.

ANY MALL
WEEKLY DELINQUENCY LIST

Month of_____

Date of Report_____

Tenant	Rent	% Rent	C.A.M.	R/E Tax	Utilities	Promo Fund	Misc	Total
____	___	____	____	____	_____	____	___	___
____	___	____	____	____	_____	____	___	___
____	___	____	____	____	_____	____	___	___
____	___	____	____	____	_____	____	___	___
____	___	____	____	____	_____	____	___	___
____	___	____	____	____	_____	____	___	___
Totals	___	____	____	____	_____	____	___	___

Grand Total Delinquency_____

Manager's Signature: _____

reports confirm or disaffirm management perceptions of center operations. Some tenants may need to expand to reach their sales potential in the center location, and others may need less space or may need to relocate to other merchandising sites.

MARKETING PLAN

The shopping center marketing plan starts with the marketing goals for the center, the strategy selected to strive for the established goals, the specific tactics required in implementing the selected strategy, and recognition of the opportunities and problems of the center.

The marketing goals for the center involve overall sales production per square foot of gross leasable area, a balance of credit and noncredit tenants, percentage share of the market, level of potential customer recognition and awareness of the existence and merchandising attributes of the center, average sales per customer trip to the center, and balanced presentation of a variety of retail goods and services. The specific marketing goals must be related to the market characteristics of potential customers within the primary and secondary

Exhibit 9-18. Sample Rent Computation Sheet

PERCENTAGE RENT COMPUTATION SHEET
INDIVIDUAL TENANT

Name of Tenant _____ Square Footage _____ Lease Year-End _____

Minimum Gross Volume: Annually $ _____ Quarterly $ _____ Monthly $ _____

Percentage Factor _____ % Tenant Is Required to Pay: * _____

Date Opened _____ *Indicate Annually, Quarterly, Monthly, or When MGV
                        Is Reached.

Month	Gross Sales	Year to Date	Amount Invoiced	Amount Paid	Balance Due
___	_____	_____	_____	_____	_____
___	_____	_____	_____	_____	_____
___	_____	_____	_____	_____	_____
___	_____	_____	_____	_____	_____

trading areas. Those market characteristics relate to both demographics and buying power in dimension. The marketing goals are subject to change over time.

The strategies for attainment of the established goals involve the balance between personal sales and impersonal sales of center attractions, the balanced use of the available advertising media, periodic changes in marketing "flights" or specific marketing programs to fit trading area needs and wants, maintenance of a balanced presentation of goods and services offered by the current storeroom merchants, and periodic scheduling of various appropriate types of mall entertainment.

Once the strategy has been planned for the attainment of the center goals, specific tactics or programs must be selected to adhere to the overall marketing strategy. For example, computerized sales, profit and loss, sources and uses of cash, and balance sheet reports may be necessary to maintain close management control. The on-site manager is, of course, aided in daily management work. The developer and other owners may maintain their business headquarters at a substantial distance from the particular center. Access to continuous management information by computer terminals and printed report output facilitate long-distance analysis and owner control. Other tactics and the identification of marketing opportunities and problems will be discussed in Chapter 10, Marketing and Promoting a Shopping Center.

Exhibit 9-19. Sales Analysis Report

ANY MALL
December 31, 19XX

Name	Term in Months	% Rent	Curr. Sq. Ft.	Current Month Sales in Thousands — This Year	Last Year	% Inc. Dec.	Year to Date Sales in Thousands — This Year	Last Year	% Inc. Dec.	1/7 Annual	Per Square Foot Current Proj.	Break Point	Curr. Cumm.	Projected % Rent
General Merchandise														
Variety Store														
McCrory	240	4.00	30,998	226.29	213.93	5.78	903.63	931.67	(3.01)	31.35	30.41	74.97	29.15	
Food														
Specialty food														
Hickory Farms	180	6.00	2,769	134.00	100.64	33.15	232.42	238.75	(2.65)	89.28	86.92	117.37	83.94	
Bakery														
Tiffany's Bakery	180	6.00	905	10.00	12.04	(16.95)	97.36	116.40	(16.36)	136.09	113.82	276.24	107.58	
Candy and nuts														
Morrow's Nut House	120	10.00	310	19.90	17.10	16.39	111.76	111.75	0.01	385.21	385.23	200.00	360.51	5,742.23
Health food														
General Nutrition	120	6.00	1,734	31.47	29.67	6.06	314.56	310.35	1.35	194.86	197.50	116.59	181.40	8,417.70
Totals			5,718	195.37	157.45	22.53	756.09	777.26	(2.72)	144.75	140.88		132.23	14,159.93
Food Service														
Restaurant with Liquor														
El Chico Restaurant	180	5.00	5,831	76.44	75.96	0.63	685.82	676.85	1.33	125.03	126.69	75.00	117.62	15,068.94
Chelsea Street Pub	180	5.00	4,670	56.63	51.68	9.58	349.09	340.64	2.48	80.13	79.86	160.00	74.75	—
Totals			10,501	133.06	137.64	4.25	1034.91	1017.49	1.71	105.06	105.86		98.55	15,068.94

TENANT MIX AND LEASE MANAGEMENT

The sales attraction of the center depends on its tenant mix. Over the 25 or more years of shopping center history, general rules of thumb have been promulgated about the optimum tenant mixes for the various sizes and types of centers. Neighborhood centers should present a balanced mixture of convenience goods and only a small portion of shopping goods. The large super-regional center may offer a larger portion of specialty goods and services along with the majority of shopping goods and services and the smaller portion of convenience goods and services. The regional center with perhaps only one or two department stores can afford the presentation of a smaller portion of specialty goods and services in comparison with the superregional center of four to six department stores. Of course, specialty centers tend to concentrate on specialty and shopping goods and services and tend to deemphasize convenience goods and services. The merchants of these centers generally do not want to compete directly with convenience and community centers.

A sample of the general rules of thumb or guidelines for tenant mix in a superregional center in 1981 compiled in a nationwide survey is shown in Exhibit 9-20. The general guidelines are quoted in percentage of total square footage of gross leasable area and in percentage of total center sales. The particular center's tenant mix is compared to the superregional suggested tenant mix. The center of the example is too high in tenant composition with respect to clothing and shoe merchandising and too low with respect to food, drugs, and personal service stores.

Lease management is an important part of center property management. Leases are signed, they end at the lease termination date, they may be renewed, and new lessees are sought to replace vacating tenants. The overall lease management objectives focus on the balanced and most desirable tenant mix for the center. When the market changes, the desired tenant mix may change, but in the meantime the manager must strive for the current ideal tenant mix.

THE OPERATING BUDGET, CASH CONTROL, AND OWNER REPORTING

Center management must account at any time for the current status of revenues and expenses of the center. A standardized set of revenue and expense accounts has developed for the various types of centers over time. The typical revenue accounts are:

Base rent
Percentage rent
Other income
    Total income

Exhibit 9-20. Tenant Mix Analysis.

Category	June 1981 Square Feet	Percent of Total Square Feet	Percent of Total Sales	1981 Superregional National Comparison (%) Percent of Square Feet	Percent of Sales
Food	5,611	2.2	2.5	8.9	18.1
Food service	24,063	9.3	14.0	6.9	7.0
Clothing					
Ladies' ready-to-wear	59,557	23.1	18.6		
Men's	12,343	4.8	4.7		
Unisex	17,485	6.8	5.7	all clothing	
Total		34.7	29.0	23.7	25.7
Shoes					
Family shoes	14,836	5.8	4.6		
Ladies' shoes	11,200	4.3	3.4		
Men's/child	4,180	1.6	2.2	all shoes	
Total		11.7	10.2	6.3	7.4
Home furnishings					
Furniture	12,067	4.7	3.2	2.2	1.5
Home appliances	8,634				
Music	6,094	5.7	5.1	3.3	4.6
Hobby/special int.	11,561	4.5	5.9	3.4	3.8
Gifts/specialties	26,525	10.3	8.4	4.5	4.6
Jewelry and cosmetics	10,978	4.3	7.5	2.3	5.2
Drugs	6,490	2.5	2.1	3.7	4.8
Other retail	2,510	1.0	1.8	3.2	0.6
Personal services	2,025	1.0	0.7	2.1	1.9
Recreation	19,247	7.5	3.4	5.2	1.6

Source: Cousins Properties Incorporated, 300 Interstate North, Atlanta, GA 30339.

The typical expense accounts are:

Management fees and costs
Leasing expense
Insurance expense
Property taxes
Maintenance expense
Common area expense
Advertising and promotion expense
Professional services expense
Bad debt expense
   Total operating expense
Mortgage and other loan interest
Ground lease payments
Depreciation expense for tax purposes
   Net taxable income or loss

In a capsule summary, these revenue and expense account balances may be maintained with respect to the current month's actual and budgeted amounts and with respect to the year-to-date dollars per square foot, actual and budgeted amounts, and the difference between actual and budgeted amounts (Exhibit 9-21). Then a more detailed management report of income and expenses may disclose greater detail about other income, management fees and costs, maintenance expense, common area expense, advertising and promotion costs, and other miscellaneous operating costs. More detailed accounting may be shown for the depreciation of the various center assets. The more detailed accounting gives more explanation of the deviations between actual and budgeted amounts shown for each standardized account (Exhibit 9-22).

Sources and uses of funds statements have been widely used by industrial corporations for the last 20 to 30 years. The shopping center developer benefits from an analysis of a similar statement, the sources and uses of cash summary report. The center owner/developer may call it the "cash flow summary" (Exhibit 9-23).

When the management and owners wish a capsule summary of the center's assets, liabilities, and net worth as of a certain date, a balance sheet must be available for scrutiny. From the center manager's office or the developer's accounting department, a balance sheet may be produced. The daily accounting results are compiled into the balance sheet report. Previously we noted that the profit and loss and sources and uses of cash accounts were compiled from the daily accounting results from the center. The balance sheet, which can be produced on a computer, shows the detailed status of the assets, liabilities, and net worth of the center (Exhibit 9-24).

Exhibit 9-21. Revenue-Expense Summary: Current Month and Year to Date

CHERRY CREEK MALL
December 31, 198X

Run Date—07/14/8X

	Current Month			Cost per Square Foot	Year to Date		
	Actual	Budget	Actual Over/(Under)		Actual	Budget	Actual Over/(Under)
Income							
Base rent	155,540	152,600	2,940	0.00	1,847,789	1,822,800	24,989
Percent rent	5,530	5,000	530	0.00	330,963	480,000	(149,037)
Net rental income	161,070	157,600	3,470	0.00	2,178,752	2,302,800	(124,048)
Other income	63,171	47,875	15,296	0.00	671,365	576,150	95,215
Total income	224,241	205,475	18,766	0.00	2,850,117	2,878,950	(28,833)
Expenses							
Management fees	4,917	4,700	217	0.00	65,447	68,700	(3,253)
Management cost	9,551	5,175	4,376	0.00	70,983	63,850	7,133
Leasing	12,498	4,500	7,998	0.00	72,931	67,450	5,481
Insurance	646	490	156	0.00	5,934	5,520	414
Property taxes	13,317	9,800	3,517	0.00	124,735	117,600	7,135
Maintenance	3,752	3,175	577	0.00	27,610	34,850	(7,240)
Common area	51,783	32,770	19,013	0.00	426,324	380,000	46,324
Advertising and promotion	2,723	2,700	23	0.00	27,897	32,400	(4,503)
Professional service	3,022	200	2,822	0.00	13,976	2,400	11,576
Bad debts	0	0	0	0.00	5,597	0	5,587
Total operating expense	102,209	63,510	38,699	0.00	841,424	772,770	68,654
Net operating increase (Loss)	122,032	141,965	(19,933)	0.00	2,008,693	2,106,180	(97,487)

(Continued)

161

Exhibit 9-21. *(Continued)*

CHERRY CREEK MALL
December 31, 198X

Run Date—07/14/8X

	Current Month			Cost per Square Foot	Year to Date		
	Actual	Budget	Actual Over/(Under)		Actual	Budget	Actual Over/(Under)
Interest and ground lease	66,115	65,460	655	0.00	790,842	790,180	662
Depreciation	9,920	15,200	(5,280)	0.00	177,230	182,400	(5,170)
Amortization	8,924	3,728	5,196	0.00	49,474	44,736	4,738
Net income (loss)	37,073	57,577	(20,504)	0.00	991,147	1,088,864	(97,717)
Cash Flow Summary							
Net income (loss)	37,073	57,577	(20,504)	0.00	991,147	1,088,864	(97,717)
Add depreciation and amortization	18,844	18,928	(84)	0.00	226,704	227,136	(432)
Less debt principal payment	19,360	19,360	0		111,899	111,899	0
Net cash flow	36,557	57,145	(20,588)	0.00	1,105,952	1,204,101	(98,149)

162

Exhibit 9-22. Detailed Revenue-Expense Analysis: Current Month and Year to Date

CHERRY CREEK MALL
December 31, 198X

Income

		Current Month			Year to Date		
		Actual	Budget	Actual Over/(Under)	Cost per Square Foot ($)	Actual	Budget	Actual Over/(Under)
Base Rent								
3000	Base Rent	155,540	152,600	2,940	0.00	1,847,789	1,822,800	24,989
	Total	155,540	152,600	2,940	0.00	1,847,789	1,822,800	24,989
Percent Rent								
3005	Rent, potential	5,530	5,000	530	0.00	330,963	480,000	(149,037)
	Total	5,530	5,000	530	0.00	330,963	480,000	(149,037)
	Net rental income	161,070	157,600	3,470	0.00	2,178,752	2,302,800	(124,048)
Other income								
3416	Temporary investments	5,945	300	5,645	0.00	19,251	3,600	15,651
3703	Insurance	88	75	13	0.00	1,013	900	113
3706	Miscellaneous	704	650	54	0.00	13,072	9,550	3,522
3710	Property taxes	13,193	6,900	6,293	0.00	89,094	82,800	6,294
3736	HVAC income	7,950	7,950	(0)	0.00	96,183	95,300	883
3740	Common area	14,626	32,000	12,626	0.00	437,304	384,000	53,304
3741	CAM Contract	(9,335)	0	(9,335)	0.00	15,449	0	15,449
	Total	63,171	47,875	15,296	0.00	671,365	576,150	95,215
	Total income	224,241	205,475	18,766	0.00	2,850,117	2,878,950	(28,833)

(Continued)

Exhibit 9-22. (Continued)

CHERRY CREEK MALL
December 31, 198X

		Current Month		Cost per Square Foot ($)	Year to Date		
		Actual	Budget	Actual Over/ (Under)		Actual	Budget	Actual Over/ (Under)

Expenses

Management Fees

		Actual	Budget	Actual Over/(Under)	Cost per Square Foot ($)	Actual	Budget	Actual Over/(Under)
5900	Management fees	4,917	4,700	217	0.00	65,447	68,700	(3,253)
	Total	4,917	4,700	217	0.00	65,447	68,700	(3,253)

Management Cost

6002	Salaries, Regular	7,482	2,900	4,582	0.00	41,419	34,800	6,619
6006	Employee benefits	241	360	(119)	0.00	4,533	4,320	213
6010	Travel and entertainment	80	350	(270)	0.00	5,801	5,450	351
6018	Miscellaneous	407	100	307	0.00	1,614	1,200	414
6020	Equipment rental	283	160	123	0.00	1,746	1,920	(174)
6021	Actuary and audit	0	100	(100)	0.00	0	1,200	(1,200)
6022	Repair and maintenance	0	20	(20)	0.00	1,644	240	1,404
6024	Supplies	813	300	513	0.00	2,243	3,600	(1,357)
6028	Contribution	0	0	0	0.00	130	500	(370)
6030	Electricity, office	405	200	205	0.00	2,311	2,400	(89)
6036	Telephone	639	385	254	0.00	5,635	4,620	1,015
6038	EDP service	(800)	300	(1,100)	0.00	3,600	3,600	0
6081	Construction T&E	0	0	0	0.00	306	0	306
	Total	9,551	5,175	4,376	0.00	70,983	63,850	7,133

Leasing

6100	Commission	12,498	4,500	7,998	0.00	72,931	67,450	5,481
	Total	12,498	4,500	7,998	0.00	72,931	67,450	5,481

Insurance

6200	Insurance	646	490	156	0.00	5,934	5,520	414
	Total	646	490	156	0.00	5,934	5,520	414

Property Taxes

6230	Real estate	13,317	9,800	3,517	0.00	124,735	117,600	7,135
	Total	13,317	9,800	3,517	0.00	124,735	117,600	7,135

Maintenance

6304	Engineering services	515	0	515	0.00	620	0	620
6330	Building	1,385	825	560	0.00	8,367	9,900	(1,533)
6336	HVAC	53	500	(447)	0.00	4,605	6,000	(1,345)
6337	HVAC electricity	1,800	1,850	(50)	0.00	14,017	18,950	(4,933)
	Total	3,752	3,175	577	0.00	27,610	34,850	(7,240)

Common Area

6400	Salary, janitor	9,163	4,850	4,313	0.00	64,567	58,200	6,367
6402	Security	10,991	6,500	4,491	0.00	59,025	52,640	6,385
6404	Salary, ground	8,699	1,700	6,999	0.00	29,949	20,400	9,549
6406	Employee benefits	1,178	1,700	(522)	0.00	17,462	16,500	962
6407	Electricity	6,903	5,975	928	0.00	51,190	63,900	(12,710)
6408	Water and sewer	69	60	9	0.00	733	720	13
6409	Lot sweeping contract	1,925	1,595	330	0.00	20,075	19,140	935
6420	Real estate taxes	4,648	4,000	648	0.00	49,296	48,000	1,296

(Continued)

Exhibit 9-22. *(Continued)*

CHERRY CREEK MALL
December 31, 198X

Run Date—07/15/8X

		Current Month			Cost per Square Foot ($)	Year to Date		
		Actual	Budget	Actual Over/ (Under)		Actual	Budget	Actual Over/ (Under)
6430	Supplies	3,252	1,400	1,852	0.00	17,604	16,800	904
6434	Lawn/garden	213	250	(37)	0.00	13,542	3,000	10,542
6428	Equipment repair	0	100	(100)	0.00	313	1,200	(887)
6442	Mall maintenance	3,727	400	3,327	0.00	51,091	32,800	18,291
6446	Lot maintenance	324	1,500	(1,176)	0.00	30,782	18,000	12,782
6454	Liability insurance	639	665	(26)	0.00	7,606	7,800	(194)
6450	Wired music	25	25	0	0.00	300	300	0
6466	Snow removal	0	2,000	(2,000)	0.00	12,606	20,000	(7,694)
6427	Landscape T&E	27	0	27	0.00	27	0	27
6398	Miscellaneous	0	50	(50)	0.00	154	600	(446)
	Total	51,783	32,880	19,013	0.00	426,324	380,000	46,324
Advertising and Promotion								
6760	Salary	456	0	456	0.00	456	0	456
6763	Travel and entertainment	57	0	57	0.00	722	0	722
6774	Miscellaneous	0	500	(500)	0.00	290	6,000	(5,710)
6776	Merchant association	2,211	2,200	11	0.00	26,429	26,400	29
	Total	2,723	2,700	23	0.00	27,897	32,400	(4,503)

Professional Services

		(1)	(2)	(3)	(4)	(5)	(6)	(7)
7212	Legal and tax	11,576	2,400	13,976	0.00	2,822	200	3,022
	Total	11,576	2,400	13,976	0.00	2,822	200	3,022
Bad Debts								
7400		5,597	0	5,597	0.00	0	0	0
	Total	5,597	0	5,597	0.00	0	0	0
	Total operating expense	68,654	772,770	841,424	0.00	38,699	63,510	102,209
	Net operating increase (Loss)	(97,487)	2,106,180	2,008,693	0.00	(19,933)	141,965	122,032
Interest and Ground Lease								
9004	Permanent expansion	662	790,180	790,842	0.00	655	65,460	66,115
	Total	662	790,180	790,842	0.00	655	65,460	66,115
Depreciation and Amortization								
9100	Building	(5,170)	182,400	177,230	0.00	(5,280)	15,200	9,920
9151	Leasing Commission	5,302	0	5,302	0.00	5,302	0	5,302
9152	Development	(564)	44,736	44,172	0.00	(106)	3,728	3,622
	Total	(432)	227,136	226,704	0.00	(84)	18,928	18,844
Net Income (Loss)		(97,717)	1,088,864	991,147	0.00	(20,504)	57,577	37,073

Exhibit 9-23. Sample Cash Flow Summary

ANY TOWN MALL
CASH FLOW SUMMARY
December 31, 1980

Description	Current Month	Year to Date
Net cash flow per summary of operations	$ 36,557	$1,105,952
Add (deduct):		
Decrease (increase) in operating receivables	58,162	(24,898)
Decrease (increase) in prepaid insurance	1,125	(118)
Increase (decrease) in operating payables	31,895	103,975
Increase (decrease) in accrued property taxes	14,912	72,577
Cash flow from operations	142,651	1,257,488
Other sources (uses) in Cash:		
Property development:		
Expansion and mall		(11,985)
Community Center net of retainage		
Payable	(206,117)	(1,696,202)
Land sale proceeds Castner Knott		49,527
Construction loan proceeds	210,763	1,716,897
Notes payable		(26,000)
Net venture cash flow	147,297	1,289,724
Less partners' distribution	(100,000)	(1,100,000)
Increase in cash for period	47,297	189,724
Add beginning cash	244,431	102,004
Cash balance at end of month	$291,728	$291,728

Source: Cousins Properties Incorporated, 300 Interstate North, Atlanta, GA 30339.

Exhibit 9-24. Balance Sheet

CHERRY CREEK MALL
December 31, 198X

Assets

Properties
  Land held for investment of future development
  Residential lot development
  Other—miscellaneous
  Residential properties
  Commercial properties—Shopping Centers

106117	2nd Expansion	2,500.84	
186216	Community center	2,678,582.77	
	Project total		2,681,083.61
140116101	Expansion	1,710,803.51	
140116103	Expansion	195,320.00	
140116200	Expansion	28,278.00	
140116300	Expansion	17,226.71	
140116301	Expansion	47,202.50	
140610101		3,385,940.58	
140610102		6,831.29	
140610103		1,655,071.61	
140610113		87,000.00	
140610114		(206,232.29)	
140610238		824,679.05	
140610301		1,399,500.20	
140610318		123,789.33	
	Project total		9,275,410.49
	Total properties		11,956,494.10
			(Continued)

169

Exhibit 9-24. *(Continued)*

CHERRY CREEK MALL
December 31, 198X

Run Date—06/13/8X

1930611	Accumulated depreciation leasing commission	(5,302.08)	
195610101	Accumulated depreciation building costs	(1,161,396.92)	
195610200	Accumulated depreciation land improvements	(363,921.09)	
Total			(1,530,620.09)
Total			10,425,874.01
Net properties			10,425,874.01
Cash and temporary investments			
101 Petty Cash		150.00	
10206101 Cash in bank (Third National)		291,577.96	
Total			291,727.96
Accounts receivable—collateralized by land			
Land mortgage notes			
Interest receivable		3,094.36	
Total			3,094.36
Accounts receivable—other			
0109951	Accounts receivable—rents	54,623.40	
010806104	Accounts receivable—198--198- CAM Reimb	(15,600.00)	
0111	Accounts receivable—other	975.00	
0111061	Accounts receivable	953.83	
01110617	Accounts receivable—Merchants Association	8,782.06	
011106183	Accounts receivable—Purolator	75.42	
Total			49,809.71
Total accounts receivable			52,904.07
0122	Estimated bad debt	(7,296.59)	
Total			(7,296.59)

Net receivables			45,607.48
Other assets			
0169	Travel advances	1,000.00	
01760614	Prepaid expenses—insurance	7,189.24	
Total			8,189.24
Total assets			10,771,398.69

Liabilities and Owners' Investment

Notes payable
Unsecured notes payable
Construction and development loans

0205061216	Construction loan, community center	2,426,350.21	
Total			2,426,350.21

Secured bank notes
Land mortgage and other notes

02030616	Notes payable—F.H.&E.C.	104,000.00	
Total			104,000.00

Permanent mortgages

0208061	Permanent mortgage loans—National Life	5,877,943.84	
02080611	Permanent mortgage loans—National Life	236,092.50	
02080612	Permanent mortgage loans—National Life Expansion	1,957,740.08	
Total			8,071,776.42
Total notes payable			10,602,126.63

Accounts payables and accrued expenses

0200	Accounts payable—miscellaneous	5,364.47	
020006103	Accounts payable—commission	4,825.90	
020006104	Accounts payable—management fees	60.40	
020006105	Accounts payable—vendors	94,086.37	
020006181	Accounts payable—198X accruals	10,390.00	

(Continued)

Exhibit 9-24. *(Continued)*

CHERRY CREEK MALL
December 31, 198X

02010611	Retainage payable—major company	64,248.66
02010612	Retainage payable—Commercial Industries, Inc.	75,214.00
020206103	Accrued property tax—198X	173,929.86
021306102	Accrued interest payable	51,898.02
02130616	Accrued interest	1,420.00
0216	Customer deposits	1,096.68
	Total accounts payable and accrued expenses	482,534.36
	Deferred income	
	Total liabilities	**11,084,660.99**

Owners' Investment

029106116	Investment by venturer	1,000.00
029106117	Investment by venturer—MH	650,000.00
029106101	Operating P/L—prior years	2,118,820.84
029206102	Operating P/L—prior years	2,118,820.84
029406101	Distribution to partners—prior years	(2,546,525.38)
029406102	Distribution to partners—prior years	(2,546,525.39)
029406103	Distribution to partners—current year	(550,000.00)
029406104	Distribution to partners—MH current year	(550,000.00)
	Current year profit (Loss)	991,146.79
	Total	(313,262.30)
	Total liabilities and owners' investment	**10,771,398.69**

172

TEN

MARKETING AND PROMOTING A SHOPPING CENTER

The center must be stocked with goods and services that fit the needs and desires of the trading area. But the existence of the center and its storerooms filled with goods and services will not be known to prospective customers if the center and its tenants with their goods and services are not marketed and promoted. The potential customer must be aware of the retail offerings and the location of the offerings before any interest in purchase can be generated. Once some interest in the available goods and services has developed, then the center and its merchants can market their offerings so that the desired actions on the part of the potential customers will take place. The prospective customers must be attracted to the center. Once they arrive at the center, they will purchase the goods and services that have been stocked which will fit their needs and desires at the appropriate price levels.

The owner, the center manager, each tenant, and each chain store organization behind specific tenants all contribute to the marketing and promotion of the center and its merchandise and services. The owner advertises through press releases and paid advertising while the land is being developed and the buildings constructed. When the center opens, the center manager tends to take over the marketing as an extension of the owner's advertising and promotional efforts. At the same time, the tenants advertise their goods and services independent of and in cooperation with the center marketing programs. Some of the chain store organizations which actually sign the leases engage in cooperative advertising with the center management and the center store operator. Other marketing programs are generated and financed by the center marketing fund, which has replaced the shopping center management association to a substantial degree in recent years.

The marketing of a center involves personal and impersonal sales efforts. In any marketing effort, personal selling is the most potent and forceful sales method. Usually personal selling is significantly supplemented by impersonal sales efforts. Impersonal selling involves public relations through giveaway items, sales promotion including news releases and counter displays, and advertising which amounts to impersonal sales presentations through paid public media where the sponsor is identified.

With these general considerations in mind, let us observe the more detailed nature of the center marketing program. Continuous feedback from market research is needed for an efficient and effective marketing effort. There must be a marketing plan whose purpose and background are well defined. The problems and opportunities of the center and its merchants must be attacked by the overall marketing plan. Goals must be established, strategies devised, and tactics established. The marketing plan must be broken into annual plans with continuity between the annual plans. Coordinated marketing flights must be created, justified, componentized, and implemented within established budgets. As a part of the annual marketing plan and the major flights planned during the calendar year, specific advertising campaigns with various media must be planned and implemented. Communications between the mall manager and the individual merchants must be continual. Legal relationships must be maintained in all business dealings. Miscellaneous management areas such as a merchants' association, a marketing fund, continued development of the center, and grand opening activities must be considered, and decisions must be made in lights of the goals and selected strategies of the marketing plan.

RESEARCH TO SUPPORT THE CENTER MARKETING

The market for the center must be studied by the prospective developer or investor. In the case of the new center, this market research is the preopening study of the trade area. After the center opens, market research of an ongoing character is required to merchandise effectively and efficiently to the changing market. Recent market studies should be the basis for changes in the tenant mix as individual storerooms become available for re-leasing. The preopening research tends to focus on trading area delineation, trading area demographic data, driving time analysis, and current consumer habits and attitudes. The ongoing market analysis tends to focus on demographic shifts, retail market shifts, and changes in consumer habits and attitudes.

The Content of the Market Study

The market study focuses on the potential buying power for the center from an appropriate trading area. After considering the developer's overall plans, the analyst is asked to assess the sales potential after establishing the trading area for the developer's overall merchandising concept.

The research points out the need for the center in light of the trading area population, current and future buying power, the comparative location of the center, the proposed center design and layout, the general center tenant composition, and the short-, intermediate-, and long-term sales potential. A sample demographic analysis for a center in Chesapeake, Virginia is shown in Exhibit 10-1. If the market research is thorough, it will analyze consumer habits, attitudes, and lifestyles. Exhibit 10-2 shows the results of a lifestyle study that was accomplished before the investment in the Greenbrier Center. The accumulated data that may come partially from personal interviews, telephone surveys, and focus group participation indicates whether the center is needed in light of the current and proposed shopping centers and other retail competition in the relevant market area. In view of the competition, what sales potential exists for what kinds of retail tenants who might locate in the proposed center? For each line of retail trade, what sales volume could be generated by the various types of center merchants? How much new square footage could be supported per line of business by the new center? What price ranges and complementary kinds of goods are suggested by the market potential? How long will it take to lease up the center?

The trading area established by the market analysis may be broken down into two or more parts for closer scrutiny. The primary trading radius usually reflects travel or driving time from the residential or business origin of the prospective customers. The primary trading radius may be supplemented by the delineation of a secondary and, perhaps, a tertiary trading radius. These delineations may be particularly appropriate for regional, superregional, and specialty centers. The trading zones for the neighborhood and community centers are less protracted or more restricted to immediate clientele who seek convenience and some shopping goods, but usually not specialty goods and services. The regional, superregional, and higher quality centers draw significantly from trading areas involving extensive driving time.

Who Benefits from Good Market Research?

The developer must wisely select the appropriate tenants for the proper combination of goods and services which will be offered to the trading area. Subsequent center owners also benefit from his or her tenant selection. The individual tenants must decide whether they can profit from the trading area after meeting their center rent obligations. More specifically, the department stores each must assess their future profitability from the trading area and the joint merchandising of all the center tenants. The survival of the key tenants determines in large part the survival of the minor tenants. The lenders each look to the profitability of the tenants whose net rental receipts secure their loans. The loans technically may be secured by the real property interests, but the real property is worth nothing without its income production from it. The ultimate consumers benefit from the market analysis because they may find in

Exhibit 10-1. Demographic Estimates for the Greenbrier Trade Area

Characteristic	1980	1985
Population	654,000	755,000
Median income*	$18,000	$18,000
Median home value*	$58,500	$59,000
Average number of people per household	2.9	3.0
Average age	40	38
Percent of families with children under 18 years of age	45%	42%
Median number of years of school completed	11.0	11.7
Occupation: Percent white collar	30%	34%
Percent of working women	39%	41%
Race: Percent of nonwhite	27%	25%
Number of housing units		
Total	225,500	251,700
Single family	169,100	176,200
Multifamily	56,400	75,500

Annual Household Income	Total	Norfolk	Chesapeake	Portsmouth	Virginia Beach
$15,000 or less	35%	44%	26%	40%	28%
$15,001 to $24,999	26	27	26	29	29
$25,000	12	8	15	13	14
$25,001 to $34,999	13	9	18	9	20
$35,000 or more	14	12	15	9	19

Age	Total	Norfolk	Chesapeake	Portsmouth	Virginia Beach
Under 25 Years of Age	11%	15%	10%	9%	8%
25 to 34 Years	29	25	35	25	34
35 to 49 Years	29	22	28	28	43
50 to 64 Years	20	23	22	24	10
65 Years of Older	11	15	5	14	5

Exhibit 10-1. *(Continued)*

Education	Total	Norfolk	Chesapeake	Portsmouth	Virginia Beach
One to eight years of grammar school	6%	5%	6%	12%	2%
One to three years of high school	15	15	18	19	7
High school graduate	39	36	40	38	43
One to three years of college	23	26	20	20	24
Four years or more of college	17	18	16	11	24

Sources: Chesapeake Chamber of Commerce, Chesapeake City Council, Chesapeake Planning Commission, 1970 Census, Virginia Department of Labor and Industry, the *VIRGINNIAN PILOT* and the *LEDGER-STAR*.
*In constant, mid-1979 dollars.

the center the goods and services which they desire and can afford. Therefore, the parties who may benefit from good market analysis include:

The developer
Other center owners
Individual center tenants
Center management
Lenders
Ultimate consumers

The market analysis underlies the feasibility analysis which becomes a part of the loan prospectus. It also underlies the leasing campaign of the developer as letters of commitment are sought from the right tenants. Once the letters of commitment are signed, the developer's attorney will follow up with detailed leases and reciprocal operating agreements for tenant signature. The tenants may view the developer's market analysis as well as their own as they negotiate for the specific storeroom and building space within the proposed center and as they plan the merchandising of that specific store. After the developer prepares or has prepared for him or her the market analysis, the lender may study the same trading area using lender analysts. In consequence, market studies of the same trading area may be prepared for all of the parties involved from their own particular viewpoints. Storerooms have to be leased, merchandise has to be ordered, and financial risks must be assessed.

Who Prepares the Market Study?

The staff of the developer, the other owners, the lender, the major tenants, or outside consultants may actually prepare the market studies. Included in this

Exhibit 10-2. Results of a Consumer Survey: Agreement with Life Style Statements

Statement	Disagree Strongly			Agree Strongly
I like to get the most for my money when I buy clothes.	1 2	9		88
I prefer comfort to fashion in my clothes.	4	11	23	62
Wise people wait for sales to buy clothes.	9	14	22	55
I really enjoy shopping for clothes.	17	14	24	45
I drive less now than I did before gasoline became so expensive.	18	19	21	42
I frequently shop at bargain areas in stores.	16	21	22	41

Statement				
I like to look a little different from other people.	8	20	36	36
I would rather go to a sporting event than go to a party.	29	24	20	27
I play golf, tennis, bowl or engage in some other athletic activity regularly.	36	20	18	26
I think of myself as being very fashion conscious.	18	21	35	26
Fashion magazines give me many ideas about clothing I would like to buy.	28	19	28	25
I probably spend more money on my clothes than I should.	34	27	16	23

Source: Cousins Properties Incorporated, 300 Interstate North, Atlanta, GA 30339.

group of firms is Real Estate Research Corporation of Chicago, a wholly owned subsidiary of First National Bank of Chicago, and Landauer & Associates, headquartered in New York, whose ownership has recently become primarily foreign in domicile. Local real estate analysts and real estate appraisers may be employed on a fee basis to do this work as may commercial brokers, real estate attorneys, and public accounts.

Sources of Data

Where do the data come from for the establishment of sales potential within the delineated trading area? Two-dimensional maps and aerial surveys may be the initial devices of market analysis. Census data on housing and income are available from the Bureau of the Census and the Bureau of Labor Statistics of the federal government for the standard metropolitan statistical areas (SMSAs). Such government studies of smaller urban areas are commissioned less frequently than are studies for the SMSAs.

The state statistical abstracts may give housing and income data as may private analyses printed in annual issues of such journals as *Sales & Marketing Management*. Several marketing directories, domestic and foreign, are continually maintained by various services and are broken down by market areas. These directories have long been useful to organizations involved in the marketing of various types of goods and services.

Local, state, and national chambers of commerce have significant amounts of data available on market areas. The U.S. Department of Housing and Urban Development frequently issues FHA housing studies of various urban areas. The Small Business Administration of the federal government has promoted market research for their purposes. Government data from any source is usually available to any citizen. Local, county, and state development offices have extensive data, particularly as related to industrial development. Some of their data concerning housing and incomes may aid the shopping center market analyst.

Local business libraries of universities, colleges, or the public library system may contain extensive market data. Bureaus of Business and Economic Research of the local university may compile state-wide and local economic data that may aid the analyst.

THE MARKETING PLAN

The marketing manager of the center should draw up a written marketing plan. This document presents in writing a detailed plan of action for the future achievement of the goals established for the shopping center. The plan is based on the problems and opportunities for the center drawn from the repeated market research studies. Exhibits 10-3 through 10-5 illustrate a summary of a center's opportunities and problems, the goals set for the same center, and the

Exhibit 10-3. Problems of and Opportunities for Willow Brook Mall

I.   New development and growth in southeast sector of DeKalb County
   A.   According to the 1980 preliminary census, the census tracts immediately inthe Franklin area show greater growth of population than any other area in the city
   B.   As a result of the Nissan Plant, with a $500 million planned cost, a $60 million payroll begins in 1985. However construction on the Nissan Plant in Centreville has already generated great interest and growth for the immediate area.
   C.   Additional development in the surrounding area of Franch has resulted in new restaurants and additional retail outlets, including K-Mart, which opened in 1983 and, possibly, Woolco, by 1986.

II.   Willow Brook Center will expand in 1983, increasing 25 percent, adding a J.C. Penney and 22 additional shops, making this the largest regional center in the Middle Georgia area.

III.   Penetration into the market and change of shopping habits to Willow Brook continue to increase steadily.

IV.   Strong and steady increases in sales volume and sales per square foot have continued; however, there are weak sales volumes in men's clothing, shoes, and home furnishings categories

V.   Competition in Franklin seems to have diminished; however, they are still drawing a great deal of tourism traffic to see the Orlando World's Fair.

VI.   Greenbrier Center, with its planned expansion and redevelopment, does provide potential for future competition for Willow Brook. Also, the additional growth and strength of retail in the Franklin area continues to be major competition for Greenbrier.

VII.   Sales in the Food Garden Area continue to be flat or declining. It is not a competitive category with the rest of the shopping center and is lagging behind the growth.

VIII.   Even though last year attempts were made to strengthen merchant attitudes and support for each promotion, this is still an area in which improvement needs to be made.

IX.   Lack of leadership and involvement with department stores in promotions, advertising, and participation persists.

X.   Target the merchants' association print advertising and increase television penetration in the market.

XI.   Get additional market exposure through media tie-ins, promotions, and community events.

XII.   The 1984 Orlando World's Fair will bring thousands of additional tourists through the area.

XIII.   Tenant mix improvements are still necessary (please refer to the tenant mix addendum for additional explanations).

Exhibit 10-4.   Goals of Willow Brook Mall

    I.   Penetrate new residential and manufacturing development to introduce the mall to potential shoppers.

   II.   A.   Involve the community in events and activities during stages of the expansion, i.e., engineering class tours, graphics on the mall, contests.

        B.   Re-Grand Opening to be major promotion for fall, strengthening Willow Brook Mall's strong position as #1 shopping center in the Southeast, with saturation in the media and the entire region.

   III.   Build market penetration by 50 percent through use of more TV.

   IV.   Focus specific promotions on category of men's clothing and home furnishings to help increase sales by 50 percent.

    V.   Continue to advertise to I-75 traffic to capture shoppers traveling those two directions.

   VI.   A.   Involve groups and people from the Franklin community in three more promotions.

        B.   Continue to target advertising into the Franklin area to reach potential shoppers.

  VII.   Increase sales in Food Garden by 10 percent and increase activities and exposure for the Food Garden in each promotion.

 VIII.   Strengthen merchants' attitudes and support by 100 percent in promotions. Increase communications with them and management through a monthly newsletter and weekly visits.

   IX.   Have regularly scheduled monthly meetings with department store managers to reinvolve them in all promotions, advertising, and participation.

    X.   Continue to pinpoint the target market with Merchant Association participatory efforts 100 percent and increase overall TV advertising in all major seasons in order to reach 75 percent of the market.

   XI.   With each mall promotion, continue to cosponsor the events with the media to gain additional free exposure for the mall.

  XII.   With the 1984 World's Fair to be in Orlando, reach the tourists coming through the area in all major hotels and motels, contact all local tour operators to include Willow Brook shopping tours.

 XIII.   See tenant mix analysis.

Exhibit 10-5. Strategy for Willow Brook Mall

    I.   Contact new businesses in the area to invite them to mall, send brochures, arrange shopping tours with VIP program.

    II.   A.   Invite engineering, landscaping, and related classes to tour stages of mall expansion. Colorful and interesting graphics on wall will increase interest on site.

            B.   Re-Grand Opening to introduce new or updated ad campaign into the market. With additional funds through initial assessment, major advertising and promotional efforts possible. Consider major advertising and promotional efforts possible. Consider theme with Broadway emphasis; utilizing Rockettes, Georgia Performing Arts Center, major noon fashion shows at Georgia Performing Arts Center, saturated media efforts, concentrating on TV, community involvement with contests, major charities, etc.

    III.   Due to the broad, regional market, TV is most efficient way to reach entire area. Recommend generic-type spot to minimize production costs and maximize coverage.

    IV.   A.   Involve all men's clothing and shoe stores in major June men's promotion, to focus on category and increase sales. Utilize ads to focus on items.

            B.   Home furnishings category still weak. Recommend re-leasing to better, more aggressive tenants. Also, focus on category during major January promotions.

    V.   Creative Displays, Inc. to continue north- and southbound billboards on I-75, as directionals to the center.

    VI.   Work with specific Franklin community organizations to bring them out to the mall. For March, host the Middle Georgia Orchid Society orchid show. Also, continue NPC Subscriber and Nonsubscriber distribution into the Northeast section.

    VII.   Utilize Food Garden in all tourism plans and program with food coupon/VIP sheet for guests.

    VIII.   To involve more tenants in the process of promotions, use the top manager in each category from 1983 as "Category Captain." They will encourage the other stores in the category to participate and the group that has the highest percentage of participation in each promotion is winner of prizes.

    IX.   Meet with department store managers each month and work closely with them for promotional support.

    X.   Continue TMC Plan with NPC, reaching all subscriber and nonsubscriber homes in sections 14, 15, 16, 18, 19, and 20 on attached map.

    XI.   Utilize radio, TV, or newspaper to cosponsor each promotion to gain additional exposure at no cost.

    XII.   Advertise in major hotel/motel tourist publications, i.e, Guest Informant, Franklin City Guide, Franklin Visitors' Guide, and Georgia Visitors' Guide. Also have mail brochures located in all major hotel lobbies and tourist information centers.

strategy devised to reach the goals. The goals for the center stem from the geographical area, the facts about the consumers in the primary, secondary, and peripheral trading areas, and the ease of accessibility of the center.

The goals, marketing plan, and formulated strategy also relate to the competition for the center. A relative draw index on a demographic basis may be drawn up when relatively reliable numbers can be attached to trading area demographic dimensions and share of the market attracted by the center from the various market segments. Exhibit 10-6 shows the relative draw indices for various demographic dimensions for the Willow Brook Mall.

$$\frac{\text{Relative draw index}}{\text{(demographic)}} = \frac{\text{Percent of mall shoppers represented by the market dimension}}{\text{Percent of market represented by the market dimension}}$$

Using the Age 14–17 dimension on the market for the mall from Exhibit 10-6, we would conclude:

$$\frac{\text{relative draw index}}{\text{(Age 14–17)}} = \frac{0.04}{0.07} = 0.6$$

In like manner, a relative draw index may be drawn up for geographic divisions of the trading area when the percent of the market and the percent of shoppers can be quantified on a relatively reliable basis. Geographic relative draw indices for Willow Brook Mall are shown in Exhibit 10-7. The relative draw index on a geographic basis rather than a demographic basis is calculated the same way.

$$\frac{\text{Relative draw index}}{\text{(geographic)}} = \frac{\text{Percent of shoppers from the particular area}}{\text{Percent of the center market from that particular area}}$$

For example, for Spartenburg County, the percent of **shoppers** from that county is 4 percent, and the percent of the Willow Brook market from Spartenburg County is 27. Therefore:

$$\frac{\text{Relative draw index}}{\text{(Spartenburg County)}} = \frac{0.04}{0.27} = 0.15 \text{ or } 0.1$$

Phone surveys and personal interviews may also divulge shopping frequency indices for the various competing shopping centers within the shopper's trading radius. The results may be shown on a geographic and a demographic basis (Exhibit 10-8). The same or similar surveys may also show the shoppers' perceptions of the following factors which they may evaluate on a four-point scale for the interviewer:

Variety of stores
Mall appearance
    Exterior appearance
    Parking lot
    Interior appearance
Mall amenities

Transportation between mall levels
   Location
   Adequacy
  Seating areas
Other mall qualities
Courtesy and helpfulness of salespeople (Exhibit 10-9)

Exhibit 10-6. Indices for Willow Brook Mall

Characteristic	Percent of Market	Percent of Shoppers	Relative Draw Index
Race			
White	82	90	1.1
Black	18	8	0.4
Other	0	2	—
Age (over 13)			
14–17	7	4	0.6
18–20	5	9	1.8
21–29	16	25	1.6
30–39	16	27	1.7
40–49	11	16	1.5
50–64	13	15	1.2
65+	9	4	0.4
Household income			
Under $10,000	17	5	0.3
$10,000–$14,999	19	13	0.7
$15,000–$24,999	41	26	0.6
$25,000–$49,999	16	45	2.8
$50,000+	7	10	1.4

Exhibit 10-7. Geographic Relative Draw Indices for Willow Brook Mall

Area	Percent of Market	Percent of Shoppers[*]	Relative Draw Index
Greenville Area	23%	50%	2.2
Greenville County—North	8%	19%	2.4
Greenville County—South	6%	14%	2.3
Total Greenville County	37%	83%	2.2
Pickens County	11%	7%	0.6
Spartenburg County	27%	4%	0.1
Anderson County	18%	2%	0.1
Laurens County	7%	3%	0.4
Total surrounding counties	63%	16%	0.3

[*]Percentage of shoppers from five-county area.

Exhibit 10-8. Shopping Frequency Indices[*]

Category	Mall 1	Mall 2	Mall 3	Mall 4	Mall 5	Mall 6	Mall 7	Mall 8	Mall 9
All Shoppers	3.2	2.6	2.3	0.7	1.0	0.5	0.6	0.7	0.9
Market									
1A Greenville Area	3.4	2.8	2.4	0.9	1.4	0.7	0.9	0.9	1.3
1B Greenville County North	3.2	2.3	2.6	0.7	1.4	0.2	0.8	0.8	1.0
1C Greenville County South	3.3	2.6	2.7	0.5	0.9	0.5	0.5	0.5	0.5
2A Pickens County	2.8	2.4	1.9	0.8	0.4	0.5	0.2	0.4	0.5
2B Spartanburg County	2.4	1.4	1.2	0.1	0.2	0.1	0.2	0.3	0.0
2C Anderson County	2.6	2.4	1.2	0.8	0.0	0.7	0.4	0.4	0.0
2D Laurens County	2.9	2.6	2.3	0.5	0.6	0.0	0.0	0.4	0.4
3 Other South Carolina	2.5	2.6	2.0	0.6	0.3	0.4	0.3	0.6	0.4
Females	3.1	2.5	2.3	0.7	1.1	0.5	0.6	0.7	0.9
Working Women	3.1	2.5	2.3	0.9	1.3	0.6	0.7	0.7	0.9
Males	3.2	2.6	2.5	0.8	0.8	0.3	0.6	0.9	0.7
Households with Children	3.2	2.5	2.4	0.7	1.1	0.5	0.6	0.7	0.9
Shopper age									
Under 20	3.3	2.3	2.3	0.6	1.0	0.3	0.5	1.0	0.7
21–39	3.2	2.5	2.3	0.8	1.1	0.6	0.7	0.7	0.9
40+	3.1	2.7	2.3	0.7	0.9	0.4	0.6	0.6	0.9
Household income									
Less than $15,000	3.0	2.5	2.1	0.8	0.7	0.5	0.3	1.0	0.7
$15,000–$24,999	3.2	2.4	2.3	0.5	0.7	0.4	0.6	0.7	0.8
$25,000–49,999	3.2	2.6	2.5	0.8	1.3	0.5	0.8	0.8	0.9
$50,000+	3.3	3.0	2.2	0.9	1.5	0.4	0.8	0.2	1.2
Ethnicity									
White	3.2	2.6	2.3	0.7	1.1	0.5	0.6	0.6	0.9
Black	3.2	2.5	2.4	1.3	0.9	0.9	0.3	2.0	1.1
Hispanic	3.3	1.8	1.5	1.3	1.5	0.5	1.0	0.8	1.8
Other	4.0	3.0	4.0	0.0	0.0	0.0	3.0	0.0	0.0

Source: Cousins Properties Incorporated, 300 Interstate North, Atlanta, GA 30339.
[*]Index: 4.0 = frequently (once a week or more); 3.0 = occasionally (once a month or more); 2.0 = seldom (less than once a month); 1.0 = first time/once; 0.0 = never.

Exhibit 10-9. Shopper Evaluation of Willow Brook Mall Features[*]

Category	Grade
Variety of stores	
Women's clothing	3.4
Men's clothing	3.1
Women's shoes	3.3
Men's shoes	3.0
Gifts	3.3
Home furnishings	2.9
Eating places	3.0
Overall merchandise selectivity	3.2
Mall appearance/amenities—exterior appearance	
Landscaping	3.6
Cleanliness	3.7
Building	3.7
Mall appearance/amenities—parking lot	
Cleanliness	3.6
Ease of parking	3.1
Directional signs	2.9
Safety	3.0
Mall appearance/amenities—interior appearance	
Lighting	3.7
Planters/landscaping	3.8
Cleanliness	3.7
Fountain	3.6
Floors	3.5
Mall amenities—getting up and down	
Escalators—location	2.8
Escalators—adequacy	2.8
Stairways—location	3.0
Stairways—adequacy	2.9
Elevators—location	2.7
Elevators—adequacy	2.7
Mall amenities—seating areas	
Adequacy	2.7
Location	2.8
Effectiveness	2.8
Other mall qualities	
Ease of finding your way around	2.9
Mall safety/security	3.1
Prices as compared to other shopping centers	2.3
Courtesy and helpfulness of salespeople	
Department stores	2.9
All other mall stores	2.9

[*]Scoring System: 4.0 = A (excellent); 3.0 = B (above average); 2.0 = C (average); 1.0 = D (below average); 0.0 = F (poor or unsatisfactory).

THE ANNUAL MARKETING PLAN

The goals for the center have been defined. They have been designed to be feasible, measurable, suitable, acceptable, flexible, and achievable. The overall marketing plan has been devised so that the specific goals may be pursued. The specific goals relate to sales volume, market share, market penetration, market research methods, special events, community relations, publicity, merchandise coordination, image, advertising, competition, tenant mix, tenant relations, and physical properties of the center. The strategies selected—specific plans in time and degree to achieve the goals—must be based upon the predefined goals; they must be capable of implementation; and the goals must be attainable with appropriate resources that must be acquired. The tactics for the implementation of the selected strategies involve (1) outlines of all market research projects, (2) the special events calendar and budget, (3) the community events calendar and budget, (4) the merchandising events, specifications, and costs, (5) rough layout for print ads and radio scripts, television story boards, and outdoor layouts, (6) media schedules including sizes of audiences at various times, reach of the media, frequencies utilized, and cost per time block, (7) sketches and cost of decor programs, and (8) tenant relations meeting schedules and preliminary agenda.

BUDGETING

Once the overall marketing plan is segmented down to the annual marketing plan, a budget must be drawn up for the selling support activities and programs for the year. Major flight components are established.

> The Flight Marketing Concept is a system of marketing planning and communication designed to increase retail activity, participatory merchandising and advertising, merchandising, collaterals, and special events to increase the center's exposure and therefore shopper response.[*]

The budget allocates sufficient dollars to the planning and implementing of the marketing flight calendar. The annual budget allocation may amount to:

General and administrative	up to 25% of the budget
Merchandising and special events	up to 33.5%
Advertising	at least 40%
Contingency	up to 1.5%
Total	100%

[*]Cousins Properties, Inc., Atlanta, Georgia, January 7, 1981

Several marketing flights may be created, but the flight budget allocations may resemble the following:

Flight Budget Allocations

Merchant communication	5%
Sales/merchandising	20
Visuals/collaterals	20
Entertainment/involvement	15
Advertising/publicity	40
Total	100%

Marketing budget allocations are also based on seasonal variations in retail sales expected for the center. Past years' seasonal trends for the center are used to adjust national or regional seasonal sales averages. The following retail peak seasons may be recognized, and the second column below lists suggested flight activity supports for the various peaks.

January	Variety clearance
February	Variety clearance, cruise, bridal
March/April	Spring fashions, shoes, accessories; sports/recreation items
May/June	Gift (Mother's Day, Father's Day, weddings, graduations, births), jewelry, home decor, home furnishings, casual lifestyle supports
July	Variety clearance
August/September	School fashions, shoes, accessories, supplies, home furnishings
October	Variety clearance (mall anniversary), outerwear, home furnishings
November/December	Gifts, toys, games, home decor, fashions, accessories, jewelry

The sales trend over the year may be reflected in a regional sales trends. The averages for a region may be seen below:

Month	Percent of Total Sales
January	5.7
February	5.7
March	7.3
April	8.0
May	7.7
June	7.7
July	7.9

Month	Percent of Total Sales
August	8.2
September	7.8
October	8.2
November	10.3
December	15.7

The mall budget matrix also must take into account the balance of the retail goods and service offerings within the center by merchandise or service category or classification. A typical regional mall merchandise formula for annual budgeting might indicate:

Men's ready-to-wear	10%
Women's ready-to-wear	25
Shoes	10
Jewelry	3
Gift/home furnishings	17
Leisure	15
Food	15
Service	5
Total	100%

SALES SUPPORT AND PLANNING

The marketing budget is based on the needs of the marketing flights planned for the coming year, the selling peaks forecast for the year, the balance of merchandise and service offerings of the center, and the merchandise and service emphasis per month and season of the year. A mall merchandise matrix covering the seasons in terms of the basic retail offerings of the center may be seen in Exhibit 10-10. From that exhibit, you can see that fashion merchandise is emphasized in marketing in the spring, early fall, and early winter primarily. Clearance sales are emphasized in other parts of the year such as late winter, late summer, and late fall. The marketing budget must reflect these seasonal expected marketing patterns as well as the more detailed expected retail sales patterns (Exhibit 10-11). Included in the monthly retail sales calendar are the religious and secular holidays which affect sales volume and the traditionally best-selling lines during each month.

MARKETING FLIGHTS

Several major communicative and comprehensive marketing campaigns are usually planned for a regional or superregional center on a yearly basis. The marketing flights may be called such things as "Season to Taste," "Le Cirque,"

Exhibit 10-10.   Mall Merchandise Matrix

Merchandise	Percent of Mall	Winter Clear January February	Spring March April	Summer May June	Summer Clear July	Fall August September	Fall Sales September October	Winter November December
Fashion			X			X		X
Gifts				X				X
Food								
Entertainment			X					
Home			X				X	
Services								
Personal								
Clearance		X			X		X	

Source: Cousins Properties Incorporated, 300 Interstate North, Atlanta, GA 30339.

Exhibit 10-11. The Retail Sales Calendar

Month	Percent of Annual Retail Sales Nationally	Percent of Annual Retail Sales— South Atlantic Region	Merchandise Emphasis and Best Sellers	Holidays
January	6.6	5.7	Variety clearance White sales TV and radio	New Year's Day
February	6.1	5.7	Variety clearance Some spring fashions and home furnishings	Lincoln's Birthday Valentine's Day Washington's Birthday
March	7.6	7.3	Spring and Easter fashions Shoes Gardening needs Recreational items	St. Patrick's Day
April	8.3	8.0	Spring and Easter fashions Housewares Outdoor items	Passover Good Friday Easter
May	8.0	7.7	Fashions Gifts Appliances Jewelry Sporting goods	Mother's Day Memorial Day
June	7.8	7.7	Men's gifts Men's wear Jewelry Luggage Bathing suits Some clearance Fast foods	Father's Day
July	7.0	7.9	Variety clearance Cosmetics	Independence Day
August	7.8	8.2	Juniors, children's and misses fashion shoes Books and stationery School supplies Furniture and bedding White sales	
September	7.8	7.8	Home furnishings Women's fashions Outerwear Books Major and small appliances	Labor Day Jewish New Year

Exhibit 10-11. *(Continued)*

Month	Percent of Annual Retail Sales Nationally	Percent of Annual Retail Sales— South Atlantic Region	Merchandise Emphasis and Best Sellers	Holidays
October	7.8	8.2	Home furnishings Women's fashions Some clearance Books and gifts	Columbus Day Halloween
November	9.4	10.3	Party apparel Gifts and books Home furnishings	Election Day Veteran's Day Thanksgiving
December	15.8	15.7	Gifts, toys, books, cameras, fashions, shoes, home furnishings, electronics, luggage	Chanukah Christmas New Year's Eve

Source: Cousins Properties Incorporated, 300 Interstate North, Atlanta, GA 30339.

"Fun on Sale," and "Fresh Face." Such flights are planned for special seasons of the year with special graphic and visual key designs. Special merchandise emphases are associated with the specific flight as are special forms of entertainment and tenant and community involvement (Exhibits 10-12 through 10-15). The flights are engineered so that every tenant's retail offerings are

Exhibit 10-12. Flight: "Season to Taste"

Title	"Season to Taste"
Season	Late fall, anniversary
Graphic/visual	
Merchandising	Gourmet cooking clinic with Arte Johnson or Vincent Price Employees in chefs' hats and aprons screened with seasonal graphic Displays of kitchen gadgets and decor items History of foods exhibit for foods available at mall Out-to-dinner fashion shows
Entertainment/ involvement	Celebrity eating contests for charity Home extension service clinics World's largest sundae, pizza, etc.

Source: Cousins Properties Incorporated, 300 Interstate North, Atlanta, GA 30339.

supported by at least one of the flights of the year. Problem areas of the center may be emphasized even more extensively in multiple flights.

For maximum marketing impact and budget economy, all flight components must mesh together and be mutually supportive of the overall flight marketing effort. The components of a single flight may be:

Income production
Merchant communications
Sales and merchandising
Visual aids and collateral support
Entertainment and involvement
Advertising and publicity

The budget is established for the flight before it commences. Once the flight is completed, a flight budget followup or recapitulation is needed for management purposes and future planning.

ADVERTISING

To support the marketing flights, the center manager will usually engage in advertising campaigns with the use of multiple media. Advertising, the paid form of nonpersonal sales presentation with the identification of the sponsor, is one of the forms of promotional devices for the marketing and promoting of a center. Advertising is usually essential for shopper recognition and awareness of the center existence, location, and goods and service offerings.

Advertising involves positioning and production of ads. As the marketing flights are designed and implemented, the various types of ads must be produced for the appropriate media after time or space has been purchased. The marketing director tailors the appearances and content of the paid messages to fit the needs of the particular flight. Numerous ads in the various media comprise the elements of the advertising campaign.

MEDIA

The vehicles for the presentation of commercial ads promoting the services, facilities, and merchandise of the center include print and broadcast media. Other media are outdoor displays, such as billboards, and sales promotion devices, such as yardsticks, beauty and cooking contests, airplane streamers, hot air balloons suspended over the center, and shopping bags with the emblem or graphic design of the center. The most commonly used print media are newspapers and direct mail flyers. Ads may be placed in various locally distributed magazines. Printed point of purchase displays may also advertise the goods, services, and facilities of the shopping center.

Exhibit 10-13. Flight: "Le Cirque"

Title	"Le Cirque" (Parisian Circus theme)
Season	Winter clearance/summer clearance
Graphic/visual	Harlequin/cabaret dancers

Merchandising	Sidewalk sale with table skirtings
	    repeat-screened with graphic
	In-store sale with rack toppers and
	    item tags screened with graphic
	Clowns parading in mall with sandwich
	    board ads of store specials
	Clowns performing at storefronts with
	    merchandise

Entertainment/
involvement
	Stage performance of "Carnival" score
	Cabaret dance performances
	Organ grinder and monkey
	Exhibit of Parisian street artist/
	    Impressionist movement (Renoir, Degas,
	    Toulouse-Lautrec, Manet)

Source: Cousins Properties Incorporated, 300 Interstate North, Atlanta, GA 30339.

Exhibit 10-14. Flight: "Fun on Sale"

Title	"Fun on Sale" For the Good Times
Season	Spring, late fall, Christmas
Graphic/visual	
Merchandising	Recreation show Toy fair Home entertainment/electronics exhibits Games People Play . . . game/party settings on the mall wiht live models Suzuki Funfair/Snowshow
Entertainment/ involvement	Chess challenge Audience participation stage games Huge Gameboard with live players in game marathon for charity Pinball Wizard

Source: Cousins Properties Incorporated, 300 Interstate North, Atlanta, GA 30339.

Exhibit 10-15. Flight: "Fresh Face"

Title	"Fresh Face"
	A slice of Spring/Summer
Season	Spring/summer
Graphic/visual	Fruit slice
Merchandising	Cosmetics makeovers
	Hat and headwear displays/shows tanning product coop
	Sundress and recreational fashion show
Entertainment/ involvement	Recreation show
	Women's sports event/clinics
	Citrus Council nutrition exhibits

Source: Cousins Properties Incorporated, 300 Interstate North, Atlanta, GA 30339.

The costs of broadcast media—radio and television—vary widely. Generally radio spots are less costly than television ad time. Television tends to be inefficient as well as expensive. The medium usually reaches a much wider market than the center management wishes to reach, but this excessive market reach must be paid for in order to cover the target market. Radio broadcast time may be selected so that the excess broadcast reach is minimized. Comprehensive statistics are usually compiled for each 15-minute block of time for each radio station airing programs and commercials within the center trade area. Those data show the age breakdown in terms of the average number of listeners within the specific time block during the 24-hour day (Exhibit 10-16). Data for

Exhibit 10-16. Sample Average Quarter-Hour and Cumulative Listening Estimates

Station Call Letters	Adults 18+						Adults 18–49					
	Total Area		Metro Survey Area				Total Area		Metro Survey Area			
	Avg. (00)	Cum. (00)	Avg. (00)	Cum. (00)	Avg. RTG	Cum. SHR	Avg. (00)	Cum. (00)	Avg. (00)	Cum. (00)	Avg. RTG	Cum. SHR
WXYZ	8	291	8	291	0.1	0.4	4	182	4	182		0.3
WAOK	74	1126	73	1062	0.5	3.5	59	809	59	765	0.6	3.9
WBIK	102	1873	62	1299	0.5	2.9	77	1394	48	947	0.5	3.2
WBKE	5	100	3	46		0.1	2	51	1	30		0.1
WCOB	13	235	13	235	0.1	0.6	9	121	9	121	0.1	0.6
WGKA	30	307	30	307	0.2	1.4	22	205	22	205	0.2	1.5
WOST	120	2716	117	2610	0.9	5.5	69	1741	66	1640	0.7	4.4
WQUN	11	287	11	269	0.1	0.5	3	136	3	127		0.2
WICO	13	393	13	393	0.1	0.6	9	285	9	285	0.1	0.8
WXLX	6	174	6	142		0.3	6	174	6	142	0.1	0.4
WPLO	125	2073	110	1809	0.8	5.2	95	1450	85	1291	0.9	5.6
WRNH	66	1272	65	1235	0.5	3.1	36	580	35	566	0.4	2.3

stations in the viewership market are usually available from the advertising agencies who produce the television ads and from the television stations themselves. Broadcast directories with comprehensive information exist.

MEASUREMENT OF ADVERTISING RESULTS

The advertisers, the media, and outside agencies measure advertising results. Consumer surveys through personal interviews or measuring equipment attached to radio and television sets give some indication to the advertiser of the effectiveness of the particular ad or series of ads (Exhibit 10-17 Advertising Recall). The results of the effectiveness surveys usually aid the advertiser in establishing the next year's advertising budget and in allocating the budget expenditures by media. The ad agencies need to know the results of their present and past ads, which influence their new ads. The media may change

Exhibit 10-17. Advertising Recall (%)

Category	Ad 1	Ad 2	Ad 3
All Shoppers	45	28	32
Market	53	31	39
1A Maryville area	53	31	39
1B Maryville County North	46	28	32
1C Maryville County South	41	33	31
2A Bartlett County	38	35	38
2B Morrison County	22	17	22
2C Allison County	22	22	11
2D Manhattan County	27	27	27
3 Other Delaware	31	15	13
Females	47	29	32
Working women	47	26	30
Males	38	25	34
Households with children	44	29	34
Shopper age			
Under 20	40	23	32
21–39	45	26	34
40+	47	34	31
Household income			
Less than $15,000	43	30	35
$15,000–$24,999	43	22	27
$25,000–$49,999	45	32	35
$50,000+	54	41	49
Ethnicity			
White	44	29	33
Black	52	24	27
Hispanic	50	50	64

their rates for various time blocks depending on the differences in advertising results at various times of the day or night over the various media.

MERCHANT COMMUNICATIONS

The center management needs to communicate with each of the center merchants in order to convey information about shopping center marketing and operations. The developer and the management may wish to prompt action of various types from the merchant. That action may pertain to rent payment—base and overage payment—or it may pertain to such things as advertising and marketing. The overall center and the individual merchants benefit from all forms of advertising and marketing. The communications may also refer to coordinated business practices and good will among the center merchants. Harmonious operations lead to better center and merchant performance.

Merchant communications may be conveyed through merchants' association meetings, written forms such as memorandums and reports, and word of mouth. Periodically the management or a group of merchant representatives usually call merchants association meetings. These meetings permit the discussion of the creation of marketing flights, their financial support, and the implementation procedures. At the meetings, tenant contributions to common area maintenance and the center promotional fund may also be discussed. Any problem or controversy about center selling practices and operating procedures may be aired and alternatives for corrective action discussed. The meetings of the tenants may merely reinforce the sales efforts and morale of the individual merchants and inspire enthusiasm for good merchandising and sales performance.

LEGAL CONSIDERATIONS IN CENTER MARKETING

When space in the center is temporarily used for marketing and sales purposes, legal agreements need to be signed by the temporary tenants and the center management. The obligations and duties of the temporary occupants are spelled out, and the center management is relieved of some liability in the performance and marketing of these temporary space users (Exhibit 10-18). Some of the temporary activity within the center is not commercial activity. The obligations and duties of these tenants who are perhaps requesting permission to use the center auditorium, conference room, or community booth may be spelled out in a legal document following an approved application for the use of the space. When the common area of the center is needed for displays and exhibits such as an antique or sports car show, an application for permission to use the common area may be used to identify the space users and their contemplated mall activities. General release and indemnity agreements may be used for temporary occupants of a center. The signatures on these release and indemnity agreements reduce the liability of the center management in the event of some legal proceedings.

Exhibit 10-18.   Example of a License Agreement for Use of Shopping Center Premises*

   This Agreement ("Agreement"), made and centered into this _____ day of _____, 19_____, by and among _____ ("Licensor"), _____ Merchants' Association, Inc. ("Association") and _____ ("Licensee"):

WITNESSETH:

   in consideration of the mutual promises, covenants and agreements hereinafter set forth, the parties hereto hereby agree as follows:

   1.   *Grant of License.* Licensor hereby grants to the Association and Licensee a license to occupy and use, subject to all the terms and conditions hereinafter stated, the premises ("premises" located in _____ ("Shopping Center") as described and designated on the sketch map which is attached hereto as Exhibit A: and by this reference made a part hereof.
   2.   *Permitted Use.* The premises shall be used and occupied solely for the following purposes, to-wit:_____
   3.   *Term.* Licensees and Association shall be permitted to use the premises during the period (the "term of this Agreement") commencing on the _____ day of _____, 19_____, at _____ o'clock _____ .m. and terminating on the _____ day of _____, 19_____, at _____ o'clock _____ .m. This license is only valid during those days and hours in which the Shopping Center is open to the public.
   4.   *Fees.*
      A.   Licensee shall pay a license fee to Association as follows:
      B.   The Association shall pay a fee to Licensee for its services as follows:
   _____

   5.   *Security Deposit.* Licensee has deposited with Licensor the sum of _____ Dollars ($_____) as security for the punctual performance by Licensee of each and every obligation of Licensee under this Agreement. In the event of any default by Licensee, Licensor may apply all or any part of such security deposit to cure the default or to reimburse Licensor for any sum which the Licensor may have spent by reason of such default.
   6.   *Utilities.* Utilities and other charges shall be paid as follows:
   _____

   7.   *Hold Harmless.* Licensee hereby assumes liability for and shall indemnify and hold harmless Licensor, the Association, the Shopping Center tenants, the owners and ground lessees of the real estate comprising the Shopping Center, and their respective shareholders, officers, directors, employees, customers and invitees (all of the foregoing being hereinafter collectively referred to as the "Indemnitees") from and against any and all liability, loss, cost, damage or expense (including, without limitation, costs of litigation and attorneys' fees) that any of the Indemnitees shall ever suffer or incur in connection with loss of life, bodily and/or personal injury, or damage to property arising out of or from the use or occupancy by the Licensee of the premises, or any part thereof, or any other part of the Shopping Center, or occasioned wholly or in part by any act or omission of Licensee, or its dealers, employees, promoters, agents, guests, invitees or contractors, or in any way relating to or arising out of any activity of the Licensee. The Licensee also agrees to release the Indemnitees from any liability in regard to any loss,

*Adapted from a similar License Agreement for Use of Shopping Center Premises designed by Cousins Properties Incorporated, Atlanta, Georgia.

Exhibit 10-18. *(Continued)*

theft, burglary, robbery or damage to equipment, supplies, prizes, merchandise, exhibits or other property of the Licensee or any of its dealers, employees, promoters, agents, guests, invitees or contractors. Licensee also agrees to indemnify and hold the Indemnitees harmless from and against any and all liability, loss, cost, damage or expense (including, without limitation, costs of litigation and attorneys' fees) that any of the Indemnities shall ever suffer or incur in connection with any claims arising out of the consumption, or existence in, on or about the Shopping Center, of any goods, products, consumables or merchandise sold or furnished by Licensee or its employees, promoters, agents or contractors.

8. *Waiver.* To the full extent permitted by law, Licensee hereby releases Licensor from any liability for damage to property of Licensee or any other person claiming through Licensee resulting from any accident or occurrence in or upon the premises or any other part of the Shopping Center.

9. *Insurance.* Licensee will provide to the Licensor prior to commencement of the term of this Agreement a certificate of insurance establishing that the Licensee carries insurance coverage with a reputable insurance company authorized to transact business in the State in which the Shopping Center is located, having coverages and limits as indicated below.

    (a) Comprehensive public liability and property damage insurance having limits of not less than \$_____ for bodily or personal injury to or death of one person, \$_____ for bodily or personal injuries to or death of more than one person in any single occurrence and \$_____ for damage to or destruction of property in any single occurrence, or a policy with combined single limits of not less than \$_____; said insurance shall include contractual liability coverage to insure Licensee's obligations hereunder.

    (b) Workmen's Compensation Insurance as required by the laws of the State where the Shopping Center is located.

    (c) Other, (specify) _____

The aforementioned certificate shall establish that the insurance will be in full force and effect at the commencement of the term of this Agreement, will name the Association (to-wit: _____) and Licensor (to-wit: _____) as additional insureds thereunder and shall provide that no such insurance may be cancelled without at least ten (10) days notice by certified mail, return receipt requested, to the Licensor.

10. *Supervision and Control.* Licensee shall at all times during its use of the premises provide sufficient supervision and maintain adequate control of its employees, guests and invitees.

11. *Maintenance.* Licensee will maintain the premises in a clean and orderly manner and will be responsible for daily cleaning and trash removal.

12. *Statutes and Ordinances.* Licensee shall at its expense obtain any licenses or permits required by any governmental agency or authority with respect to the type of activity to be conducted on the premises.

13. *Removal of Goods.* Licensee agrees that upon the termination of this Agreement, Licensee shall remove its goods and effects from the premises, repair any damage caused by such removal and peaceably yield up the premises in clean condition and in good order and repair, ordinary wear and tear excepted. Any personal property of Licensee not removed within two (2) days following such termination shall, at Licensor's option, become the property of Licensor.

Exhibit 10-18. *(Continued)*

14. *Rules, Regulations and General Conduct.*

(a) Licensee agrees not to harm the premises, or commit or permit waste, or create any nuisance, or make any use of the premises which in Licensor's judgment is offensive, or do any act tending to injure the reputation of the Shopping Center. Licensor reserves the right to terminate this Agreement at any time upon notice to Licensee.

(b) Licensee shall not use any vehicle, motor, camera, lighting device or projector within or about the Shopping Center without the prior consent of Licensor. Licensee shall not engage in any fighting or use physical force or abuse or obscene language toward any person or engage in any form of objectionable behavior, such as the making of loud noises or coarse or offensive utterances, gestures or displays, any of which cause or may cause public inconvenience or annoyance or alarm. In addition, Licensee shall not permit the emission of noise or odors from the premises or use any devices or paraphernalia such as loudspeakers, sound amplifiers, radios, televisions or phonographs without the prior written consent of Licensor. No unlawful activities shall be permitted on the premises, nor shall gambling or the consumption of alcoholic beverages be permitted.

(c) Licensee agrees not to make any alterations or additions to the premises, or make any holes in walls, partitions, ceilings or floors, or paint or place in, on or about the premises any signs, placards or other advertising media, banners, pennants, awnings, aerials, antennas, or similar items, without obtaining the prior written consent of Licensor.

(d) Licensee shall not obstruct the free flow of pedestrian or vehicular traffic on walkways, sidewalks, stairways, escalators, roads, driveways, parking lots, or any other area regularly used for such traffic with the Shopping Center. Exhibits are limited to _____ feet in width, with a cross-over space at intervals of fifteen to twenty feet. The height of any exhibit over four feet shall be subject to Licensor's approval.

(e) Licensor reserves the right to require the withdrawal from display of any item, object, person, printed matter or any other thing of any nature which in the opinion or Licensor might be detrimental to the appearance or reputation of the Shopping Center.

(f) All loading and unloading shall take place within such times and at such place as shall be designated by Licensor.

(g) Licensee shall obey all of the rules and regulations set forth herein or hereafter promulgated from time to time by the Licensor governing or pertaining to the Shopping Center or the Shopping Center's licensees.

15. *Liens.* Licensee agrees not to permit any mechanics' or materialman's lien to be filed against the premises by reason of any work, labor, services or materials performed at or furnished to the premises for Licensee or anyone occupying the premises under Licensee. Nothing in this Agreement shall be constructed as a consent on the part of the Licensor to subject the Licensor's estate in the premises to any lien or liability under the lien laws of the State in which the Shopping Center is located.

16. *Default.* In the event of any failure of Licensee to pay any sum due hereunder, or any failure to perform any other of the terms, conditions or covenants of this Agreement to be observed or performed by Licensee or if Licensee shall become bankrupt or insolvent, or file any debtor proceedings, or take or have taken against Licensee in any court pursuant to any statute either of the United States or any State, a

(Continued)

Exhibit 10-18. *(Continued)*

petition in bankruptcy or insolvency or for reorganization or for the appointment of a receiver or trustee of all or a portion or Licensee's property, or if Licensee makes an assignment for the benefit of creditors, or petitions for or enters into an arrangement, or if Licensee shall abandon said premises, then Licensor, in addition to all other rights and remedies it may have, shall have the immediate right of reentry and may remove all persons and property from the premises and such property may be removed and stored in a public warehouse or elsewhere at the cost of, and for the account of, Licensee, all without notice or resort to legal process and without Licensor being deemed guilty of trespass, or becoming liable for any loss or damage which may be occasioned thereby. Licensee agrees to pay on demand all expenses (including attorneys' fees) incurred by Licensor in enforcing any obligations of Licensee under this Agreement.

    17. *Relationship Between Parties*. Nothing contained herein shall be deemed or construed as creating the relationship of principal and agent or of partnership or of joint venture between the parties hereto, it being understood and agreed that nothing contained herein, nor any acts of the parties hereto, shall be deemed to create any relationship other than the relationship of licensor and licensee.

    18. *No Personal Liability*. Anything to the contrary elsewhere herein notwithstanding, there shall be absolutely no personal liability on the part of the persons, firms, or entities which constitute Licensor with respect to any of the terms, covenants, conditions and provisions of this Agreement, and Licensee shall look solely to the interest of Licensor, its successors and assigns, in the Shopping Center for the satisfaction of each and every remedy of Licensee in the event of default by Licensor hereunder, such exculpation of personal liability is absolute and without any exception whatsoever.

    19. *Miscellaneous Provisions*. (attach additional pages if needed.)

    In Witness Whereof, the parties have executed this Agreement as of the day and year first above written.

LICENSOR_____   LICENSEE_____

By:_____   By:_____

Its:_____   Its:_____

ASSOCIATION_____   ADDRESS OF LICENSEE:_____

By:_____   _____

Its:_____   _____

MERCHANTS' ASSOCIATIONS AND PROMOTIONAL FUNDS

The success of a shopping center requires the harmonious functioning of the merchants' association or promotional fund. Some centers operate more smoothly to the increased profitability of all parties involved when the merchants and the owner join together in a merchants' association. They periodically discuss their common problems and jointly sponsor advertising and promotional efforts which benefit the overall center and its merchants individually. Other centers function better with a promotional fund and less merchant participation in center management. Disputes and differences of opinion among the individual merchants are avoided, and the monies contributed by each merchant under the lease agreement to the promotional fund are advantageously spent by the professional management of the center in support of the management's plans for the various well-defined marketing flights.

Usually the regional and superregional centers utilize the merchants' association mechanism while the neighborhood center tends to have no merchants' association or promotional fund at all. About 60 percent of all community centers maintain merchants' associations. Promotional funds have been established in lieu of merchants' associations in a small percentage of all types of U.S. centers, according to recent statistics of the Urban Land Institute (Exhibit 10-19). Canadian centers use promotional funds more often than U.S. centers, even though the majority of Canadian centers utilize merchants' associations or have no joint marketing arrangement.

Most of the assessments for the association of the promotional fund are allocated to the tenants on the basis of square feet of GLA leased, but a few centers base their assessments on front footage, percent of sales, or other allocative means. For regional and superregional centers, the department stores usually contribute 20 to 25 percent of the funds raised for the association or promotional fund. Regardless of the type of center, the center management contributes a comparable portion—20 to 25 percent—of the total funds raised.

FLEXIBILITY FOR DEVELOPMENT LATER OF THE EXISTING CENTER

The legal and design bases of the shopping center should provide the flexibility needed for possible future expansion and renovation of the center. The reciprocal easement agreements may have to be expanded to allow for the functioning of new and expanded stores. Leases should provide flexibility in center

Exhibit 10-19.   Frequency of Merchants' Associations/Promotional Funds in U.S. Shopping Centers

Number of Centers in Sample	Superregional 69	Regional 80	Community 234	Neighborhood 316
Centers with merchants' association	98%	95%	58%	22%
Centers with promotional fund	1	3	4	3
Centers with no association	1	2	38	75
Total	100%	100%	100%	100%

Source: Merchants' Associations/Promotional Funds, *Dollars & Cents of Shopping Centers* (Washington, D.C.: Urban Land Institute, Second Printing, 1981), Section H, Table 8H–1, p. 305.

construction and design. For example, dividing partitions may have to be moved as the storeroom dimensions and shape are changed to accommodate more sales and more neighboring merchants. Existing merchants may have to be imposed on in order to develop and construct new storerooms. Customer entranceways may be blocked temporarily; loading docks may be closed temporarily to accomodate storeroom enlargement and new construction. Construction equipment and vehicles may temporarily hinder existing merchant functions and operations. Part of the parking lot may have to be used temporarily for the construction vehicles and equipment. The violations of the various legal agreements of the lease contracts must be amicably managed so that the new development can be accomplished to the betterment of the total center.

The initial design of the center may account for possible future expansion. Temporary roofing systems may accommodate later construction of additional floors of the center buildings. The layout of the storerooms may accommodate the addition of other department store tenants. The plot plan could be flexible enough to accommodate the additions of large retail units that would develop their own "pads" or ask the developer to build for them.

GRAND OPENINGS

The grand opening is the principal event that acquaints the potential customer with the benefits of the center and its convenient location. The unusual amount of marketing makes the grand opening a gala event. The marketing director or center manager wants to involve as many community residents in the trading area as possible in the events planned for the grand opening; the event should offer something for everyone. The planned attractions must bring prospective customers to the center to view for themselves the magnificent assortment of new goods and services.

Part of the developer's problem is the coordination and timing of the construction and furnishing of tenant storerooms so that all merchants may have their doors open for business at the grand opening. Every merchant needs to gain from the initial advertising and promotional extravaganza as much as the developers, the other owners, and the lenders do.

ELEVEN

VALUATION OF
SHOPPING CENTER

Situations arise where the current value of the center is needed. When the developer wishes to finance or refinance the center, the lender will want to know the present value of the proposed collateral for the loan. After the lender views the appraisal, he or she may find what portion of the collateral value is not yet pledged for outstanding obligations. A new loan may be made if sufficient collateral value is available to secure it. A first mortgage or a junior mortgage may be under negotiation.

When the state government decides to reappraise taxable property, the tax appraiser from the county, township, or parish assessor's office will place on the center property a new estimated value. This new value may be called the "fair market value," "appraised value," "assessed value," "market value," or "fair value." The system for tax appraising approved by the state legislature is followed in reappraising the center. On the records, separate values are recorded for the land and the improvements.

If one of the owners of the center dies, the estate of the deceased will be subject to probate or estate settlement. In order to distribute the assets of the estate to the heirs and assigns, all assets must be appraised at their current dollar values, including the equity in the center. The total value of the equity in the center is usually appraised. The equity position or proportional share of the deceased is ascertained, and a value is attributed to that ownership interest. If controversies ensue among the family members and friends of the deceased, more than one appraiser may be asked to estimate the current value of the deceased's ownership interest in the center. Court hearings may take place with statements of value from appraisers of opposing parties. The judge of the particular court may finally decide upon a reasonable value for the ownership interest in the center.

In a similar manner, the center may undergo appraisal as a result of the exercise of the power of eminent domain by a state-approved party. The pursuit of an approved public project may require the taking of land in total or in part from a shopping center tract. The condemning authority must legally pay just compensation to the landowner whose property is acquired voluntarily or involuntarily for the development of the public project, such as the widening of a street or the construction of a state or interstate highway. If the land and improvements are not voluntarily sold to the development authority by the landowner, the authority may condemn the property, estimate a fair market value for the property taken, and pay the landowner this amount. Such condemning authorities either have professionally trained real estate appraisers on their staffs or in their employ on a temporary basis. The landowner may wish to contest the financial settlement, in which case he or she may employ one or more real estate appraisers to estimate the fair market value of the condemned property. In eventual court hearings, the appraisers each may have to testify as to their estimates of current value. The system of analysis for condemnation appraising is different from that of estate settlement appraisal analysis, but the controversial nature of appraised values may seep into the condemnation situation.

Some ground, storeroom, and building leases are revised periodically by reappraisal of the property. If the property value has risen since the original lease terms were negotiated, new lease terms may be drawn up to reflect the inflationary conditions. Usually the landlord and the tenant wish impartial real estate appraisers to reevaluate the premises so that the original lease may be renewed on amicable terms. The reappraisal lease renewal may occur every three to five years. If the reappraisal were commissioned less often, the forces of inflation might cause a sharp rise in the property values during the reappraisal interval. Long reappraisal periods would tend not to give the landlord the desired inflation protection.

Hazard insurance protection is needed for the center. The insurance company representative bases the policy on the risks and values associated with the center. If the insurance company wishes to cover the center, it must first establish the center's current value. Then the premiums may be set for the insured party's payment on an annual or semiannual basis.

If a party wishes to purchase or sell an interest in the center, the value of the center at that time must be estimated. The buyer wants to know what a reasonable bidding price would be, and the seller wants to know what a fair sale price would be. If the seller's offering price is higher than the buyer's bid price, the final negotiated selling price may be a dollar value in between the two. The seller and the buyer may be experienced in real property valuation, but nevertheless they may seek an outside appraisal opinion to refute or substantiate their initial opinions.

USE OF THE THREE APPROACHES TO APPRAISED VALUE

There are three approaches to the appraisal of the center: (1) the cost approach, (2) the market comparison approach, and (3) the income approach. The cost approach requires a depreciated replacement cost new for the center. Contractors who have recently finished comparable centers in nearby urban areas may estimate the current reproduction or replacement cost of the subject. The appraiser may assess the dollars associated with the physical deterioration and the functional and economic obsolescence realized by the subject.

The market comparison approach is based either on grid analysis using recently sold comparable centers or on ratio analysis such as gross income multiplier (GIM) analysis. Since many centers have sold in many parts of the country recently, the market comparison approach may be used by the appraiser in many instances. For example, centers originally belonging to Dayton Hudson, Federated Department Stores, General Growth Properties, Earnest Hahn and Company, and Monumental Properties have recently been sold to domestic and foreign investors. If comparable centers have recently been sold in the general area of the subject, the use of the market comparison approach to value may be extremely significant.

The income approach involves income capitalization or discounting of cash flows. Future revenues and expenses must be estimated. The type of financing used by the typical investor must be ascertained from the marketplace.

Now, let us look at each of these approaches to appraised value in greater detail.

The Cost Approach to Value

The cost of constructing the center today must first be estimated. Then the current depreciation in dollars is subtracted from the reproduction or replacement cost new in order to find the desired depreciated reproduction or replacement cost new.

The real estate appraiser may use several different methods to find the current reproduction or replacement cost. The reproduction cost is the cost of replicating or creating exactly the same building as was originally built. The replacement cost is the cost of creating the same functional utility in the new building as in the original building.

The first method we will consider is the quantity survey method. We take the individual building components such as the brick, each of the sizes of concrete block used, or a length of electrical wiring, and multiply the total cost of the separate item times the number of items used in the building. The total cost associated with each individual component includes the profit and overhead costs of the general contractor and the subcontractor. The total cost for all the items integrated into the completed construction of the finished building is called the reproduction cost. Then the total cost new should be depreciated to reflect the current condition of the subject. Dollar amounts representing the existing physical depreciation and functional and economic obsolescence should be subtracted from the total cost new. The depreciated cost new is the appraiser's value from the cost approach.

Another way to calculate the total cost new is to add the total costs of all of the basic units of the finished building. A unit, for example, might be the heating, ventilating, and air-conditioning system. The total cost of each unit is added to the others to find the total reproduction cost by the unit-in-place method.

Another method of finding the current reproduction cost of the subject is the trade breakdown or segregated cost method. Each of the subcontractor totals used in bidding on the construction of a comparable property today are added to the other subcontractor totals. For example, the total expense associated with the completed work of the plumbing company is added to the total cost submitted by the electrical contractor. The other subcontractor totals are added in with all costs reflecting subcontractor profit and overhead. A total reproduction cost new may be derived by this trade breakdown method.

The most often used method, the market comparison or cost-per-square-foot method, employs estimates of current square footage costs of recently completed construction of comparable structures with similar interior and exterior features and amenities. Local contractors who have recently finished comparable buildings can convey the costs to the appraiser who adjusts the costs received in terms of any unique features of the subject.

Depreciation adjustments for physical, functional, and economic depreciation and obsolescence must reflect current market conditions. The appraiser uses selling price differences recently perceived in the marketplace to identify the dollars of depreciation of the three types that the center currently reflects: physical deterioration, functional obsolescence, and economic obsolescence. Even new shopping centers may indicate elements of depreciation and obsolescence.

Items of depreciation and obsolescence may be curable or incurable. The dollar amount of depreciation may reflect the cost of curing a defect which could be accomplished today. Other forms of depreciation may only be economically curable after the passage of a time interval, such as roof replacement. Roof replacement may be needed every 15 years. The appraisal may be conducted part of the way through the roof's economic life. Some items of depreciation of the center may be economically incurable. The foundation may have settled, and cracks in the concrete foundation may show when storerooms are recarpeted. The defects in the foundation and the "bone structure" (walls holding up the roof and resting on the foundation) of the center usually are considered economically incurable. Once the appraiser has estimated the accrued depreciation and obsolescence, the estimated amount of dollars of depreciation and obsolescence is subtracted from the estimated reproduction cost new in order to derive the value from the cost approach. A brief summary is given in Exhibit 11-1.

Exhibit 11-1. Calculation of Depreciated Reproduction Cost New in Summary

	Cost per Square Foot of GLA	Dollar Amount
Reproduction Cost New		
Land—20 acres at $50,000 an Acre	$ 1.15	$1,000,000
Predevelopment cost (legal, interest, etc.)	1.40	280,000
Improvements—200,000 sq. ft. of GLA	30.00	6,000,000
Architectural and engineering work	1.00	200,000
	$33.55	$7,480,000
Depreciation and obsolescence		
Physical depreciation, 5 percent of cost excluding land cost, $6,480,000	$ 324,000	
Functional obsolescence, 2 percent of cost excluding land cost, $6,480,000	129,600	
Environmental or economic obsolescence—none	—	453,600
Total depreciated reproduction cost new		$7,026,400

The Income Approach to Value

The net operating income can be capitalized into value or the future net cash flows can be discounted into present value in order to find the value from the income approach.

Capitalization of Net Operating Income. Income capitalization is the derivation of value from the net operating income and an appropriate capitalization rate through the use of a formula:

$$\text{Value} = \frac{\text{Stabilized Net Operating Income}}{\text{Capitalization Rate}} \quad \text{or} \quad V = \frac{I}{R}$$

The cash flow analysis from the feasibility study or another profitability study is the usual source of the stabilized net operating income. The capitalization rate can be derived in numerous ways.[*]

The best method of finding the "cap rate" is the use of recent sales prices and the concurrent net operating income from several comparable properties. Perhaps several recent sales of comparable shopping centers may be located where data may be acquired about the net operating income at the time of sale. This derived overall rate may be applied to the stabilized net income of the subject to derive the market value from the income approach to value.

Often a recapture rate is added to the investor's required yield. For example, the typical investor may require a total yield of 16 percent on the invest-

---

[*]*Capitalization Methods & Techniques,* an Educational Memorandum of the American Institute of Real Estate Appraisers of the National Association of Realtors (Chicago: American Institute of Real Estate Appraisers, 1979).

ment in the center. The recapture rate may be a straight-line rate based on the remaining economic life of the center or it may reflect a sinking fund or level annuity rate which assumes investor reinvestment of the periodic returns of capital. The level annuity rate reflects reinvestment at the going market yield. The sinking fund rate reflects reinvestment of the funds periodically set aside for capital recapture at a passbook savings or other conservative rate of interest. If the remaining economic life of the center is assumed to be 30 years, the straight-line recapture rate would be calculated by dividing 100 percent by 30 years which would give 0.033 a year capital recapture.

 If the appraiser assumes that the investor will reinvest the periodic recapture payments at an interest rate equal to the investor's required yield, or 16 percent, the level annuity recapture factor at 16 percent for 30 years would be 0.001886. This factor is found in present value tables for 16 percent in the sinking fund column across from 30 years. If the reinvestment rate was perceived to be more conservative, say, 8 percent, the sinking fund recapture rate for 30 years at 8 percent would be 0.007686. Therefore, depending on the recapture assumption, the appropriate cap rates using the yield recapture method would be

Straight-Line Recapture Assumption (No Reinvestment)		Level Annuity Assumption (Reinvestment at 16%)		Sinking Fund Assumption (Reinvestment at 8%)	
Investor's yield reqt.	0.16	Investor's yield reqt.	0.16	Investor's yield reqt.	0.16
Straight-line recapture rate	0.033	Level annuity recapture rate, 16%	0.001886	Sinking fund recapture rate, 8%, conservative rate	0.007686
Cap rate	0.193	Cap rate	0.161886	Cap rate	0.167686

If the stabilized net operating income were $100,000, the value of the center would vary with the selection of the appropriate capitalization rate.

Straight-line Recapture (No Reinvestment)	Level Annuity Assumption (Reinvestment at 16%)	Sinking Fund Assumption (Reinvestment at 8%)
$V = \dfrac{I}{R} = \dfrac{\$100,000}{0.193}$	$V = \dfrac{I}{R} = \dfrac{\$100,000}{0.161886}$	$V = \dfrac{I}{R} = \dfrac{\$100,000}{0.167686}$
Therefore, $V = \$518,134$	Therefore, $V = \$617,719$	Therefore, $V = \$596,353$

If the real estate appraiser can justify the assumption that the investor will invest the payments from cash flow each period which represent the return of capital at a market rate of interest, say, 16 percent, the value of the center will be the highest. The level annuity cap rate, 0.161886, is the lowest; the straight-line cap rate, 0.193, is the highest. The lower the capitalization rate, the higher the resulting value for the property.

Another method of deriving the cap rate is called the band of investment method. The costs of the various funds invested in the center are weighted and combined into one capitalization rate. An example of the use of this method in a simple appraised valuation for a shopping center may be found in Exhibit 11-2. If the equity represents 40 percent of the total capital, for example, the borrowed funds would represent 60 percent (100%–40%). The current total equity dividend requirement might be 17 percent. The loan constant for typical mortgage financing at a 16 percent rate for 20 years with annual debt service payments is 0.168667. The weighted cost of the funds is found from the band of investment method of deriving the capitalization rate.

Source of Funds	Percentage of Total Capital	Cost of Funds		Weighted Cost
Equity funds	0.40	× 0.17	=	0.068
Mortgage money	0.60	× 0.168667	= +	0.1012
	1.00			0.1692

If the stabilized net operating income is $100,000, the value of the center is $V = I/R$ or $100,000/0.1692 = $591,017$. Other methods of deriving the capitalization rate abound. The appraiser may use the Ellwood formula which incorporates the expected depreciation or appreciation of the center, a mortgage coefficient, and a sinking fund factor.[*] The Ellwood formula and tables may be used when the appraiser has good data from typical investors of comparable shopping centers concerning annual rates of center appreciation over typical holding periods, typical and current mortgage financing terms, and current overall yield requirements of typical investors.[*] The same data are useful for discounted cash flow analysis in the determination of the equity value and the loan value. The total of these two current values equals the present value of the center.

Loan data are available from life insurance industry sources about mortgage terms, including capitalization rates over recent years. The uncertainties and risks of shopping center investment and lending are abstracted into the rates finally used for loans of recent periods. Exhibit 11-3 shows that recent cap rates have tended to lower for the largest commercial retail mortgage loans. The average cap rates have tended to be a little less than the average loan constants. The terms to maturity of the surveyed shopping center loans have tended to decline. The debt coverage ratio has generally approximated 1.20 to 1.35 in

[*]Hines, M. A., *Real Estate Appraisal* (New York: Macmillan Publishing Co., 1981), pp. 292–309.
[*]Ellwood, L. W., *Ellwood Tables for Real Estate Appraising and Financing* (Cambridge, Mass. Ballinger Publishing Company, 1977).

Exhibit 11-2. Valuation of a Shopping Center Using the Band of Investment Method to Find the Capitalization Rate.

Gross Income		
Major tenants 500,000 Square Feet of GLA Average $5.00/sq.ft.		$2,500,000
Other tenants 100,000 Square Feet of GLA Average $15.00/sq.ft.		1,500,000
Total gross income		$4,000,000
Vacancy and bad debt loss		
2% Major tenants (2% of $2,500,000)	$ 50,000	
10% Other tenants (10% of $1,500,000)	150,000	200,000
Effective gross income		$3,800,000
Operating Expenses (25% of EGI)		950,000
Net operating income		$2,850,000

Capitalized value:

$$\frac{NOI}{R} = \frac{\$2,850,000}{0.14169} = \$20,114,334 \text{ or rounded to } \$20,500,000$$

Debt service: 14%—20-year term—5 year call option
             Annual Payments Loan Constant 0.150986
             Loan-to-value ratio: 70%
             Loan amount = 0.70 × $20,500,000 = $14,350,000
             Debt service amount = $14,350,000 × 0.150986 = $2,166,649

Cash flow before taxes:	Net operating income	$2,850,000
	Annual debt service	2,166,649
	Cash flow before taxes	$ 683,351

Calculation of Capitalization Rate (R) Using the Band of Investment Method

Source of Funds	Percent of Funds		Cost of Funds		Weighted Cost
Mortgage	0.70	×	0.150986	=	0.1056902
Equity	0.30	×	0.12	=	0.036
					0.14169

recent years; lenders have tended to require higher debt coverage ratios from the borrowers of the largest shopping center loans.

Mortgage loan data on shopping centers of five or more stores show that average loan-to-value ratios are tending to decline as interest rates and loan constants have been increasing (Exhibit 11-4). The term of the average center loan made by a life insurance company appears to decline as the average loan amount has risen to approximately $6,500,000.

If the value of the center from the income approach is found by discounting cash flows, the appraiser must first ascertain the net cash flows from each period of the expected cash flow stream that belong to the owners and to the lenders. At the end of the holding period, a net cash amount will represent the proceeds from the sale less the current mortgage balance. The equity investor receives the net amount, and the lender's mortgage balance outstanding is paid. If the appraiser does not know the tax status of the center owner, the before-tax net cash flows should be discounted at the investor's before-tax

Exhibit 11-3. Average Mortgage Loan Terms on Commitments of $100,000 and over on Commercial Retail Mortgage Loans

Size of Mortgage Loan	Average Cap Rate			Average Interest Rate			Average Percent Constant			Average Term (Years/Months)			Average Debt Coverage		
	4Q 1981	1Q 1980	1Q 1979	4Q 1981	1Q 1980	1Q 1979	4Q 1981	1Q 1980	1Q 1979	4Q 1981	1Q 1980	1Q 1979	4Q 1981	1Q 1980	1Q 1979
Average	13.7	12.3	10.2	14.93	12.36	9.96	15.5	12.6	11.1	11/7	19/11	21/1	1/36	1.18	1.20
Less than $1 million	*	*	10.4	*	*	10.07	*	*	11.8	*	*	18/9	*	*	1.19
$1 million– $3,999,000	13.5	12.2	10.1	15.38	12.71	9.94	14.6	12.6	11.0	7/3	15/10	21/3	1.38	1.24	1.18
$4 million– $7,999,000	*	12.9	10.3	*	12.1	9.93	*	12.7	11.7	*	26/8	18/4	*	1.08	1.18
$8 million and over	NA	12.1	10.0	NA	11.69	9.99	NA	12.3	10.2	NA	21/0	25/2	NA	1.21	1.29

Source: American Council of Life Insurance.

*Data not shown where there are fewer than three loans.

required rate of return to find the value of the equity. For example, the expected net cash flows might be:

Year	Net Cash Flow before Federal Income Taxes
1	$ 10,000
2	15,000
3	22,000
4	20,000
5	350,000

If the investor's required rate of return is assumed to be 16 percent, these net cash flows can be discounted into the present value of the equity using an income approach.

Year	Net Cash Flow before Federal Income Taxes	Present Value Factor at 16%	Present Value of the Net Cash Flow
1	$ 10,000	0.862069	$ 8,620.69
2	15,000	0.743163	11,147.45
3	22,000	0.640658	14,094.48
4	20,000	0.552291	11,045.82
5	350,000	0.476113	166,639.55
			$211,547.99

When the net cash flows before taxes are discounted at 16 percent, the value of the equity is $211,547.99, or $212,000 rounded off. The present value of the mortgage financing, $400,000, is then added to the value of the equity, $212,000, to obtain the total current property value, $612,000.

Exhibit 11-4. Average Mortgage Loan Terms on Commitments of $100,000 and over on Shopping Centers of Five or More Stores Made by 20 Life Insurance Companies.

	Selected Year		
Mortgage Term	1981	1979	1977
Average capitalization rate	13.0	10.3	9.8
Average interest rate	14.0	10.28	9.27
Average percentage constant	14.5	11.1	10.2
Average debt coverage	1.28	1.26	1.31
Average term (year/month)	13/6	20/8	22/10
Average loan-to-value ratio	69.8	74.3	73.9
Average loan amount ($000,000)	$6.41	$5.73	$5.01

Source: American Council of Life Insurance.

The Effect of Different Capitalization Rates on Property Value. The appraiser is very much aware that, if the capitalization rate increases due to the investment risks and yields required and/or due to the rising cost of debt financing, the appraised value of the center from the income approach will decline. In reverse manner, if the derived cap rate declines, the appraised value will rise. One can see this by assuming a given net operating income and dividing it by assumed cap rates. If the net operating income is $100,000 and the cap rate is 10 percent, the value of the property—$100,000 divided by 0.10—is $1,000,000. But if the net operating income remains at $100,000 and the cap rate increases to 20 percent, the value of the property—$100,000 divided by 0.20—is only $500,000. As the rate increases from 10 to 20 percent, the value declines from $1,000,000 to $500,000.

The Market Comparison Approach

If comparable centers or comparable portions of similar centers have sold recently, the appraiser may compare three or four of the "comparables" to the subject to observe the relative value of the subject.

Land Valuation. If the land needs to be valued, the following units of comparison may be used: sale price per acre, sale price per square foot, and sale price per front foot. The subject land is compared in all differentiating respects to the comparable parcels of land which have sold recently.

Valuation of Land and Improvements. If the improvements and the land must be valued, analysis employing gross income multipliers may be used. The gross income multipliers (GIMs) reflected by the recent sales of comparable properties may suggest the correct multiplier for the subject. An example follows.

Comparable Property	Recent Sale Price	Gross Annual Revenue at the Time of Sale	Gross Income Multiplier
A	$8,500,000	$1,200,000	7.08
B	7,200,000	1,070,000	6.73
C	9,000,000	1,320,000	6.82

If the gross annual revenue of the subject is $1,250,000 and the GIM that most closely fits the characteristics of the subject is 6.8, the value of the subject would be $8,500,000.

Reconciliation of the Three Values from the Three Approaches

The values derived from each of the three approaches—cost, market comparison and income—must be digested into a single value or a range of possible values for the center. The three different values may be rather close to one another. The reconciliation of the three values then may be relatively easy; a single value is chosen which best fits the subject. If the values from the three approaches are rather different, the appraiser may give more weight to one or two of the values than to the third one. The values from the market comparison and the income approaches may be given more significance than the value from the cost approach. A shopping center is usually built so that the owners reap a reward from the market or income value being higher than the cost to develop the center. An example follows.

Value from the Cost Approach	$6,000,000
Value from the Income Approach	7,000,000
Value from the Market Comparison Approach	6,800,000

The appraiser, downplaying the significance of the value from the cost approach, may decide that the center is presently worth $6,800,000.

TWELVE

FINANCING SHOPPING CENTERS IN GENERAL

Financing is a key factor in shopping center development and investment. The creation or development of a new center depends on the financing available. The parties involved analyze all of the financial features to find out if the "numbers will work." Will all parties receive a reasonable return on the funds they must invest? The sale of an existing center depends on the financing available to the buyer. Most center buyers require financing; some do not, but they tend to be in the minority. If the current owner wishes to "unlock some of the equity" in the center, the current financing terms will determine whether advantageous refinancing is possible. If market and sales trends encourage expansion and renovation, current financing is the key to current or delayed changes in the center.

UNIQUE QUALITIES OF SHOPPING CENTER FINANCE

Even though the financing patterns for all types of income properties in the United States tend to be similar, shopping center finance has unique features. Lenders and investors are enticed by the shopping center because it offers inflation protection from percentage net leases that are relatively short in duration. As the prices of consumer goods and services rise with inflation, the overage lease payments received by the landlord rise. There is a trend toward indexed base rents, also. At the end of the year or the initial lease term, the tenant who is a good merchandiser or service unit can afford to enter into a new lease with a higher base rent and, perhaps, higher overage payments because the tenant is profiting from the financial prosperity of the American consumer.

If an individual lessee is not prospering in the inflationary environment of the community, the landlord can replace this tenant quickly because of the relatively short lease term.

Even though the purchase of durable goods such as cars, houses, and household appliances tends to fluctuate widely with the change in economic conditions, purchase of consumer nondurable goods and services tends to be more stable. The shopping center lender and investor can benefit financially from this stability. Cash flows are more stable, and the forecasting of future cash flows is less hazardous than in the case of predominantly durable goods.

The shopping center industry is maturing with a good record of profitability behind it. In the 25 years since the formation of the International Council of Shopping Centers, the industry has exhibited a relatively steady trend of development in comparison with the housing and office building sectors. In housing and office building development, periods of overbuilding have created gluts of space on the market. Shopping center development in the United States has been less speculative. Booms and busts have not generally characterized shopping center development. Not all centers have been profitable, but the industry earnings records have generally pleased lenders and investors.

THE ECONOMY AND THE COST OF MONEY

The U.S. economy continues to be one of the most stable in the world. This conclusion may be reached even though the United States has experienced inflation rates of 10 to 12 percent in the last few years, during the latter 1970s and the early 1980s. Business and economic cycles have occurred in the United States throughout its relatively short history. The rest of the developed nations of the world have also experienced economic and business cycles over their long economic histories, but generally with longer periods between peaks and troughs of adjacent cyclical fluctuations.

Since the Accord of 1954, the U.S. Treasury Department and the Federal Reserve System have pledged to coordinate fiscal and monetary policy for economic stability. The Treasury Department, under the Secretary of the Treasury, is principally responsible for the financing of the federal government and its agencies. Its principal means of financing are (1) the sale of Treasury securities of varying maturities and (2) the taxation of incomes of individuals and business enterprises. The formulation of and the implementation of monetary policy lie mainly with the Federal Reserve System. Since the passage of the Financial Institutions Deregulation Act in 1980, monetary policy has been determined jointly to a degree and implemented by the Federal Reserve System, the Comptroller of the Currency, the Federal Home Loan Bank System, the National Credit Union Administration, the Federal Deposit Insurance Corporation, the Federal Savings and Loan Insurance Corporation, and the Treasury Department.

Disturbing economic fluctuations of the past two decades have prompted recent changes in the administration of monetary and fiscal policy. The alarming recession with inflation of 1979 through 1982 was preceded by similar economic downturns in 1974 through 1975 and 1969 through 1970. These economic downturns took their tolls in terms of unemployment, squeezes on business profits, declines in personal incomes, declines in industrial productivity, negative international balances of payments for the United States and bankruptcies among major American financial institutions and industrial companies.

The instability of the American economy has been partially traced to the overregulation of the financial institutions, partially traced to the lack of flexibility of debt financing, and partially traced to inadequate financing from the money and capital markets. For example, the heavy regulation of the commercial banks and savings and loan associations is being phased out over a period of years during the 1980s. At the same time, the Federal Reserve Board plans to gain better control over monetary conditions. In the debt financing area, congressional and state legislative statutes passed during 1981 permit more flexibility in mortgage financing. For example, new types of variable-rate and shared equity residential mortgages permitted by the legislation may give the mortgage lenders protection against the disastrous effects of inflation. Financing of income properties depends on changes that permit adequate financing from the money and capital markets. For example, needed changes are beginning to occur in the secondary mortgage market. Home-improvement and seller-financing loans can now be sold to the secondary mortgage market under new programs. (The trading of existing mortgages is accommodated by the secondary mortgage market.) A subsidiary of the Mortgage Guaranty Insurance Corporation is acting as a private secondary mortgage institution for the trading of all kinds of mortgage loans, particularly mortgages insured by private companies or government agencies. Such money and capital market changes give more liquidity to mortgage lenders and more stability to the mortgage market and the economy.

THE MORTGAGE MARKET OVER THE PAST 20 YEARS

Since the early 1960s, the United States mortgage market has experienced major changes. In the decade of the 1960s, mortgage lenders and borrowers negotiated variable-rate mortgages for income properties including shopping centers. The debt service was periodically recalculated by the lender and paid by the mortgagor on the basis of an established number of points above the base rate which was the floating New York bank prime or commercial paper rate. Therefore, if the mortgage rate floated two points above the bank prime rate and the bank prime rate was 14 percent at the end of the payment period, the next mortgage payment would be calculated by the lender at 16 percent. In

1979 and 1980, mortgage lenders of state and federally chartered financial institutions started underwriting variable-rate mortgages for one- to four-family residential units. Today, many single-family residential mortgages have variable rates. The lending community and their regulators state that the current and future mortgage markets are oriented significantly to that type of mortgage on residential as well as commercial properties.

Long-Term, Uninsured Mortgage Loans

Long-term mortgage loans have been in vogue for commercial and residential properties since World War II. The 30-year level-payment fully amortized residential mortgage began with the Housing Act of 1934, which called for such mortgages and the establishment of the Federal Housing Administration to administer the mortgage insurance program. The few shopping center mortgages covered by FHA mortgage insurance were neighborhood centers integral to the success of FHA-insured mortgages for adjacent low- and moderate-income housing projects. These centers were minor developments of the major housing projects.

Flexible Shopping Center Mortgage Terms
Preclude Active Secondary Mortgage Market

Over the last 20 years, the provisions of shopping center mortgages have been flexibly negotiated between the mortgagees (lenders) and the mortgagors (borrowers). The mortgage terms open to negotiation have been:

Contract interest rate	Prepayment provisions
Interest-only period	Nature of the equity participation
Basis for the floating rate	Nature of the lender's purchase option
Term of the loan	Loan-to-value ratio
Call provision	
Full or partial amortization with a balloon payment possible	

The individually negotiated features of shopping center mortgages and the absence of mortgage insurance have precluded active trading of shopping center mortgages in a secondary mortgage market.

High Degree of Leverage

The majority of shopping center deals have been highly leveraged in the past. Multiple mortgages have financed centers so that many developers have mortgaged out. Mortgage monies have equaled or exceeded development costs of the owner who has often been the development company. The developer found that the center cash flows could financially support the multiple mortgages since very little equity participation was required by the lender until the 1970s. Equity participation became increasingly significant during this decade. The payment of multiple mortgages became increasingly costly.

Effects of Changes in Federal Tax Laws on Mortgage Lending

The tax laws affecting mortgage lending and real estate investment have changed dramatically during the last 20 years. The real estate investment trust (REIT) was created by the tax laws of 1960. These tax-exempt lending and investing institutions have financed various phases of various shopping center developments since 1961. The tax laws related to pension fund investments are being changed to make tax exempt the pension fund income from income-producing real properties. Then the pension fund managers will be more willing to invest a larger portion of their funds in such assets. Currently their income from stocks and bonds is tax exempt.

The tax position of savings and loan associations is gradually being increased to the level of the tax position of some of their competing institutions. Over the phase-in period, less and less of their reserves for losses may be deducted from otherwise taxable net income. At the same time, the taxpaying financial institutions are subjected to decreasing federal corporate income taxation. Corporate income tax rates, particularly for firms with smaller net profit positions, are gradually being reduced. Details can be observed in Chapter 15.

As of the passage of the Economic Recovery Act of 1981, the depreciation methods for real and personal property are favorable to increased investment in centers. The investment tax credit applied to an income property may be as high as 10 percent. The renovation of older buildings for later commercial use justifies substantial tax credits for the investor. Preservation of historical buildings is encouraged by income tax legislation. The maximum rate applicable to investment income or earned income through salaries and wages has been set at 50 percent. The maximum rate applied to investment income was earlier 70 percent.

When an owner wishes to sell or liquidate an income property investment, the tax laws remain favorable to long-term capital gains. To defer income taxation, the seller may negotiate an installment sale or arrange for an exchange of real properties. The prospective seller may refinance the center before putting it up for sale. In this manner, the purchase will require less equity from the buyer and the seller may take tax-free cash out of the property before the sale is consummated. Refinancing before the sale is particularly easy to get if the center has increased in value since the original mortgages were placed on the property and the current level of the outstanding mortgage indebtedness has been paid down to a relatively low level. The refinancing also increases the amount of mortgage interest that may be deducted for federal income tax purposes.

The Usefulness of the Secondary Mortgage Market

The secondary mortgage market of the last 20 years has generally not involved the trading of commercial nonresidential loans. The shopping center loans that have been purchased by the government-affiliated secondary mortgage market have been centers financed in big residential project loans where the small centers were an integral part of the newly developed community. Otherwise, the trading of shopping center loans is accomplished through private channels unrelated to the Federal National Mortgage Association, the Federal Home Loan Mortgage Corporation, or the Government National Mortgage Association. Most of these loans have been funded by the original mortgage lender, who negotiated with the shopping center owner-developer as construction plans became final, and have been held until maturity. An active secondary market for shopping center and other nonresidential mortgage loans has never materialized in the private or public sector.

The government-affiliated secondary mortgage market involving FNMA, FHLMC, and GNMA has been useful to lenders wishing to make shopping center loans or wishing to purchase participations in shopping center loans. The secondary market institutions have been available for lender sale of their approved residential loans. In this way lenders have gained liquidity; these newly acquired funds could be placed in shopping center loans as such advantageous lending opportunities arose. The yields on shopping center and other commercial property loans have ranked higher over time than yields of most residential loans; the percentage rent and equity participation clauses have generally afforded the lender higher yields than those on multifamily or other types of commercial and industrial mortgages. With the liquidity from approved residential loans, even local savings and loan associations and commercial banks could invest in small center loans and participate in larger center loans.

Tax-Exempt Financing

During the latter part of the 1970s, tax-exempt financing of commercial development became common. New business enterprise and the expansion of existing businesses were encouraged by many local and state governments through industrial development financing on a tax-exempt basis. These tax-exempt funds raised by industrial development authorities on a revenue bond basis reduced the cost of funds to the shopping center owner-developer. The cost of mortgage money might be found to be three percentage points or 300 basis points cheaper than money acquired at current market rates for the development. (A basis point is one one-hundredth of a percent or 0.0001; that represents one ten-thousandth of the integer one.)

Some of the tax-exempt municipal financing was associated with Urban Development Action Grants where cities encouraged redevelopment or development of areas of proven poverty levels. If the center developer would show the anticipated future employment of poverty-level, currently unemployed residents of the poverty area, the future increased levels of sales to the local community and the subsequent increase in sales and income tax receipts, and the need for tax-exempt funds to make the development possible, the local city government could arrange for the sale of a municipal bond issue and/or a HUD grant for the development of the center.

The Cost of Commercial Mortgage Money During the Past 20 Years

In terms of nominal or contract interest rates, the rates on commercial mortgages more than doubled over the last 20 years during the 1960s and 1970s. The rates in the early 1960s approximated 6 percent, and they exceeded 12 percent by 1979. Over that period, taking into account inflation in the United States, this contract rate in real terms declined to even a negative amount by the mid-1970s. In other words, at 12 percent lenders were losing money on their investments. By 1981, long-term mortgage rates on income properties surpassed 14 percent and, therefore, the current rate of inflation that approximated 12 to 13 percent.

As the lenders noticed this gradual erosion of purchasing power in the use of the fixed-rate commercial mortgage, they added inflation protection features such as "floating" interest rates and equity participation. Originally the rates were permitted to "float" over the bank prime rate or the commercial paper rate. Later in this period, the rate "floated" over an index comprised of various market short- and long-term rates or other individual market rates viewed as more reflective of mortgage market conditions.

Equity participation has meant various things to various people. After receiving their mortgage interest based on the contract fixed rate, the lenders may receive extra income from a percentage of the gross revenues in total, the gross revenues over a base amount, the net operating income, or cash flow before taxes. As a reminder of the origins of these various balances, we may note Exhibit 12-1, Derivation of Cash Flow and Taxable Income. The real estate investor usually wishes to know the cash flow before and after taxes and the investor's tax position. If the shopping center investment has a tax shelter aspect, the investor's taxable income will be negative at least one of the tax periods. In Exhibit 12-1, the cash flow before and after taxes and the taxable net income are positive. After the payment of federal income taxes at an assumed overall rate of 50 percent, the owners would jointly pocket $868,560. The lenders would receive a total of $1,809,280 in fixed-rate debt service and equity participation.

THE MORTGAGE MARKET IN THE 1980s

A forecaster's job is always a difficult one. The economic patterns established in the United States in recent years, though, tend to make a forecaster's job

Exhibit 12-1.   Derivation of Cash Flow and Taxable Income.

Gross revenues ($8 a Square Foot for 500,000 Square Feet)		$4,000,000
Less: Vacancy and bad debt loss		
Majors: credit tenants	3% (80% of GLA)	
Locals: noncredit tenants	12% (20% of GLA)	
0.03 × 0.80 = 0.024		
	0.12 × 0.20 = 0.024	
.048 × $4,000,000		192,000
Effective gross income		$3,808,000
Less: operating expenses (20% of effective gross income)		
(cash operating expenses including *ad valorem* taxes)		761,600
Net operating income		$3,046,400
Less: Annual debt service (loan remaining $10,000,000)		
Current debt service: Floating rate basis		
($10,000,000 × 0.15 loan constant)		1,500,000
Cash flow before lender participation (equity participation)		$1,546,400
Lender participation in the cash flow, 20%		309,280
Cash flow before taxes for owners (cash throwoff)		$1,237,120
Less: Federal income tax payment (overall 50% rate assumed)		368,560
Cash flow after taxes (spendable income)		$ 868,560

Calculation of Taxable Income

Net operating income			$3,046,400
Less: Depreciation (200% declining balance method, economic life 40 years)			
current depreciable base, $10,000,000; rate, 5%		$ 500,000	
Less: Mortgage interest			
Fixed-rate debt service	$1,500,000		
Lender participation	309,280	1,809,280	2,309,280
Taxable net income			$ 737,120
Federal income taxes at 50% overall rate			368,560
After-tax income			$ 368,560

easier. The continuing high level of inflation seems to have enough momentum behind it that we foresee at least 6 to 7 percent inflation per year during the 1980s. The level of inflation may even be higher if conflicts around the world require more U.S. financial and military aid than is already being given. High levels of inflation have always been associated with wartime conditions.

Deregulation of commercial banks, savings and loan associations, mutual savings banks, and credit unions—which engage in mortgage lending—has started as the decade opens. The federally sponsored deregulation is currently being implemented by a gradual plan. While the financial institutions are permitted more competition with each other, the federal monetary policy makers are attempting to get better control over monetary conditions. The financial institutions need more inflation protection which should be derived from less government regulation. More competition among institutions will probably result in the demise of some lending institutions and the expansion of other lending institutions. One of the results that may be forecast is the increased competition for commercial mortgage yields. During the past 20 years, the yield competition for mortgages has been intense in the money and capital markets. The intensity of this yield competition will probably increase as the traditional lenders are given permission to devise other competitive investment instruments in order to attract funds. For example, the yields on savings accounts of banks and savings and loans, with complete deregulation and the demise of Regulation Q, will probably rise to competitive levels. At that time, mortgage yields will have to be advantageous or the traditional mortgage lenders with their new investment freedom will shift their investments normally devoted to residential and commercial mortgages to stocks, bonds, and other negotiable and nonnegotiable instruments.

Changes in Flows of Funds

The competition among financial institutions may change the overall flows of money and capital market funds. In recent years, for example, monies have been flowing out of commercial banks, savings and loans, mutual savings banks, and credit unions and into money market funds sold by stock brokerage firms and into pension funds and term life insurance policies. "Intermediation" rather than "disintermediation" has been going on as investors and businesses have placed their funds in the hands of financial institutions who invest the funds for them using their specialized investment skills. But the "intermediation" or investment of funds by financial intermediaries has resulted in a shift in capital flows and a shift in traditional investment patterns. The funds placed in money market funds are usually invested in short-term, relatively liquid securities such as commercial paper and certificates of deposit.

The insurance companies and industrial firms normally invest pension funds in stocks and bonds of companies headquartered in the United States and abroad and in long-term securities offered by governments at home and abroad. Life insurance companies historically invest the monies in their general accounts in numerous forms of securities including construction and development loans and commercial mortgages. Therefore, life insurance companies have been major sources of commercial mortgage money.

Pension funds have historically invested only 1 to 2 percent of their huge portfolios in real estate and real estate interests; these investments often take the form of commercial mortgages. With the recent passage of legislation that requires further diversification of pension fund portfolios, these institutions are forecast to become important sources of real estate investment and mortgage monies during the 1980s. The terms of commercial mortgages and the circumstances of real estate investment may give the pension funds and the life insurance companies (who invest their own funds as well as the funds of pension fund clients) the inflation protection, portfolio diversification, and yield that they seek.

The flows of funds will return to the thrift institutions and the commercial banks when they are able to give competitive investment returns on the deposits made. Until that time, the mortgage market will *not* be supported by these traditional mortgage lenders with the needed volumes of funds. The mortgage market will be financed by the lenders who have the necessary funds and who wish to purchase commercial mortgages with competitive yields. The decision making with regard to pension funds is normally based on the tax exemption of their investment returns. Life insurance companies have normally not been subject to a federal income tax burden as high as that of the thrift institutions and commercial banks. Therefore, the institutional decision making about competitive investment yields takes on a new dimension in the 1980s.

The Effect of Inflation on Debt Finance

If the mortgage lenders have to pay competitive returns on the investments of their depositors, insured parties, and pension fund contributors, they must realize inflation-protected yields on their mortgage investments. As the cost of money changes with inflation, the mortgage yields must change. Therefore, analysts expect underwriting of variable-rate or "floating rate" commercial mortgages to continue. The risk/return relationship of each mortgage may be reviewed frequently. This review will probably result in relatively short mortgages for the permanent financing of commercial development or call provisions in mortgages with long-term amortization. Since the pension funds and the insurance companies will have increasing sums to invest over time, these investors may wish to take larger equity positions and reduced debt positions. They seek inflation protection and investment outlets involving large sums of money placed for relatively long periods.

THIRTEEN

SOURCES OF SHOPPING CENTER FUNDS AND THEIR REQUIREMENTS

Financial institutions, industrial corporations, individuals, and groups of individuals and businesses finance shopping centers. They may loan money or they may take ownership interests. The source may loan money and, at the same time, become an owner of the center, or the source of funds may take an ownership interest without loaning any money.

GENERAL CONDITIONS RELATED TO THE SOURCES OF FUNDS

When monies are loaned to the center owner, the lender may prefer to loan on a first mortgage or trust deed basis. The regulations to which the lender is subject may specify only first mortgage lending. On the other hand, the regulations over the lender may permit a first or junior mortgage interest of any degree of subordination. That source of funds may consider the distinguishing investment characteristics among first, second, and third mortgage lien positions. Higher risk assumption and loan subordination may be associated with higher yields for the investor. Some lenders can aggressively pursue higher risk investments while other people or institutions do not seek higher risk or their government regulations do not permit it.

The pattern of center ownership is changing. Historically, the shopping center department stores have been owned and operated by the department stores themselves. Sometimes the developer or center owner has owned the buildings of the anchor tenants and has left the operation of these department stores to the merchandising companies. Usually the developer, the development company, a joint venture, or a limited partnership with the developer as general partner owned and leased the mall buildings to the mall tenants. The developer or a joint venture often has developed the center and constructed the buildings, perhaps including the department store buildings to their specifications. Today some of the major financial institutions are developing and constructing shopping centers for their own accounts. The life insurance company in particular, for its own account or for its pension fund accounts, is acting as its own developer. This is forecasted by many to become more prevalent in the future as more shopping centers are needed and as mortgage monies are becoming more scarce and more costly. In like manner, as public and private limited partnerships accumulate more investible funds, they may wish to develop and hold centers for their own account. One or more general partners of the group may act as the developer for the group.

The changes in investment patterns are not exclusive of foreign investors. Foreign investors, during the early and mid-1970s, bought existing centers or employed an American developer to put together a shopping center for them. As we entered the 1980s, the foreign investors had gained enough expertise in the United States that they were developing U.S. centers for their own accounts.

SOURCES OF CONSTRUCTION AND DEVELOPMENT LOANS

The main source of construction and development loans is the *commercial bank*. The commercial loan departments of most commercial banks have become very familiar with construction lending. The loans are not collateralized with real estate since the real estate does not exist but is being created. Therefore, the commercial loan department handles these loans rather than the mortgage department, division, or company.

Savings and loan associations and *mutual savings banks* may provide construction and development loans for shopping centers particularly when they are financing the permanent loans. The *real estate investment trust*, particularly in the form of the mortgage trust, has made millions of dollars available for construction and development loans on income-producing properties in the past. The trust may have the authority and the monies to fund construction and development loans even for the sizable shopping center. The *life insurance companies* entered construction lending for income properties in the late 1970s. This has been a part of their recent diversification within the real estate and mortgage sectors of the economy.

SOURCES OF PERMANENT MORTGAGE LOANS

The majority of the financial institutions may provide permanent financing for the shopping center. The institutions with the most constraints on the amount of funds invested in a single project would cater to the financing of the smaller centers or participate in larger mortgage loans with some institutions. The savings and loan associations and the mutual savings banks would tend to fall into this group. The commercial bank can usually provide permanent financing for the center but usually prefers to avoid it because of their liquidity and reserve requirements. Pension funds, endowment funds, foundations, and life insurance companies have provided most of these monies historically. Finance companies particularly have catered to the financing of junior mortgage loans on residential and smaller income properties. Financial subsidiaries of industrial corporations, such as General Electric Credit Corporation, have provided first and junior mortgage loan funds for income properties for a number of years. They have been supplementary sources of long-term mortgage funds rather than primary sources as the life insurance companies and pension funds have been. In the heyday of the REITs, most of the trusts provided sizable amounts of long-term mortgage monies to developers of all kinds of income properties; the profitable and active trusts today do considerable permanent financing of income properties. Credit unions usually prefer not to permanently finance income properties because of the lack of the necessary funds and their preferences for short-term loans. Off-shore investors may finance permanent loans on any income property in the United States; the investment depends upon their preferences, their regulations abroad, and their cash flow positions.

In summary, the usual sources of permanent financing are:

Saving and loan associations and mutual savings banks (smaller centers usually)
Pension funds, endowment funds, and foundations
Life insurance companies
Financial subsidiaries of industrial corporations
Finance companies (smaller junior mortgage loans)
Real estate investment trusts
Offshore investors

SOURCES OF EQUITY FUNDS

The life insurance company, the pension fund, the joint venture, and the public or private limited partnership have historically invested in the ownership of the center of any dimension. The life insurance company and the pension fund have often entered into purchase-leasebacks with the developer. Individuals and business entities have often engaged in the full or partial ownership of the center. Individuals may combine under the syndicate or partnership relationship. If some individuals and businesses want limited legal and financial liability, often the limited partnership or syndicate is set up. The other owners may act as the general partners of the limited partnership. The partnership entity may be a joint venture for the single project. Usually the syndicate has a single general partner. The REIT and the offshore investor may take a direct ownership position or these parties may finance purchase-leasebacks.

Recently equity funds have been established for real estate investment by life insurance companies, commercial banks, and other real estate intermediaries. Many clients contribute monies to the equity fund or separate account, and the underlying financial sponsor invests the monies for the group of clients. Many of these investments by equity funds have found their way into shopping center ownership and finance. More will be said about this topic later.

To summarize, the following are sources of equity funds for shopping centers:

> Life insurance companies, general and separate accounts
> Pension funds
> Joint ventures
> Public or private limited partnerships
> Real estate syndicates
> Developers and their development companies
> Real estate investment trusts
> Offshore investors
> Equity funds sponsored by banks, life insurance companies, and other real estate companies

UNIQUE CHARACTERISTICS OF THE CHIEF SHOPPING CENTER LENDERS AND INVESTORS

Each of the chief sources of funds for the shopping center has its own unique characteristics. These unique characteristics are subject to change, particularly since the financial reform legislation of 1979 and 1980 was passed by Congress and signed into law by the president. Let us, therefore, examine more closely the shopping center lending and investing practices of the commercial bank, the thrift institution, the pension fund, the life insurance company, the real estate investment trust, the equity funds, the syndicate, the limited partnership, and the offshore investor.

The Commercial Bank

Commercial banks are vital institutions in the financing of shopping centers of all sizes and types. The developer can aid the commercial bank, and the bank can aid the shopping center developer. Usually the bank is a source of construction money; maybe its mortgage company will locate the permanent lender for the center. The commercial bank may act as a lender and, at the same time, as an investor in the form of a joint venture partner. One or more commercial banks may be needed for the successful financing of the small, medium, or large shopping center.

The Commercial Bank as an Investor. The bank's commercial loan department may offer construction money once a permanent takeout or its substitute is presented. The substitution may be a gap loan or a standby permanent loan commitment. The appraisal for the center will be studied along with the feasibility analysis, market studies, tenant lease commitment letters, and other parts of the loan prospectus. The construction loan finally offered may represent total costs of development. Recent construction loans for approximately 75 percent of appraised value have paid all or a majority of the developer's construction costs.

If the developer does not have in-house mortgage brokers or other mortgage brokers associated with him or her on a continuing basis, the developer may request the services of the bank's mortgage company or department. Most commercial banks have established or bought mortgage companies during the past 10 years, if not before. The mortgage bankers and brokers affiliated with the bank usually have correspondent lenders and investors who have need for sound, inflation-protected shopping center mortgages. (Mortgage bankers originate, sell, and service mortgages while mortgage brokers merely originate mortgages and sell them to investors without retaining the loan servicing.) The shortest way to find a permanent lender or an appropriate group of investors for a limited partnership or joint venture may be to contact a bank related mortgage company. They maintain working relationships over the years with numerous lenders and investors and constantly seek new investor-correspondents. As the new contacts are made, the potential lender-correspondents indicate the types of mortgages and other investment situations they are seeking.

A few commercial banks still have affiliated real estate investment trusts. These REITs may have the money on the right terms for less traditional investments. Many bank REITs have been chartered to offer junior mortgage financing, gap loans, standby commitments, sale-leaseback deals, joint venture participation, and direct sole property ownership. The developer may wish to tap this bank source of funds.

If an agency of the local or state government floats municipal bonds to help finance the shopping center, the local commercial bank will be one of the first clients to be interested in the purchase of these bonds. Bank portfolios are generously filled with tax-exempt municipal bonds. More often than not, the municipal bond financing for the center will be tax exempt for federal income tax purposes. As the investment banking firm markets the bonds, they may consider private placement with a commercial bank rather than a public offering of the bonds. By means of a private placement, the bank may be able to negotiate in advance of the bond issuance their preferences for the bond terms. The bank may be in a position to ask for a little higher yield in return for reduction of investment banking flotation expense accomplished by means of the private placement.

The bank has some vested interests with respect to a center of substantial size and community impact. The bank will want to be represented at the center. It may want a small location on the interior mall along with a corner site for a regular branch building with drive-in service or a nonmanned satellite branch. A bank branch or two at this shopping center location may serve the local residents and business customers coming and going from the center and the merchants and employees doing business in the center. Deposits can be taken, services rendered, and loans negotiated easily at this well-located site. The bank appreciates the fact that the shopping center is a good traffic generator.

The merchants in the center, the developer, as well as other parties associated with the center will need checking accounts for the processing of payroll and other operating expenses. The check clearing service of a local commercial bank is needed by the new and existing businesses attracted to the center.

Regulation and Portfolio Composition in General. Because of the supervision of the nationally chartered commercial bank by the Federal Reserve, the Comptroller of the Currency, and the Federal Deposit Insurance Corporation, national banks have a low percentage of their portfolio committed to intermediate- and long-term mortgage loans. The same thing is generally true for state-chartered banks which are subject to regulation and supervision by the state department of financial institutions and the Federal Deposit Insurance Corporation. Their need for a high level of liquidity for the maintenance of reserves precludes a high-level commitment to longer-term loans of any kind, secured or unsecured. The profitability of a shopping center mortgage might attract their attention, but the commercial banker usually has to settle for the short-term, high-yield construction and development loans. They have learned to control the risks of construction and development loans and benefit from the quick turnover and high yield of these loans.

In pursuing their threefold objectives—safety, liquidity, and profitability—the commercial bankers hold relatively low-risk and relatively short-term Treasury securities, federal agency securities, and municipal bonds. Their investment portfolios epitomize liquidity and safety. To gain profit for the bank's many stockholders, the commercial bank makes relatively short-term loans to ultimate consumers, other financial institutions, businesses, and government entities. The commercial bank tends to be a chief source of financing for the mortgage company, the finance company, and the real estate investment trust.

Since it serves the Federal Reserve Board in the implementation of monetary policy and the U.S. Treasury in the implementation of fiscal policy, the commercial bank is permitted to deduct justifiable loan loss reserves from its otherwise taxable income. In this way, the commercial bank is not subject to the total impact of the corporate federal and state income tax laws even though it is a private corporation. All financial institutions, which are regulated by the government on one level or another, are sheltered totally or partially from corporate income taxation.

Joint Venture Partners. Joint ventures for shopping centers often have commercial banks as venture partners. As a partner, the bank usually contributes the construction and development monies. That may be the commercial bank's only financing role. A yield higher than the construction loan yield may be forthcoming as the partners each benefit in the participation in the equity from the operating center. In a joint venture, the bank often joins with the developer, a life insurance company, and perhaps a pension fund. While the life insurance company provides the intermediate-term monies and perhaps some equity, the pension fund invests in the permanent loan and may provide equity. If the commercial bank provides equity, it would probably originate from the bank's trust department from unrestricted funds or the bank-sponsored real estate investment trust.

Thrift Institutions—Savings and Loan Associations and Savings Banks

The thrift institutions—savings and loan associations and mutual savings banks—account for approximately one-fourth of the commercial mortgage debt outstanding (Exhibit 13-1). In comparison, commercial banks and life insurance companies each account for approximately 30 percent of the commercial mortgage debt.

The savings and loan association provides about three-fourths of the commercial mortgage money per year emanating from the two thrift institutions which recently totaled $63 billion (Exhibit 13-2). While the nonresidential mortgage debt per year of the S&L industry has steadily climbed to $44 billion, most of this money has gone into loans on permanent site improvements rather than into loans on land (Exhibit 13-2). More than half of the portfolio holdings of commercial mortgage debt represent construction loans for nonresidential structures; the rest represents permanent first and junior mortgage financing of nonresidential real estate (Exhibit 13-3). The S&L holdings of commercial mortgage loans have declined markedly since 1978. This portion of the portfolio reached a peak of $110 billion in that year. The portfolio holdings of commercial mortgage loans of mutual savings banks have declined but far less significantly from the peak year of 1979 (Exhibit 13-4). In the peak year they contributed $17.3 billion to the commercial mortgage market.

The Operating Conventions and Regulations of the Savings and Loan Association. The savings and loan association has been labeled a "thrift institution" because most depositors are saving so that they may finance a house. The S&L encourages personal, business, and government thrift or saving in order to consume on a higher scale later. The S&L takes demand and time deposits of individuals, businesses, and government organizations and invests these funds mainly in residential mortgages. The Internal Revenue Service has encouraged

Exhibit 13-1.   Commercial Mortgage Debt Outstanding (in millions of dollars, at end of period)

Holder	1978	1981	1982
All holders	$211,851	$279,096	$294,641
Major financial institutions			
Commercial banks	66,115	90,717	100,269
Mutual savings banks	16,319	17,150	15,200
Savings and loan associations	40,461	46,691	47,557
Life insurance companies	62,232	88,991	92,322
Federal and related agencies			
Farmers Home Administration	101	506	377
Mortgage pools or trusts*			
Farmers Home Administration	3,560	6,161	7,011
Individuals and others†	22,883	28,880	31,905

Source: Table 1.55, Mortgage Debt Outstanding. *Federal Reserve Bulletin*, May 1981, p. A39; March 1982, p. A41; March 1983, p. A41.
*Outstanding principal balances of mortgages backing securities insured or guaranteed by the agency indicated.
†Other holders include mortgage companies, real estate investment trusts, state and local credit agencies, state and local retirement funds, noninsured pension funds, credit unions, and U.S. agencies for which amounts are small or separate data are not readily available.

Exhibit 13-2.   Nonresidential Mortgage Debt Held by All Operating Savings and Loan Associations by Type of Property (in Millions of Dollars)*

End of Year and Quarter	Total	Nonresidential Mortgage Debt		
		Total	Land	Other
1972[†]	$206,182	$18,721	$1,814	$16,907
1973[†]	231,733	21,876	2,294	19,582
1974[†]	249,301	24,506	2,643	21,863
1975[†]	278,590	29,140	3,064	26,076
1976[†]	323,005	33,786	3,392	30,394
1977	381,163	37,964	4,002	33,962
1978				
March	392,418	38,771	4,120	34,651
June	407,940	39,447	4,324	35,123
September	420,934	39,989	4,420	35,569
December	432,808	40,641	4,458	36,183
1979				
March	441,358	40,958	4,590	36,368
June	456,544	41,956	4,839	37,117
September	468,307	43,038	5,058	37,980
December	475,797	43,773	5,281	38,492
1980				
March	479,078	43,740	5,366	38,374
June	481,184	43,980	5,437	38,543
September	491,895	44,271	5,460	38,811
December	502,812	45,253	5,531	39,722
1981				
March	507,152	45,694	5,680	40,014
June	514,803	46,435	5,920	40,515

Source: *Federal Home Loan Bank Board Journal Annual Report 1980*, Vol. 14, No. 4, p. 107, and March, 1982, Vol. 15, No. 3, p. 113, Table S.4.7.
*Distribution is estimated primarily on the basis of data reported semiannually by FSLIC-insured associations.
[†]Data for the indicated period reflect an increase in total mortgage balances caused by an addition of newly organized associations, or a decrease caused by conversion or merge into mutual savings banks or by liquidation.

Exhibit 13-3.   Commercial Mortgage Loan Activity of Savings and Loan Associations (in Millions of Dollars)

| | | FSLIC-Insured Associations | | |
| | | | Loans Closed for the Purpose of: | |
Period	All Operating Associations' Total Loans	Total	Construction of Nonresidential Structures	Purchase of Nonresidential Real Estate
1977	$107,368	$105,287	$2,252	$1,908
1978	110,294	108,273	2,168	1,676
1979	100,546	98,730	2,106	1,430
1980	72,537	71,270	1,979	1,265
1981	53,283	52,333	2,263	1,223
1982				
January	2,369	2,327	161	201

Source: Table S.4.5., Mortgage Loan Activity of Savings and Loan Associations. *Federal Home Loan Bank Board Journal Annual Report 1980*, April 1981, Vol. 14, No. 4, p. 106, and March 1982 Vol. 15, No. 3, p. 48.

Exhibit 13-4.   Commercial Mortgage Loans of Mutual Savings Banks (in Millions of Dollars, at End of Period)

Year/Quarter	Total Mortgage Debt Outstanding	Total Commercial Mortgage Debt Outstanding
1978	$ 95,157	$16,529
1979	98,908	17,340
1980	99,827	17,180
1981	100,000	17,150
1982	294,641	15,200

Source: Table 1.55, Mortgage Debt Outstanding. *Federal Reserve Bulletin*, May 1981, p. A39; March 1982, p. A41; March 1983, p. A41.

this practice through tax regulations. A portfolio heavily laden with single- and multifamily mortgages has resulted in the lowest federal income tax incidence. The financial reform of 1978–1982 gives the S&L new asset and liability powers for future changes in institutional operations.

Historically, the federally chartered S&L has been regulated and supervised by the Federal Home Loan Bank Board and the Federal Savings and Loan Insurance Corporation. The state-chartered associations have been regulated by the appropriate state department of financial institutions and the Federal Savings and Loan Insurance Corporation since most state-chartered S&L wish federal insurance coverage of their deposits. With the financial reform of 1978 the reserves of this depository institution will be subject to control of the Federal Home Loan Bank Board and by a federal financial committee of which the Federal Reserve Board is a member.

The Current Status of the S&L as a Commercial Mortgage Lender. The S&L is tending to finance business more and to finance purchasers of residential real estate less. In light of the financial reform, they are tending to invest in higher yielding mortgages whose yields are protected against the inroads of inflation. In addition to variable-rate home and apartment project mortgages, they tend to view favorably construction and development loans for shopping centers and other commercial properties and variable-yield shopping center loans of intermediate term with equity participation.

Currently many savings and loans are merely trying to stay solvent as their funds costs, particularly the current cost of money market certificates, are higher than their average mortgage portfolio yield. Because of the money market competition, the large deposits over $100,000 move quickly in and out of financial institutions, including the savings and loans. Many are seeking, therefore, the protection and aid of the Federal Home Loan Bank Board and the Federal Savings and Loan Insurance Corporation to maintain even a low amount of equity while trying to underwrite as many variable-rate, relatively short-term renegotiable loans as possible. Little shopping center financing is expected from them in the near term, even on a participation basis.

The Operating Conventions and Regulations of the Mutual Savings Banks. Since the vast majority of mutual savings banks are state chartered, they are primarily subject to the regulation and supervision of the appropriate state department. Since most of the deposits of savings banks are insured individually up to $100,000, that insurance protection comes from the Federal Deposit Insurance Corporation or state-chartered savings bank insurance corporations. Most of the savings banks are located in the Northeast and Middle Atlantic states. Since most of the state insurance agencies for mutual savings bank deposits are located in the Northeast, most savings banks deposits are covered by the state agencies. The Federal Deposit Insurance Corporation primarily insures deposits of commercial banks, but it insures sizable sums of savings bank deposits. The insurance coverage gives these insurance corporations the right to regulate and supervise the insured savings banks.

The Current Status of the Savings Bank as a Commercial Mortgage Lender. As thrift institutions, the savings banks historically have divided the majority of their portfolios between industrial corporation bonds and mortgages. Most of the mortgages have been residential in nature and insured by the Federal Housing Administration or private mortgage insurance companies or guaranteed by the Veterans Administration. As a part of their bond portfolios, the savings banks, like the savings and loans, have purchased GNMA-guaranteed mortgage-backed securities.

Commercial mortgage debt has been permitted for investment by the state regulators and the deposit insurance corporations. In the late 1970s, this commercial mortgage debt amounted to approximately $17 billion (Exhibit 13-4).

Generally the savings bank can finance shopping center construction and development as well as permanent first and junior mortgages for the center. Like all mortgage lenders, they desire inflation protection through variable rates and equity participation. Like the savings and loans, they invest a very small amount of their assets in real estate ownership. Usually the real estate investment is confined to the ownership of their headquarters and branch office buildings. The financial reforms may result in major changes in the future of their real estate and mortgage investment policies.

The Pension Fund

The assets of pension funds are second only to the assets of commercial banks among the financial institutions of the United States. It is estimated that the various types of pension funds currently have assets approximating $750 billion. It is a rapidly growing financial institution as increasing numbers of employers and employees contribute increasing amounts of money each year to public and private funds. The four categories of pension funds are: (1) Old Age and Survivors Insurance trust fund (Social Security); (2) disability trust fund; (3) private pension funds (individual and business); and (4) other public funds. In 1969, the category with the largest asset volume was the private fund. Second was the public fund other than OASI and the disability trust fund (Exhibit 13-5). The monies in the private and other public fund categories have more than doubled every 10 years in recent decades.

General Pension Fund Investment Practices. The various types of pension funds follow different investment policies and practices. Many of the state and local government pension funds confine their investments primarily to Treasury and federal agency securities. Some of these funds have recently been permitted by their state legislatures to invest in more risky securities such as common stocks. The Social Security fund has been known to invest primarily in Treasury and federal agency securities underwritten especially for Social Security Administration investment. Private pension funds generally confine the bulk of their investments to corporate stocks and bonds. For example, private noninsured pension funds have recently invested half of their funds in common stock, one-fourth in corporate bonds, and 10 percent in Treasury securities (Exhibit 13-6). The remaining 15 percent was invested in cash, institutional deposits, preferred stock, mortgages, and other assets.

The press has recently said that pension funds are increasingly investing in real estate and mortgages with inflation protection features. If the pension funds invested as much as 5 percent of their estimated assets of $750 billion in

Exhibit 13-5. Assets of Private and Public Pension Funds by Type of Fund (in Billions of Dollars, End of Year Book Value)

Type of Pension Fund	1950	1960	1970	1979
Total, all types	$37.8	$108.3	$264.1	$639.6
OASI trust fund*	13.7	20.3	32.5	24.7
Disability trust fund*	†	2.3	5.6	5.6
Private and public funds	24.2	85.6	226.0	609.3
Private funds	12.1	52.0	138.2	362.7
Insured	5.6	18.8	41.2	139.2
Noninsured	6.5	33.1	97.0	223.5
Public funds	12.1	33.7	87.7	246.6
State and local government	5.3	19.3	60.3	178.9
U.S. government	6.8	14.3	27.5	67.7

Source: U.S. Social Security Administration, *Social Security Bulletin*. Represents trust funds under the Federal Social Security Act; OASI: Taken from the *Statistical Abstract of the U.S., 1980,* Table No. 554, p. 344.
†Not applicable.

Exhibit 13-6. Assets of Private Noninsured Pension Funds.

Assets	3rd Quarter 1978	3rd Quarter 1979	3rd Quarter 1980
In Millions of Dollars			
Cash and deposits	$ 7,400	$ 8,741	$ 7,854
U.S. government securities	19,862	21,357	27,287
Corporation and other debt	51,511	58,091	63,422
Preferred stock	1,119	1,324	1,521
Common stock	97,728	108,161	123,038
Mortgages	2,705	2,991	3,669
Other assets	15,668	17,342	21,643
Total Assets	195,993	218,007	248,434
As Percent of Total Assets			
Cash and deposits	3.8	4.0	3.2
U.S. government securities	10.1	9.8	11.0
Corporation and other debt	26.3	26.6	25.5
Preferred stock	0.6	0.6	0.6
Common stock	49.9	49.1	49.5
Mortgages	1.4	1.4	1.5
Other assets	8.0	8.0	8.7
Total assets	100.0	100.0	100.0

Source: *SEC Monthly Statistical Review*, Vol. 40, No. 2, February 1981, p. 5.

real estate and mortgages, the real estate-related investment would amount to roughly $38 billion. Five percent of their assets would be a very insignificant portion of their possible investible assets. But that portion has never been invested in real estate-related interests in the long history of U.S. pension funds. Foreign pension funds often invest 25 to 30 percent of their assets in mortgages and real estate, particularly income-producing property interests. The potential for pension fund investment in real estate and mortgages is great. Even 25 percent of the current estimated asset volume of $750 billion would amount to approximately $188 billion.

Ways That a Pension Fund Can Invest in Real Estate. There are four ways that the pension fund can invest in real estate. First, it can invest in commingled funds currently managed by life insurance companies and large commercial banks. These commingled funds usually borrow funds on the strength of the equity and expand the asset base in this way. Second, the pension fund may hire independent fee advisors to manage their funds. The advisor working for a fee would be aware that the pension fund may be subject to taxation on any unrelated business income from leveraged properties the advisor purchases for the fund. Third, the pension fund may purchase units of a public real estate partnership. Units may be purchased of a partnership which offers its units to the general public. Balcor Pension Investors is an example of such a current public real estate partnership. The fourth way is direct equity investment by the fund itself without no assistance from outside advisors and fund managers. The pension fund itself would worry about the consequences of unrelated business income taxation.

Pension funds may escape taxation of "income attributable to acquisition indebtedness or unrelated business income" in the following manner. The pension fund monies may be combined with other monies from other sources in a common trust. Commercial bank trust departments invest significant volumes of funds, for example, in common trust funds. The pension fund may ask the life insurance company to manage the investment of its funds through insurance company separate accounts. The pension fund may enter into partnership agreements such as joint ventures. A special debt vehicle such as a convertible mortgage may be utilized for investment by the fund in order to escape the taxation of unrelated business income.

The pension fund can also invest in real estate through purchase-leasebacks. The pension fund may purchase the land and lease it back to the original owner. Then the pension fund may finance the leasehold mortgage on the improvements. This type of financing fits many shopping center situations.

Ways the Pension Fund May Invest in Commercial Mortgages. Commercial mortgages in their entireties may be purchased. An alternative is the purchase of a commercial mortgage participation where the underwriter of the mortgage and other lenders may invest in the same mortgage. Whole mortgages or participations may be purchased as financing for a shopping center. The pension fund may wish inflation protection in the form of call options at 5- or 10-year intervals with equity participation in addition. Even though call options may be negotiated for the pension fund, the shopping center mortgage may be amortized for 25 or 30 years. The first and/or junior permanent mortgages may be financed while the pension fund also contributes equity to the financing of the center. Part of the equity may be committed as the mortgage is funded; the rest of the equity may be acquired at a later date.

Delayed equity purchase by the pension fund may take the form of an investment in a convertible mortgage. The pension fund enters the picture as a mortgage lender, but has the option later to convert the debt interest to an equity interest. After the center is finished and establishing a successful track record from operations, the pension fund may or may not wish to exercise the option of converting the debt position to an equity position.

Regulation and Taxation of the Pension Fund. Generally there is no governmental regulation of private pension funds. Public pension funds are usually subject to governmental or legislative regulation. If the pension fund seeks a tax-exempt institutional status, it must report its existence to the Internal Revenue Service and qualify for tax-exempt status. The investment income of qualified pension funds is tax free for federal income tax purposes. The tax status is related to the fact that the fund is accumulated from the periodic contributions of the employer and the employee as the employee remains on the payroll.

Mortgage and Real Estate Investment Trends. In the past, the pension fund has needed little inflation protection since a guaranteed income was payable to the retired employees and their beneficiaries at their deaths. Now the retired employee is faced with the erosion of fixed incomes due to the runaway inflation. The pension funds see that they will be faced with demands for increasing pension fund payments to protect the retirees from the disastrous effects of inflation. To gain inflation protection for the pension fund portfolios, the administrators or managers will have to demand indexed mortgages rates, equity participation, and call options in relatively shorter shopping center mortgages.

Since employer and employee contributions to the pension fund continually arrive for investment, sizable commercial real estate investments, such as the regional or superregional shopping center, will be sought for efficient, timely investment. Liquidity will be needed to some degree because retired persons continually are paid retirement benefits. The income from the shopping centers or shopping center mortgages may meet this demand for liquidity.

Some corporate pension funds have a high proportion of their assets in mortgages, mortgage securities, and direct real estate investment. In October 1979, a widely distributed shopping center magazine reported on 10 corporate funds which had a high proportion of assets in real estate vehicles (see Exhibit 13-7).

Exhibit 13-7.   The Real Assets Held by 10 Corporate Funds in 1979

Corporation	Total Pension Fund Assets (in Millions of Dollars)	Real Estate Investment* (Percent of Total Assets)
Southland Corporation	$125	85%
Greenwood Mills	30	75
Mirro Aluminum Co.	12	70
Continental Group, Inc.	424	50
Butler Manufacturing Co.	27	50
E-Systems, Inc.	75	47
Neptune International Corp.	6	42
Sperry Rand Corp.	500	41
Solo Cup Corporation	7	39
Hesston Corporation	6	30

Source: Money Market Directory. Quote taken from *Shopping Center World*, October 1979, p. 26.
*Includes mortgages, mortgage securities, and direct investments.

The Foundation or Endowment Fund

The tax-exempt foundation or endowment may invest in a shopping center in several ways. It may engage in a land sale-leaseback with or without subordination to the leasehold lender. The foundation may invest in the first or subordinated leasehold mortgage on the improvements on leased land. If the land is owned by the shopping center developer and other owners, the endowment or foundation may merely finance the first or subordinated mortgages on the fee estate. The endowment fund may purchase the land and buildings of the center and lease the whole entity back to the developer over a relatively long period, possibly with renewal options, at a good yield to the beneficiaries of the endowment fund.

The Life Insurance Company

The life insurance company in the United States has a long history beginning in 1759 with the establishment in Philadelphia of The Corporation for Relief of Poor and Distressed Presbyterian Ministers and of the Poor and Distressed Widows and Children of Presbyterian Ministers. Now their assets total approximately $480 billion. These assets are represented primarily by government securities, corporate bonds, and mortgages. Other assets include corporate stock, policy loans, real estate, and other assets. They invest for their own account and for separate accounts maintained and managed for outside clients.

Income and Expense Sources of the Life Insurance Company. The income of the life insurance company is derived from two principal sources: (1) life and health insurance policies and variable annuity sales, and (2) investments. The well-diversified life insurance company sells ordinary, group, industrial, and credit life insurance. Term insurance sales have been increasing while other ordinary life policy sales have been declining. Group life insurance sales have been increasing while industrial life insurance sales have been declining. Credit life insurance has been increasing, but it still accounts for only 6 percent of total life insurance sales.

Premium income is derived from three main sources: (1) life insurance sales, (2) annuity sales, and (3) health insurance sales. About half of the premium receipts come from life insurance sales. Another third of the premium receipts come from health insurance sales, and the remaining premium receipts come from annuity considerations.

The expenses of the life insurance company may be categorized as operating expenses, cash withdrawals based on policy loans to insured parties, and policy payments to insured parties and their beneficiaries. Actuarial tables permit the close and reasonably accurate forecasting of current and future policy payments to insured parties and their beneficiaries. Policy loans are difficult to forecast because of the discretionary behavior of the insured parties. Financial conditions and the relative levels of interest rates of the various portions of the interest rate structure have a strong bearing on the demand for policy loans, though. Operating expenses can be managed and can be forcasted to increase with inflation.

The Cash Flow Situation of the Life Insurance Company. The life company can expect a continuous, reliable cash inflow from the ordinary life and the group life insurance policies. The inflow of variable and fixed annuity receipts is less predictable as is the inflow from term and credit life insurance policies.

Advisory fees from the management of affiliated real estate investment trusts and separate accounts for investment clients are less certain than ordinary life insurance premiums. Clients for investment management tend to shift their business from one investment advisor to another over short intervals. The advisory fees from a prosperous real estate investment trust are more certain to stabilize or increase than fees from a marginal REIT operation.

Withdrawals on the basis of policy loans have disastrous consequences when those cash outflows have not been forecast accurately. They can be a steady drain of life insurance company resources, particularly in times of relatively high interest rates in the money market.

When interest rates in the capital market are at a high level and tending to increase, the value of the bond holdings of the life insurance company declines. At the same time, the market value of the common stock may increase with the inflationary condition of the stock markets. Existing fixed-income mortgages, like fixed-income corporate industrial bonds, decline in value with rising interest rates in the capital market. Real estate values may increase with inflation and give the life insurance company some relief from inflationary erosion of the dollar.

Therefore, the net cash flows of a life insurance company have become more unpredictable in a period of rapid inflation and high interest rates than they were in earlier economic periods. The portfolio composition and asset requirements, therefore, tend to change in order to protect the life company from the financial risks of the economic environment. In shopping center finance, we may expect them to want variable-rate mortgages with relatively short terms or call options at 5- to 10-year intervals of the permanent mortgages. We may expect them to participate in the equity of the center in numerous ways. The life company may wish to participate in the gross revenues of the owner from the tenants, the net cash flows after fixed debt service, the tax-free refinancing proceeds, and the net cash proceeds from the sale of the center. They may desire investment in convertible mortgages where they can look forward to complete or partial equity participation in a profitable center after it has operated a period of time. They may wish to develop their own centers to benefit from all sources of cash flows and profits. Or they may wish to take a heavy portion of the ownership of the center with the developer who retains only a minority ownership position.

As the operation expenses and the demands of life insurance policyholders for increased future payments rise, the life company must generate higher incomes from their investments which reflect the pattern of inflation. The stockholders of the stock life insurance companies expect continuously rising market prices for their stock. The owners of mutual life insurance companies expect ever higher dividends from their life insurance company investment. The variable annuity purchasers expect inflation protection from their future annuity payments. The ownership of real estate and variable-yield mortgages may help the life company meet these investor demands.

The Regulation and Taxation of Life Insurance Companies. Life insurance companies are state-chartered stock or mutual companies. Therefore, the state insurance commission wherever the life insurance company does business regulates the company. The insurance commission of the state in which the life company is domiciled has the most regulatory authority. Since most life insurance companies do business in the state of New York because of the large number of residents and businesses, the investment regulations of the New York insurance commission have a great bearing on the investment policies and practices of most large life insurance companies.

The Internal Revenue Service permits the life company to deduct its necessary policy reserves against its otherwise taxable income. The life company is subject to corporate income taxation, but the huge reserves against possible policy payment contingencies reduce the possible tax obligations of the company. Like the other taxable financial institutions, the life insurance company is not subject to the full force of the corporate federal income taxation.

The Commercial Real Estate and Mortgage Lending Policies and Practices. The life company has recently filled between 25 and 30 percent of its portfolio with mortgages. The vast majority of the mortgages purchased in the last seven or eight years have been commercial mortgages rather than residential mortgages. Since 1960 the real estate holdings of the life companies have approximated 3 percent of assets (Exhibit 13-8). In early 1981 the holdings of mortgages and real estate approximated $150 billion. Every month recently another $1 billion of assets are added to the mortgage and real estate accounts. In 1980, 125 U.S. life companies maintained separate accounts for clients which contained sizable amounts of real estate and mortgages (Exhibit 13-9). Admittedly, the assets of the separate accounts were primarily common stock and bonds, but real estate and mortgage holdings exceeded $3.3 billion. Some of the largest commingled real estate funds are being managed by Aetna, Equitable, John Hancock, and Prudential life insurance companies.

The Real Estate Investment Trust

In 1960 Congress modified the Internal Revenue Code to permit the establishment of a new financial intermediary specially designed for real estate and mortgage investment. Some call the real estate investment trust a "real estate mutual fund."

The Nature of the Real Estate Investment Trust. The REIT is a tax-exempt business trust that is owned by at least 100 different shareholders at least 300 days of the year. The financial institution may not actively manage any of its real properties; it must be a passive investor. It must derive at least 75 percent of its income from real estate-related sources and must distribute at least 95 percent of all taxable income to maintain its tax-exempt status. More than 75 percent of its assets must be real estate related. The REIT may sell up to five properties a year provided that the properties have been held by the REIT for four or more years without disqualification as a REIT.

Exhibit 13-8. Real Estate Holdings of U.S. Life Insurance Companies

Year	Dollar Amounts (in millions)	Percent of Assets
1890	$ 81	10.5%
1900	158	9.1
1920	172	2.3
1940	2,065	6.7
1960	3,765	3.1
1970	6,320	3.0
1978	11,764	3.0
1979	13,007	3.0
1980	15,007	3.0
1981	18,278	3.5

Source: 1982 Life Insurance Fact Book, p. 83.

Exhibit 13-9.   Distribution of Assets Held in Separate Accounts by U.S. Life Insurance Companies (in Millions of Dollars)

Year	Total Assets	Real Estate	Mortgages	Common Stock	Bonds
1981	$44,094	$5,030	$1,401	$16,909	$18,244
1980	35,772	3,341	687	17,665	12,392
1979	25,644	2,097	410	12,868	9,187
1977	17,358	803	268	10,946	4,569
1975	12,973	563	200	9,277	2,553
1973	10,030	186	171	7,900	1,581
1971	7,523	24	87	6,416	763
1969	3,619	1	36	2,745	638
1967	1,207	—*	14	1,055	114

Source: *1982 Life Insurance Fact Book* and *1980 Life Insurance Fact Book* (Washington, D.C.: American Council of Life Insurance, 1982 and 1980), p. 88.
Note: In 1981, 144 companies; in 1980, 140 companies, and in 1979, 125 U.S. life insurance companies had assets in separate accounts compared with 123 companies in 1978, 125 in 1977, and 123 in 1976.
*Less than $500,000.

This unique type of business trust, which is created solely for the investment in real estate and mortgages, is controlled by a board of trustees, is managed on a daily basis by an advisory company, and is owned by the holders of shares of beneficial interest. The declaration of trust established the investment guidelines for the individual REIT. These investment guidelines may describe any of three basic types of real estate investment trusts: (1) equity trust, (2) mortgage trust, and (3) hybrid trust. When the REIT industry reached its peak in operations in about 1974, all types of REITs held more than $20 billion in assets. The mortgage trusts tended to thrive on construction and development loans; the equity trusts, on real estate ownership; and the hybrid trusts, on real estate ownership and all types of mortgage debt. By the early 1980s the most prominent, profitable REITs were described primarily by equity or hybrid trusts. The industry assets had declined to approximately $11 billion, according to the National Association of Real Estate Investment Trusts.

Congress created this "real estate mutual fund" so that individuals and businesses with modest investment capital could invest on a joint ownership basis in real estate and mortgages with only small investment outlays. These investors would expect to realize some capital appreciation and dividend income from the holding of their shares of beneficial interest. REIT share prices usually range from $10 to $30. Many trusts trade their shares of beneficial interest on the New York and American Stock Exchanges. The investor could also participate in the good fortunes of real estate by investing in the commercial paper, debentures, convertible debentures, short-term promissory notes, and mortgages sold by the REIT in order to raise funds for real estate and mortgage investment. The industry balance sheet of Exhibit 13-10 shows the predominant assets and liabilities of the REITs.

The Current Financial Status of the REITs. Many REITs are thriving currently. Hybrid and equity REITs are tending to perform best in the current recession with inflation. The top 15 REITs in terms of the market value of their shares of beneficial interest are described briefly in Exhibit 13-11.

Many REITs have had institutional sponsors such as life insurance companies, commercial banks, and financial conglomerates. At the end of 1979, about 15 percent of the REITs had institutional sponsors of this type (Exhibit 13-12). About half of the REITs at that time had no outside advisor.

The Financing of Shopping Centers by Real Estate Investment Trusts. Quite often the REIT declaration of trust permits the financing of income properties, such as the shopping center, with many types of financial agreements. The REIT declaration may also permit the total or partial ownership of any type of center. In other words, REITs usually have a great deal of latitude for the financing of shopping centers.

The shopping center developer may approach the REIT for many types of loans and equity funds. The developer may inquire about land loans, construction and land development loans, gap loans, standby commitments, wrap-around loans, convertible mortgages, and permanent mortgages of first and junior subordinated priorities. The REIT may be interested in purchase-lease-backs or outright ownership of all or part of the equity in the center. The purchase-leasebacks may involve only the land or the land and the permanent improvements to the land. The REIT may have a lot of flexibility in equity and debt investment. Usually, though, they are restrained by the tax code from taking active roles in the management and development of the center. The developer may retain full operational control of the center even though the REIT may make a major commitment of equity and debt funds.

Offshore Investors

In the last four years, huge sums of money have been invested in U.S. real estate and mortgage debt by foreign investors. For investment returns, they have looked to the investment in all types of U.S. income properties. But many of these foreign investors have shown preferences for shopping center investments, debt and/or equity investments. This trend has alarmed some Americans and has pleased others. Some Americans fear takeover of American industry or segments of American business and industry by foreign parties. Some have feared the takeover of American farms, the origin of vital foodstuffs. Other Americans who have seen the scarcity of domestic investment capital have welcomed the infusion of capital from abroad.

Americans have long invested tremendous sums in real estate and operating businesses around the world. Every year the outflow of American investment capital far surpasses the inflow of foreign investment capital. Whether the capital is flowing out or in, the investor seeks to gain a higher yield on the capital than it would receive if placed elsewhere. When the foreign investor sees profitable opportunities in real estate in the United States and invests

Exhibit 13-10. REIT Industry Balance Sheet (in Millions of Dollars).

Assets	Most Recent	1st Quarter 1980	Liabilities	Most Recent	1st Quarter 1980
First mortgages			Commercial paper	$ 572.1	$ 647.8
Land and development	$ 541.6	$ 602.2	Bank borrowings	2,566.1	2,869.6
Construction	884.6	974.0	Senior nonconvertible debt	586.8	531.8
Completed properties			Sub. nonconvertible debt	238.1	284.1
0–10 years	669.0	685.6	Convertible debt	566.1	600.4
10 + years	1,509.0	1,500.9	Mortgage on property owned	2,564.8	2,557.8
Junior mortgages	658.2	692.6	Other liabilities	344.8	413.2
Loan loss allowance	(626.5)	(684.4)		$7,438.8	$7,904.7
Property owned	6,551.1	6,675.6	Shareholders' equity	3,657.2	3,641.1
Cash and other assets	909.0	1,099.3			
Total assets	$11,096.0	$11,545.8	Total liabilities and equity	$11,096.0	$11,545.8

Source: REIT Industry Monthly Review, October 1980, p. 12.

Note: The published financial statements of all REITs of which NAREIT has any record including trusts which are not currently qualifying as REITs for federal tax purposes. For the most recent quarter 218 trusts are included. The totals in this table and all other REIT tables do not necessarily equal the sum of their parts due to rounding. "Property owned" includes $1.0 billion of property acquired by or in lieu of foreclosure. Joint venture and partnership interests are also included in "property owned" at the amounts reported on REIT balance sheets.

Exhibit 13-11. A Brief Characterization of the Top 15 REITs in Terms of the Market Value of Their Shares (Fall 1980)

Type of Sponsor	Type of Trust	Data Date	Total Assets (millions of dollars)	Share Price, 12/31/80	Annualized Dividend Yield
Life insurance company					
Connecticut General REIT	Hybrid	9/80	$372.9	$26.500	8.30%
MONY Mortgage REIT	Hybrid	8/80	208.6	7.000	13.14
Equitable Life REIT	Hybrid	7/80	319.1	10.875	12.87
Massmutual REIT	Mixed Mortgage	10/80	170.5	12.625	13.31
Bank					
Wells Fargo REIT	Hybrid	9/80	233.5	24.500	8.16
Bankamerica REIT	Hybrid	10/80	167.1	26.375	7.58
Other					
General Growth	Equity	9/80	405.9	20.500	NA
First Union	Equity	9/80	243.5	21.125	6.63
Santa Anita	Hybrid	9/80	76.4	41.500	7.33
Consolidated Capital, Inc.	Mortgage	9/80	91.6	24.500	13.80
Lomas Nettleton	Hybrid	9/80	318.0	18.750	14.08
ICM Realty	Hybrid	8/80	58.2	21.500	13.02
Hubbard REIT	Equity	7/80	105.7	15.875	12.60
Consolidated Capital Realty	Hybrid	8/80	133.4	31.500	8.38
Washington REIT	Equity	9/80	43.1	38.875	7.00

Source: REIT Industry Investment Review, January 1981, p. 1.

Exhibit 13-12. REIT Assets by Type of Advisor (Year-End, 1979)

Category	Number of REITs	Percentage of Industry Assets
Commercial bank	16	12.0%
Independent mortgage banker, broker, or real estate-oriented company	35	13.3
Advisor owned by individuals	18	7.6
Conglomerate	5	1.6
Life insurance company	11	14.0
No advisor	110	47.0
Other including unknown	23	4.5
Total	218	100.0%

Source: REIT Industry Monthly Review, October 1980, p. 10.
Note: In many instances indirect ties, overlaps, and partial ownership of the advisor impede efforts to place an advisor in any one category. Any REIT whose advisor was at least 50 percent owned by a bank, bank holding company, or bank holding company subsidiary was considered to fall into the "commercial bank" category.

capital here, he or she views comparable investments at home less favorably. Therefore, the flows of funds worldwide will continue as long as the investor is gaining financial advantage.

Motivations of the Foreign Investor. Some motivations behind U.S. real estate investment are personal; most are financial. Sometimes a foreigner buys a home in the United States where he or she and perhaps his or her family can reside while attending to business in the United States. Very few American homes are purchased by foreigners for recreational and social purposes. Some of the homes are purchased to facilitate quick exit from the native country in case of military insurrection, government nationalization of business and industry, and political upheaval. Some residential buildings in major cities are purchased for embassy personnel. Foreign government and financial representatives need temporary homes while visiting the United States on business. As the foreign government, company, or individual establishes a temporary home in the United States, the investor may realize that profit may be possible from the capital appreciation in that residential real estate over time. The investment and the costs of operating the residence may amount to less than the rental costs of space for numerous company or government representatives.

Foreign entities purchase and rent U.S. real property much as Americans do. They seek profits from investment. They seek capital appreciation, equity buildup perhaps from mortgage reduction, positive net cash flows from building rental and operation, and tax benefits. Foreign entities have developed, built, purchased, and operated American income properties, including shopping centers, with these motivations in mind.

Tax Benefits. Most foreign investors in U.S. real estate escape all or the majority of the U.S. real estate tax regulations. They may escape the impact of U.S. capital gains and ordinary income taxation if they consult with tax accountants and attorneys who are experts in this area. Many American investors join or set up investment organizations in foreign countries so that they may be treated as foreign investors. American real estate investment companies are domiciled in the Cayman Islands, the Netherlands Antilles, and other Caribbean islands with favorable tax codes. These American investors may be joint owners with other American and foreign investors by means of limited partnerships, corporations, or other business organizations favorable for tax purposes.

Many of the current foreign investors of U.S. real estate and mortgages are pension funds. U.S. pension funds are usually tax free. Foreign pension funds may be tax free or lightly taxed by the central government at home. These pension funds may enjoy definite tax advantages with regard to real estate and mortgage holdings.

Financial Background of the Foreign Investor. The foreign investor may represent a central government, a central bank, a financial conglomerate, a commercial bank, an investment bank, an industrial corporation, a business or personal trust, a personal holding company, a family foundation or trust, an international oil company, or other financial entity. Many types of financial backgrounds are represented by the foreign investors in U.S. real estate.

The foreign investor may have the means to find suitable real properties, such as prime shopping centers, and may have access to the appropriate analytical data. If the foreign investor has the requisite financial background in U.S. real estate analysis, he or she may purchase or lease suitable real properties without outside consultation and advisement. Other foreign investors may know the rudiments of U.S. real estate laws, financing, cash flow analysis, and tax regulations. These investors may seek financial, accounting, economic, and legal advice from American representatives. Many advisors in the United States are available to advise the foreign investor, among them commercial real estate brokers, investment bankers, real estate consultants, feasibility analysts, tax accountants, and real estate attorneys. Many of these counselors specialize in shopping center acquistion and financing. Some of the foreign investors are well equipped to develop shopping centers in the U.S. They may acquire centers by means of joint ventures for a time before they begin to develop their own centers and keep the many financial returns for themselves.

Geographical Origins of the Offshore Investors. Most of the offshore investors come from Canada, Great Britain, Central and South America, and Western Europe. Some come from the Caribbean. Some investors domiciled elsewhere around the world may form a subsidiary in the Caribbean isles for any possible tax advantage. In other words, the domicile of the business entity associated with the shopping center may or may not be the original country of the investor. Several layers of subsidiary companies may be used for real estate and mortgage investment in order to gain tax and/or financial advantages or to disguise the actual sources of the monies invested. Full business disclosure is less prevalent around the world than it is in the United States.

A foreign investor interested in center financing or ownership may come from any country of the world. Foreign investors in U.S. real estate within the last four or five years have come from such places as South Africa, Australia, Venezuela, Guatemala, Japan, Taiwan, India, and Italy.

Foreign Investment in Shopping Center Debt and Equity. In recent years the most active competition in the shopping center arena has come from American life insurance companies and pension funds and from foreign investors. All three entities have wished to purchase all or part of the equity in prime centers. They have financed mortgages and sale-leasebacks, also. The American real estate press has repeatedly charged that this competition has forced shopping center purchase prices sky high and has forced capitalization rates and dividend yields down sharply. The shopping center developers who have recently sold all or part of their equity to foreign investors have tended to gain relatively high prices. With the decline in retail sales with the recession, the rising construction and land costs, the rising storeroom rents, and the resistance of shopping center developers to parting with substantial portions of their equity interests, the investment focus may be off the shopping center. If the foreign investor cannot find prime centers to buy and prime locations for centers to be developed by their development subsidiaries, this investor may turn to other inflation-protected, profitable forms of income-producing properties.

Equity Funds

The equity fund is a commingled real estate fund which may be a closed- or open-end mutual fund that invests primarily in real estate assets. The real estate may be leveraged or nonleveraged, depending on the preferences of the fund managers and the clients. The primary sponsors of an equity fund are commercial banks, life insurance companies, limited partnerships, and real estate companies. Usually the equity fund caters to private and public pension funds, though other clients may be served. The client buys units of the open- or closed-end fund whose value is appraised periodically, perhaps as often as monthly. The fund may permit purchases and sales of units on a monthly basis. Since the equity fund is a relatively new phenomenon, most units are purchased rather than sold.

The bank-sponsored equity fund is usually associated with its trust department operations. The insurance fund may be part of the company's general account and provide guaranteed interest income to the client, or it may be a separate account subject to different insurance commission regulations and investment policies. The real estate company and limited partnership funds manage individual equity funds on specific investment policies. A large financial institution is not available on an in-house basis for real estate consultation.

Advantages of Equity Funds over Pension Funds. The equity fund may return a yield higher than the overall stock market performance. Real estate returns during the last decade have often exceeded the returns from common stock. The stability of the income from the invested funds may be enhanced. Specialized management personnel may be acquired for a cost less than that for the pension fund. Greater investment liquidity may be gained through investment unit acquisition and liquidation. Purchase or participation in large-scale commercial projects, such as regional shopping centers, may be possible, and these may yield higher investment returns. Combined monies from several sources may permit acquisition or development of large, profitable income properties. Combined funds from several sources may permit more geographical and property diversification than would be possible for a single pension fund.

Major Differences Among the Equity Funds. The equity funds currently in existence differ on the bases of:

Closed- or open-end nature of the fund
Sponsor competence
Cost of management
Investment strategy
Geographical and property diversification
Investment return

The life insurance company and commercial bank separate accounts tend to be open-end in nature. Clients may enter the fund at any time, and additional properties may be acquired at any time that more monies are available. The real estate company or limited partnership situation usually describes a closed-end fund. A limited amount of money is raised at one time. Once that money has been invested, another fund-raising drive must be initiated.

Some fund managers have more successful trade records over longer periods of time than other fund managers. For example, major life insurance companies have managed sizable real estate and mortgage portfolios for decades. Their investment returns may surpass the investment returns of other managers. There is no conclusive evidence of this industry relationship, though. Exhibit 13-13 shows that Prudential Life Insurance Company gained a 23.9 percent return on its open-end commingled real estate fund while Aetna Life Insurance Company gained only a 12.6 percent return on its similar fund. At the same time, Wachovia Bank's equity fund received a 20.3 percent return on its fund, but Crocker National Bank received only a 10.0 percent return on its fund.

Growth of the Equity Funds. In the early 1981 there was an estimated $5 to $6 billion invested in equity funds. Since the pension fund total in early 1981 is estimated to be $750 billion, the equity funds probably have less than 1 percent of the total pension fund assets. It has been estimated, though, that roughly 1

Exhibit 13-13. Real Estate Fund Growth and Performance, 1978 through Early 1980; Open-End Commingled Real Estate Funds.

Name of Sponsor	Real Estate Assets (millions of dollars)		Real Estate Fund Performance (Percent)		
	1978	Early 1980	1979 Income	Appreciation	1979 Total
Aetna Life Insurance	$ 58	$ 280	9.6%	3.5%	12.6%
Bank of America	46	60	9.0	4.1	13.1
Crocker National Bank	23	50	8.1	1.9	10.0
Equitable life	378	1,033	9.3	5.5	14.8
First National Bank of Boston	27	73	9.6	2.1	11.7
First National Bank of Chicago	65	249	7.9	7.2	15.1
Hancock Life Insurance	60	250	10.2	8.8	19.0
Prudential Life	1,090	2,000	8.8	15.1	23.9
Travelers Insurance	50	150	9.8	0.5	10.3
Wachovia Bank	58	75	7.1	13.2	20.3

Source: Hansen A. S. "Pensions and Investments," Appraisal Briefs, Vol. 15, No. 15, July 23, 1980 (a newsletter of the Society of Real Estate Appraisers).

percent of pension fund assets are invested in real estate at present. Some of the money, therefore, is managed by sources other than real estate equity funds.

At the end of 1979, a survey of equity funds showed six insurance companies and twelve commercial banks managed in 20 commingled real estate funds approximately $4 billion of equity funds, primarily from pension funds. In 1979, the life insurance companies managed in separate accounts $26 billion of pension funds, including $2.5 billion in real estate and mortgages (Exhibit 13-14). In contrast, in 1974 equity funds totaled only $750 million. At least half the equity funds in operation now did not exist in 1974.

The Prudential PRISA separate account and Equitable Life's Separate 8 Account continue to dominate the equity funds. In 1975, Separate 8 Account at Equitable contained only $45 million in 16 properties; now it owns more than 160 properties valued at approximately $1.25 billion. Prudential's PRISA fund has increased in leaps and bounds to more than $2 billion by 1980.

Equity Fund Characteristics. The insurance company funds tend to be much larger in asset volume than do the commercial bank funds. In 1979, the average insurance fund was seven times larger than the average bank fund. The average overall equity fund was approximately $280 million. The time of existence of the insurance company funds and the bank funds on the average was the same - six years.

The equity funds diversify across income property types, project size, and geographic location. Whether the fund is sponsored by a life insurance company or a commercial bank, for example, one-fourth of its assets tend to be in each of the following types of property: retail properties, office buildings, hotels and motels, and industrial properties. The bank equity funds tend to stay more liquid with greater portions of their clients' assets invested in cash and marketable securities. The insurance funds do reflect extreme portfolio conditions with respect to retail property holdings. An insurance equity fund may have as much as three-fifths of its portfolio in retail properties or another fund may have no investment in retail properties. In essence, the same extreme in

Exhibit 13-14.   Net Asset Size of Commingled Real Estate Funds, 1980

	Insurance Company Funds	Bank Funds	Both
Largest	$2,178,844,267	$290,311,817	$2,178,844,267
Smallest	74,188,690	5,017,596	5,017,596
Mean	679,207,974	84,855,612	329,588,937
Median	352,761,633	64,796,690	88,534,530

Source: Estey, Arthur and Miles, Mike, "How Pension Funds Invest Through CREFs," *Commercial Investment Journal*, Winter 1982, p. 9. Realtors National Marketing Institute, 1982.

retail property investment may prevail among the bank equity funds. The vast majority, though, hold one-quarter of their assets in retail properties, including shopping centers.

The majority of the equity funds tend to concentrate to an extent their real property investments in the Sunbelt. The South alone may account for all of the investments of a single equity fund or only 2 percent of the investments of another. But the South, on the average, attracts one-third of the acquisitions of the fund. The region with the fewest overall fund commitments is the East. The life insurance company sponsors tend to favor investment properties in the East more than do the commercial bank sponsors. The larger the fund, usually the greater the geographic diversification within the fund properties.

The life insurance fund tends to invest more money per property than does the bank fund. This may reflect the fact that the insurance fund generally is much larger than the bank fund. For example, 40 percent of the insurance fund investments may be over $10 million in size while 8 percent of the bank fund investments may be that size.

The investment return performance of both the bank and the insurance company funds has approximated overall 13 to 15 percent a year. The percent return from capital appreciation is usually less than the cash-on-cash return from net income. As an exception to that generality, the capital gains realized in 1979 by the Wachovia Bank fund and the Prudential Life funds were close to double the cash-on-cash returns.

The clients and the fund managers usually negotiate short contracts of one or two years, but the management contracts range from one to five years. The management fee may be 3 to 5 percent of "defined" income or collections, plus perhaps an incentive arrangement based on investment performance.

Examples of Equity Fund Investment in Retail Properties. Let us observe the portfolio mix of five equity funds and what proportions are devoted to retail properties including shopping centers.

1. *Equitable Life's Separate 8 Account.* Of the 160 properties valued at $1.25 billion, 64 percent was invested in retail stores, 16 percent in office buildings, 18 percent in other commercial and industrial real estate, and 2 percent in hotel properties. Of all the properties owned in all portfolios of Equitable, 42 percent of the assets were devoted to retail properties.

The management of the Separate 8 account can undertake many diverse real estate activities, including:

Assuming debt
Issuing forward commitments to buy properties
Developing real properties
Making purchase-money mortgages on properties that it wishes to sell
Making construction loans to developers if the loan converts into equity
    when the property is finished
Entering into joint ventures, mainly with developers

Therefore, the monies of the Separate 8 Account can be invested in shopping centers in all of these ways.

2. *First National Bank of Chicago's Fund F.* This equity fund was started in 1973 by the Real Estate Research Corporation, a subsidiary owned by First National Bank of Chicago, and the Trust Department of First National Bank of Chicago. This equity fund buys only 100 percent fee simple interests in income properties, 5 percent of which are shopping centers. Fund F does not use leverage and takes no depreciation or investment tax credits because the pension fund participants of Fund F cannot use tax benefits and are careful to avoid taxation of unrelated business income from leveraged property.

The management of this open-end equity fund, which currently holds $250 million is assets, plans during the 1980s to concentrate first on office building investment and, second, to invest in neighborhood and convenience shopping centers. They plan to avoid regional shopping centers or any other centers that sell primarily shopping goods.

As a cosponsor of the fund, Real Estate Research Corporation provides the market analyses, the consulting services, and the appraisal services. The Real Estate Group of the First National Bank of Chicago's Trust Department takes care of the acquisition, operation, and sale of the real properties of the portfolio.

3. *Rosenberg Real Estate Equity Funds (RREEFs).* The Rosenberg Capital Management Company of San Francisco started closed-end equity funds in 1974. For the Western fund they raised about $200 million in four separate closed-end funds. In July, 1979 they opened in Chicago RREEF Mid America and have raised approximately $150 million for the Midwest and Texas real property markets. For properties worth more than $15 million, they opened RREEF USA (also in 1979) and raised about $140 million by fall 1980.

Of the 21 investors, 18 were U.S. corporate pension funds. They had purchased 46 properties in the West and Midwest. Most of these properties were located in the West. The purchases of real properties were made with all cash. The RREEF funds owned 1.1 million square feet of shopping centers, 1.5 million square feet of office buildings, and 2.6 million square feet of industrial properties. They do not buy properties, including shopping centers, which are located on leased land. The management wants tenants on short-term leases with kickers. The RREEF funds do not act as developers of shopping centers or any other property type. Before acquisition, the finished property usually must attain at least 70 percent occupancy.

The four founders of the equity funds and their associates work with mortgage brokers on many of their deals. Almost all deals involve real estate brokers. The management prefers close association with the real estate brokers.

4. *Aetna's Real Estate Separate Account (RESA).* The open-end, commingled real estate equity fund held approximately $300 million in assets for qualified pension funds by 1980. The fund, initiated in mid-1977, buys existing real estate on a leveraged or unleveraged basis. The amounts of their individual transactions vary widely from $5 million to $30 million. Recently their portfolios have contained 65 percent in the form of retail properties. They plan to cut

the portion devoted to retail properties down to 40 percent of the total portfolio. In the future, they plan to have 34 percent of their portfolio invested in commercial and industrial properties with most of this amount devoted to industrial properties. Aetna's RESA does not purchase multifamily apartment buildings, but has purchased hotels. The management buys existing properties as sole owner. They avoid joint ventures for existing properties.

Since Aetna's RESA management has had difficulty finding appropriate properties at reasonable prices, 50 percent of their equity units have been committed to to-be-built properties which have been joint ventures with substantial developers.

The Hartford-based operation has committed about 30 percent of its volume through mortgage loan correspondents and the rest through real estate brokers and developers. On existing property purchases, the management usually wants a minimal cash-on-cash return the first year of 8 to 10 percent. On to-be-built properties, they are now requiring 10 to 11 percent cash-on-cash return the first year. They usually employ a holding period of approximately 11 years for analysis so that the short-term leases may turn over two to three times. They usually capitalize the free and clear return from the specific property at 9 percent. Generally 15 percent is the minimum hurdle rate used. By the fifth year of real property operation, the management would want to see a 12 percent cash-on-cash return. These requirements change over time.

5. *Prudential Life's PRISA Fund*. Through this fund equity investments are made by Prudential for the general and separate accounts of the large life insurance company. Even though PRISA purchases existing properties, development activities have become dominant. PRISA builds more than it buys.

The open-end, commingled equity fund has more than 200 investor-clients. Many of these clients are Fortune 500 corporations. A number of unions also contract for their investment services.

The real properties in the PRISA portfolio are located all over the United States and cover every property type. The target portfolio contains 20 to 30 percent of retail properties along with 20 to 30 percent of office buildings, 20 to 30 percent of industrial properties, and 20 to 30 percent in all other kinds of properties.

The Real Estate Syndicate

When the shopping center developer needs capital, he or she may turn to numerous sources. We have previously surveyed the sources of funds associated with commercial banks, the thrift institutions, the life insurance companies, the pension funds, the real estate investment trusts, the offshore investors, and the equity funds. The commercial banks and thrift institutions generally have only debt financing available. The other sources may have both equity and debt financing available for the shopping center developer.

The developer of existing centers or centers to be built may arrange to sell one or more of his or her shopping centers to the real estate syndicate. The existing or proposed real estate syndicate would merely make arrangements to purchase the shopping center "product" of the developer. Sale of a center to a real estate syndicate would be similar to sale of a center to a life insurance company, a real estate investment trust, or a domestic or foreign-domiciled pension fund.

The Nature of the Shopping Center Syndication. One or more centers may be syndicated at one time in one offering. Shopping centers may be combined with other income properties in a single syndicate offering. Any size of center may be syndicated. The ownership vehicle may be a corporation, a limited partnership, a joint venture, or some other legal form of business organization.

Real estate syndication amounts to the sale of ownership interests in one or more real properties by the sponsor of the syndication. A third-party marketing organization may be employed by the syndicate sponsor to actually sell the ownership interests. The developer may cosponsor the syndication with a professional real estate syndicator. This cosponsorship may take the form of a joint venture.

A Source of Shopping Center Financing from Public or Private Offerings. The developer or the syndicator employed by the developer may make a public or private offering of the equity of a center to individual, business, and institutional investors. The public offering may involve security sales in interstate commerce; even a private offering may go across the state lines and be treated as an interstate offering. A private offering may deliberately be restricted to investors within the boundaries of the state in which the developer and the property reside. If a limited number of in-state investors are acquired and the characteristics of the private offering fit the state securities regulations, only the state department for securities regulation will regulate the offering, the sponsor, and the marketing program. If the marketing program, property acquisition, and investor arrangements take on interstate dimensions, the public or private offering is subject to the regulation of the Securities and Exchange Commission of the federal government as well as the state's securities regulation.

If the syndication of the shopping center ownership is classified as a public offering and regulated by the SEC, the cooperation and counsel of sophisticated syndicators, syndication attorneys, and syndication accountants will probably be needed. Since 1971 and 1972, the recent peak years for real estate syndication, the SEC has added many syndicate regulations further to protect the "consumer," the prospective or current syndicate investor. The regulations have proliferated since the slump in real estate of 1974 through 1975. Many syndication sponsors went out of business during that period and perpetrated many losses for syndicate investors. The federal and state securities regulators have sought since that time to correct the syndication conditions leading to the numerous "consumer" losses. Therefore, more disclosure and reporting requirements are now in effect for syndicate sponsors.

The Marketing System and the Security Offered. The syndicator may market the offering alone, or he or she may employ the marketing services of professional marketing organizations. For example, there are approximately 18 active sponsors of public syndications at present. More than two-thirds of the money for public syndications has been raised by only 6 of the 18 sponsors. They include JMB Realty, Balcor, Integrated Resources, Consolidated Capital, Fox & Carskadon, and Robert A. McNeil. The publicly traded company of this group, Integrated Resources, trades its securities on the American Stock Exchange. The other five real estate syndicate sponsors are private companies. These sponsors plus Merrill Lynch raised over $1 billion in public offerings and over $200 million in private placements in 1981.* They all sell their limited-partnership interests through securities dealers, such as E.F. Hutton, Paine Webber, and Shearson Loeb Rhoades. Paine Webber, Merrill Lynch, and Smith Barney as well as other investment banking-brokerage firms have now developed their own real estate products through their real estate subsidiaries. They therefore sell their own real estate limited-partnership interests, also.

The limited partnership may involve leverage when the sponsor borrows money on the basis of the equity capital raised. The security interest may, on the other hand, amount to an unleveraged partnership interest. E.F. Hutton, Merrill Lynch, and Paine Webber have sponsored unleveraged limited partnership interests which they have offered for sale to the public. In contrast, JMB and Paine Webber Income Properties partnerships have invested only in joint ventures, and most of the joint ventures have been financed with borrowed money. The return on the investment depends largely on the acquisition of reasonably priced long-term permanent mortgage financing.

Funds may be raised publicly or privately with specific properties under option or no specific properties in mind. The latter type of offering takes the form of the "blind pool." The syndicator is merely promising that the investor's monies will be used to acquire and operate income properties. In 1980 it is said that Wall Street raised over $1 billion for public blind pool limited partnerships. The estimate for 1981 sales of this type of limited partnerships is even higher. The largest public partnership raised $100 million in 1980, according to the press. The blind pool security is offered, for example, by the various Robert A. McNeil Funds that Pacific Investments has sponsored since 1965.

The minimum public partnership investment may be $2,500 to $5,000, but the average investment ranges from $10,000 to $20,000. Private placements which are typically limited to 25 to 35 wealthy or relatively wealthy individual investors usually involve minimum investments of $50,000. In many cases, the investment is substantially more. Obviously, the public offerings appeal to a much broader cross-section of American investors.

Recently several limited partnerships have raised $50 million to $100 million. In the early 1970s, the offerings resulted in only $10 to $20 million being

---

*Jarchow, Stephen P., "Real Estate Syndications: Structure of Public Real Estate Offerings," *Real Estate Review*, Vol. 11, No. 4, Winter 1982, p. 17.

raised by the syndicators per offering. Real estate syndications faded to a low number in the recession of 1974 through 1975. They are now reviving with accumulated investible capital seeking inflation hedges in the form of real estate investment. Public and private offerings have amounted to several billions of dollars in the early 1980s. The amounts of syndication funds seeking good existing income properties have combined with large foreign sources of capital to drive the prices of many prime shopping center prices unusually high. In the late 1970s, the initial yields from prime properties that were accepted by such equity funds were relative low—4 to 6 percent on invested capital. They looked for the majority of the investment yield to come from the future sale of the property at a substantial capital gain.*

The formation and operation of the real estate syndicate involve at least three phases: planning, operating, and terminating. Various duties must be performed and various types of people may be employed to get the necessary work done. During the planning and operating phases, reports must disclose syndicate information to prospective and current investors that is appropriate and sometimes required by the regulators. The sponsor is compensated on several bases. Finally, the investor is rewarded for the syndicate use of the invested capital. Let us look at the three phases of formation and operation, compensation, and investment returns in greater detail.

The Three Phases of the Syndicate Formation and Operation. The planning phase includes the conception and visualization of the syndicate offering and management. During this phase, the objectives of the syndicate operation and the sponsor are finalized in the printed prospectus or syndicate offering. In order to put together the offering, the sponsor may employ an attorney familiar with registered securities sales and an accountant familiar with real estate accounting for syndications and required disclosure. An appraiser may value income properties that the sponsor proposes to purchase for the syndicate. The sponsor may consider mortgage financing for the anticipated acquisition of proposed properties. Current mortgage terms and prospective equity yields must be ascertained by the sponsor. The syndicate offering in printed form must disclose the detailed expectations for the real estate syndicate's investment. The regulators have recently encouraged even the forecasting of possible investor yields from the various possible real estate sources. If the investment yield is expected to come from income, tax shelter, and capital gains sources, this must be estimated for the holding period according to the individual sources of investment yield.

The sponsor may be compensated by the investors for the planning and underwriting work of this phase. A commission may be payable as a percentage of the purchase price of the properties acquired for the syndicate by the sponsor, for example. In this work, the sponsor is acting as a real estate broker for the syndicate group. Actually, the sponsor may hire a commercial broker to

*Ibid.

handle the real estate brokerage details for the syndicate. Part of the real estate planning may be accomplished by recognized real estate consultants. The accounting and public disclosure system may be set up by nationally recognized public accounting companies. The distribution system for the security sales may be subcontracted to nationwide stock brokerage firms such as Bache, Halsey Stuart, and Merrill Lynch. An investment banking firm may undertake the sale of the securities through the specific brokerage houses. A commercial printing company will probably be engaged to print in sufficient volume the required printed offering or prospectus.

The operating phase starts as soon as the offering is subscribed at least adequately enough that desirable real properties may be purchased. The assets may include shopping centers whose financial characteristics fit the investment objectives of the offering and the investors themselves. The syndicate sponsor and his or her associated officers and employees may manage the acquired properties. If not, professional firms must be employed for efficient property management. The sponsor assumes the role of a fiduciary with responsibility to the investors who have placed their funds in the hands of the syndicate manager-sponsor. Good property management is part of the regulated process which must serve the interests of the syndicate investors. The property management reports become a part of the periodic reporting system for the investor group.

The offering may give the investor a right to decide on strategic changes in the management of the syndicate properties as the operation of the syndicate proceeds. If a general manager or property management company proves incompetent, the investor may have a right to participate in the replacement. If original properties do not prove to be sufficiently profitable for the pursuit of the syndicate objectives, the original properties may need to be sold and additional properties purchased as replacements. Refinancing may be desirable. Other changes during the operating phase may be desirable, and the limited partners may be permitted limited management participation.

Generally, to preserve the limited legal and financial liability of the limited partner, active management involvement is not permitted by the courts and the Internal Revenue Service. If the vast majority of the active management rests with the general partner, the sponsor, the Internal Revenue Service will permit exemption of the syndicate itself from taxation and taxation of the proceeds to each investor only. The real estate syndicate may be a type of limited partnership and subject to the usual limited partnership rules and limitations.

The sponsor may be compensated during the operating phase. A management fee may be earned. A brokerage commission may be earned if properties must be replaced. The sponsor may be entitled to a share of the operating cash flows generated by the individual properties.

For six recently completed syndications, the life cycle of the syndicate on the average was fourteen years. The sales phase and part of the planning phase lasted about two years; the operating phase lasted seven years; and the collection or termination phase encompassed five years. The six real estate syndicates permitting this summary of experience were Consolidated Capital's

California Realty Fund; Fox & Carskadon's Century 70 and 71 Funds; JMB's Carlyle 71 Fund; and McNeil's Pacific Plan Investors' Funds 1 and 2. The funds commenced during 1970 and 1971 and have recently come to an end of the total cycle.

The collection or termination phase is the last of the three phases of the typical real estate syndicate. A buyer is sought for each property. When the syndicate must finance the buyer of syndicate property, the financing period may be as long as five years. The purchase monies are collected from the buyer over this period with interest on the financed amount. Part of the return to the syndicate investor is the interest income on the financed purchase.

The sponsor will probably be compensated during the collection phase. A part of the net sale proceeds will usually go the syndicate manager. An incentive agreement may call for special compensation if the investment performance exceeds specified minimum levels. The sponsor may also receive a brokerage commission for the sale of each property which brings the syndicate life to an end. This commission will probably represent a percent of the sale price of the individual property. The management fees for the sponsor usually run until the properties are all sold. Outside brokers may be employed and compensated for the detailed closing arrangements. Attorneys and accountants may again be employed to bring the syndicate to an end with the proper reports to the regulators and the investors. The proper cash distributions must be made to the investor.

The Types of Compensation for the Sponsor. In public real estate syndications, the sponsors may receive 20 to 35 percent of the benefits from the syndication. For example, if the investors receive a 17 percent after-tax annual return on a public syndication, they would have received a 21 to 26 percent return if they had owned and managed the same properties and had had the same investment results through direct ownership. The sponsor fees and share of partnership performance may be 10 percent during the planning phase for organization and underwriting, 10 percent of the cash flow from operations, and 15 percent of the property appreciation during the termination phase. In the planning phase, most of the organization and underwriting fees go to sales representatives of unaffiliated securities firms, lawyers, and accountants. Recent competition among sponsors and pressure from state and federal regulatory agencies have resulted in reduction of sponsor compensation in the planning phase, particularly acquisition fees.

Investment Returns. The limited partnerships may be classified as income deals or income tax shelter deals. The income tax shelter fund may have a life cycle of approximately 14 years, which covers the three typical phases of the cycle. The income deal may have a longer life and involve less leverage. The income deals tend to emphasize steady, tax-sheltered cash flow from operations through net leases. The Integrated Resources' American Property Investors Fund is an example of this type of fund. The typical life cycle is about 17 years. The shopping center investment could fit into either type of fund since any degree of leverage can be employed and net leases are typical.

In recent months the income tax shelter deal might earn a 17 percent after-tax average annual yield, uncompounded, for the 50-percent-tax-bracket limited partner. Over a 14-year period, this investor might easily earn the total after-tax return of 240 percent in addition to repayment of principal. In contrast, during the 1970s, income deals had an average annual after-tax return of 12 percent, uncompounded, for the investor in the 35- to 40-percent tax bracket.

The investment returns in the 1980s may not be quite as impressive even though vacancy rates are very low and the recent low levels of construction point to rapidly escalating rents in the near future. The recent tax revisions offer faster depreciation write-offs and lower capital gains taxation. Since large investors have recently been eager to acquire good income properties, the prices of such properties have been forced very high. The cost and terms of mortgage monies have been ominous. Lenders, at the same time, are reducing their loan-to-value ratios so that down payments may reach 40 percent of value in the future.

There has been a change in the purchase ratios associated with public syndication of leveraged properties. In the early 1970s, it was possible to purchase syndicate property for about 3.5 times the gross proceeds of the syndicate offering. Gradually this factor dropped to 2.2 by 1980. In other words, in 1971 the ratio of gross syndicate proceeds to total property purchase price was as low as 29 percent. Less leverage property can be purchased with every dollar of syndicate money. The state of the mortgage market has caused this declining relationship (Exhibit 13-15).

Over the same period of time, the 1970s, the yields from tax savings from tax write-offs have declined because of changes in the federal income tax laws (Exhibit 13-16). For example, construction period property tax expense and construction loan interest expense must be amortized over a relatively long period rather than expensed immediately. Because of the decrease in the cash yields over the 1970s and the uncertainty about future appreciation of income property values, the real estate syndicate yields of the 1980s may not be as spectacular as those of the 1970s. Over the next decade, the expected annual after-tax return of standard real estate syndications may be 11 to 12 percent. The key is the capital appreciation of income properties, such as shopping centers, in the future.

Current Trends in Shopping Center Financing Through Real Estate Syndication and Limited Partnerships. Over time, many real estate syndications, limited partnerships, and joint ventures have been formed for the holding of leveraged and unleveraged income properties. Many of the income properties have been shopping centers. Records are kept on only a small portion of these offerings and investment situations.

Exhibit 13-15.   Public Syndication Leveraging

Year of Deal	Gross Proceeds as a Percentage of Total Purchase Price	Purchase Prices as Multiple of Gross Proceeds
1971	29.0%	3.45 times
1972	30.6	3.27
1973	33.7	2.97
1974	35.3	2.83
1975	26.6	3.76
1976	35.0	2.86
1977	34.4	2.91
1978	39.4	2.54
1979	39.8	2.51
1980	45.0	2.20
Summary		
1971–1972	30.0	3.30 times
1973–1977	35.0	2.85
1978–1979	40.0	2.50
1980	45.0	2.20

Source: Friedman, Jack, "Syndications: Hot Performers Cool Off,"
Table II, *Barron's*, January 5, 1981, p. 14.

**Exhibit 13-16.   First Three-Year Tax Benefits for Public Syndications
Beginning Operations 1970–1976 and 1977–1979 (50% Tax Bracket).**

	Year 1	Year 2	Year 3	Average
Cash distributions from operations				
1970–1976	1.2%	2.8%	3.8%	2.6%
1977–1979	2.0	2.3	3.2	2.5
Cash tax savings from write-offs				
1970–1976	17.4%	10.8%	7.1%	11.7%
1977–1979	7.2	5.3	5.8	6.1
Total cash benefits				
1970–1976	18.6%	13.6%	10.9%	14.3%
1977–1979	9.2	7.6	9.0	8.6

Source: Friedman, Jack, "Syndications: Hot Performers Cool Off," Table 1,
Barron's, January 5, 1981, p. 12. Reprinted by permission of *Barron's*, © Dow
Jones & Company, Inc., 1981.

Trend data from the National Association of Securities Dealers show that
syndicate offerings registered with the NASD peaked in 1972 and again in
1978. The NASD offerings exclude public programs that are sold by companies
and persons not affiliated with the NASD. Comparable figures for private

offerings are even more difficult to acquire since centralized reporting is not required for many of the issues. There is evidence that the ratio of nonpublic real estate offerings to fully registered SEC offerings may well be ten to one.

The Role of the Mortgage Broker

The mortgage broker is a financial intermediary who underwrites mortgage loans and places them with investors. These investors may be mortgage correspondents of the mortgage broker on a continuing basis. In other words, the mortgage broker finds prospective mortgage borrowers, helps them gather the necessary information for a proper mortgage loan application, and then locates investors for the loan. In serving the prospective borrower, the broker attempts to find the investor with the mortgage terms which best satisfy the needs of the borrower. For example, the cash flow forecasts of the borrower need to be matched by the amount of periodic debt service over the appropriate time frame so that the borrower can easily meet the loan provisions.

The Functions of the Mortgage Broker. In serving both the prospective borrower and the prospective lender, the mortgage broker needs full information about the borrower's needs, the value of the property to be mortgaged, the income potential of the property to be pledged, the income and wealth status of the borrower, and the credit standing of the tenants and the mortgagor. The mortgage broker is familiar with typical lender requirements and the specific mortgage requirements of the particular lender who may be interested in the subject loan.

Certain loan ratios must generally be met by the prospective mortgagor. Usually a prospective lender wants to see (1) the debt service coverage of the income property for the expected holding period, (2) the prospective stabilized operating ratio, (3) the prospective cash-on-cash return for the investor-mortgagor for the first and subsequent years, and (4) the breakeven ratio for the expected holding period. The lender will also analyze the requested loan amount in light of the size, tenancy, and location of the shopping center. The appraised value of the center, rendered by an approved real estate appraiser, will establish the amount of loan in general. Each mortgage lender has conventional loan-to-value ratios for typical shopping center loans of different configurations. Each lender likewise has rules of thumb for each of the strategic ratios in view of the type of income property involved.

If the loan requested generally fits a specific investor's needs, the mortgage broker sends the loan application with all the necessary data to the prospective lender. If the lender sends in the return mail a letter of commitment, the broker will earn a placement fee from that lender. Earlier, an origination fee will be charged the prospective mortgagor for originating or underwriting the loan for prospective lenders. Therefore, the mortgage broker may earn a fee from both the borrower and the lender. These are the chief sources of income to the mortgage broker.

The mortgage banker also earns servicing fees from the lender when the lender commits to the funding of the loan and leaves the mortgage servicing with the mortgage company. The mortgage banker earns origination fees, servicing fees, and possibly mortgage placement fees. The mortgage broker and the mortgage banker serve the same functions except for the servicing of the mortgage over the term of the mortgage agreement. Servicing the mortgage entails loan payment collection and conveyance of net proceeds to the lender less the servicing fee.

While mortgage bankers originate, sell, and service primarily residential mortgage loans, they also deal in commercial mortgage loans including shopping center loans. The mortgage broker tends to concentrate on commercial mortgage loans and only occasionally deals in residential mortgage loans. Residential properties and borrowing circumstances tend to more unusual than typical when the mortgage broker is involved in the transaction. Mortgage bankers, on the other hand, deal continually in typical VA, FHA, and privately insured conventional residential mortgage loans.

Licensing of Mortgage Brokers by States. Individual states license mortgage brokers. The state may wish to control and regulate the mortgage brokerage business. This may be particularly true if the state has experienced considerable litigation about possible illegal and unscrupulous dealings concerning mortgage brokers. The state of Florida, for example, has licensed mortgage brokers in past years.

The Background and Associations of Mortgage Brokers. Many mortgage brokers eventually affiliate with mortgage companies. In reverse, many mortgage bankers leave their mortgage companies and become independent businessmen as mortgage brokers. Such individuals may be well versed in mortgage underwriting and well acquainted with mortgage lender needs and loan requirements. They may personally be acquainted with a sufficient number of mortgage investors and prospective mortgagors that their fee business on a continuous basis is well assured.

The Future of the Mortgage Broker. The mortgage broker may continue to serve well the commercial mortgagor. The developer of a shopping center may continue to count on the fine service of an established and well-informed mortgage broker. The business of the mortgage broker is likely to expand, though. As equity funds become as important to the shopping center developer as debt financing or perhaps more so, the mortgage broker may become an equity broker, also. The broker may find that a client needs only equity sources or both equity and debt monies. The broker's investor list then needs to expand to those who can invest equity funds. The earlier investors of the broker may have been prepared to offer only mortgage funds. The same or some of the same investors may wish to invest equity monies or a combination of equity and debt funds.

FOURTEEN

FINANCING PATTERNS

Since the shopping center is an attractive investment, many alternative financing methods are available regardless of the state of the American economy. In prosperous periods with moderate amounts of inflation, certain methods are favored over others. This is true in recessions and in periods of runaway inflation.

The economic climate is only one variable in decision making. The investor reviews the financing alternatives from his or her background of personal or institutional tax burdens, government restrictions from the country of domicile, and portfolio risk/return preferences. A number of financing alternatives are always available, and the final selection has to be made by the investor.

THE SPECTRUM OF FINANCING ALTERNATIVES

The alternatives range from all equity financing to all debt financing. In between these extremes we find alternatives presenting varying degrees of financial leverage. In other words, borrowing from lenders may comprise the majority of the financing (high degree of leverage) or it may comprise only a minor portion of the total financing (low degree of leverage). The developer-owner may trade on the equity to a high degree by acquiring a significant portion of borrowed money, or the developer-owner may finance with a high portion of equity and trade very little on the equity in acquiring borrowed funds.

In any stage of the economic cycle, many shopping centers are owned outright. At the same time, many centers will be financed with multiple mortgage loans where the developer "mortgages out." In this case, the developer may pocket money from the lenders or at least have very little equity in the center. The only monies that the developer has in the project may amount to some front-end planning and architectural costs that the lenders did not fund under their mortgages.

The borrowed monies may be collateralized or not. If the lender makes the money available because the owner pledges the center improvements as security for the loan, the investor has given a mortgage or deed of trust to finance the center. The lender may make the monies available without the pledge of the owner's real property. In this case the owner is not giving a mortgage to the lender in return for funds. This may represent a personal loan or it may represent a debenture agreement if the borrower is incorporated. In either instance, the credit standing and development capability of the borrower are accepted for the loan approval in lieu of the pledge of the financed property.

GENERAL CONSIDERATIONS

The developer may plan to take only a short-term position in the completed center, or he or she may take a long-term position by holding a minor portion of the equity where his residual financial interest may be minimal. The subsequent owners who originally finance the center or who invest monies later may have a long-term, an intermediate-term, or a short-term interest in the center. Their selection from the financing opportunities will tend to reflect the extent of their financial interest and their financial motivations.

FINANCIAL MOTIVATIONS OF SHOPPING CENTER INVESTORS

As the center is financed for land acquisition, land development, building construction, and permanent operation as a profitable entity and an economic force in the community, the investor may have some or all of the following considerations in mind:

Management control of the center operation
Investment profitability
Assumption of risk and its promised compensation
Tax shelter
Need for capital
Demand for shopping center investments

The center owners who assume the most risk and provide the majority of the capital may wish to reduce their risk by keeping management control over the center operations. Other investors may seek silent partner status where they invest their money and stay aloof from the management.

The investor may have a target rate of return in mind for a shopping center investment. There may be a target cash-on-cash return in mind for the first year; another and perhaps higher cash-on-cash return may be expected by a later year in the expected holding period; and an overall yield from all sources of benefit may be expected from the investment by the time the property interest is refinanced and sold. A projected cash flow analysis for the entire expected holding period may indicate the possible returns from the first year and the intermediate years of the holding period, and the accumulated return at sale time. The profitability expected may depend on the sources of funds and the nature of the investor's existing portfolio. The profitability of the contemplated investment may be important to a single individual or to an investment committee.

The current profitability of the shopping center may be a secondary feature to the investor. A capital gain may be desired because periodic income is not needed. Tax shelter may be utmost in the mind of the investor. If the investor is not subject to American taxation for the most part, the U.S. tax attributes of the center are irrelevant. A rather low cash-on-cash return during the first few years of the investment may be approved as long as a sizable amount of money may be invested for the long term in a country of relatively stable economic and political climate. Offshore funds which actually represent monies acquired by American and foreign citizens from trafficking in illegal drugs may be seeking immediate, sizable investment outlets with few questions asked. Newer regional and superregional shopping centers can absorb many millions of dollars in equity funds.

Some investors can assume substantial amounts of financial risk and may be looking for extra compensation for it. Real estate investment trusts—mortgage and equity alike—in the past have been able by their state charters to assume high levels of shopping center risk. The same has been true of foreign and domestic pension funds whose investment practices are regulated on a minimal level. Domestic life insurance companies are also in most instances subject to minimal regulation from the state insurance commissions of the states in which insurance policies are sold. The investments covered by the applicable investment "legal lists" are broad in scope. Investors such as domestic commercial banks, savings and loan associations, and mutual savings banks usually have investment and regulatory restrictions which preclude a high amount of risk taking with shopping center investments.

Tax shelter is a feature important to investors with high tax burdens. Not all parties interested in shopping center investment feel the burden of high income taxes. For example, very high income individuals may pay very little in income taxes, and that taxation is attributable to the minimum taxation of tax preference items and excess itemized deductions passed by Congress in the 1976 Tax Reform Act. High-income people may benefit from good tax counsel and already have otherwise taxable income sheltered by the ownership of cattle farms, oil exploration companies, or other natural resource firms. The tax counsel may point out the advantages of depletion allowances and investment tax credits.

The developer may or may not need capital. The domestic life insurance companies are now developing income-producing properties that they have long purchased or financed in existing form. Foreign investors during the mid-1970s tended to purchase existing properties or form joint ventures with American construction and development companies to develop shopping centers and other income-producing properties. Today many institutional investors from abroad are developing their own centers in the United States with their own employees for their long-term holdings. A joint venture is no longer needed. Using their own expertise, they retain all profits involved in the development. If the developer locates a lender with reasonable terms who will fund the total development costs permanently, little equity capital is needed. The development circumstances dictate the demand for more capital.

The shopping center may be the investment of greatest demand among investors. This may be so because of the inflation protection afforded by shopping centers in general. If there is a lot of investment demand, the financing of the center with all equity or a mixture of debt and equity may be very easy to accomplish at very reasonable cost. Investor demand may increase the gross income multipliers and reduce the required immediate cash-on-cash returns. The perceived low inflationary risk of the shopping center investment· may reduce contract mortgage rates and increase the funds offered for a single center.

THE MARKET FORCES OF THE 1980s

Several factors seem to point to more equity investment and less mortgage financing of centers during the 1980s. The traditional sources of mortgage monies have become very inflation sensitive. They are demanding shorter mortgages, perhaps with balloon payments, and more equity participation in order to protect the real value of their investment returns. Since the cash flows from the property are often insufficient to cover the debt service requirements of those shorter loans with traditional loan-to-value ratios of 70 to 80 percent, the borrower is being forced to settle for lower ratio loans and, of course, commitment of more equity funds.

Equity funds during the 1980s may be plentiful from pension funds and life insurance companies which invest as fiduciaries pension fund monies as well as their own monies from their general accounts. Under phased-in deregulation statutes, the thrift institutions and credit unions are attempting to diversify their portfolios with commercial and personal loans and to steer away from high portfolio percentages of mortgage loans.

The new sources of equity may wish more control over center operations. The developer may lose some control to those contributing large sums of equity. Leverage positions will probably become more modest; trading on the equity will bring less favorable results to the equity returns because of the inflation-protected terms of the mortgage lenders. Tax shelter may become less important as the equity sources are not burdened with income taxes. More equity capital will be needed as mortgage loans contribute a lower portion of the permanent financing. The yield requirements of the increased equity sources will have to be met by the developer, perhaps as the developer's yield is reduced from normal levels. As these changes occur, the demand for shopping center investments will probably continue.

The demand for profitable shopping centers may not be met because good sites for profitable centers are becoming scarce. Many densely populated, affluent areas are already served by good centers. The equity funds available may have to be placed in the major renovation of well-located older centers and in expansion of existing centers where the market potential has increased and more retail units can be integrated into existing centers. More declining central business districts of major metropolitan areas may be redeveloped into viable "superregional shopping centers." Because of energy conservation and the convergence of all public transit systems in the central business district, the debt and equity monies may be well spent in that general location.

COMPONENTS OF SHOPPING CENTER FINANCE AND THE PARTIES RESPONSIBLE

The shopping center consists of developed land, buildings, and site improvements. When a site is selected by a developer, land for the center is usually supplemented with land on the fringes of the shopping center site which also may be zoned for commercial use. The developer realizes that the development of a profitable center may be the catalyst for increased values of the adjoining land. Therefore, the developer often acquires more land than is directly needed for the integrated retail complex "under one roof."

The shopping center buildings include the department store main and satellite service building plus the mall building housing the other retail and institutional tenants. The site improvements include the parking lot, striped for parking spaces, the interior and exterior landscaping, and the traffic control islands, signs, and traffic lights. The character and construction expense of the buildings and site improvements depend upon the type of center. The neighborhood, community, and specialty centers may involve only one or two separate structures because they contain no spacious department stores. Several buildings are involved in regional and superregional centers because of the presence of one or more department stores.

The land may be financed separately from the buildings and site improvements. Each building may be financed separately or all of the necessary buildings may be financed as a "package." The wishes of the developer and the tenants are pursued. Quite often, the department stores find it more advantageous to build and finance their own buildings. Then the developer finances as an integrated whole the mall buildings and the site improvements—if the land is financed independently from the developer's improvements.

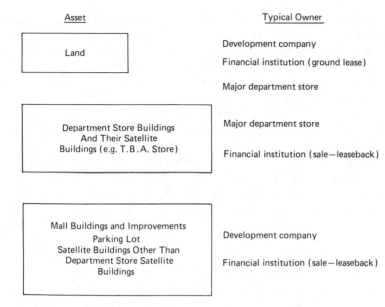

Asset   Typical Owner

Land — Development company / Financial institution (ground lease) / Major department store

Department Store Buildings And Their Satellite Buildings (e.g. T.B.A. Store) — Major department store / Financial institution (sale–leaseback)

Mall Buildings and Improvements, Parking Lot, Satellite Buildings Other Than Department Store Satellite Buildings — Development company / Financial institution (sale–leaseback)

Exhibit 14-1.   Common Shopping Center Ownership Patterns

DEBT FINANCING IN GENERAL

Financing a center with borrowed funds may involve various kinds of negotiable instruments. In order to acquire money, the prospective borrower goes through a loan acquisition process. The center is valued usually by a real estate appraiser, and the credentials of the developer and other owners are scrutinized for loan repayment purposes. The borrower soon recognizes that there is a normal commitment process pursued by the lenders. The commitment process may change, but a system for approving the loan and funding the project remains. The commitment from the lender specifies the acceptable loan terms from the lender's point of view. If the center owner agrees to the lender's terms, the schedule for the loan funding is placed on the lender's calender and becomes a part of the lender's future cash flow obligations. Not all loans made stay on the lender's books as they were originally committed. Therefore, a part of this chapter is the discussion of loan refinancing and foreclosure.

The Nature of the Various Debt Instruments Which May Be Employed

Earlier in the text, we discovered that a shopping center can be financed with all equity, all debt or almost all debt, or a good mixture of debt and equity. The equity can be raised through the sale of stock, common and preferred, if the developer is a corporation. It can also be raised through the sale of syndicate shares, limited partnership interests, and general partnership interests as well as through joint venture participations. We can look at the subject of equity in greater detail later in the text.

The debt instrument may be very different in character from that of an equity agreement or, in today's money and capital markets, the terms of the debt may closely approximate the return characteristics reserved historically for the equity contributors. Convertible debentures and convertible mortgages are two hybrid debt/equity instruments.

Creditors can make loans to shopping center owners which do not involve the pledge of real property. We tend to call them either debenture or revenue bonds. In debenture financing, the repayment of the loan with interest depends on the good faith and credit of the debtor. A long history of profitable business usually must lie behind the good faith and credit. In revenue bond financing, the net revenue generated by the income-producing property will pay the interest and repay the principal borrowed.

Mortgages and Deeds of Trust. Assuming that most loans made to shopping center owners are collaterized with real property interests, let us concentrate on mortgage instruments. The most common mortgage instruments are the mortgages and the deed of trust. They both represent collaterized debt financing, but the deed of trust involves a trustee who holds the title during the financing while the mortgage does not. Both the mortgage and the deed of trust are two-part negotiable instruments. A pledge of real property with a recital, perhaps, of the repayment terms is joined with the promissory note. If the mortgage financing is accomplished in a title theory state, the instrument pledging the real property is called the deed of trust. In a lien theory state, the contract is merely called the mortgage; in a hybrid theory state, a mortgage deed. Regardless of the name of the pledging agreement, a promissory note must accompany the pledge agreement. When deeds of trust or trust deeds are employed for the financing, the pledging agreement is labeled the deed of trust, the borrower is called the trustor, the lender is the beneficiary, and the third-party intermediary is the trustee. A note also must accompany the deed of trust to make the financing arrangement enforceable and complete.

Some states employ mortgages exclusively; some use deeds of trust exclusively. Other states of the nation use both mortgages and deeds of trust for real property financing. The lender's attorneys and the attorneys for the center owners will be cognizant of the current state legal practices.

In mortgage lending, three types of states are identified by the attorneys and mortgage lenders: the title theory states, the lien theory states, and the hybrid theory states. Title theory states assume that, when a mortgage or deed of trust is given by the borrower to the lender or trustee, the title to the property is transferred by the borrower to that party. The lender permits the borrower to occupy the mortgaged property until a default on the mortgage or note occurs. There is no equitable right of redemption for the mortgagor because the title already is held by the lender or trustee. In a lien theory state, the borrower gives a mortgage or deed of trust to the lender or trustee and keeps the title to the property pledged as collateral. In this case a lien is placed on the title. The borrower retains possession until a default on the mortgage or note occurs. Upon default, the borrower may repay the overdue amount during the grace period before the lender forecloses or may exercise the equitable or statutory right of redemption after the foreclosure sale. Hybrid theory states combine the characteristics of mortgage lending of the title theory and the lien theory states.

Mortgage loans may be made by the lender or the lender's investment committee on the basis of the value of the real property alone, the credit standing of the borrower alone, or the property and the borrower's credit standing together. Often we hear comments about "real estate" loans and "credit" loans. Even though the lender may be financing on the basis of the credit standing of the shopping center owner, the lender usually takes into account the value and economic viability of the center property. It is more likely that the mortgage loan decision was made primarily on the expected income potential of the center where the borrower and the borrower's credentials remain relatively unknown.

The Process of Loan Acquisition and Negotiation

Once the developer has acquired the land for the center, or at least has the land under option for future lease or purchase, he or she must proceed to finance the proposed center. The options and any other forms of financing for the land should take into account the possibility that the developer cannot get the zoning changed or reasonable financing arranged. The developer may also invite the land owner to contribute the land as a center partner, co-owner, or stockholder. Option and other land financing arrangements might be avoided this way.

The Use of Mortgage Bankers or Brokers. The land, the development of the land for subsequent building construction, building construction, and permanent operations of the center may need financing as a whole or in component parts. Knowledge is needed about current lender and equity financing terms. More than one approach may be taken to assess current lender and investor conditions. In-house mortgage brokers may accomplish the job. If the development company's mortgage brokers on the permanent staff need assistance, mortgage bankers with mortgage companies or local lending institutions may be asked for advice and counsel. If these sources of information are insufficient, the developer can contact friends in the shopping center industry, friends in the financial community, or prospective lenders themselves.

The Loan Prospectus with Pro Forma Statements. When the mortgage bankers, financial institutions, or other people are approached about possible financing and the current terms of equity and debt alternatives, the developer should have a loan prospectus available for the person's scrutiny and detailed study.

This prospectus may be professionally designed and compiled. A substantial sum of money may be expended for the architectural renderings for the prospectus and the plat of the center with the proposed improvements laid out by planned phases of development. Pro forma statements with the names of key tenants and the lease terms of their letters of commitment may be shown along with aerial photos of the site and its environs. Data from market and feasibility studies should be incorporated in the prospectus so that the lender's questions in these areas may be quickly and explicitly answered. Data from the recently completed environmental impact study may be incorporated to answer lender questions in that strategic area. Flood plain maps may show the propensity of the site to be inundated with flood water. Road maps of the community, metropolitan area, and region of the state may be used to indicate the location of the trading area boundaries and the existing and proposed competition. In-house or outside commercial artists may design the cover and motifs which carry through the prospectus. The binding of the numerous pages of up-to-date exhibits may be professionally done. The developer is preparing the prospectus as a sales tool as well as a source of information for project presentation. Skilled merchandising of the center's lending proposal can prompt timely and generous commitments for equity and debt financing. Merchandising is applied appropriately to the loan acquisition process as well as to the retail tenant's sale of goods and services.

Developer Motivation. Even though the mortgage banker may locate alternative sources of the desired financing, the developer personally discusses the possible loan terms with the most promising sources. The mortgage banker may shorten the path to the best current sources. This middleman may be acquainted with the portfolio needs of various mortgage company correspondents and know the terms that they can offer on a competitive basis.

The developer may move forward in demonstrating the financial attributes of his or her current and proposed centers. More than one center may be financed with the loan commitment from the lender. Larger developers work on more than one center at a time. Each of these centers will have its unique financing characteristics from the viewpoint of the lender-investor. The developer will point out some of these unique characteristics; more than likely, the lender-investor may note other unique features. Therefore, extended phone calls and personal trips to the lender-investor's offices are usually required for the negotiation of the final loan "package," the acquisition of the loan commitment, and the closing of the loan.

The Negotiable Terms of the Loan "Package"

The negotiation of the various types of mortgage loans varies widely. The residential mortgage loan for the owner-occupied house has been a very standardized loan, particularly if the lender wished to underwrite the loan for possible sale to the secondary mortgage market institutions. The Federal

National Mortgage Association (Fannie Mae) and the Federal Home Loan Mortgage Corporation (Freddie Mac or The Mortgage Corporation), for example, have established guidelines for the standardized residential mortgage loans that they can purchase from approved mortgage sellers. The mortgages must be relatively standardized so that mortgage-backed securities may be formed with a pool of mortgages as its base, so that mortgage participations and whole loans may be sold from the FNMA and FHLMC portfolios to outside investors, and so that the subsidized loans can be sold by the tandem plan to the Government National Mortgage Association (Ginnie Mae). The secondary mortgage market caters primarily to the trading of the standardized residential mortgage loan. Nonstandardized loans have not been actively traded in the secondary market. Lenders do not know what product they are buying and, therefore, must take the time for analysis of each individual unstandardized loan. An active, mass market cannot function on the basis of unstandardized mortgage loans.

As residential mortgage loans are becoming unstandardized with the variable-rate and equity participation features, they are entering the same market as the other income property loans, including the shopping center loans. Here the terms of the mortgage loan have always been specially negotiated to cater to the wishes of the lender-investor, the unique risk/return characteristics of the particular shopping center, and the special needs of the developer and the other parties to the center ownership. Since the center loans are highly individualized, there has never been active secondary market trading of these loans like the active trading of FHA and VA loans.

What terms of the shopping center mortgage loan are negotiable? The loan consists of a "package of terms." The lender-investor may consider complete negotiation of all the terms, or the monied source may be firmly committed to certain loan terms but open to negotiation of other terms of the loan package. In some situations, the lender-investor is found to be very unyielding to persuasive negotiation. Shopping center money may be scarce, interest rates high, loan terms short, and shopping center investments out of favor.

The following loan terms are traditionally open to negotiation:

Term to maturity	Contract interest rate
Amortization period	Prepayment provisions
Interest-only period	Payment period
Loan-to-value ratio	Terms of equity participation (Exhibit 14-2)

Terms that have been open to negotiation during the 1960s and 1970s have included:

Variable interest rate provisions
    Index
    Period for the indexing of the loan
    Initial rate concession from the market rate
Distribution plan for the tax-free proceeds from refinancing

Exhibit 14-2. Commitments of $100,000 and Over on Shopping Center Mortgages Made by 20 Life Insurance Companies

Year	Number of Loans	Amounts Committed ($000)	Loan Amount ($000)	Interest Rate (by #)	Interest Rate (by $)	Loan/Value	Capitalization Rate	Debt Coverage	Percent Constant	Term (Years/Months)
1982										
1st quarter	14	50,028	3,573	15.38	14.39	69.6	13.7	1.45	15.9	13/0
2nd quarter	15	84,982	5,665	16.33	15.04	82.5	15.1	1.27	15.5	18/6
3rd quarter	15	48,481	3,232	14.92	14.51	64.9	12.2	1.29	15.1	7/10
1981										
1st quarter	16	$108,995	$ 6,812	13.58	13.33	72.6%	12.8%	1.27	13.8%	10/11
2nd quarter	10	112,520	11,252	14.58	13.59	71.0	13.1	1.22	14.8	19/1
3rd quarter	6	24,424	4,071	13.68	13.55	75.7	11.8	1.25	14.0	14/0
4th quarter	10	23,238	2,324	15.26	14.93	66.6	13.7	1.36	15.5	11/7
1980										
1st quarter	14	71,260	5,090	12.23	11.69	70.7	11.6	1.29	12.0	17/1
2nd quarter	2	21,125	10,562	NA	NA	NA	NA	NA	NA	NA
3rd quarter	14	68,284	4,877	12.84	13.08	70.4	12.3	1.32	13.3	15/10
4th quarter	9	29,228	3,243	12.92	12.85	73.5	12.1	1.26	13.2	11/1
1979										
1st quarter	86	557,958	6,488	9.99	9.96	74.5	10.1	1.25	10.9	21/1
2nd quarter	105	511,036	4,867	10.17	10.20	74.8	10.3	1.24	11.1	20/4
3rd quarter	70	419,535	5,993	10.39	10.34	74.3	10.5	1.28	11.0	21/0
4th quarter	45	266,210	5,916	10.90	10.79	73.1	10.7	1.25	11.6	20/0
1978										
1st quarter	79	412,162	5,217	9.23	9.13	73.7	9.7	1.33	10.1	23/1
2nd quarter	93	308,599	3,318	9.39	9.42	72.6	9.8	1.39	10.4	22/11
3rd quarter	66	310,765	4,709	9.71	9.68	73.1	10.0	1.31	10.5	21/11
4th quarter	70	290,740	4,153	9.90	9.89	74.5	10.2	1.24	11.0	20/9

Source: Investment Bulletins, Table L. Washington, D. C.: American Council of Life Insurance, 1979–1982.

Recently, as lenders have tended to shorten center loans, they have considered call options. The call options at perhaps five-year intervals permit the lender to renegotiate the loan terms before the loan is extended further. The market has been changing so rapidly with inflation and credit conditions that lenders are tending to add this item to negotiation.

Convertible debt features have recently been considered. The investor may purchase the debt obligation of the developer. This debt may be convertible or exchanged for the stock of the development company or ownership entity at the option of the investor. The time for the exchange of the debt for the equity interest depends on the conversion ratio and the possible capital appreciation from the holding of the stock in the future. Therefore, the purchase price of the stock at conversion and the possible equity yield from the stock ownership are important components of the negotiation.

Any of the mortgage terms may be negotiated at the wish of any of the involved parties. Even more or less standardized provisions, such as those related to insurance coverage and the payment of insurance proceeds, are always subject to negotiation. Another example is the usual provision for lender approval of assignment or subletting of major tenant leases. Such a mortgage provision may be part of the "boiler plate" or the provisions may be negotiated for a special advantage or disadvantage for a certain party to the negotiations.

The Loan Constant. The negotiation of the loan constant results in loan provisions for the term to maturity, contract interest rate, and amortization plan. The loan constant is the portion of the original loan amount which represents the level payment debt service for each repayment period of the fully amortized mortgage for the life of the mortgage at the contract interest rate. For example, the loan constant for an 11 percent loan for 30 years with level annual payments is 0.115025. The loan constant for the same 11 percent fully amortized loan for 30 years but with level monthly, quarterly, and semi-annual payments is given below.

Annual payments	0.115025
Semiannual	0.057307
Quarter	0.028603
Month	0.009523

The reader can readily see how fast the loan constant drops as the payment periods per year increase. The loan constant also changes as the term to maturity changes. Below we may see the change in the loan constant for the 11% fully amortized loan with level annual payments as the term to maturity shortens.

Years	Constant
30	0.116025
25	0.118740
20	0.125576
15	0.139065
10	0.169801
5	0.270570

The center obviously must generate a much higher annual net operating income in order to cover the shorter annual debt service requirements. The prospective borrower must always keep in mind the lender's debt coverage requirement for the granting of the loan. The negotiated loan terms must adhere to the established debt coverage ratio even if the debt service is relatively high with relatively high interest rates and a relatively short term to maturity.

Another loan constant relationship is the change in constant with the change in the interest rate given an established term to maturity. The constants for 10- and 20-year fully amortized loans with level annual payments are shown below for contract interest rates of 10, 12, 15, 18, and 20 percent. As the contract rate increases, the loan constant increases.

Contract Interest Rate	20-Year Term	10-Year Term
10%	0.117460	0.162745
12	0.133879	0.176984
15	0.159761	0.199252
18	0.186820	0.222515
20	0.205357	0.238523

The lender examines the expected net operating income each year of the projected holding period. At the same time, the lender considers the interest rate return required for this portion of the lender's portfolio. Usually a debt coverage ratio is established for each type of mortgage loan that the lender makes. The preferences of the borrower for interest expense and loan term are recognized in light of the debt service the net operating income from the property will carry. The lender and the investor alike realize that any one loan constant represents several interest rate–loan term combinations. Rate and term combinations for an annual loan constant of 0.20 (assuming level annual payments) are given below.

Interest Rate (%)	Loan Term (years)
20	30
18	13½
16	10½
14	9½
12	8½
10	7½

If the net operating income is projected at $600,000 and the debt coverage requirement is 1.2, the debt service cannot exceed $500,000. If the developer thinks that $5 million should be borrowed for the permanent financing of the center, the loan constant that the net operating income can support would be $500,000/$5,000,000 or 0.10. What possible financing would be permitted with a loan constant of 0.10? The following rate-term combinations (again assuming level annual payments) are available to the lender.

Interest Rate (%)	Loan Term (years)
10	60
9½	33
9	26
8½	23
8	21

If the lender sees that an annual loan constant means a maximum of 10 percent interest if the loan is underwritten for 60 years and the lender currently needs a much higher interest rate return, the next thing that can be considered is reduction of the size of the original mortgage loan. In today's market this phenomenon occurs frequently so that many centers subsequently have more equity committed and less leverage than is possible in an economic period of lower interest rates.

If the original mortgage loan could be reduced from $5 million to $2.5 million with the additional equity contribution from the owner or ownership group of $2.5 million, the net operating income could carry a debt service with a loan constant of 0.20 ($500,000/$2,500,000). The lender might be able to fund a loan with a rate-term combination given above. For example, the lender might settle for a 16 percent contract rate with 10½-year maturity or an 18 percent rate with a 13½-year maturity. The debt service coverage would be 1.2 with a net operating income of $600,000 and a loan of $2.5 million.

If the lender and the borrower think these terms, which both result in a 0.20 loan constant, are too stringent and will settle for a lower interest rate and longer term as long as there is a strong likelihood of significant equity participation, the loan offered might have a loan constant lower than 0.20. A 13 percent loan for 20 years might be offered the borrower; the loan constant would be 0.142354. The lender would have to feel assured that the rest of the desired yield would come from equity participation. If the coverage requirement of 1.2 was met, the loan amount would go up to $500,000/0.142354 = $3,512,374, roughly $3.5 million. More equity would have to be invested than first thought, but the additional equity would have to be only $1.5 million with a loan constant of 0.142354 rather than $2.5 million if the loan constant were held at 0.20. The catch would be the source of the extra $1.5 million in equity.

Amortization. The repayment of the money borrowed, called amortization, may be scheduled in a number of ways. A straight term loan may be set up. The borrower would pay only interest each payment period and the total principal at the maturity of the loan. In contrast, the loan might provide for payment of interest only for the first five years followed by interest and amortization payments for the rest of the loan life. Another way of repaying the principal is the establishment of a fully amortized level payment loan where an increasing amount of each debt service payment goes toward principal repayment while an interest payment makes up the residual portion of the payment.

Points. If the lender agrees to a contract interest rate which is less than the market rate of interest, that lender may require the payment of points at the closing of the loan. The payment of discount points means prepaid interest to the lender (called the mortgagee) from the borrower (called the mortgagor). One discount point equals 1 percent of the original mortgage amount. If a lender requires five points from the mortgagor at the closing and the initial loan amount is $5,000,000, the mortgagor pays the mortgagee $5,000,000 × 0.05 or $250,000 at the closing. Usually discount points are required by the mortgagee only in the case of residential mortgages covered by FHA (Federal Housing Administration) mortgage insurance or VA (Veterans Administration) guarantees. Here the contract rate of interest is set by the U.S. Housing and Urban Development in consultation with Congress. This administered rate is usually below the market rate of interest, and the lender must charge points to bring the loan yield to the current market yield.

Once the lender amortizes the prepaid interest across the expected life of the mortgage, perhaps 12 years, the annual yield to the lender goes from the contract rate up to the effective market rate of interest in some cases. One discount point approximates ⅛ percent of yield when the prepaid interest is amortized in the above mentioned manner. Therefore, if the mortgagor had paid five points on the $5,000,000 loan and the contract rate had been 15 percent, the approximate yield would be 15⅝ percent. The mortgagor may not mind the prepayment of mortgage interest if the tax laws permit the immediate deduction of this expense for federal income tax purposes.

Usury Rates. Usury rates established by the state legislatures beyond which the lender's yield could not trespass existed for many years for the various types of lending. Most business mortgage loans over $100,000 and corporate mortgage loans of any amount were exempt from these interest yield ceilings, which applied primarily to residential mortgages. At any time, though, state legislatures could declare that the contract rate plus the prepaid interest plus other direct loan fees for commercial mortgage loans could not exceed a statutory ceiling. In 1980, however, Congress eliminated mortgage usury ceilings set by state legislatures; federal authority preempted state authority in this matter. The usury ceilings were choking off mortgage money needed for permanent residential financing in states with ceilings below the going mortgage market rates. It was better to take federal action quickly than to wait for the individual state legislatures to reform or eliminate their existing usury statutes.

Due-on-Sale Clauses and Loan Assumption. As mortgage lenders have sought to protect themselves from inflation risk, they have not permitted loan assumptions on the original terms of the mortgage. In most instances, since the existing mortgage was negotiated, mortgage yields have moved up with inflation. Therefore, most commercial mortgages on shopping centers have due-on-sale or similar clauses concerning loan assumption by subsequent center purchasers. The due-on-sale clause, which has recently gained notoriety in the residential mortgage market, states that the outstanding balance of the mortgage comes due when the mortgaged property is sold to a new party. In this way, the lender gains notice of the change in ownership and may consider continuation of the outstanding loan on current market terms or may call the loan for immediate payment of the outstanding balance. A new mortgage with the new mortgagor can then be negotiated. Generally, the lender is trying to protect his or her portfolio against lower yielding mortgages underwritten in earlier years.

Prepayment Penalty. Mortgagors often wish to prepay their loans if extra funds are available to reduce the outstanding balance. Often the mortgagee will permit a certain amount of early payment without any prepayment penalty. Beyond this established amount of early payment, the lender may negotiate prepayment penalties to discourage the mortgagor from further prepayment and early sale of the mortgaged property. This is particularly true if mortgage interest rates are forecasted to drop decisively. If interest rates are expected to continue upward, the mortgagee may avoid putting a prepayment penalty in the mortgage so that the mortgagor is encouraged to pay the total mortgage off early. The sooner the lenders get the money back, the sooner they can put that same money in higher yielding investments.

Prepayment penalties take different forms. One of the most common forms in shopping center finance is the prohibition of any prepayment for the first few years of the loan, and then progressively lower prepayment penalties. Assuming mortgage lenders only make loans whose yields they are currently satisfied with, the lenders wish to keep those loans on the books and in their cash flow distributions for at least a few years. After, say, a five-year "lockout," the lender might permit prepayment in total or in part at a 5 percent penalty on the prepaid loan amount after five years of the loan have passed. This penalty might be related to Year 6; a 4½ percent penalty might be placed on prepayment during Year 7; 4 percent on Year 8; 3½ percent on Year 9; and so on. After 12 years or the calculated average length of a mortgage, the mortgagee may permit any amount of prepayment without penalty. Thus prepayment penalties become an obstacle to mortgagors' overall flexibility in future sale and refinancing.

Mortgage Kickers and Equity Participation. When the mortgage lender needs more investment yield than the contract rate on the mortgage and the prepaid interest in the form of points allow, the mortgage lender may negotiate for part of the mortgagor's equity. Recently about two-thirds of the loan amounts of commercial retail mortgages have reflected equity kickers (Exhibit 14-3). The provisions for additional lender return beyond the stated interest rate span a wide range (Exhibit 14-4).

Equity participation may take several forms, including (1) participation in the landlord's gross revenues from the center beyond a certain amount; (2) participation in the landlord's net operating income; (3) participation in the landlord's cash flow before taxes but after the contractual debt service payment; (4) participation in the increase in cash flow to the landlord on a rising, sliding scale; (5) participation in the landlord's tax-free proceeds from property refinancing; (6) indexation of the loan amount outstanding (participation in the property value which increases with inflation); (7) participation in overage rents; and (8) indexation of the loan amount outstanding. Let's look at each in detail.

1. *Participation in the Gross Revenues beyond a Certain Amount.* If the annual gross revenues received by the landlord from the center tenants are $4,800,000 ($8 per square foot × 600,000 gross leasable square feet) and the base for the participation is $3,500,000, then the landlord would pay the mortgagee an extra $350,000 if the percent of participation above $3,500,000 was 10 percent. The lender collects this amount in addition to the regular annual debt service.

2. *Participation in the Net Operating Income.* The lender may wish to participate in the net operating income before the regular debt service payment is made. The lender knows that it is difficult to participate in the net taxable income from the center because the landlord may seek to reduce this amount

Exhibit 14-3.   Percentage of Total Commercial Retail Mortgage Loans That Have Provisions for Additional Return (Reported by 20 Life Insurance Companies)

Year	Percent of Total Loans in Terms of Total Number of Loans	Percent of Total Loans in Terms of Total Loan Dollars
1981		
1st quarter	11.4%	66.8%
2nd quarter	38.5	79.3
3rd quarter	30.8	29.3
4th quarter	50.0	62.1
1980		
3rd quarter	17.4	22.8
4th quarter	54.5	60.1

Source: Investment Bulletins, 1980–1982 (Washington, D.C.: American Council of Life Insurance.)

Exhibit 14-4. Provisions for Additional Lender Return beyond the Stated Interest Rate (Reported by 20 Life Insurance Companies in the Period 1980–1982)

Contingent interest
  Income participation
  Equity participation without equity purchase
Joint venture loans
  Less than 10% equity participation
  10 to 25% equity participation
  Over 25% equity participation
  Existing joint venture
Purchase-leaseback of land
Renegotiable/adjustable rate
  Every 3 years
  Every 5 years
  After 10 years
Discount loans
Shared appreciation
Variable rate

Combination of Features

Purchase-leaseback of land with equity participation
Income and equity participation
Purchase-leaseback of land with equity purchase
Income participation with renegotiable rate
Income participation and shared appreciation

Source: Investment Bulletins, 1980–1982 (Washington, D.C.: American Council of Life Insurance).

by every possible tax deduction. Participation in the net operating income may be a little easier, but it may still be difficult to audit the deduction of reasonable operating expenses as the landlord arrives at the income figure for the lender's participation. The landlord's accountant has every motivation to deduct as much as possible in order to decrease the base amount for lender participation. If the mortgage permits 5 percent participation in the net operating income (otherwise called "NOI") and the NOI for the center the previous year was $500,000, then the landlord would have to pay the lender $25,000 extra as part of the mortgage yield.

3. *Participation in the Cash Flow*. The lender may participate in the cash flow after normal debt service but before federal income tax payments.

Net operating income	$1,000,000
Less: contractual debt service	500,000
Cash flow before federal income taxes	$ 500,000

If the lender's percent of participation is 20 percent, the landlord pays extra mortgage debt service of $500,000 × 0.20 or $100,000 immediately after the end of the established accounting period. The lender could participate in the equity at the end of any monthly, quarterly, semiannual, or annual accounting period.

The rate of participation in the cash flow depends upon such things as the participation in the increases in the cash flow, the level or increasing schedule for the participation in the cash flow, the participation in the net sales proceeds, the participation in the refinancing proceeds, the indexing of the outstanding loan balance, the relative level of the original loan-to-cost ratio, and other such considerations.

The mortgagee may consider a basic relationship between contingent interest in total and the loan-to-cost ratio represented by the original mortgage amount. The more leverage the mortgagor acquires, the higher the percentage of contingent interest for the lender, generally speaking. The following relationship might generally prevail.

Loan to Cost	Contingent Interest
100%	50%
95	45
90	40
80	30

4. *Participation in the Increase in the Cash Flow on a Rising, Sliding Scale.* As the cash flow before taxes of the center changes from accounting period to accounting period, the lender may participate in the extent of increase. As the percentage of increase over the prior accounting period increases so may the participation in this increase by the lender. For example, if the cash flow increase is 10 percent from the prior period, the lender may participate in 10 percent of the increase. If the cash flow increase is 25 percent, the lender may participate in 12 percent of the increase. If the cash flow increase is 50 percent, the lender may participate in 15 percent of the increase. This participation in the center's equity is an additional part of the the lender's overall yield from the property in addition to the normal participation in the basic cash flow.

Cash flow before taxes, Year 1988	$550,000
Cash flow before taxes, Year 1987	500,000
Dollar increase in the cash flow	$ 50,000

Increase in the cash flow = 10 percent ($50,000/$500,000)

The lender's participation schedule for cash flow
   15% in all cash flow before taxes generated
   Additional participation in the increase in cash flow:
      10% in percentage annual increases up to and including 10%

12% in percentage annual increases over 10% and up to and including 25%

15% in percentage annual increases over 25% and up to and including 50%

20% in percentage annual increases over 50%

In the example, then, the landlord would pay the lender for Year 1988:

Basic cash flow participation $550,000 × 0.15	= $82,500
Participation in the cash flow increase	
$50,000 increase from last year (10% rise) × 0.10	5,000
Additional lender compensation from cash flow participation	$87,500

5. *Participation in the Refinancing Tax-Free Proceeds to the Landlord.* When the landlord refinances the existing mortgage and walks away with tax-free cash proceeds, the lender may reserve the right through the mortgage to participate in this cash receipt. For example, at the time of the refinancing, the original mortgage balance may be down to $4,000,000 and the new mortgage balance may be raised to $6,000,000 after the refinancing. The landlord of the center would walk away with $6,000,000 − $4,000,000 or $2,000,000 tax free after the refinancing. The original mortgage lender may reserve the right to participate in these receipts. If the percentage participation is 25 percent, then the mortgage lender must receive from the landlord $500,000 extra compensation. This equity participation also becomes part of the overall yield to the mortgage lender.

6. *Participation in the Landlord's Net Sales Proceeds.* When the center is sold while the mortgage is still outstanding, the lender may take part of the sales proceeds as part of the mortgage agreement. Any percent of the proceeds for the lender may be agreed upon. For example, if the center sells for $10 million, the outstanding mortgage balance at the time is $5 million, taxes payable are $2,000,000, the net cash proceeds would be:

Sales price		$10,000,000
Less: Mortgage balance	$5,000,000	
Taxes payable	500,000	5,500,000
Net cash proceeds after taxes		$ 4,500,000

If the lender is entitled to 10 percent of the net cash proceeds after taxes, the lender would expect $450,000 (0.10 × $4,500,000) from the seller-mortgagor.

Quite often the lender participates in the realized or increased cash flow as well as the sales proceeds or residual. The cash flow and residual combinations in the equity participation may reflect the following:

1. Fixed percentage of the *realized* cash flow plus fixed percentage of the residual (net cash proceeds from sale)

2. Fixed percentage of the *increase* in the cash flow plus a fixed percentage of the residual

3. Increasing percentage or "sliding kicker" on the increase in cash flow plus a fixed percentage of the residual

If there is no participation in the residual or net cash proceeds from sale, then the contingent interest from a fixed or scaled percentage of the realized or increased cash flow may be negotiated on a higher level.

7. *Participation in Overage Rents*. Instead of participation in the gross revenues, cash flow, increases in the cash flow, or net operating income, the lender may be entitled to a part of the overage rents. Most shopping center tenants pay rent on the basis of net, indexed percentage leases, so successful tenants will probably generate significant overage rents for the landlord. The mortgagee may participate with the landlord in these overage payments. The lender may take 40 percent of the overage. An example is below.

Base gross rents (average $6/sq. ft. × 700,000 sq. ft. GLA)	$4,200,000
Overage rents received	1,400,000
Lender participation in the overage rents at the rate of 40 percent	$ 560,000

8. *Indexation of the Loan Amount Outstanding*. The lender may participate in the increased value of the property as the term of the loan passes. The initial debt service is paid including the contribution to principal repayment and the contribution to the lender's interest income. As the index changes, the outstanding loan amount and the debt service change. The lender's capital is protected from inflation while the landlord receives only part of the capital appreciation that the property may gain over time. An example follows.

Hypothetical Index Changes

End of Period	Index Amount	Percent Change from Prior Year
1	100	—
2	110	10%
3	123	12
4	133	8

Original mortgage amount, $10,000,000, 13 percent contract interest, 15-year term with an annual loan constant of 0.1518291 with monthly payments.

Annual Payment Period	Annual Debt Service with Monthly Payments	Principal Repayment	Interest Payment	Outstanding Loan Balance	Indexed Loan Balance
1	$1,518,291	$218,291	$1,300,000	$ 9,781,709	$10,759,880
2	1,633,663	234,879	1,398,784	10,525,001	11,788,001
3	1,789,762	257,322	1,532,440	11,530,679	12,453,133

Other Mortgage Terms

The mortgage or deed of trust is a complicated document with numerous provisions. Sometimes its significance is facetiously measured by the total inches of the document or the total poundage of the file containing the mortgage.

The Relationship between the Period of Financing and the Time of the Payment. Mortgages can be payable in advance or in arrears. That is to say, the payment may be made in advance of the financing period or the payment may follow the financing period. According to general mortgage lending practices, most mortgage payments are made in arrears. The period of financing takes place—that is, the month, quarter, six months, or year of financing passes—and then the mortgage payment for that period is due. Residential mortgage payments are usually payable in arrears by the month. Commercial mortgages including shopping center mortgages may be payable in arrears by the month, quarter, semiannual period, or year. Many shopping center mortgages are payable in arrears less frequently than a month. The payment period depends on the cash flow preferences of the mortgagee and mortgagor. Trading conventions of the secondary market have less influence over the payment period in commercial mortgages than they do in residential mortgages.

The Tax-Free or Taxable Rate of Interest. The interest received by the investor from the mortgage or industrial development bond may be free from federal income taxation or it may not be. Usually the interest payable under a mortgage or deed of trust agreement is taxable when received by the investor. The interest received after the purchase of a tax-exempt municipal or industrial development bond is free from taxation by the Internal Revenue Service. The developers and owners are usually financed in this advantageous way because the center (1) provides increased sales and property tax receipts for the local governmental jurisdictions, (2) provides increased employment opportunities for unskilled, previously unemployed workers, and (3) raises the economic level of a neighborhood otherwise described as economically deprived or depressed. The rate of interest to the developer usually reflects the municipal bond rate of interest for that bond issue plus the investment banking fees charged. Recently the cost of tax-free financing to the developer has approximated two points (or two percentage points or 200 basis points) below current taxable rates of interest in the marketplace. This type of below-market-rate financing has developed for residential and commercial development during the extended period of chronic inflation and increased levels of unemployment.

Restrictions on Lease Assignment and Subleasing. The lender whose repayment schedules are based on the cash flows from net, indexed percentage leases of the tenants of the center are sensitive to lease assignments and subleasing agreements between the landlord-mortgagor and the various individual tenants. The mortgagee often requires the right to give approval or disapproval to the proposed assignment or subleasing agreement. The mortgagee is concerned with the credit status and sales performance of those from whom the landlord acquires rental receipts. Before the landlord-mortgagor can approve the new tenancy of the storeroom, the mortgagee must be consulted for lease approval. Subletting or subleasing means that the original tenant remains financially responsible for the payment of rent in the various forms under the original lease. Assignment is more significant to the mortgagee because the original tenant is released from the financial obligations of the original lease and the new occupant assumes the full financial responsibility for the storeroom lease. The mortgagee may want to oversee the provisions in the lease for the default by the tenant due to bankruptcy or other financial conditions.

Subordination Clauses. There are two parties associated with mortgage financing who may subordinate their financial positions: the landowner and the mortgage lender. If the developer-owner leases the center land or any part of it, the leasehold mortgage lender may require that the landowner subordinate his or her financial interest to the leasehold mortgage. Leasehold lenders often will finance only on the basis of first mortgages or deeds of trust. Without a subordination agreement with the landowner, the landowner retains the first priority to the receipts from the shopping center in case of ground lease default. In other words, if the lessee defaults on the ground lease conditions, the landowner may foreclose on the lessee's shopping center with first priority on the proceeds from its sale.

If the landowner subordinates his or her interest to the leasehold mortgage lender, the landowner takes a second priority or residual position in the event that default occurs. If the landowner does not subordinate, the leasehold mortgage lender usually wants the privilege of satisfying the lease agreement to cure the ground lease default for the lessee so that the landowner does not foreclose on the center with first priority to the sale proceeds. If the leasehold mortgagee cures the default with the payment of money, that lender merely adds the amount to the outstanding leasehold mortgage balance and charges interest on this additional amount advanced for the lessee-mortgagor, but default on the ground lease may be prevented.

One mortgagee financing the center may subordinate to another mortgagee purposefully. If the lender does not want to finance as a first mortgage lender, that lender permanently subordinates to the lender with first priority on the receipts from the property in case of loan default. This subordinated lender may enjoy the additional investment yield from the assumption of additional financial risk as a junior mortgagee. Or the lender is restricted by portfolio or other regulations from assuming a first mortgage position. For example, the portfolio regulations may permit only a second mortgage position or the amount of the mortgage will have to fit into the "basket clause" provisions. If the lender is a life insurance company, it may not want to use the flexibility of investment afforded by the basket clause for this particular mortgage. More will be said about basket clause provisions in the discussion of lending by life insurance companies for their own accounts later in the text.

Reciprocal Easement Agreement. As the center has become a multi-owner, multiple financed commercial enterprise with department store ownership and financing of its own premises and land, the reciprocal easement agreement or overall operating easement has assumed strategic importance. The individual lease and operating agreements between each tenant and landlord and between each department store and developer are subordinated to the overriding reciprocal easement agreement (REA) which integrates all the property and financial interests of the total operating center. Since all parties to the operation, ownership, and financing of the center are dependent upon the successful operation of the center as a whole, each of the parties benefits from the detailed documentation of the agreement and its enforcement.

As the development of the center evolved into such a segmented financial entity with segmented ground leases, divided land ownership, multiple building ownership, multiple mortgages per property, and enclosed mall space serving all operating entities, the overall operating agreement arose. This reciprocal easement agreement is usually recorded at least in memorandum form for the legal protection of all interests and for public notice. The extensive, detailed portions of the agreement may remain private to the parties involved, particularly the agreements for maintenance of exclusive operating clauses and the minimal conditions for department store operation and merchandising. The owners and mortgagees, for example, gain considerable security from the overall agreement. The restrictions on future changes and modifications of the center tend to assure continued financial success.

Significant future changes in almost every area of center operation, ownership, and financing are subject to restrictions from the reciprocal easement agreement (REA). Some of the relationships controlled by the REA are:

Lease assignment
Property ownership transfer
Foreclosure conditions for mortgagees and mortgagors
Renovation after fires, condemnation, or other calamities

Remodeling conditions
Expansion of the center with additional stores
Changes in the parking lot
Changes in street ingress and egress

The clauses of the REA constrain cancellation or modification of any of the existing agreement for the financial security of the center as a whole.

TYPES OF LOANS AVAILABLE FOR CENTER FINANCING

Various types of loans, secured and unsecured, are available for various stages of center development and operation. Some of the loan types are associated

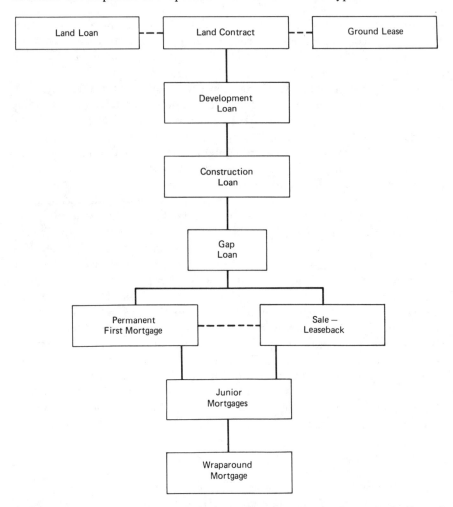

Exhibit 14-5.   Construction and Development Financing—Income Properties in General

primarily with land acquisition and financing. Some are connected principally with land development and improvement construction. Other types are associated with the operating stage of the development.

Land Acquisition

A *commercial loan* from a commercial bank, finance company, savings and loan association, or real estate investment trust (also called a REIT, pronounced "reet") may enable the prospective center developer to acquire the fee interest of the proposed site. This loan often covers only 40 to 50 percent of the land value. A business associate or other individual may also provide the funds for this short-term loan. Many developers start project development with the outright ownership of the fee of the proposed development site.

If a *land loan* is not acquired, the seller may wish to negotiate an *installment sale* of the property. The seller finances the sale at 100 percent of value with a relatively low down payment and agrees to accept installment payments which encompass a reasonable rate of return on the loaned money for the seller. The seller may gain favorable tax treatment through the installment receipt of cash and a relatively high sale price with the interest rate set at the market or lower. The developer receives the benefit of no immediate, total cash outflow for the land purchase. Other costs of development must be covered by the developer at the same time.

The seller may also agree to a *land contract* with the purchaser. Unlike the installment sale where the buyer immediately takes title to the fee, the vendee (buyer) of the land contract takes title to the property after the vendor (seller) has received all payments on the installment contract. If a low down payment is permitted, the seller is providing almost 100 percent financing. The vendor may permit the vendee to take title after a sufficient amount of the payments have been made and the vendee is in a position to acquire traditional financing with a financial institution. The vendee may be paid in full with the proceeds from the new mortgage monies. The vendor receives periodic interest income and principal repayment. The vendee benefits from tax-deductible interest payments and the slow cash outflow for subsequent land ownership.

The developer may ask the landowner to become a partner in the center development. The landowner, who contributes the land to the venture, therefore, would become a *joint venture partner*, a *limited partner*, or other such partner. As a partner in the venture, the landowner would expect to receive a return on the investment and perhaps share in the equity of the operating center and the residual proceeds of the future sale.

The land could be *syndicated* if the developer finds that its value is exorbitant. The developer could negotiate with the landowner for an option to purchase. Then the developer could proceed to syndicate the ownership. Investors might be attracted to the land ownership by the proposed rental rate to be paid on the ground lease arranged with the developer. The rate of investment return built into the lease payments might prove very attractive to investors wishing to increase their cash flows. These same investors may wish to increase their assets which may be subject to the favorable capital gains taxation at the time of the future sale.

The developer might acquire the deed to the land through the offer of a *purchase money mortgage* by the original landowner. To reduce the cash outflow, the developer might negotiate for a high ratio mortgage. (This refers to a relatively high loan-to-value ratio for mortgage lending purposes.) A low down payment might lead to acquisition of a valuable property. Seller financing is always a possibility.

To reduce the developer's current cash outflow, he or she might also consider *deferred acquisition* with the current landowner. An installment purchase might be arranged where the seller would finance delayed payment in the purchase installments. The seller might be motivated by tax considerations to defer the installment receipts to periods when his or her overall rates for federal income taxation might decline to a lower level. For example, the first payment might be delayed one year from the effective time of purchase.

A three-party agreement might be devised so that the developer would take an option to purchase on the land intending to sell the land to an investor so that it could be leased back over a long period. The three parties to the *sale-leaseback* would be the original landowner, the developer with the option to purchase, and the individual investor or financial institution which agrees to buy the land and lease it back to the developer.

If the developer acquires the fee to the land, a mortgage may be placed on the fee interest. As an alternative, a leasehold mortgage may be placed on the real property estate created by the ground lease. A subsidiary of the developer may lease the fee from the development company and then sublet to the tenants of the center. A mortgage could then be placed on the fee and another mortgage on the leasehold estate.

Land Development

A commercial loan may be separately acquired for the development of the proposed site from its original condition as raw land. A short-term loan, unsecured like the land loan, may be acquired at a rate in excess of the bank prime rate. The developer may face the lender's use of a relatively low loan-to-value ratio. The loan cannot be secured by the proposed center because it does not yet exist in saleable form. The financial institution or individual may require collateral in the form of other property or assets of the developer. If the developer is well known by the commercial bank or other source of funds, the land development loan may be merely a personal loan. The land is prepared for the construction of the permanent improvements with the money from this loan and equity from the owner. The utility lines are installed after the drainage improvements are made. The land is graded and landscaped. Preliminary drives and parking lots are constructed for the construction crew parking and the ingress and egress of construction-related vehicles.

Since land development for the proposed construction usually takes a short period of time, the interest rate on the loan is usually fixed. The loan rate will be set at so many points above prime or some other selected rate.

Interim Loan for Construction of the Improvements

Usually the developer gets a permanent loan commitment and takes it to a construction lender to get interim financing. Some interim loans for construction are acquired without the permanent commitment in the hands of the developer. The developer always stands the chance of construction loan rejection or higher than normal interest rates when a permanent commitment is not acquired earlier. The lender is not assured of repayment without the permanent commitment unless the developer gets a standby commitment or gap loan from a source.

Construction Loan. The construction loan may span two to five years because construction may take that long. This short-term, unsecured loan which covers total construction costs is usually underwritten at so many points above the bank prime or bank commercial paper rate. Quite often the base rate is a composite of rates from the most active New York banks. The loan amount is often 75 percent of the appraised value.

When construction is completed and the developer has the building permits and the certificate of occupancy, the construction loan is due. Interest is paid to the lender as the interim loan amounts are taken from the institution or individual in the form of advances. The principal amount of the loan is totally repaid at the completion of construction. Permanent loan proceeds usually fund the construction loan. A gap or standby lender may extend the monies that repay the construction loan.

The construction lender advances money as the architect, owner, and general contractor vouch for the completion of individual phases of the construction. A title company often makes the loan advances with a percentage holdback, such as 5 to 15 percent, after it has assured itself of the clear ownership of the property of the borrower. The title company usually checks the docket for mechanic's liens before it considers advancement of the next requisitioned monies. The owner is notified of the filing of any liens against the property by the title company as the construction proceeds. (A mechanic's lien is a claim that a laborer, material supply house, or other party engaged in the construction of a land improvement has upon the property of the owner as security for a debt or outstanding obligation such as overdue wages.) Mechanic's liens can usually be satisfied through sale of the project, but this is seldom done. The lender wants the owner to clear any liens filed against the property so that the lender's lien position is secure. For example, the construction lender wants to maintain lien priority over any construction workers or material supply houses.

Gap Loan. Another type of interim loan is a gap loan. The money from a gap loan is used to repay the construction and other prior loans. The gap loan may be required because a permanent loan commitment has not yet been acquired. The gap loan has substantial risk associated with it because a permanent lender has not yet appeared, so it is usually short and is underwritten at a higher rate than the land, land development, and construction loans. The lender is compensated for the generally high-risk status of the financing. The REITs may be sources for this type of loan. Other relatively unregulated real estate lenders who may assume relatively high-risk investments may be able to accommodate a developer with this type of short-term loan. This loan can be secured by the time of its funding by the lender because the center will be completed and the construction lender is being paid.

Standby Commitment. If the total permanent financing is not yet committed, a standby commitment may be acquired from a lender. If monies are needed to pay off earlier loans and a permanent loan or equity is not available at the appropriate time, a lender may be paid to stand by with interim loan funds. Real estate investment trusts have had the inclination to fund such standby positions in the past. A nonrefundable fee is usually charged for the standby commitment, and then a relatively high rate is placed on the loan if monies eventually have to be advanced. The standby commitment may be required by the construction lender in order for the developer to acquire the interim loan for construction.

PERMANENT FINANCING

Permanent financing is needed to pay back the amount due on the construction loan and to finance the long-term operation of the center. This permanent financing takes many forms. As time goes by and inflation persists, new forms of financing are added to numerous traditional forms.

The Takeout or Permanent Loan Commitment

Before permanent financing in any form is placed on the property, the developer-owner has to get a takeout or permanent loan commitment. This commitment usually must precede the acquisition of the interim financing. The construction lender usually wants to know that he or she will be repaid from the permanent loan proceeds when construction is finished. This commitment is a document, perhaps in the form of an extended letter, which irrevocably pledges the source of permanent loan funds to make the loan described when the construction is finished or a certain occupancy level is reached or, in the case of an existing center, when a certain closing date is reached. The developer will more than likely permit the execution of the promised action. But it is possible that, if the developer gets a commitment later which promises more favorable terms, the prior commitment will be cancelled by the developer. Since the original permanent lender may thereafter question the integrity of that developer, this action does not often occur.

The Kinds of Takeout Commitments. Actually there are several kinds of takeout commitments. Some of them are related to permanent debt financing. Some are related to partial or total equity financing from the lender involved. Names of some of the types follow.

Permanent debt financing commitments
    Standard long-term permanent loan commitment
    Junior mortgage commitment
    Commitment to participate in permanent financing
    Combination construction loan and permanent loan commitment
Total equity financing commitments
    Purchase-leaseback commitment
    Commitment to purchase upon completion
    Commitment to syndicate upon completion
    Commitment to purchase a fee with or without subordination
Other types of commitments
    Standby commitment
    Purchase-saleback commitment
    Land-purchase-leaseback-leasehold mortgage commitment
    Commitment to joint venture

The Typical Lenders Who Issue Takeout Commitments. Through custom in the United States, these financial institutions give takeout commitments that indicate their promise to provide funds to the prospective borrower at a later date:

Insurance companies
Commercial banks
Mutual savings banks
Savings and loan associations
Pension funds
Real estate investment trusts
Corporations
Foundations and endowment funds

The Content of the Takeout Commitment. The document conveyed by the lender to the prospective mortgagor usually states the loan amount that will be provided, the contract rate, the loan term, and the repayment provisions. The prepayment provisions are pointed out. The other terms of the takeout commitment are mentioned below.

Refundable and nonrefundable fees
Description of the pledged property
Termination date of the commitment and the provisions for possible extension
Lender approval of the plans and specifications or any required modifications

Necessary payment by the mortgagor of outstanding taxes and assessments

Tax and insurance escrow deposits required

Floor loan amount and the leasing requirements for the funding of the floor loan

Leasing requirements for the funding of the maximum loan amount

Terms and conditions for the tenant leases

Assignment of rents

Assignment and sublease requirements for the tenant leases

Corporate or personal liability or exculpation from liability

Hazard and rent insurance requirements

Contingent interest or loan participation conditions

Requirements for reciprocal easement and other operating agreements

The buy-sell agreement among the mortgagor, permanent lender, and construction lender

All of the clauses necessary to the complete understanding of both mortgagor and mortgagee about the promised financing should be set forth. As soon as the takeout commitment is accepted by the mortgagor, the mortgagee may work this cash flow situation into his or her overall cash flow distribution for future periods.

Variable Rate Mortgage

The interest rate on the mortgage and therefore the debt service payments vary with a selected index of interest rates. If the selected index goes down over the mortgage payment period, the interest rate for the mortgage payment for the next period may be adjusted downward. Quite often the mortgage will state the minimum change in the index which will cause a change in the mortgage rate. If the change upward or downward in the index is less than the established differential, the mortgage rate and the mortgage payment will remain the same. If the change in the index is equal to or greater than the minimum differential change, the lender is required to change the rate on the mortgage a given amount and the dollar amount of the next debt service payment.

During the 1960s and the early 1970s, commercial mortgage rates often floated over either the New York bank prime rate or the New York commercial paper rate by an established number of interest points. As the index rate changed, the debt service requirements changed for the mortgagor. Often permanent loans on shopping centers carried variable rates. Developers became accustomed to the common phenomenon, particularly in scarce money and high interest rate periods. Center owners have never favored variable rate mortgages, but they have been forced to agree to them to get the right amount of financing for the right loan term with lesser equity participation then otherwise.

Blanket Mortgage

A mortgage may rest on the collateral of several real and personal properties of the mortgagor. The lender may not be able to make the loan unless the equity or structures of more than one property are pledged as collateral for the center mortgage. The equity or real property may take the form of several existing centers whose mortgages have been paid down to relatively low levels or whose values have risen beyond the value of the original loan collateral.

As the blanket mortgage payments are made and the loan is reduced to a sufficient level, one or more of the underlying properties collateralized for this loan may be released. The lender may continue to maintain a loan relationship where the loan balance is approximately 75 percent of the pledged property, if the original loan-to-value ratio was 75 percent.

Rollover Mortgage

A rather short mortgage may be renewed repeatedly by the given lender. The constant renewal or rollover of the three- or five-year mortgage amounts to the same financing as a loan for an extended period, such as 30 to 40 years. Canadian residential mortgages have taken this form for years. The lender is not obligated to renew the mortgage on the original terms or on changed terms. If mortgage monies are scarce for the lender or if the mortgagor's credit standing has deteriorated significantly during the last mortgage period, the lender may elect not to renew the loan. The mortgagor has recourse to approach another mortgage lender to continue the financing of the subject property with a new mortgage from another lender.

First Mortgage

A first mortgage is the mortgage lien with first priority on the real property pledged in case of loan default and foreclosure. If a mortgage is foreclosed, the lienor or mortgagee with first priority is paid first from the proceeds from the property sale. If the mortgage is considered in good standing, the first mortgagee has the first right to the net operating receipts of the center as funds are distributed to mortgagees.

A first mortgage may be on the fee, on the leasehold estate, or on a subleasehold estate. A loan may be made to the party holding the fee simple absolute or, in short form, the fee interest in the center or land. The loan may not be made on the basis of the ownership of the fee interest, but on the basis of a leasehold interest. If the party that owns the leasehold estate wishes to mortgage that interest in order to build the permanent improvements on the land, the lender would make a leasehold mortgage. The party that wants to make the improvements may be a subleasehold entity rather than a leasehold owner. The landowner may lease to a tenant who may lease to a prospective shopping center developer. The developer wants to improve the land but only holds a subleasehold estate in the land. A lender, therefore, could make a first subleasehold loan. There can be junior mortgage interests in the fee, the leasehold, and the subleasehold. The subleasehold loan of any priority is a rarity.

In order for a lender to make a *first* leasehold mortgage loan on the land, the lender would have to require the subordination of the fee interest in the land. The fee owner of the land may or may not be willing to subordinate to the leasehold mortgagee. Sometimes the landowner will subordinate his or her fee interest in exchange for high lease payments and, therefore, a higher rate of return from the leased land. If a first subleasehold loan were financed, the fee owner and the leasehold estate owner would both have to subordinate their interests to the subtenant. It is not going to happen often.

Junior Mortgage

A junior mortgage is a mortgage lien that has less priority over the property sale proceeds in foreclosure or the current net operating income than the first mortgage lien. A junior mortgage may be a second, third, or any other subordinated mortgage. A wraparound mortgage (discussed later in this chapter) may be a second mortgage; therefore, it is a junior lien. At lease one lien is already on the center when the wraparound mortgage is financed with the center as collateral. A junior mortgage lien can be attached to any real property interest just as a first mortgage lien can.

Junior mortgage financing is based on the amount of appraised value of the center that the junior mortgage lender perceives as collateral for the junior mortgage loan. For example, the first mortgage lender may look to 60 percent of the appraised valuation of the center to cover the amount of the loan. Forty percent of the appraised valuation would remain as possible collateral for junior mortgage lenders. A second mortgage lender may agree to fund a loan which would represent 25 percent of the appraised valuation. This lender might feel relatively secure in his or her lending position. Fifteen percent of the appraised valuation remains as a buffer zone against exigencies of the future including possible decline in the market value of the center. If the appraised value of the center is $5,000,000, the first mortgage loan may represent 60 percent of value or $3,000,000. The second mortgage loan at 25 percent of value could represent $1,250,000. Smaller third and fourth mortgage loans— junior mortgage loans—may also possibly be placed on the property. Such junior mortgage financing depends on the risk-return status and the wishes of the mortgagor and the particular mortgagee. An example follows.

First Mortgage Financing. $3,000,000 first mortgage loan at 60% of value at 15% interest for 20 years annual payments, fully amortized.

Loan constant: 0.159761
Annual debt service: 0.159761 × $3,000,000 = $479,283

Net operating income from the center	
(20% of value)	$1,000,000
Annual debt service	− 479,283
Cash flow before taxes (and possible participation)	$ 520,717

$$\text{Return on equity} = \frac{\text{cash flow}}{\text{equity investment}} = \frac{\$520{,}717}{\$2{,}000{,}000} = 26\%$$

This mortgage might call for contingent interest (equity participation) such as the following alternatives:

1. 10% of gross revenues in excess of $300,000
2. 20% of net operating income in excess of $250,000
3. 5% of total gross revenue
4. 25% of percentage rents

Second Mortgage Financing. $1,250,000 second mortgage loan at 25% of value at 17% interest for 10 years annual payments, fully amortized.

Loan constant: 0.214657
Annual debt service: 0.214657 × $1,250,000 = $268,321.25

Net operating income from the		
center (20% of value)		$1,000,000
Annual debt service:		
First mortgage	$479,283	
Second mortgage	268,321	747,604
Cash flow before taxes (and possible participation)		$ 252,396

$$\text{Return on equity} = \frac{\text{cash flow}}{\text{equity investment}} = \frac{\$252{,}396}{\$750{,}000} = 33.7\%$$

The regular junior mortgage is separate from the prior mortgage. The wraparound mortgage which wraps around the prior mortgage is a newer variation of a junior mortgage. The regular junior mortgagee receives only the debt service for the junior mortgage principal repayment and interest income. Debt service is not paid to the prior mortgagee by the regular second mortgage lender.

Combined First and Second Mortgages

Today, a lender who wishes to take a deep financial interest in the center may finance both the first and second mortgages on the center. He or she may take a substantial equity interest in the property at the same time. Shopping center financing has been a favored form of institutional financing because of its inherent inflation protection. The lender mentioned might really have in mind total ownership of the center within a certain time frame. The developer and the lender may wish to have the developer and other associated owners hold the ownership for a few years before the lender exercises an option to purchase the remaining outside equity. For various financial and tax reasons, the lender may finance both the first and second mortgages at one time. Separate mortgages may need to exist rather than a single mortgage because of portfolio restrictions and institutional or governmental regulations.

Intermediate-Term Callable Loans

The shorter term permanent loans that are callable at specific intervals after the loan origination are variations of the Canadian rollover mortgage. The loan intervals between the call times are longer than the three- to five-year intervals on the Canadian rollovers. The mortgagee is attempting to provide permanent financing but must be assured of inflation protection. At the call times, the lender can terminate the loan or negotiate for different loan terms, such as higher interest and a higher percentage of equity participation. If the mortgagor's credit has deteriorated, the mortgagee can terminate the loan outright with no chance for renegotiation of the original loan. The adjustment of the loan can be made at specified call times. The mortgage may be callable every so many years or at given times at unequal intervals. For example, the mortgage may be callable every 10 years through a total loan period of 40 years.

Level-Payment, Fully Amortized Permanent Loans

Some shopping centers have been financed on this basis, while many others have been financed on the basis of an interest-only period followed by partial amortization. The level mortgage payments start at the closing of the loan. Even though the periodic mortgage payments are the same, the interest and principal composition of those equal payments changes. By the end of the loan term, perhaps 25 years, the lender has totally recouped the principal amount loaned and has received interest income each payment period. The last payment is the same amount as the first payment. The loan term is the same as the amortization period. For example, if the loan term is 25 years, the amortization period is 25 years.

Balloon Mortgages

The last payment, the balloon payment, is larger than the prior mortgage payments because the loan has been only partially amortized. If the lender receives all of the prescribed mortgage payments on time and paid in full, the lender will receive only part of the amount loaned to the mortgagor. The mortgagor and the mortgagee have agreed to partial amortization. Quite often the two parties have also agreed to an interest-only period at the start of the loan. The mortgagor may pay only interest in the prescribed periodic payments for the first three to five years of the loan. Then the amortization of the principal starts. Balloon mortgages with early interest-only periods are commonly used. The amortization period may be 30 years while the term of the loan is only 20 years. The use of the 30-year loan constant would result in a balloon payment the 20th year of the loan.

Wraparound Mortgage Loan

When the mortgagor is financing with a prior mortgage, a new mortgage may be placed on the property which gives more money to the mortgagor but leaves the prior mortgage in effect. The wraparound mortgage lender gives the mortgagor more money and assumes the obligation of paying the prior mortgage debt service after collecting the debt service for the wraparound mortgage. The wraparound loan amount is the outstanding amount due on the prior mortgage plus the new monies advanced.

There are two kinds of wraparound mortgages: (1) those giving more monies to the mortgagor over the remaining term of the original mortgage, and (2) those giving more monies to the mortgagor where the wraparound mortgage extends beyond the original mortgage. The latter type of wraparound mortgage might have a call option at the end of the original term of the prior mortgage. The wraparound lender would then be in a position to renegotiate new financing for the total needs of the mortgagor into the future. Until this time, the mortgagor would benefit from a lower debt service for the wraparound loan due to its extended term.

Why have wraparound loans become popular for the financing of all kinds of properties?

The Borrower's Viewpoint. The borrower may have a relatively favorable loan on the property already and may find it wise to continue financing with it. Since interest rates have risen faster in 1980 and 1981 than in the prior 35 years, the rates on many early loans are very favorable. Equity participation has increased in the last few years so that any new loans have automatically incorporated that feature where the older loans do not. The existing loan may have a fixed rate and level payments and be fully amortized over 30 to 40 years originally.

The Lender's Viewpoint. The wraparound lender writes a loan for an amount larger than the original loan he or she is wrapping around. For example, the outstanding balance on the original loan may be $1,000,000. The wraparound loan may be underwritten for $1,400,000, but the wrap lender advances only $400,000 in new money to the mortgagor. The wrap lender arranges for the payment of the debt service on the wrap loan to be made to the wraparound lender who is obligated to pay first the required debt service to the first mortgage lender. The wrap lender retains the surplus of the wrap loan debt service as his or her return on investment. The investment is the sum of new monies actually provided by the wrap lender.

The wraparound lender may finance the advancement of the new money at a contract rate below, at, or above the market rate for the loan. The yield to the investor varies with the loan rate selected for the wraparound loan. Exhibit 14-6 shows the variety of results which are possible when the original loan rate is 9 percent and the wrap loan rates are 11, 15, and 17 percent. The variation in yields may also result from differences in loan terms, differences in loan amounts outstanding, and the relative difference between the rate on the original loan and the rate on the present wraparound loan.

Mortgage Bonds

Sometimes a bond issue, based on the appraised value of the center, is sold by the developer to interested investors. Since these bonds pledge as security the financed real property, they are mortgage bonds. The indenture agreement calls for repayment of the amount borrowed with interest over the legal life of the bond. The bonds can be bought like any other industrial or utility bond on the market. The investor should find the interest yield competitive with other bonds of similar risk and marketability.

SHARING THE EQUITY

Mortgage kickers, equity participation, or contingent interest is a part of most permanent financing today. The developer-owner shares his equity in a number of ways which we will review. When a sale-leaseback is engaged in, when a bondable net lease is turned into mortgage debt, when a developer-owner becomes a partner in a joint venture, and when a partnership takes the ownership interest, we find that the developer is sharing the equity with other investors. As we continue into this topic, we will consider the debt arrangements where the lender obtains an option to purchase all or part of the equity.

Mortgage Kicker

The lender may expect more than the contract interest on the debt. If the lender has financed a 13 percent mortgage for 25 years for $5,000,000, for example, that lender may expect more than a 13 percent return on the $5,000,000

Exhibit 14-6. Illustration of Yield Calculations When the Wraparound Loan Rate is below, at, or above the Market Rate for the Loan.

Wrap Loan Rate under the Market Loan Rate

Terms of the original mortgage loan: 30 years, 9 percent, annual payments, level payments, fully amortized, $2,000,000 original amount
Current loan balance: $1,500,000
Remaining term: 20 years

Terms of the wraparound mortgage loan: 20 years, 11 percent, annual payments, level payments, fully amortized, $2,500,000 loan amount

Type of Loan	Annual Loan Constant	Annual Debt Service
Wraparound loan, 11 percent, 20 years	0.125576	$313,940
Original loan	0.097336	194,672
	Difference	$119,268

Basic yield to the wraparound lender: $\dfrac{\text{debt service retained}}{\text{new monies advanced}} = \dfrac{\$119,268}{\$1,000,000}$

$= 11.9\%$

Wrap Loan Rate at the Market Rate, Assuming the Market Rate is 15 Percent

Type of Loan	Annual Loan Constant	Annual Debt Service
Wraparound loan, 15 percent, 20 years	0.159761	$399,403
Original loan	0.097336	194,672
	Difference	$204,731

Basic yield to the wraparound lender: $\dfrac{\text{debt service retained}}{\text{new monies advanced}} = \dfrac{\$204,731}{\$1,000,000}$

$= 20.5\%$

Wraparound Loan above the Market Rate

Type of Loan	Annual Loan Constant	Annual Debt Service
Wraparound loan, 17 percent, 20 years	0.177690	$444,225
Original loan	0.097336	194,672
	Difference	$249,553

Basic yield to the wraparound lender: $\dfrac{\text{debt service retained}}{\text{new monies advanced}} = \dfrac{\$249,553}{\$1,000,000}$

$= 25\%$

invested if the shopping center is successful. In the typical current mortgage, there will be a "mortgage kicker." The lender may also call this additional income from the mortgage "equity participation" or "contingent interest." This mortgage kicker may take the following forms:

A percentage of shopping center gross revenues in excess of a stated amount
A percentage of the net operating income in excess of a stated amount
A percentage of the total gross revenue
A percentage of the cash flow before taxes (cash throwoff)
A portion of the overage rents (the rents paid as a percentage of sales
      achieved over and above the square footage rents for the store space)

Sale-Leaseback Arrangements

The developer gives up some ownership when the land and/or the improvements of the center are sold to an investor and leased back.

Land Sale-Leaseback with a Leasehold Mortgage. The developer may originally own the land. He or she may sell the land to an investor and arrange to lease it back. The substantial sum of money tied up in the land is released for other development purposes, but the developer must keep it under long-term lease for the development and operation of the center. All lease payments are totally deductible for federal income tax purposes unless the Internal Revenue Service finds that the lease payments are essentially installment payments for the purchase of the land. Therefore, the developer may put a clause in the agreement reciting the option to purchase at a reasonable future price at given time intervals.

When the developer sells the land and leases it back for the shopping center, he or she will probably need financing to construct the shopping center improvements. An outside investor may put up all of the cash needed in the form of equity. If only part of the needed money takes the form of equity, debt funds must be acquired. Since the buildings will rest on leased land, the developer must find a lender who will finance leasehold mortgage. Not all long-term lenders will have the facility to make the necessary first or junior leasehold mortgage. Long-term lenders more readily finance mortgages on the fee. Leasehold mortgage financing is hinged to the continued and timely lease payments to the landowner. If the mortgagor defaults on the ground lease payments, the landowner has the right to foreclose on the buildings built on the leased land. The landowner will take title to the center improvements. Therefore, leasehold lenders usually anticipate higher risk in a leasehold mortgage compared to a mortgage on the fee.

The party who buys the land and leases it back may agree to subordinate the fee interest to the leasehold interest of the developer who is seeking a leasehold mortgage. Most lenders prefer a first leasehold mortgage. If the new landowner will not subordinate the fee interest, the leasehold mortgagee is definitely taking a high financial risk as junior mortgage financing is provided.

An illustration of the financial calculations leading to investment returns available for the landowner, the leasehold mortgage lender, and the center owners is shown in Exhibit 14-7. The small center of 125,000 sq. ft./GLA costing $5,500,000 has a free and clear return of 13.54 percent. The cash-on-cash return to equity may be 6.0 percent, the return to the landowner may be approximately 30.4 percent, and the return to the leasehold mortgage lender may be approximately 15.5 percent.

Fee Mortgage and Leasehold Mortgage. If the developer or the ownership group already owns the land for the center, they may lease to a shopping center subsidiary. At the same time, monies may be derived from the land from the mortgaging of the fee. The lease payments can be set so that the mortgage payments are met and there is a return to the equity in the land. As the developer finances the permanent structures, the leasehold lender will be sought if borrowed funds are needed. The developer or ownership group may subordinate their equity interests in the land to the leasehold lender in order to acquire funds on the best terms. There is some evidence that leasehold lenders are becoming accustomed to financing junior leasehold loans for shopping centers. Subordination of the landowner's interest may not be necessary in order to acquire good financing for the buildings.

Sale-Leaseback. The land and the improvements of the shopping center may be sold to an investor or financial institution and leased back on a long-term basis. The previous owners—the developer and partners—may ask for an option to purchase at an agreed price at various times in the future. The developer would have no funds in the project once the sale-leaseback agreement is executed. Often such an agreement is negotiated with a life insurance company or pension fund as the center is being planned. The investor takes title when the developer gets the certificate of occupancy at the completion of construction. There may be a lease-up requirement that must be met before the investor takes title and leases the center back.

If the developer sells the center land improvements in total for $5,500,000 to an investor in return for a 15 percent, 30-year renewable lease, the developer will have no equity invested in the center but may reap a sizable return. Using the basic data from Exhibit 14-7, we see that:

Gross income for the 105,000 sq. ft. at $10/sq. ft.	$1,050,000
Less: Lease payment for land and improvements	
$0.15 \times \$5,500,000 =$	825,000
Residual to the developer before taxes	$ 225,000

Since the developer has no money invested, the rate of return is infinite.

Exhibit 14-7. Illustration of Financing by Means of a Land Sale-Leaseback with a Leasehold Mortgage.

Property description: A proposed 125,000 sq. ft. community shopping center covering 10 acres

Development costs

Land: Approximately 10 acres (435,600 sq. ft.) at $20,000 an acre = $200,000
Sold to an investor for $200,000 and leased back at a rate of 12% for 30 years, annual payments, plus 5% of net operating income available for annual debt service

The constant for the ground lease = 0.124144
Annual ground lease payments = 0.124144 × $200,000 = $24,829

Building cost: 125,000 sq. ft./GLA at $40/sq. ft.	$5,000,000
Land development and other development costs	500,000
Total costs	$5,500,000

Pro forma income and expense

Income: 105,000 sq. ft. at $10.00/sq. ft.	$1,050,000
(including first year overage payments)	

Vacancy and bad debt loss:

Major tenants: None
Minor tenants, 30% of space with 15% estimated vacancy and bad debt loss
0.30 of total space (NLA) 105,000 = 31,500 sq. ft.
31,500 × estimated $12/sq. ft. = $378,000

$378,000 × 0.15 (vacancy) =	56,700
Effective gross income	$ 993,300
Operating expenses including real estate taxes (25% of EGI)	248,325
Net operating income available for debt service and ground rent	$ 744,975
Less: Fixed ground rent	24,829
Balance before participation by the landowner	$ 720,146
Less: Participation by landowners	
(5% of net operating income available for debt service)	36,008
Net operating income available for leasehold mortgage debt service	$684,138

Calculation of leasehold mortgage payment:
Value of leasehold estate:

$$\frac{\text{NOI available for A.D.S.}}{R} = \text{value} = V$$

If NOI available for annual debt service = $684,138
and R = capitalization rate = 0.13
then V = value = $5,262,600

Leasehold loan terms:
70% of value, 14% interest rate, annual payments, 25-year amortization schedule
15-year loan term, 20% participation in NOI available for annual debt service over $500,000

Exhibit 14-7. *(Continued)*

Loan amount = $5,262,600 × 0.70 = $3,683,820
Loan constant = 0.145498
Fixed annual debt service = 0.145498 × $3,683,820 = $535,988

NOI available for annual debt service			$684,138
Less: Leasehold mortgage fixed payment		$535,988	
Leasehold mortgage equity participation			
NOI available for A.D.S.	$684,138		
Base amount	500,000		
Amount subject to participation	$184,138		
Times participation (20%)	× 0.20	36,828	572,816
Cash flow to equity before taxes			$111,322
Value of leasehold estate		$5,262,600	
Mortgage, leasehold		3,683,820	
Value of the equity		$1,578,780	
Total development cost	$5,500,000		
Leasehold mortgage	3,683,820		
Equity contributed	$1,816,180		

Return to equity before taxes:

$$\frac{\text{cash flow before taxes to equity}}{\text{equity investment}} = \frac{\$111,322}{\$1,816,180} = 6\%, \text{first year return}$$

(other forms of return not included here: equity buildup, possible tax shelter, and long-term capital appreciation)

Return to landowner before taxes:

Cash flow before taxes to landowner:	fixed payment	$24,829
	equity participation	36,008
		$60,837

$$\frac{\text{cash flow before taxes to landowner}}{\text{investment in the land}} = \frac{\$\ 60,837}{\$200,000} = 30.4\%, \text{first year return}$$

Return to leasehold mortgage lender

Cash flow before taxes to leasehold lender:	fixed payment	$535,988
	equity participation	36,828
		$572,816

$$\frac{\text{cash flow before taxes to leasehold lender}}{\text{investment in leasehold loan}} = \frac{\$572,816}{\$3,683,820} = 15.5\%, \text{first year return}$$

Joint Venture. When two or more investors pool their talents and financial resources for a single real estate venture, the arrangement is called a joint venture. The partners usually each provide a vital element to the overall financial success of the project. Often shopping centers of some size are developed and financed by this means.

The parties joined together for a shopping center venture are often a developer, a commercial bank, a life insurance company, and a pension fund. Other parties may be represented and the life insurance company or the pension fund may be missing from the group. The developer provides the marketing, construction, and administrative expertise to pull the elements together for a successful center. The commercial bank usually provides the construction loan. The life insurance company may provide the permanent financing for the first years of the center operation. The pension fund may contribute the permanent funds for the later years of the center operation. An architect may join the group with equity capital and architectural and construction expertise. This person and his or her firm may supervise the construction progress. The developer may have a construction company that does the construction work outside of the department store construction. The developer may actually be the real estate subsidiary of a major department store chain such as Homart Development Company of Sears Roebuck or the J. C. Penney development subsidiary.

The venture partners expect to benefit from the financial success of the center. Each party that offers managerial expertise and/or money will expect participation in the equity of the resulting projection. The lenders will probably want a preferred, fixed return on their monies plus some equity participation. They will want to participate in the operating cash flows, gross revenues, overage rents paid, or other such dollar amounts generated by the center. Exhibit 14-8 shows the possible lender and developer returns from equity participation in cash flows before taxes and net sale proceeds before taxes at the end of 10 years. The returns from the small center of 100,000 square feet of GLA depend upon the cash flows generated and the capital appreciation realized at the end of 10 years.

The joint venture agreement may be set up like a limited partnership. The limited partners may be tenants in common with unequal cash contributions. Any partners who join in the active management of the center development and operations take general partnership status with unlimited legal and financial liability. The financial risk of the limited partners is limited to their financial investments usually. Any debt obligations of the partnership are negotiated on a non-recourse basis so that the personal and other business assets of the individual partners cannot be reached to satisfy joint venture obligations. Therefore, exculpatory clauses are generally put in the mortgages.

Limited Partnership. The developer may form a limited partnership for the financing of the center. The developer will probably take the status of the general partner while the limited partners will contribute the equity capital. The limited partnership shares may be sold to any number of individuals and

Exhibit 14-8.   An Illustration of Joint Venture Financing.

Basic Assumptions of the Illustration

Size of center: 100,000 sq. ft./GLA
Land cost $ 200,000
Building cost   2,800,000
Total cost $3,000,000
Total value: Gross income $5/sq. ft. $500,000
              Operating expenses $1/sq. ft.   100,000

              Net operating income $4/sq. ft. $400,000
Capitalization rate: 13%

$$\text{Value:} \quad \frac{\text{NOI}}{R} = \frac{\$400,000}{0.13} = \$3,076,923 \text{ or, rounded off, } \$3,100,000$$

Lender contributes $250,000 to the deal and shares (1) the cash flow after the first mortgage loan payment of $336,307 50/50 with the developer, and (2) 10% of the after-tax cash proceeds from the sale of the property in 10 years.
  First mortgage: 70% LTV, 14% interest, 25 years, annual payments
                   Closed first 10 years, open 105% declining 1/2 of 1% per year
                   Loan constant: 0.145498
                   Mortgage amount: 0.70 × value = 0.70 × $3,100,000 = $2,170,000
                   Annual debt service: $336,307
  Total financing: First mortgage $2,170,000
                    Equity from lender   250,000

                                               $2,420,000
Cash flow available for annual debt service $400,000
Less: Annual debt service   336,307

Cash flow remaining $ 63,693
                  Developer receives $ 36,846
                  Lender-owner receives   36,846

Investment Returns from Operating Cash Flows

Return to lender as an equity partner:

$$\frac{\text{cash flow received}}{\text{lender's equity investment}} = \frac{36,846}{250,000} = 0.147 \text{ or, rounded off, } 15\%$$

Return to lender on total first-year investment:

$$\frac{\text{cash flow received}}{\text{lender's total first-year investment}} = \frac{373,153}{2,420,000} = 15.4\%$$

(Continued)

Exhibit 14-8. *(Continued)*

Return to developer:

$$\frac{\text{cash flow received}}{\text{value of equity contributed}} = \frac{36,846}{680,000} = 0.054 \text{ or } 5.4\%$$

Value of center		$3,100,000
Less: First Mortgage	$2,170,000	
Equity from lender	250,000	2,420,000
Value of equity contributed by developer		$ 680,000

$$\frac{\text{cash flow received}}{\text{cash equity contributed}} = \frac{36,846}{580,000} = 0.064 \text{ or } 6.4\%$$

Cost of center		$3,000,000
Less: First Mortgage	$2,170,000	
Equity from lender	250,000	2,420,000
Cash equity contributed by developer		$ 580,000

Other possible forms of return for the developer: long-term capital gain, tax shelter, management fee, tax-free refinancing proceeds, leasing commission

Investment Returns after Sale Proceeds

A. Indicated sale price at end of 10th year based on a 10% annual appreciation

Present value factor at 10% for 10 years: 2.5937

$3,100,000 × 2.5937 = estimated sale price at end of 10 years =		$8,040,470
Estimated loan balance at end of 10 years:		
10.9% paid off - 89.1% remaining (using mortgage handbook)		
$2,170,000 × 0.891 = estimated loan balance at end of 10 years		1,933,470
Indicated equity for lender and developer before taxes		$6,107,000
Taxes payable:		
Capital gains taxes	$1,075,016	
Ordinary income taxes - tax loss		
No depreciation recapture; straight		
line depreciation used		
Less: Tax benefit or savings	46,000	$1,029,016
Equity after taxes for lender and developer		$5,077,984
Calculation of adjusted sale price		
Sale price	$8,040,470	
Selling expenses		
(4% of sale price)	321,619	
Adjusted sale price	$7,718,851	

Calculation of adjusted basis

Cost − depreciation taken = adjusted basis

$3,000,000 − (0.06 2/3 × 10) =

$3,000,000 − 2/3 ($3,000,000) = $1,000,000

Exhibit 14-8. *(Continued)*

Long-term capital gain (held 10 years)

Adjusted sale price	$7,718,851		
Less: adjusted basis	1,000,000		
Long-term capital gain	$6,718,851		

Long-term capital gains taxes

Capital gain taxable		
($6,718,851 × 0.40)	$2,687,540
Ordinary income tax rate assumed	× 0.40
Capital gains taxes payable	$1,075,016

Calculation of taxable income or loss for year 10

Net operating income			$400,000
Less: Depreciation $3,000,000 × 0.06 2/3 =	$200,000	
Mortgage interest − estimate for year 10	315,000	515,000
Tax loss		($115,000)

Tax benefit or savings:

Tax loss × ordinary income tax rate

$115,000 × 0.40   = $46,000

Lender participation in after-tax cash proceeds from property sale

10% × $5,077,984 = $507,799

Developer receipts from the sale proceeds

Total after-tax equity for lender and developer	$5,077,984
Less: Amount to lender (10%)	507,799
Net to developer from the sale	$4,570,185

Indicated sale price at end of 10th year based on <u>10%</u> annual appreciation

Cash received by lender as a part owner:

Other income	$ 36,846
Cash flow from sale	507,799
Total	$544,645

Return to lender: $\dfrac{\$544,645}{\$250,000} = 218\%$

Cash received by developer:

Other income	$ 36,846
Cash flow from sale	4,570,185
Total	$4,607,031

Return to developer based on value equity contributed $= \dfrac{\$4,607,031}{\$680,000} = 677.5\%$

Return to developer based on cash equity contributed $= \dfrac{\$4,607,031}{\$580,000} = 794.3\%$

(Continued)

Exhibit 14-8. *(Continued)*

B. Indicated Sale Price at end of year 10 based on 5% annual appreciation

Present value factor at 5% for 10 years: 1.628895

$3,100,000 × 1.628895 = estimated sale price at end of 10 years =	$5,049,575
Estimated loan balance at end of 10 years	1,933,470
Indicated equity for lender and developer before taxes	$3,116,105
Indicated equity for lender and developer after taxes	$2,546,490

Cash received by lender:

Other income	$ 36,846
Cash flow from sale	254,649
Total	$ 291,495

$$\text{Return to lender overall} = \frac{\$291,495}{\$250,000} = 117\%$$

Cash received by developer:

Other income	$ 36,846
Cash flow from the sale	2,291,841
Total	$2,328,687

$$\text{Return to developer overall - value equity} = \frac{\$2,328,687}{\$680,000} = 342\%$$

$$\text{Return to developer overall - cash equity} = \frac{\$2,328,687}{\$580,000} = 401.5\%$$

Calculation of adjusted sale price:

Sale price	$5,049,575
Selling expenses (4% of sale price)	201,983
Adjusted sale price	$4,847,592

Adjusted sale price	$4,847,592
Adjusted basis	1,000,000
Long-term capital gain (held 10 years)	$3,847,592

Calculation of long-term capital gains taxes:

Capital gains taxable $3,847,592 × 0.40 =	$1,539,037
Ordinary income tax rate assumed	× 0.40
Capital gains taxes payable	$615,614.80

Tax loss = (115,000)

Tax benefit: tax loss × ordinary income tax rate assumed = tax savings

$$($115,000) \times 0.40 = 46,000$$

Calculation of lender participation in after-tax cash proceeds from sale

Indicated equity before taxes	$3,116,105

Exhibit 14-8. *(Continued)*

Taxes payable:		
Capital gains taxes	$615,615	
Less: Ordinary income tax savings		
(No depreciation recapture)	46,000	
Balance		569,615
Equity after taxes for lender and developer		$2,546,490
Lender participation (10%)	$254,649	
Calculation of developer receipts from sale		
Equity after taxes for lender and developer		$2,546,490
Less: Lender participation		254,649
Net to developer from the sale		$2,291,841

business entities. If the investors reside within the boundaries of the state in which the center lies, the developer usually will not have to register with the Securities and Exchange Commission, a federal government agency. The marketing of the investment shares would fall under the jurisdiction of the state securities agency. The state's blue-sky laws usually require disclosure including the principals of the development, the proposed nature of the development in which the monies will be invested, and the risks involved in the investment. Most states want the prospective investor to receive a copy of a prospectus for the investment project before the investor must make a decision about investment. The state may not render a judgment as to the soundness or financial feasibility of the proposed investment. The Securities and Exchange Commission regulations are similar to the state's regulations, but are more detailed and costly to perform.

The limited partnership may be a public or private one in another sense. The shares may be privately placed or privately subscribed. No public marketing of the shares may even take place. A few friends and acquaintances from a single community may provide the capital with no public fanfare. In contrast, many New York investment banking firms have publicly marketed limited partnership shares for larger projects on a nationwide basis. For example, Merrill Lynch's thousands of stock brokers around the country have repeatedly marketed public limited partnership shares in various real estate ventures.

More than one limited partnership class may be associated with the financing of a regional or superregional shopping center. Two classes of limited partners may be called Tenants-in-Common Class A and Tenants-in-Common Class B. An example of a projected cash flow distribution for such a Class A and Class B partnership is shown in Exhibit 14-9. Class A partners benefit from more tax shelter than do Class B partners. Class B partners benefit from more cash flow than Class A partners do.

Exhibit 14-9. Projected Taxable Income and Cash Flow Positions for Two Classes of Partners in the Cherry Hills Regional Shopping Center (Years Ending March 31).

Years	NOI	Mortgage Interest	Mortgage Amortization	150% Depreciation	Total Deductions	Taxable Income or (Loss)	Cumulative Income (Loss)	Net Cash Flow
Tenants-in-Common (Class A)								
198X	$—	$ 66	$—	$ 67	$133	$(133)	$(133)	$—
198X	239	152	36	183	335	(96)	(229)	51
198X	239	150	38	171	321	(82)	(311)	51
198X	239	147	41	162	309	(70)	(381)	51
198X	239	145	43	152	297	(58)	(439)	51
198X	239	142	46	143	285	(46)	(485)	51
198X	239	140	48	135	275	(36)	(521)	51
198X	239	137	51	127	264	(25)	(546)	51
199X	239	134	54	120	254	(15)	(561)	51
199X	239	131	57	113	244	(5)	(566)	51
199X	239	128	60	107	235	4	(562)	51
Tenants-in-common (Class B)								
198X	$—	$ 66	$—	$ 67	$133	$(133)	$(133)	$—
198X	287	152	36	183	335	(48)	(181)	99
198X	287	150	38	171	321	(34)	(215)	99
198X	287	147	41	162	309	(22)	(237)	99
198X	287	145	43	152	297	(10)	(247)	99
198X	287	142	46	143	285	2	(245)	99
198X	287	140	48	135	275	12	(233)	99
198X	287	137	51	127	264	23	(210)	99
199X	287	134	54	120	254	33	(177)	99
199X	287	131	57	113	244	43	(134)	99
199X	287	128	60	107	235	52	(82)	99

Syndication. A syndicate manager with some investment objectives may sell syndication shares totaling a given amount to a number of investors intrastate or interstate. The manager will invest the amount of money raised by this "closed-end fund" in one or more properties. One or more shopping centers may be purchased by the manager on behalf of the syndicate members. Some good properties may have been located by the manager before the syndicate offering. The manager may locate the properties with the desired investment characteristics after the offering is fully subscribed.

All of the capital subscribed may or may not be invested at the end of the subscription period. The manager may hold back funds for his or her own management fees and commissions payable over the years of the syndication and for investment in good properties which become available over time. In order to raise more funds after the first monies are fully invested, the syndicate manager must make an entirely new offering of shares.

The real estate syndicate is similar to a real estate limited partnership. The syndicate manager may contribute only managerial and marketing expertise as the general partner of a limited partnership might. The syndicate member usually assumes the limited legal and financial liability that the limited partner also assumes. While the syndicate may own a few dissimilar properties, the limited partnership may only own one regional shopping center. Another limited partnership may be established for a second property.

Shopping Center Condominium. Condominium ownership is spreading to all kinds of commercial properties. Since the developer is tending to lose owner- ship and control to the major investor-lenders, some developers may consider the condominium legal arrangement as an alternative to investor-lender fi- nancing. Each tenant or investor could own the airspace used for merchandis- ing and pay common area maintenance and management fees to maintain the public areas such as the mall and parking space. The airspace sold to investors would primarily be horizontal since the majority of shopping center space is one story in height. Multilevel centers would have horizontal and vertical airspace dimensions to the marketing effort.

Convertible Mortgage. A lender who agrees to finance a center permanently may wish to own all or part of the center later. The developer-owner could offer the lender a convertible mortgage, similar to a convertible bond, with an option to purchase. The purchase price could be established in the option so that the lender could make a decision as to when to exercise the option. The lender would probably wait until the center attains a value in excess of the option price and then exercise the option, as holders of convertible bonds tend to do. The lender would gain fixed and contingent interest for a period. If the opportunities of ownership appear to be good, the lender could take investor status. The cash flow and tax differences would be studied before mortgage conversion would take place.

The developer would gain debt capital for a time. The fixed and contingent interest paid would be fully tax deductible. When the developer wishes to invest in additional centers which seem to offer more cash flow, capital gain, and tax shelter opportunities, the lender might convert the bond to equity. The lender could operate the center and relieve the developer of a major capital commitment in the center. Even though the lender might take the ownership on a deferred basis, the developer might be requested to continue the management. A developer subsidiary could stay with the center to manage it and retain fees for that management.

Sale and Repurchase on an Installment Sales Contract. The developer and investor may wish to agree to the sale of the center by the developer with repurchase by the developer from the investor on an installment basis. The cash flow return from the project would help the developer buy back all or a portion of the equity. The developer gains cash flow for investment in other projects while the cash flow and tax savings from the center may be paid to the investor for gradual ownership accumulation. After the installment payments which incorporate a reasonable return to the investor are made, the developer may benefit from the long-term capital gain from the property. This gain would be dependent upon the installment purchase price agreed to by the investor. The interest on the installment debt would be tax deductible to the developer. The developer probably would not want to sell to the investor until a long-term capital gain were available.

REFINANCING

Refinancing is part of the evolution of the shopping center. The center was originally financed, and it has been in operation for some time. Now the time has come to refinance.

Reasons for Refinancing

Several reasons may prompt this refinancing of the center. Among them are:

1. *Expansion*. An existing center may need expansion to serve the increased customer clientele and to permit more tenants to offer more goods and services in the center.

2. *Renovation*. New capital may be needed to refurbish and renovate in order to maintain or improve the competitive market position of the center.

3. *Buy-out of Partners*. One or more of the current partners may wish to release their capital investment from the center so that they may go to other investments. They may seek other real estate investments or other types of investment media entirely. They will no longer be owners of the center.

4. *Working Capital for Other Projects*. An owner may need working capital to finance other projects. Other projects, including other shopping centers, may need capital for current operation or construction.

5. *Return of Existing Equity*. The owners may wish to release much of their capital even though they plan to remain owners of the center. They may have other uses for the capital.

6. *Repurchase of Land*. To reduce the leverage on the center, the current state of profitability will permit refinancing to get more capital so that the land under the center can be bought rather than leased. The leased land no longer will be part of the burden of debt on the center.

7. *Tax-Free Dollars*. The owner may carry away from the currently operating center tax-free proceeds from refinancing. The Internal Revenue Service regulations permit this tax effect of refinancing.

8. *Impending Sale of the Center*. Better financing on the center may entice more buyers and higher offers for the purchase of the center. The original mortgages may have relatively low outstanding balances. A purchaser may want more leverage and less required equity in order to buy.

Types of Centers Particularly Needing Refinancing

As retail markets are slowly becoming saturated with up-to-date shopping centers, several types of existing centers are needing expansion, renovation, and refurbishing. Among them are the central business district, older suburban malls, and older central city malls.

The Central Business District. Central business district retailing has existed for many years in most metropolitan areas. Ultimate consumers and merchants are quickly realizing, with the continuing energy crisis, that the central business district is readily accessible to a majority of the consumers. The mass transit systems all converge in the central business district. The bus lines, the subways, the elevated trains, the electric streetcars, and the trolley cars all converge downtown. Therefore, a number of the larger shopping center developers, including Rouse Company, are redeveloping the CBDs of a number of the older cities with modern shopping centers for the expected consumer increase as the price of gasoline increases. The Rouse Company, for example, has redeveloped the downtown retailing of Boston and Baltimore. The Urban Development and Investment subsidiary of Aetna Life Insurance Company redeveloped North Michigan Avenue in Chicago with Water Tower Place. The renovation and expansion of CBD retailing requires mortgage refinancing and new financing. In most cities, the central business district already has major retail tenants, but the physical facilities have become outdated. The existing mortgages often need refinancing for the work that needs to be done.

Older Suburban Malls. Some of the older suburban malls need major renovation and remodeling. Existing mortgages may need refinancing in order for the developer to acquire the money needed. For example, Melvin Simon, a major shopping center developer, has taken on the task of major renovation and expansion of the Greenwood and Eastgate Malls of Indianapolis recently. The buying power exists in the normal trading areas, but the older centers have lost their old competitive positions in the market.

Older Central City Malls. Existing neighborhood and community centers in the older central city areas today may need renovation and refurbishing to meet the demands of the consumers within the immediate trading area. Some of these smaller centers are losing customers to suburban malls because the older merchants are no longer providing the goods, services, attractive facilities, and parking desired by consumers in the nearby trading area. Considerable profits may be made from the renovation of such centers to increase the gross sales potential, to increase the storeroom rents, and to reduce the operating costs.

The Loan Acquisition Process

Refinancing a loan is much like financing a center from scratch. Some say that refinancing, especially with the original lender, is much easier than the original financing.

To acquire new funds through a refinanced mortgage, the lender approached will want to see the following documentation:

Income statement for the current and recent years
Expense statement for the current and recent years
A cost breakdown for the impending expenditures associated with the land and buildings
An income and expense statement for the center after the proposed changes
Lease review forms for each current tenant

Quite often the refinancing involves new construction or storeroom modification where a construction loan is needed. The application for a construction loan requires considerable data from the prospective borrower. For the closing of the construction loan, considerable data and expense are also required of the borrower and lender. The application and closing of the new permanent loan also require a lot of preparation and expense on the parts of the borrower and the lender.

In brief, the underwriting of the new construction and permanent loans— refinancing loans—involves the following considerations:

Borrower. The past experience of the developer, the quality of product delivered, his or her financial strength, the depth of the developer's organization, and the ability of the developer.

Use of the refinancing proceeds. Is the new money going into the financed property or into another investment? Is the new money just the recapture of earlier cash investment?

Appropriateness of the current location.

Balance or imbalance of basic industry.

Accessibility of the center.

Adequacy of traffic circulation.

Objections from environmental protection groups.

Sale trends.

Strength of the tenants in the relevant market.

Competitive resiliency.

Neighborhood or trade area trends.

New or proposed competition.

Reliance on percentage rents. Is the fixed rent relatively high with less reliance on variable rents?

Lease terms remaining.

Existence and continuance of reciprocal easement and other operating agreements.

Releasing prospects.

Current and proposed tenant mix.

Expense protection. Are most of the current leases net, indexed percentage leases? Could they be changed into this inflation-protected form?

GOVERNMENT FINANCING

As federal and state governments seek to reduce and eliminate poverty among its citizens and residents, its representatives have devised community development block grants and other such government financing programs. To qualify, state and city governments are required to present worthwhile and qualified residential, commercial, and industrial projects to the appropriate offices of the U.S. Department of Housing and Urban Development and certain state agencies. The appropriate HUD or state offices review the requested funding by the cities and states and the projects which would receive financial assistance. The city or state may receive a federal government grant on the strength of the need for the project presented to HUD. Under other circumstances, block grants may be given cities or states based on the presence of a specified level of poverty or economic distress.

From 1978 through 1980, two federal government programs provided funding for shopping center rehabilitation or development through city or state implementation. Community development block grants (CDBGs) were given to states after applications were approved; urban development action grants (UDAGs) were given to cities whose applications and projects were accepted. In 1981, as the federal budget was trimmed by the new administration, the funds for the UDAG program were reduced. At the time of this writing, merger of the UDAG program with the CDBG program was expected.

General Requirements

The shopping center owner or developer could acquire funds under the UDAG program only if the project would not take place unless UDAG monies were available on the needed terms. In other words, the expansion of the center or the center's development would not take place "but for" the developer's receipt of UDAG money on the desired terms. The funds could be offered by the city in the following forms:

Equity funding
Loan
Interest subsidy
Other approved subsidy

Most of the funding since the 1978 creation of the UDAG program has taken the form of loans.

Certain requirements for the UDAG funding must be met by the city. The funding must help revitalize the stagnant economy of the area and/or must help reclaim deteriorated neighborhoods. Generally the city must be on the UDAG list of economically distressed cities published periodically in the Federal Register by the U.S. Department of Housing and Urban Development. The local residents as well as the local taxing jurisdictions must be aided by the financing plan. The project must be located in the distressed neighborhood or immediately adjacent to the delineated "pocket of poverty."

How do shopping centers justify special funding by the city or state? New, expanded, or remodeled shopping centers lift the current distressed economic status of the neighborhood. Employment is increased, particularly among the unemployed or underemployed unskilled residents of the local community. Most shopping center employees are unskilled. The city and the developer, furthermore, may pledge the employment of a specific percentage of shopping center workers from CETA workers from the local community. The improved property is subject to increased *ad valorem* taxation. The sales and services are subject to retail sales taxation, and the employee incomes are subject to state and federal income taxation. In addition, the new, expanded, or rehabilitated center provides greater community facilities which supplement the housing, community social services, and other commercial and industrial enterprises.

The federal grants and loans may be used for land improvement for the shopping center by the city. The city may use the money for the extension and expansion of sanitary and storm sewer, electric, gas, and water lines to the site. Any needed pedestrian malls or overhead walkways may be financed with the money. The costs of changing traffic patterns may be met with these sources of funds. The shopping center developer may benefit from the use of the government monies but may not receive them directly as grants or loans. Federal monies merely supplement sources of state and city monies.

Energy-saving projects often receive special consideration. Recently a shopping center was completed that was heated and cooled by a solar component system. Future centers will probably incorporate into their construction solar heating and cooling systems. The installation of such a system may only be possible with federal and state funding on a supplementary basis. Private funds would have to meet the majority of the required cost.

Federal grants are available generally where more private investment funds are attracted to the given project than public funds. The ratio of private funds per project versus public funds has been approximately six to one through 1980. The government puts in "seed money" which attracts a significant amount of private money. The shopping center investment may attract the necessary private funds to establish a sizable "leverage" ratio.

Industrial Revenue Bond Financing

Since the Revenue Act of 1978 which amended the Internal Revenue Code of 1954, the federal grants to a project may be supplemented by industrial development bond financing. A center remodeling or construction job may cost up to $20 million. Up to $10 million may be raised through the issuance of industrial revenue bonds. Even though tax-exempt municipal bonds recently have sold for prices which establish only a small margin of yield difference between tax-exempt bonds and taxable bonds, there still may be an interest saving to the shopping center developer. In today's mortgage market of 14 percent rates, the tax-exempt bond sale would probably lower the developer's financial cost about two percentage points to about 12 percent. The shopping center development might be possible only if such reasonable long-term financing were available.

Financing by means of industrial revenue bonds sales is possible without the request and receipt of other government funding. In recent years many commercial enterprises including shopping centers of smaller size have been funded with tax-free bonds, but no funds may have been received from federal block or UDAG grants. The two financing plans may be totally independent of each other.

FHA Mortgage Insurance under a Comprehensive Redevelopment Project Mortgage

The shopping center developer may obtain Federal Housing Administration mortgage insurance for his or her center if the center is a small part of a comprehensive redevelopment project financed with FHA mortgage insurance. During the 1960s, many federal urban renewal projects around the country involved primarily multifamily residential development, but neighborhood or community shopping centers were an integral part of the developments. If the same developer built both the residential and the commercial buildings, the center's permanent financing was obtained on particularly good mortgage terms with FHA mortgage insurance coverage.

FIFTEEN

INCOME AND
AD VALOREM TAXATION

Several types of taxes have an impact upon the profitability of the shopping center. The center is subject to sales, ad valorem, income, estate and inheritance, inventory, and payroll withholding taxes. Other local, state, and federal forms of taxation may also have a bearing on the center ownership and its operation.

State and federal income taxes are powerful forces for the reduction of owner yields. If taxable income in substantial amounts is derived from the center and the owner is faced with high ordinary income tax rates, the sizable net taxable income may disappear after the payment of income taxes. If the center generates a tax loss, the owner must consolidate the income or loss from the center with other sources of income and loss so that the shopping center loss may offset other sources of taxable income. The loss has no favorable effect unless it offsets other sources of income as large or larger in dollars than the tax loss.

Ad valorem taxes are also potent forces toward the reduction of the owner's yield. These real property taxes may represent a sizable portion of the gross income derived from the center. For example, *ad valorem* taxes may account for 15 to 25 percent of the center's effective gross income. (Effective gross income, as one recalls, is the gross income less estimated vacancy allowance and bad debt expense.)

TAX INCIDENCE AND THE STAGE OF DEVELOPMENT OF THE CENTER

Tax payments are required through the three principal stages of center development, (1) the planning and construction stage, (2) the operating stage, (3) the termination stage, when the owner sells the center or exchanges it for another real property.

During the planning and construction stage, the owner sees money flowing to outside suppliers of funds, materials, and labor. Little taxable revenue is coming in to the developer. The owner of the land is faced with *ad valorem* taxes due to the ownership. If the landowner has leased the land, the ground lease payments represent taxable income.

During the operational stage of the center development, the owners are receiving cash flow distributions from the property. The lenders receive standard debt service payments plus equity participation payments. All of these income flows are taxable under state and federal income tax regulations. At the same time, operating expenses are being paid by the owners and the lenders which may be deducted from the gross revenues. The owner of the center buildings particularly gains tax relief from the tax deduction of depreciation. If the lender does not hold an ownership interest in the center, no depreciation deductions are permitted the lender. Only the buildings are depreciable, not the land.

At the end of the tax years during the operation of the completed center, income tax returns must be filed with the Internal Revenue Service and the state revenue departments. These returns itemize such things as the cost of repairs, the costs associated with the mall management and supervision, management fees to outside management companies, computer lease payments and maintenance costs, office supplies, advertising and promotional expense, and mortgage debt service payments. Each of these dollar items may be deducted from the gross revenue from the center before adjusted taxable income is derived. Once the depreciation expense is worked into the tax return, there may remain no "adjusted taxable income" against which tax rates are applied. Then again, taxes may be payable if the return shows a taxable net income.

During the operating stage, *ad valorem* taxes are payable on both the land and the land improvements including the buildings. Tax statements are received by the recorded owners of each of the real property assets. When the mall owner receives the *ad valorem* tax bills, he or she usually distributes the proportional costs to each of the mall storeroom tenants so that the bill is paid from contributions from the tenants, not the owner. The net leases usually provide for tenant proportional payment of property taxes, hazard insurance premiums, and common area maintenance expenses. Each tenant bears a proportional part of the total operating costs in these areas.

During the termination stage, the capital gain is calculated. If a capital gain accrues to the owners, what kind of capital gain is defined by the time the asset has been held since its purchase? Is it a short- or long-term capital gain? When the lender receives the final payment of debt service from the original owner, that sum of money may be taxable to the lender if the lender is subject to income taxation. Some of our mortgage lenders are fully tax exempt. Others are subject to relatively low income tax incidence. The final *ad valorem* tax payment is made by the original owner. At the closing, the original owner will probably pay the property taxes for the part of the tax year in which the center was owned by that party. The ordinary income tax rates of the owner may apply to the net taxable income from operations as well as the recapture of depreciation of the center buildings that has already been taken for income tax purposes.

INCOME TAXATION

The income tax regulations significantly affect the cash flow distributions to the owners of the center. The net income from operations is taxed at the ordinary income tax rate of the owner. Depreciation expense deductions and the recapture of depreciation deductions at the time of property sale are covered by certain IRS regulations. Capital gains, short and long term, are treated separately and differently from operating income. When an owner refinances the center, income tax regulations apply to this separate transaction. Exchanges are covered by special tax rulings and regulations. The same thing is true of property exchanges for assets of like or unlike kind. Tax credits are available for certain types of income property rehabilitation and the purchase of energy-saving equipment and mechanical systems to be incorporated in the existing center.

Taxation of Operating Income

If a taxable profit is derived from the operation of a center, the income tax rate of the ownership entity for the tax year of center operation is applied to the net taxable income. If the owner is a corporation, the corporate income tax rate of the owner is applied to the taxable amount. The owner may not be a corporation. If the ownership entity is a partnership, a proprietorship, or any other taxable organization, the cash flows distributed to the owner are taxable at the individual's or organization's ordinary income tax rates. The net unincorporated income of the business entity is not subject to federal income taxation. Any profit distributions made to individuals or companies who are partners in the venture are subject to federal income taxation, though.

The corporate federal income rates applicable in 1983 for the tax year 1982 and for subsequent years until changed by the IRS are summarized in Exhibit 15-1. The schedule for married individuals filing joint returns is shown in

Exhibit 15-2; the rate schedule for unmarried individuals other than surviving spouses and heads of households, is given in Exhibit 15-3.

During the planning and construction stage of the center development, some items of expense are immediately deductible for federal income tax purposes and some are capitalized and amortized like capital expenditures. Generally ordinary and necessary business expenses of any stage of center development and operation are immediately deductible in the current tax year. These items from the planning and construction stage include:

Fee for preliminary studies such as the market study, the feasibility
    study, and the environmental impact study
Real estate appraisal fee
Loan origination fee
Deed and mortgage recording fees
Insurance premiums for title insurance
Attorney fees for closing the loan and transferring the title
Brokerage commissions
Advertising and sales promotion costs

Exhibit 15-1. Corporate Federal Income Tax Rates Applicable in 1983 for the Tax Year 1982

15% on taxable income not in excess of $25,000
18% on taxable income in excess of $25,000, but not in excess of $50,000
30% on taxable income over $50,000, but not in excess of $75,000
40% on taxable income over $75,000, but not in excess of $100,000
46% on taxable income over $100,000

Exhibit 15-2. Tax Rates Applicable to Married Individuals Filing Joint Returns in 1983 for the 1982 Tax Year

If taxable income is:	The tax is:
Not over $3,400	No tax
Over $3,400 but not over $5,500	11% of the excess over $3,400
Over $5,500 but not over $7,600	$231, plus 13% of the excess over $5,500
Over $7,600 but not over $11,900	$504, plus 15% of the excess over $7,600
Over $11,900 but not over $16,000	$1,149, plus 17% of the excess over $11,900
Over $16,000 but not over $20,200	$1,846, plus 19% of the excess over $16,000
Over $20,200 but not over $24,600	$2,644, plus 23% of the excess over $20,200
Over $24,600 but not over $29,900	$3,656, plus 26% of the excess over $24,600
Over $29,900 but not over $35,200	$5,034, plus 30% of the excess over $29,900
Over $35,200 but not over $45,800	$6,624, plus 35% of the excess over $35,200
Over $45,800 but not over $60,000	$10,334, plus 40% of the excess over $45,800
Over $60,000 but not over $85,600	$16,014, plus 44% of the excess over $60,000
Over $85,600 but not over $109,400	$27,278, plus 48% of the excess over $85,600
Over $109,400	$38,702, plus 50% of the excess over $109,400

Exhibit 15-3. Tax Rates Applicable to Unmarried Individuals Other Than Surviving Spouses and Heads of Households to Be Used in 1983 for the 1982 Tax Year

If taxable income is:	The tax is:
Not over $2,300	No tax
Over $2,300 but not over $3,400	11% of the excess over $2,300
Over $3,400 but not over $4,400	$121, plus 13% of the excess over $3,400
Over $4,400 but not over $8,500	$251, plus 15% of the excess over $4,400
Over $8,500 but not over $10,800	$866, plus 17% of the excess over $8,500
Over $10,800 but not over $12,900	$1,257, plus 19% of the excess over $10,800
Over $12,900 but not over $15,000	$1,656, plus 21% of the excess over $12,900
Over $15,000 but not over $18,200	$2,097, plus 24% of the excess over $15,000
Over $18,200 but not over $23,500	$2,865, plus 28% of the excess over $18,200
Over $23,500 but not over $28,800	$4,349, plus 32% of the excess over $23,500
Over $28,800 but not over $34,100	$6,045, plus 36% of the excess over $28,800
Over $34,100 but not over $41,500	$7,953, plus 40% of the excess over $34,100
Over $41,500 but not over $55,300	$10,913, plus 45% of the excess over $41,500
Over $55,300	$17,123, plus 50% of the excess over $55,300

Insurance premiums for hazard and casualty insurance coverage for the construction effort

Items from the operating stage of the center that are immediately deductible can be fixed or variable.

Fixed expenses (those that do not vary with occupancy level) include:

Insurance premiums
Ad valorem tax payment
Depreciation of land improvements

Variable expenses (those that vary with occupancy level) include:

Property management fees
Utility expense
Mall and parking lot maintenance expenses
Advertising and promotional expenses
Other ordinary and necessary business expenses

The items from the planning and construction stage that the Internal Revenue Service requires to be capitalized and amortized over a period of years include:

Real estate syndication sales expense
Construction loan interest
Ad valorem tax payments during construction

The expense associated with the sale of partnership interests or syndicate shares must be capitalized and amortized over a period of not less than 60 months. For 1982 and later years, the construction loan interest and *ad valorem* tax payments during construction of the center must be capitalized and amortized over a 10-year period. In other words, this expense must be spread over the coming 10 years rather than totally deducted for federal income tax purposes in the immediate year of expense payment. This does not apply to development of low-income housing.

Depreciation Expense

Even though the owner may not put money every year into the renovation of the center to eradicate any depreciation or obsolescence, the Internal Revenue Service permits the deduction for federal income tax purposes of amounts for depreciation expense. Land improvements, but not land, may be depreciated. New or existing land improvements may be written off over a 15-, 35-, or 45-year period. Straight-line depreciation may be utilized for the depreciation of any structure or land improvement. Under the Accelerated Cost Recovery System (ACRS), an accelerated method of depreciation may be used for each type of income property as an alternative to use of the straight-line method. The 175 percent declining balance method or the straight-line method of depreciation calculation may be used for shopping centers and other non-residential real property. The accelerated depreciation is calculated by use of a special table (Exhibit 15-4, ACRS Cost Recovery Table for All Real Estate except Low-Income Housing). Generally the same recovery period and method must be used for each component of the structure; component depreciation methods are no longer permitted for use.

If the center is depreciated using the 15-year accelerated method of depreciation, all of the depreciation expense taken for federal income tax purposes, not just the excess depreciation expense over straight-line depreciation, is recaptured at the sale of the property at the taxpayer's ordinary income tax rate. If the straight-line method of depreciation is used over the 15-, 35-, or 45-year period, there is no recapture of depreciation.

Four classes are established for the depreciation of tangible personal property: 3-, 5-, 10-, and 15-year recovery period classes. The 3-year class of personal property contains automobiles, light-duty trucks, and machinery and equipment used in connection with research and experimentation. All other machinery and equipment with an asset depreciation range midpoint life of 4 years or less is also included in the 3-year class. The 5-year class includes all tangible personal property that is not assigned to the 3-, 10-, or 15-year classes. This property includes single-purpose agricultural structures and horticultural structures as well as petroleum storage tanks and other storage facilities for oil-related assets. The 10-year class contains public utility property with an asset depreciation range midpoint life of 18½ to 25 years, manufactured

Exhibit 15-4. ACRS Cost Recovery Table for All Real Estate

Table I
All Real Estate (Except Low-Income Housing)

The applicable percentage is: (use the column for the month in the first year the property is placed in service)

If the Recovery Year is:	1	2	3	4	5	6	7	8	9	10	11	12
1	12	11	10	9	8	7	6	5	4	3	2	1
2	10	10	11	11	11	11	11	11	11	11	11	12
3	9	9	9	9	10	10	10	10	10	10	11	11
4	8	8	8	8	8	8	9	9	9	9	9	9
5	7	7	7	7	7	8	8	8	8	8	8	8
6	6	6	6	6	7	7	7	7	7	7	7	7
7	6	6	6	6	6	6	6	6	6	7	7	6
8	6	6	6	6	6	6	6	6	6	6	6	6
9	6	6	6	6	5	6	6	6	6	6	6	6
10	5	6	5	6	5	5	5	5	6	5	6	5
11	5	5	5	5	5	5	5	5	5	5	5	5
12	5	5	5	5	5	5	5	5	5	5	5	5
13	5	5	5	5	5	5	5	5	5	5	5	5
14	5	5	5	5	5	5	5	5	5	5	5	5
15	5	5	5	5	5	5	5	5	5	4	4	5
16	—	—	1	2	2	3	3	4	4	4	4	5

Table II
Low-Income Housing

The applicable percentage is: (use the column for the month in the first year the property is placed in service)

If the Recovery Year is:	1	2	3	4	5	6	7	8	9	10	11	12
1	13	12	11	10	9	8	7	6	4	3	2	1
2	12	12	12	12	12	12	12	13	13	13	13	13
3	10	10	10	10	11	11	11	11	11	11	11	11
4	9	9	9	9	9	9	9	9	10	10	10	10
5	8	8	8	8	8	8	8	8	8	8	8	9
6	7	7	7	7	7	7	7	7	7	7	8	8
7	6	6	6	6	6	6	6	6	6	6	6	6
8	5	5	5	5	5	6	6	6	6	6	6	6
9	5	5	5	5	5	5	5	5	5	5	6	6
10	5	5	5	5	5	5	5	5	5	5	5	5
11	4	5	4	4	4	5	5	5	5	5	5	5
12	4	4	4	4	4	4	5	5	5	5	5	5
13	4	4	4	4	4	4	4	4	4	5	5	5
14	4	4	4	4	4	4	4	4	4	4	4	4
15	4	4	4	4	2	2	3	3	4	4	4	4
16	—	—	1	1	1	2	2	3	3	3	3	4

Source: Higgins, J. Warren, "Depreciation of Real Estate and the Economic Recovery Act of 1981," Real Estate Tax Corner, *The Real Estate Appraiser and Analyst*, Spring 1982, p. 72.

homes, and railroad tank cars. The 15-year class of personal property contains public utility property with an asset depreciation range life of more than 25 years.

Businesses may elect to expense up to $5,000 of personal property cost in 1982 and 1983; $7,500 in 1984 and 1985; and $10,000 thereafter. The expensed property does not qualify for the investment tax credit.

Investment Tax Credits

A credit against the federal income tax payment is allowed for a stated percent of qualified investment in personal property, a stated percent of qualified investment in energy savings systems or equipment, a stated percent of qualified investment in substantially rehabilitated structures, and a stated percent of qualified investment in rehabilitated certified historic structures. The maximum tax credit for regular investment in qualified personal property is 10 percent. This regular 10 percent credit may be combined with a similar tax credit for investing in qualified energy-saving property. Rehabilitation tax credits may be 15, 20, or 25 percent of qualified rehabilitation expenditures depending on the age of the existing structure and its certification as a historic structure.

The Regular 10 Percent Investment Tax Credit

The regular 10 percent investment tax credit is available for 5- and 10-year recovery property according to the provisions of the Economic Recovery Tax Act of 1981. Three-year recovery property qualifies for a 6 percent investment tax credit. Items possibly associated with shopping center investment that may be covered by the investment tax credit are:

Elevator	Roadways within the shopping center complex
Escalators	Fire extinguishers
Boiler facilities	Office equipment
Display racks and shelves	Wall-to-wall carpeting
Neon and other signs	Window-washing equipment
Refrigerators	

For the tax year 1982 and thereafter, the regular 10 percent tax credit applies against the first $25,000 of tax liability plus 90 percent of the tax liability exceeding $25,000. Any part of the investment tax credit which is not applied as a credit against the tax because of the limitations just mentioned may be carried back 3 years and forward 15 years, as of the 1981 tax act. The investment tax credits are to be used up in the following order: first, the carryovers from earlier years are used; then credits earned during the current tax year; and then carrybacks from the earliest years first. An unused investment credit that arises from a net operating loss carryback can be carried back 3 years and forward 15 years. The maximum investment tax credit for used property is $125,000 through 1984; after 1984, it is $150,000. The full recapture of the investment credit is reduced by 2 percent for each year the property is held. No recapture of the investment credit is required for eligible 5-, 10-, or 14-year property actually held for at least 5 years, or eligible 3-year property held for at least 3 years.

In general, the regular investment tax credit applies to expenditures on "Section 38 property." This refers to depreciable or amortizable property having a useful life of three years or more and includes: (1) tangible personal property; (2) other tangible property (not including a building or its components) used as an integral part of (a) manufacturing, (b) extraction, (c) production, or (d) furnishing of transportation, communications, electrical energy, water, or sewage disposal services; (3) elevators and escalators; and (4) research facilities and facilities for the bulk storage of fungible commodities, including liquids and gases.

Business Energy Investment Tax Credit

Special investment tax credit rules and regulations apply to business energy property. If the business energy property qualifies as a Section 38 property, both the regular 10 percent investment tax credit and the business energy credit may apply to that business energy property. After 1985, the business energy tax credits associated with solar, wind, geothermal, ocean thermal, and small-scale hydroelectric generating property are scheduled to expire. Business energy property generally falls within one of the following categories: (1) alternative energy property, (2) solar or wind energy property, (3) specially defined energy property, (4) recycling equipment, (5) shale oil equipment, and (6) equipment for producing natural gas from geopressured brine. Alternative energy property is equipment used to generate fuels produced from sources other than fossil fuels (petroleum and natural gas). To be eligible for this credit, the property must be depreciable or amortizable and have a useful life of three years or more. The business energy investment credit is equal to 10, 11, or 15 percent of the taxpayer's qualified investment in the property depending on the property classification under the IRS regulations. The appropriate percentage by property classification may be reduced if the property is financed with tax-free industrial development bonds. The investment credit for business energy property is limited to 100 percent of tax liability reduced by the credit allowed that is not attributable to business energy property. The limitations on the amount of total allowable investment credit and the carryover and carryback provisions are applied first to the regular investment credit, next to the business energy investment credit for property other than solar or wind energy property, and finally to the business energy investment credit for solar or wind energy property.

Rehabilitation Investment Tax Credit

Many shopping centers that are 15 to 25 years old are currently subject to renovation. The renovation of these existing centers has started in recent years, and it tends to continue as construction costs of new buildings have risen to relatively high levels. In many instances it pays to renovate and perhaps expand rather than construct totally new premises. Some of the projects in the inner city and central business districts of our major cities have involved center development in certified historic structures. For example, some of the recent Rouse Company retail developments in central business districts have revolved around historic sites. As older buildings in densely populated urban areas are renovated for current merchandising centers, the rehabilitation investment tax credits will become more significant.

Application of Rehabilitation Tax Credit Regulations. The 1981 Economic Recovery Act created the new schedule of rehabilitation credits for non-residential and certified historic residential buildings. A brief summary is given below:

Type of building	Rehabilitation
30-year nonresidential buildings	15%
40-year nonresidential building	20%
Certified historic structure	25%

If the rehabilitation of a building began before January 1, 1982 and the building was at least 20 years old, but less than 30 years old, a special rule allows a credit for this building under the prior law.

The investment tax credit currently depends on the age of the nonresidential structure or on its certification as a historic structure. Only 15-year straight-line depreciation may be used for the recovery of the rehabilitation expenditures. For renovation of nonhistoric nonresidential structures, the basis for the building is reduced by the amount of the investment tax credit taken (Exhibit 15-5). Qualifying rehabilitation expenditures are treated as new rather than used property.

The rehabilitation expenditures must substantially rehabilitate the building. There is "substantial rehabilitation" if one of the following conditions exists:

1. The qualified rehabilitation expenditures during the 24-month period ending on the last day of the taxable year exceed the greater of the adjusted basis of the property or $5,000.

2. The rehabilitation meets the requirements under the first alternative by substituting 60 months for 24 months. The alternative 60-month period will be available only if there is a written set of architectural plans and

Exhibit 15-5. Property Rehabilitation Tax Credit Categories

	Nonresidential Structures 20 to 29 Years	Nonresidential Structures 30 to 39 Years	Nonresidential Structures 40+ Years	Certified Historic Residential or Nonresidential Structures
Prior law	10% investment tax credit plus straight-line depreciation	10% investment tax credit plus straight-line depreciation	10% investment tax credit plus straight line depreciation	10% investment tax credit plus straight-line depreciation or 60-month amortization
1981 Economic Recovery Act (effective for rehabilitations beginning after 12/31/81)	No credit	15% investment tax credit plus 15-year straight-line depreciation and basis reduction for investment tax credit taken	20% investment tax credit plus 15-year straight-line depreciation and basis reduction for investment tax credit taken	25% investment tax credit plus 15-year straight-line depreciation with no basis reduction
Transitional Rule (for qualifying expenditures made before and continuing after 1/1/82)	Prior law rules apply	Prior law rules or election of new rules for expenditures after 12/31/81	Prior law rules or election of new rules for expenditures after 12/31/81	Prior law rules or election of new rules for expenditures after 12/31/81

Source: Braitman, Howard L., and Stine, John B., II, "The Tax Legislation Benefits Real Estate Investors," *Commercial Investment Journal,* Winter 1982, Table III, p.6. ©Realtors National Marketing Institute ® of the National Association of Realtors ® 1982. All rights reserved. Reprinted from *Commercial Investment Journal,* Winter 1982. Table III, p. 6 with permission of the Copyright Proprietor.

specifications for all phases of the rehabilitation and there is a reasonable expectation that all phases of the rehabilitation will be completed within the 60 months.

Certified Historic Structures. A certified historic structure that is residential or nonresidential is defined as a structure which is (1) listed in the National Register of Historic Places; (2) located in a district listed in the National Register; or (3) located in a local or state historic district approved by the Secretary of the Interior. Under the 1981 act, the historic building rehabilitation does not have to be certified rehabilitation under the rules of the Secretary of the Interior. The rehabilitation may be certified by the Department of the Interior, though.

The National Register of Historic Places operates under the aegis of the National Park Service and was created in 1966. The National Register is said to include such properties as the Statue of Liberty and Alcatraz Island. Since special treatment for register properties was first enacted in 1976, register listings have increased 80 percent—from 13,538 in 1977 to 24,347 late in 1981.[*] Within that period, more than 2,500 projects with a total investment of $1.2 billion qualified for tax benefits. The U.S. Treasury Department estimates that annual construction eligible for the 25 percent credit will balloon from $800 million in 1982 to $2 billion in 1985.[†]

Refinancing the Center

When the mortgage terms become favorable or when the value of the center has risen measurably while the outstanding debt has fallen to a low level from the previous periodic mortgage payment, the owner may refinance the center with same or a different lender. Refinancing usually means that the outstanding amount of the debt is increased. The periodic mortgage payments may increase if the term of the mortgage is not extended significantly at the same time that the loan amount is increased. The borrower may wish to take money out of the project, may wish to expand or renovate the center with the new money, or may wish to increase the leverage on a favorable basis. Increased leverage may mean increased return on equity. Refinancing usually means tax-free cash proceeds from the new mortgage financing even after refinancing costs are paid.

Capital Gains Taxation

The taxation of capital asset transactions is dependent on the net capital gains position of the taxpayer and the corporate or individual status of that taxpayer.

---

[*] Smith, Randall, "Preserving the Past: Tax Breaks Spur Developers to Work on Projects Eligible for National Register of Historic Places," *The Wall Street Journal*, Thursday, May 27, 1982, p. 56.
[†] *Ibid.*

Different capital gains regulations apply depending on the corporate or individual status of the taxpayer (Exhibit 15-6). Four net capital gains positions for the taxpayer are possible: (1) net long-term gain, (2) net long-term loss, (3) net short-term gain, and (4) net short-term loss. Most taxpayers anticipate gains. According to the current tax regulations for individual taxpayers, 40 percent of long-term capital gains are subject to taxation at the ordinary income tax rate of the taxpayer. Capital gains are considered long term if the capital asset is held over one year. All (100 percent) of short-term capital gains of individual taxpayers are subject to the taxpayer's ordinary income tax rate.

The amount of the capital gain is calculated by subtracting the adjusted basis from the adjusted sale price. Capital gains are only recognized and realized for income tax purposes when a center is sold. The adjusted sale price amounts to the sale price less selling and fix-up expenses. The adjusted basis is equal to the

Exhibit 15-6. Taxation of Capital Asset Transactions

Individuals

Net long-term gain:	40% of gain treated as ordinary income
	60% of gain treated as a tax preference item subject to minimum tax rules
Net long-term loss:	Offset against ordinary income 50 cents on the dollar, with a maximum deduction per year of $3,000; balance carried over to future years until it is used up
Net short-term gain:	Taxed at regular rates
Net short-term loss:	Up to $3,000 deducted in the tax year incurred against ordinary income dollar for dollar; balance carried over to future years until it is used up

Corporations

Net long-term gain:	Taxed at 28% rate or taxed with other ordinary income at regular rates, whichever is lower
Net long-term loss:	Offset against ordinary income dollar for dollar; adjustments to ordinary income cannot create a net operating loss
	Balance subject to three-year carryback and then five-year carryover
Net short-term gain:	Taxed at regular rates
Net short-term loss:	Offset against ordinary income dollar for dollar; adjustments to ordinary income cannot create a net operating loss
	Balance subject to three-year carryback and then five-year carryover

Source: Hines, M.A. *Real Estate Investment* (New York: Macmillan Publishing Co., 1980), Exhibit 14-4, p. 235.

cost of the center development plus the cost of later improvements less depreciation deductions for income tax purposes. Once a net gain is established, then the length of the holding period is observed. The gain is then classified as a long- or short-term capital gain for tax purposes.

If a net long-term capital gain is realized at the sale of the center, 40 percent of that gain is subject to the taxpayer's ordinary income tax rate and 60 percent is subject to the alternative minimum tax. The 60 percent of the long-term capital gain not previously taxed is considered a tax preference item and is subject to the minimum tax regulations. Other tax preference items are derived from:

Excess intangible drilling costs
Excess accelerated depreciation over straight-line depreciation
Exercise of qualified stock options
Depletion
Rapid amortization on railroad rolling stock, child-care, and pollution control facilities

To calculate the tax due under the alternative minimum tax, the non-corporate taxpayer totals taxable income that year less total deductions for that year plus capital gains preference items and adjusted itemized deductions preferences. From this total may be deducted a $30,000 exemption ($40,000 for joint returns) from taxation. The resulting balance is subject to an alternative minimum tax rate of 20 percent.

Installment Sale of a Center

In order to delay the payment of income taxes, a property may be sold on an installment basis. If at least one payment is received by the seller in a tax year other than the year of sale, the income tax due on the sale is payable on a proportional basis when each of the installments is received. For example, if a long-term capital gain is realized on the sale of a center in Year 1, but the sale price is payable in two installments, one in Year 2 and one in Year 3, then a proportional part of the capital gains taxes is payable when the first payment is received in Year 2 and a proportional part of the taxes is payable when the second payment is received in Year 3. The seller may arrange for the receipt of the payments in the years when the seller's ordinary tax rate is lower than usual. When the seller's ordinary tax rate is lower, it may mean that the seller's income for those years is relatively low. The relatively low incomes of those years are better supplemented by the installment payments from the property sale. If the total payment is made in the year of property sale, the seller's ordinary tax rate may be driven unusually high with this large injection of income. This is more significant if the property gain is short term in nature. The maximum long-term capital gains rate is now 20 percent.

The Exchange of a Center Rather Than Outright Sale

Instead of an outright sale of a center, the owner may wish to exchange the center for another property. Part or all of the exchange may be tax deferred. The amount of boot received by each of the exchanging parties to balance the values of the exchanged properties will be subject to income taxation. The term "boot" refers to unlike property received as part of the property exchange. Boot may be cash, notes receivable, or other personal assets. Since the exchange of real properties of like kind may mean the deferral of income taxes, the center owner should consider this method of disposal of his or her center ownership interest with a real estate attorney or accountant well versed in tax-free exchanges.

THE *AD VALOREM* TAX SYSTEM

The state, country, and local governments may support their operating expenses with the proceeds from *ad valorem* taxes. The various governmental bodies, agencies, and authorities estimate their operating expenses for the coming fiscal period. Then they examine the forecast sources of income to cover these expenses other than *ad valorem* taxes. The portion that must be raised through *ad valorem* taxes is established.

Each real property is inventoried regarding its current *ad valorem* tax status. Normally church, education, and other governmental properties are not subject to property taxation. Of course, governmental properties include parks, fire stations, court houses, city halls, public libraries, highway and street right-of-ways, water towers, hospitals, prisons, and water treatment centers. The taxable property must be valued by tax appraisers according to specified appraisal systems so that equality of tax assessment may be maintained for taxpayer benefit. The fair market value of the taxable properties may be the same as the assessed value. Then again, assessed value may be only a portion of fair market value. The portion of fair market value that assessed valuation represents may be determined by the land use. Some states establish varying assessment ratios for the various types of land uses. For property tax purposes, the land uses may be divided into owner-occupied single-family residential, commercial including rental residential units, industrial, public utility, farmland, and timberland. Fewer or more categories may be used depending on the wishes and statutes of the particular state legislature.

A tax rate is set by each taxing jurisdiction that depends upon the property tax revenue for support of its operating expenses for the coming fiscal year. Several tax rates may be combined to form the total tax rate applicable to the assessed valuation of a single taxable real property. The tax rate may be quoted in mills per dollar of assessed valuation, dollars per hundred dollars of assessed valuation, or dollars per thousand dollars of assessed valuation. For example, the rate quoted may be $50 per $1,000 of assessed valuation. If the assessment ratio is 30 percent and the fair market value of the center is $20,000,000, the assessed valuation would be $6,000,000 and the *ad valorem* taxes payable would be 6,000 × $50 or $300,000. The portion of fair market value represented by the *ad valorem* taxes would be 0.30 × 50/1000 or 0.015 or 1½ percent of fair market value.

When a government service is rendered to only a small number of real properties, each of those properties is usually assessed its proportional part of the cost of the government service or improvement in the form of special assessment taxes. Therefore, a real property may be subject to regular *ad valorem* taxes and to special assessments. The special assessment is a special lien against the property that may be paid immediately or delayed by means of installment payments. The installment payments will normally involve the payment of statutory interest charges for the use of government funds.

Special assessments are placed against real properties whose value benefits from such local government services and improvements as extension of the sewer line, paving of the street or road, or installation of street lights. The cost of the government service may be allocated among the benefiting properties on the basis of front feet or total square feet. Each standard size lot may be charged the same amount; larger lots such as double lots may be charged a proportionally higher amount. A reasonable method of allocation will be utilized. Normally hearings involving the neighborhood residents are held prior to the government improvement. The approval of the affected property owners must be gained before the project may proceed and the special assessments levied in an equitable manner against each benefiting property.

SIXTEEN

INVESTMENT RETURN ANALYSIS

From the cash flow analysis, it is possible to determine the return on the shopping center investment. Several methods of determining the investment yield may be employed. A single investor may use one or more of the investment yield measurement methods. Each method tends to measure a different dimension of the investment yield. For example, the payback method tends to indicate the relative liquidity of the venture. In contrast, the internal rate of return does not indicate the liquidity of the investment, but does measure the long-term profitability of the project.

The first part of this chapter is, therefore, devoted to investment return measurement. The second part is devoted to indications of shopping center profitability over time. In this part, the yields from shopping center investments are compared to the yields from other types of real estate investments. The relative profitability of the several classifications of shopping centers is reviewed. Then the yield expectations from real estate portfolios including shopping center investments of various major real estate investors are considered. Survey data from 18 major real estate investors from spring 1982 are presented. It is noted that shopping center yields are usually competitive with medium- and high-grade corporate bond yields. The recent trend in corporate bond yields is presented to show the proximate yield requirements for shopping center investments.

METHODS OF INVESTMENT RETURN MEASUREMENT

According to several surveys made during the 1970s, five methods of measuring real property investment returns are employed. The three most frequently used methods are:

Total dollar return
Cash-on-cash return or average annual return
Cash payback

The other two methods which are increasingly used are:

Net present value
Internal rate of return or discounted rate of return

Generally, the internal rate of return method is used more frequently than the net present value method because it does not require the derivation of the investor's required rate of return. The internal rate of return method requires finding the rate of interest which equates the investment cost to the expected future net cash benefits from the investment.

Let us use the following situation to distinguish among the various measurement measures and the ways they are employed. The cash investment in the shopping center is $50,000. Five years of periodic cash flows after taxes are assumed. No sale of the property is assumed during these five years. The ordinary income tax rate is 50 percent.

Year	Cash Flow after Taxes (CFAT)	Cash Flow before Taxes (CFBT)
1	$ 5,000	$ 10,000
2	12,000	24,000
3	20,000	40,000
4	25,000	50,000
5	38,000	76,000
Total	$100,000	$200,000

Total Dollars Return

The total of the annual dollar returns after taxes is $100,000, which is the five-year return on the initial investment of $50,000.

Cash-on-Cash Return

This investment measure may be based on after-tax or before-tax cash flows. It may also measure the first-year return or the average cash return over the holding period, the five-year period in our case. The analyst may wish to compare the cash return against either the initial cash investment or the average cash investment in the project.

Let us first use the after-tax cash flows and the initial cash investment. The first-year measurement would be Year 1 CFAT $5,000 divided by the initial investment $50,000 or 10 percent. Let us then compare the average annual cash flow after taxes to the initial cash investment.

Average annual cash flow after taxes:

$$\text{total CFAT divided by 5 or } \frac{\$100,000}{5} = \$20,000$$

Initial cash investment = $50,000

$$\text{Average annual CFAT to initial cash investment} = \frac{\$20,000}{\$50,000} = 40 \text{ percent}$$

Now let us consider the ratio of the average annual cash flow to the average cash investment over the holding period.

Average annual cash flow after taxes: (see above) $20,000
Average cash investment = initial investment divided by 2
                        = $50,000 divided by 2 = $25,000
Average annual cash flow after taxes to the average cash investment

$$= \frac{\$20,000}{\$25,000} = 80 \text{ percent}$$

Now let us use the before-tax periodic cash flows. The first-year return ratio, using the initial cash investment, would be Year 1 CFBT $10,000 divided by the initial investment $50,000 or 20 percent. If the average annual cash flow before taxes to initial cash investment were calculated, it would be $40,000/ $50,000 or 80 percent. If the average annual cash flows before taxes were compared to the average cash investment, the ratio would be $40,000/$25,000 or 160 percent.

If the analyst knew the investor's overall tax rate, the after-tax calculations would be appropriate. If the analyst is not aware of the current tax position of the investor, the before-tax calculations would be necessary. If the analyst were measuring the returns from several properties, and several investors with their individual tax positions might be interested in those properties, the before-tax measurements would be meaningful.

Cash Payback

If $50,000 was invested in the shopping center and the owner was expecting to receive the after-tax cash flows during years 1 through 5 as set forth above, the cash payback period would be 3.5 years. The cash flow of $5,000 from Year 1, the cash flow from Year 2 of $12,000, and the cash flow from Year 3 of $20,000 would return only $37,000 to the investor. The investor would need to wait for an after-cash flow of $13,000 from the expected total cash flow of Year 4 of $25,000 in order to get all of the original cash investment back. You might say the cash payback period is 3.5 years.

Net Present Value

The net present value of the center is found by deducting the cash investment in the center from the present value of the expected future annual net cash flows from the center including the net after-tax cash proceeds from the sale of the center. We must know, therefore, how to calculate the net cash sale proceeds after taxes. Let us use the previous illustration, but add useful information.

Calculation of Net Cash Proceeds Before Taxes

Sale price of the center		$1,000,000
Less: Sales commission (5% of sale price)	$ 50,000	
Mortgage loan balance	400,000	450,000
Net cash proceeds before federal income taxes		$ 550,000

Calculation of Federal Income Taxes Payable. Capital gains calculation:

Sale price of center			$1,000,000
Less: Sales commission (5% of sale price)		$ 50,000	
Adjusted basis:			
Investment cost	$700,000		
Less: Depreciation	300,000		
Adjusted basis		400,000	450,000
Capital gain (long term because the center has been owned for more than 12 months)			$ 550,000

Recapture of Depreciation Taken on Nonresidential Property

Total depreciation expense taken	$300,000	
Ordinary federal income tax rate assumed	× 0.50	
Taxes payable for depreciation recapture		$ 150,000

Calculation of Capital Gains Taxes Payable

Long-term capital gain (calculated earlier)	$550,000	
40% of the long-term capital gain is taxable	× 0.40	
Taxable long-term capital gain at ordinary tax rates		$ 220,000
Application of ordinary income tax rate = assumed 0.50		× 0.50
Federal income taxes payable on 40% of the LTCG		$ 110,000
Tax preference income subject to minimum or alternative minimum taxation		330,000

If the taxpayer-owner is subject to ordinary income taxation at a 50 percent rate, then:

Federal income taxes payable at the ordinary rate of 50%:

Depreciation recapture: $300,000 × 0.50	$150,000
Taxes payable on other taxable income or loss	

for Year 5 at 50% rate ($76,000 × 0.50)   38,000
40% of long-term capital gain × 0.50 or
$220,000 × 0.50   110,000 $ 298,000

Federal income taxes payable on tax preference items:

Adjusted gross income	$76,000
Plus: Depreciation tax preference item	330,000
Balance	$406,000
Less: Exemption (not filing jointly)	− 30,000
Taxable at 20% rate	$376,000
Taxes due	$ 75,200
(20% × $376,000)	

Calculation of Net Cash Proceeds After Taxes

Net cash proceeds before federal income taxes	$ 550,000
Less: Total federal income taxes payable	373,200
Net cash proceeds after federal income taxes	$ 176,800

Therefore, the periodic cash flows for the calculation of net present value would be

Year	Cash Flow after Taxes (CFAT)	
1	$ 5,000	
2	12,000	
3	20,000	
4	25,000	
5	214,800	($38,000 + $176,800)

To find the present value of these cash flows using a 10 percent discount rate, you multiply each annual net cash flow by the respective 10 percent factor taken from the Present Value of $1 interest tables.

Year	CFAT	Present Value Factor at 10%	Present Value in Dollars
1	$ 5,000 ×	0.909	$ 4,545
2	12,000 ×	0.826	9,912
3	20,000 ×	0.751	15,020
4	25,000 ×	0.683	17,075
5	214,800 ×	0.620	133,176
			$179,728

Net Present Value Calculation.

Present value of the periodic net cash flows after taxes discounted at the investor's required rate of return of 10 percent	$179,728
Cash investment	− 50,000
Net present value	$129,728

Internal Rate of Return

The analyst finds the rate of return which equates the cash investment with the periodic net cash flows expected from the investment including the net cash proceeds from the sale.

By the trial and error system, we first select a possible internal rate of return. We know, from the above calculations, that 10 percent is much too low to equate the cash investment to the present value of the periodic cash flows after taxes. Therefore, let us start with a 20 percent discount rate

Year	CFAT	Present Value Factor at 20%	Present Value at 20%	Present Value Factor at 30%	Present Value at 30%
1	$ 5,000	0.833	$ 4,165	0.769	$ 3,845
2	12,000	0.694	8,328	0.592	7,104
3	20,000	0.578	11,560	0.455	9,100
4	25,000	0.482	12,050	0.350	8,750
5	214,800	0.401	86,135	0.269	57,781
			$122,238		$86,580

When we subtract the cash investment of $50,000 from the present value of the cash flows after taxes discounted at 30 percent (the highest rate in our interest tables) of $86,580, the surplus of $36,580 indicates that the discount rate must be higher than 30 percent to equate the investment to the present value of the expected future net cash flows. The very favorable initial financing and the favorable sale price have resulted in an unusually good after-tax rate of return to the investor, an after-tax internal rate of return over 30 percent.

RECENT INVESTMENT RETURNS FROM SHOPPING CENTERS AND OTHER INCOME PROPERTIES

Some evidence of investment returns from real properties as a whole and shopping centers in particular is available from current sources.

Yields from Income Properties in General

Over the last few years, 1970 to 1982, income property returns on a current dollar basis or on a constant dollar basis have outperformed the Consumer Price Index, Treasury bills, long-term bonds, and the Standard and Poor 500 Common Stock Index, according to the investment yield calculations of the management of the Property Investment Separate Account (PRISA) of The Prudential Insurance Company of America. The analysis started on July 31, 1970 and covers yields from equity ownership of income property. The managers of PRISA select real properties with attractive rates of current income as well as good prospects for long-term growth for this pension fund and other investor clients.

Some 1979 yield data from selected open-end real estate funds show an average yield on income property holdings that year of 18.7 percent. The yield was approximately split between the cash yield and the capital appreciation. Only 1 percent more of the total yield was attributable to appreciation than to periodic cash return (Exhibit 16-1, Characteristics of Open-End Real Estate Funds, 1979). The PRISA fund outperformed the other funds by turning in an overall yield of 26 percent.

Annualized returns from commingled real estate funds in 1980 ranged from 69.4 percent to 9.5 percent and averaged 17.9 percent.˙ When the return of each fund was weighted by the fund's asset size, the average return was 18.5 percent. At the same time the Consumer Price Index increased 13.5 percent. In light of the fact that the stock market returns have fluctuated widely over the decade of the 1970s, the return shown by the Standard and Poor 500 Stock

Exhibit 16-1.   Characteristics of Open-End Real Estate Funds, 1979 (Averages Weighted by Assets)

Open-End Real Estate Fund	Real Estate Assets (millions)	Cash Yield	Appreciation	Total
PRISA	$1325.5	9.2%	16.8%	26.0%
The Equitable	929.7	8.5	4.4	12.9
Fund F	198.1	7.9	3.2	11.1
Continental Illinois	48.7	9.2	3.8	13.0
Wachovia Bank	60.2	4.5	9.2	13.7
Bank of America	59.7	9.3	4.6	13.9
Wells Fargo	54.0	8.5	4.0	12.5
Crocker	38.0	7.9	1.4	9.3
First National Bank of Boston	32.2	9.2	2.0	11.3
Travelers Insurance	106.6	10.3	(1.2)	9.1
	$1852.7	8.8%*	9.9%*	18.7%*

Source: John McMahan Associates, "Institutional Strategies for Real Estate Equity Investment," *Urban Land*, Vol. 40, No. 6, June 1981, p. 17.
*Varying fiscal year closing periods during 1979.

Exhibit 16-2. The Yield Trend for Seasoned Issues of Two Grades of U.S. Corporate Bonds

	YEAR						
Bond Rating	1977	1978	1979	1980	1981	February 1982	February 1983
A	8.49	9.12	10.20	12.89	15.29	16.35	13.52
Baa	8.97	9.45	10.69	13.67	16.04	17.18	13.95

Source: *Federal Reserve Bulletin*, March 1982 and March 1983.

Index for 1980 was 31.5 percent.[*] Since income property yields tend to compete most closely with corporate bond yields, we see from Exhibit 16-2 that these competitive yields generally doubled in the period 1977 through 1982 to arrive at the 16- to 17-percent level. The rates fell to 13.5−14 percent by early 1983.

Yields from Shopping Center Investment

A recent institutional investor and advisor survey showed that the major investors in income properties in 1982 had major holdings in shopping centers (Exhibit 16-3, Survey Results). Some of the major investors listed are taxable parties; some are not. Their investment return preferences, therefore, differ by their tax positions. Generally, on a taxable basis, the survey showed that the major investor expected a return from 16 to 18 percent overall in early 1982 from an income property portfolio. On a nontaxable basis, they appear to want 8 to 10 percent investment returns. Since shopping centers are major components of the individual portfolios, the investors expect substantial returns from these entities.

If the investment analyst or investor looks over a number of issues of *Dollars & Cents of Shopping Centers*, published by the Urban Land Institute and cosponsored by the International Council of Shopping Centers, it might seem evident that more dollars are pocketed by square foot of gross leasable area for the superregional center than for the other four major types of centers (Exhibits 16-4 and 16-5). The net operating balances for the smaller community and neighborhood centers, though, are higher as a percent of total receipts than that for the regional centers. The investor derives more profit per dollar invested on a percentage basis from the smaller centers (Exhibit 16-5). The average rent for the larger center is higher than the average rent for the smaller center (Exhibit 16-4). The development costs for the larger center are also higher than those for the smaller centers.

[*]Estey, Arthur, and Miles, Mike, "How Pension Funds Invest Through CREFs," *Commercial Investment Journal*, Vol. 1, 1982, p. 11.
[*]*Ibid.*

Exhibit 16-3. Real Estate Institutional Investor/Advisor Survey.

Company, Address	Contact, Phone	Number of Institutional Clients*	Total Real Estate Assets† (millions)	Percentage of Real Estate Holdings — Income-Producing Properties	Other	Breakdown of Real Estate Holdings (%)	Major Type of Shopping Center Holdings‡	Geographic Preference	Preferred Return on Investment	How Shopping Center Properties Managed	Will Investor Company or Advisor Firm's Clients Take on Development Role?
Ackerman Advisory Assoc. 3340 Peachtree Rd. N.E. Tower Place. Suite 100 Atlanta, GA 30026	Paul H. Saylor (404) 262-7171 (404) 266-0800	6	$ 282	100%		Shopping centers 36, Office buildings 48, Industrial properties 16	Regional	Continental U.S.	10%+	Professional management firm	Possibly
Alex Brown Realty, Inc. 7 North Calvert St., 5th Flr. Baltimore, MD 21202	John M. Prugh (301) 727-4083		92	100		Shopping centers 5, Office buildings 22, Multifamily residential 73	Neighborhood	Sunbelt	10% leveraged	Shopping center development/ management firm	Yes
Consolidated Capital 1900 Powell St. Suite 1000 Emeryville, CA 94608	Richard Wollack Phil Maher, Sr. (415) 652-7171		1000	100		Shopping centers 5, Office buildings 10, Multifamily residential 85	Community	Southeast South Southwest Northwest		In-house management	Doubtful
Richard Ellis, Inc. 200 E. Randolph Dr. Suite 6545 Chicago, IL 60187	Edward P. Meyer (312) 861-1105	6	600	100		Shopping centers 40, Office buildings 50, Industrial properties 10	Regional	Nationwide	8.25–8.75	Professional management firm; Shopping center development/ management firm; In-house management	No
Equitec Properties Co. P.O. Box 1109 Lafayette, CA 94549	(415) 283-8700		600	100		Shopping centers 1, Office buildings 80, Industrial properties 18, Multifamily residential 1	Community, Regional	Sunbelt West	20% IRR over 5 years	In-house management	Possibly
Equity Corp. First American Center 25th Floor Nashville, TN 37238	Linda G. Chesnut (615) 242-4417	14	125	100		Shopping centers 50, Industrial properties 25, Multifamily residential 25	Community	Southeast	8-10%	In-house management	Yes
Grosvenor International 44 Montgomery St. Suite 4284 San Francisco, CA 94104	William J. Abelman Geoff Goddard (415) 434-0175	4		100		Shopping centers 20, Office buildings 70, Industrial properties 10	Neighborhood, Regional	West of Chicago/ New Orleans border	15-16% IRR; minimum 6% cash on cash	Shopping center development/ management firm	No
Grubb & Ellis Property Services Co. 1333 Broadway Suite 2400 Oakland, CA 94612	Perry P. Noyer (415) 839-9600	3	100	100		Shopping centers 20, Office buildings 40, Industrial properties 40	Community	West Southwest	11% yield 18% IRR	Professional management firm	No
Landauer Advisors, Inc. 200 Park Ave. New York, NY 10166	Patrick J. Callan (212) 687-2323	3	500	100		Shopping centers 14, Office buildings 60, Industrial properties 2, Multiuse complex 24	Regional	Continental U.S.	15-18% IRR	Professional management firm	No

Landsing Properties 431 Burgess Drive Menlo Park, CA 94025	(415) 323-8313		250	100		Shopping centers Office buildings Hotels Multifamily residential Agriculture, mixed-use complex	20 35 4 28 13	Neighborhood Community	TX, OK, CO, ID, OR, Northern CA		In-house management	No
Loeb Partners Realty 521 Fifth Ave. New York, NY 10175	Gary L. Naughton (212) 883-0371	6	960	90	10	Shopping centers Office buildings Industrial properties Hotels Multifamily residential	35 40 10 5 10	Neighborhood Community Regional	Sunbelt	8-12%	In-house management	No
Noro Realty Advisors, Inc. 250 Piedmont Ave., NE Suite 1410 Atlanta, GA 30308	Frederick D. Clemente (404) 586-0900		200	100		Shopping centers Office buildings Industrial properties Multifamily residential	24 31 13 32	Neighborhood Community	Southeast Southwest Western and Rocky Mountain States	13-15% IRR	Direct and supervisory management	No
Norris Beggs & Simpson 243 Kearny St. San Francisco, CA 94108	Garrett P. Scales	20	500	100		Shopping centers Office buildings Industrial properties	35 30 30	Neighborhood Community Regional	West		In-house management	Yes
Paine Webber Properties 100 Federal St. Boston, MA 02101	S. Douglas Weil George H. Bigelow (617) 423-8150	7	100	100		Shopping centers Office buildings Multifamily residential	51 8 41	Community Regional	Nationwide	16-20% IRR	Shopping center development/ management firm	No
RepublicBank Dallas, N.A. P.O. Box 241 Dallas, TX 75201	David J. Pittman Stan D. Miller (214) 643-7526		205	33	67			Neighborhood	Southeast Southwest	8-9%	In-house management	No
RREEF 650 California St. San Francisco, CA 94108	(415) 781-3300	40	1300	70	30 (uncommitted)	Shopping centers Office buildings Industrial properties Multifamily residential	20 54 25 1	Neighborhood	Major metro areas only	Real discounted return minimum 4%	In-house management	No
The Peckham Boston Co. Four Longfellow Place Boston, MA 02114	John M. Peckham, III (617) 523-4440	4	30	100		Shopping centers Office buildings Industrial properties Multifamily residential	50 20 10 20	Regional	Nationwide	Varies with risk	In-house management	
The Travelers Insurance Co. One Tower Square Hartford, CT 06115	Thomas Montgomery (203) 277-0111	100	7000	100		Shopping centers Office buildings Industrial properties Multifamily residential Agricultural	20 40 25 5 10	Community		16-18%	Professional management firm	No

Source: "Institutional Investor/Advisor Survey," *Shopping Center World*, Vol. 11, No. 3, March 1982, pp. 56–59. © 1982 Communication Channels Inc., 6285 Barfield Road, Atlanta, GA 30328.

*Appropriate for advisory firms only.

†Total dollar assets are given for investor firm or for combined assets of advisory firm's investor clients

‡For purposes of this survey, neighborhood centers are defined as those under 100,000 square feet; community centers as those from 100,000 to 300,000 square feet; and regional centers as over 300,000 square feet.

Exhibit 16-4. Operating Receipts of Shopping Centers

Shopping Center Type	Median Expected Operating Receipts per Square Foot of Gross Leasable Area		
	1981	1978	1975
Superregional	$11.64	$7.41	$7.52
Regional	7.04		
Community	3.48	4.83	—
Neighborhood	4.07	4.48	—

Source: *Dollars & Cents of Shopping Centers* (Washington, D.C.: Urban Land Institute, 1981, 1978, and 1975).

Exhibit 16-5. Net Operating Balance of the Various Types of Shopping Centers, 1981

Type of Center	Dollars per Square Foot of Gross Leasable Area	Percent of Total Receipts
Superregional	$6.71	61.4%
Regional	4.01	60.4
Community	2.40	70.3
Neighborhood	2.99	73.8

Source: *Dollars & Cents of Shopping Centers* (Washington, D.C.: Urban Land Institute, 1981), pp. 19, 63, 115, and 165.

GLOSSARY

Accelerated depreciation methods. Methods of calculating depreciation expense which permit more generous deductions than the straight-line method does.

Adjusted basis. Investment cost less depreciation taken for federal income tax purposes.

Advantageous refinancing. *See* Refinancing, advantageous.

Alternative minimum taxation. Tax regulations covering special payment of federal income taxes on special "tax preference" items which real property accounting may involve. Regular taxes are calculated; then the taxpayer must figure the taxes due based on alternative minimum tax rules.

Amortization. The repayment of the borrowed principal amount of a loan. In layman's language, the term "amortization" often is used interchangeably with "debt service."

Amortized expense. Expense spread out over a selected and appropriate time period.

Assignment. Sale of a security in its original form with no modifications.

Balloon payment. A payment of principal that is due the lender to complete the amortization of the loan at the maturity of the loan. When a balloon payment is called for, the original loan was not fully amortized in level payments over its term. The amortization period was probably longer than the loan term.

Band of investment. A method of deriving a capitalization rate for real estate appraisal that uses a weighted cost of funds as the rate. The proportional amount of each source of funds is weighted by its cost. The weighted costs of all the funds invested in the project are totaled to find the appropriate capitalization rate.

Bank prime rate. The interest rate that the commercial bank may quote to its industrial corporation clients with the highest credit ratings.

Basis point. One one-hundredth of a percent.

Beneficiary. The lender associated with a trust deed.

Bond. An indenture agreement issued and then sold by a business or government entity which promises interest income and the repayment of principal to the investor. The industrial corporation bond is usually secured only by the good credit standing of the issuer and not by the real estate or other collateral. The term "bond" usually implies that the debt obligation is relatively long term.

Business cycle. The fluctuations of business conditions in general. The four phases of the business cycle tend to match the four phases of the economic cycle. *See* Economic cycle.

Call provisions. The clauses in the mortgage which permit the lender to accelerate the maturity of the outstanding loan amount upon certain conditions.

Cap rate. An abbreviation for "capitalization rate."

Capital appreciation. The increase in market value of an asset over time.

Capital depreciation. The decrease in market value of an asset over time.

Capital gains taxation. The taxation more favorable than ordinary corporate or personal income taxation which is usable for long-term capital gains treatment at tax time.

Capital market. The market for longer-term securities with a range of credit ratings from high to low which are issued by industrial corporations, other businesses, financial institutions, the U.S. Treasury, and other issuers.

Capitalization. The spreading out over time of an expense. As an asset is used, the expense associated with the asset is taken as a tax deduction. The present value of an asset may be often determined by income capitalization methods. The stabilized net operating income is divided by an appropriate capitalization rate.

Capitalization rate. An appropriate rate which represents the required investment rate plus the rate of recapture of the invested principal. The rate may also reflect the mortgage and equity financing of the particular or typical property, the expected value depreciation or appreciation, the mortgage loan-to-value ratio, and the appropriate sinking fund factor for the investment recapture.

Cash flow. The flow of cash in or out of a business in the form of rents, operating costs, mortgage payments, or other such cash requirements. Often the term "cash flow" refers to the amount of cash generated by a business over a period of time after the cash operating expenses and mortgage payments are deducted from the cash revenue from various sources. The "cash flow" may be calculated before or after federal income taxes are paid.

Cash investment. The investor's contributed cash. The cash invested in the project from equity and debt sources.

Cash-on-cash return. The initial year's net cash flow divided by the cash investment from the owner(s). The stabilized annual cash flow before or after federal income taxes divided by the cash investment of the owner(s).

Cash payback. The period of time over which the investors receive the return of their invested capital from the net cash flows of the investment.

Certificate of deposit. A document written by a depository financial institution that shows that a time deposit was made by the depositor and a certain rate of interest is payable per year on that deposit. This document may be negotiable for future trading in the money market by the institution.

Chain retailers. Retailers whose stores are associated under a holding or operating company. The various retail store locations are financed and operated from a central office of the organization.

Collateral. Assets pledged to secure a loan.

Commercial banks. Depository institutions which serve the consumer, business, government, and other financial institutions that are chartered either by the Comptroller of the Currency or the appropriate state department of financial institutions. The vast majority of their deposits are insured up to $100,000 each by the Federal Deposit Insurance Corporation. The national bank is regulated by the Comptroller of the Currency, the Federal Reserve Board, and the FDIC. The state bank is regulated by the appropriate state department of financial institutions and the FDIC.

Commercial paper. The short-term negotiable promissory notes sold by commercial banks, finance companies, and other issuers with high credit standings for the financing of their private businesses. The paper term to maturity usually does not exceed 270 days and usually runs for only 30 to 90 days.

Common stock. The ownership interests of a corporation. Usually common stock has associated with it voting and dividend rights.

Community shopping center. The retail complex of numerous stores which attracts customers from a driving time radius of five to ten minutes who are attracted to the convenience and shopping goods and services which are available. The anchor tenants may be a supermarket, a drugstore, and a discount department store.

Component depreciation method. The depreciation method which calls for the separate depreciation of each depreciable component of the property using its individual economic life and the remaining depreciable value. The various depreciation methods such as straight-line, 125 percent straight-line through 200 percent straight-line declining balance, and sum-of-the-years-digits may be used with the component depreciation system. Became obsolete in 1982.

Comptroller of the Currency. The federal agency of the executive branch of the federal government that charters and supervises nationally chartered commercial banks.

Constant. *See* Loan constant.

Consumer Price Index. An index maintained by the Bureau of Labor Statistics of the U.S. Department of Labor which shows the relative change in the prices of consumer goods and services over a period of time. The BLS usually recalculates the index every month and publishes it in several journals and newspapers. The change in the index is often used to show the change in U.S. inflation and to adjust indexed rents and mortgage rates.

Contract rate. The stated interest rate in contrast with the effective interest rate.

Convenience goods and services. The consumer goods and services that are bought with little forethought in a handy and convenient location. They are usually relatively inexpensive and are bought frequently (e.g. cigarettes, milk, bread, dry cleaning).

Conversion. Change from the original condition, state, or financial interest to another condition, state, or financial interest. For example, the holder of a convertible bond may convert it into stock ownership at a given time or stock price to be reached in the future. The debt turns into equity with the exercise of the conversion right.

Convertible debenture. An unsecured bond which is convertible into stock of the corporation.

Corporation. A business organization with an infinite life whose owners are stock holders. A board of directors is its policy-making group while the day-to-day operation is accomplished by the professional management of the enterprise. The business entity's taxable income is subject to federal and state corporate income taxation.

Cost approach to value. The approach to value which results in the depreciated replacement cost new of the subject.

Credit union. A financial intermediary which takes in deposits from a related group of employees or other individuals and makes personal and home mortgage loans to the same or other members. The tax-exempt financial institution may be a member of the National Credit Union Administration. If it is, the individual credit union pays a fee to the NCUA and submits to its supervision, regulation, and insurance on deposits.

Debt. Borrowed money whose return of capital must usually be accompanied by the payment of interest for the use of the capital.

Debt service. The periodic payment toward the principal and interest on an unpaid loan.

Declining balance depreciation method. A method of depreciating real property for tax and internal business purposes where the succeeding depreciation amounts are calculated on the declining balance of the undepreciated value of the asset. According to the current tax laws, 175 percent and 200 percent declining balance methods may be used for depreciation of specific types of real properties.

Depreciation. Loss in market value. A noncash tax-deductible business expense. Loss in value from physical deterioration, functional obsolescence, or environmental obsolescence.

Depreciation allowance. The business expense associated with depreciation of a property.

Deregulation. Elimination of regulations which were originally in force.

Developer. The person who directs the planning, organizing, financing, and constructing of a new, expanded, or remodeled income property.

Development. Creation of something that did not exist before. With respect to a shopping center, the planning, organizing, financing, and construction of a center using the appropriate skilled personnel under the direction of a person called a developer.

Discount rate. The rate of interest which is used to change future expected net cash flows from a property into present value. The discount rate usually reflects the current investor's overall yield requirement for the type of property and its characteristics.

Discounted rate of return. *See* Internal rate of return.

Disintermediation. The withdrawal of funds by individuals and businesses from the traditional depository institutions and the direct placement of these monies by the investors in such direct investments as stocks, bonds, and mortgages.

Durable good. An asset whose useful life extends a relatively long period. Such an asset might include a car, a house, an apartment building, electrical appliances, or furniture.

Economic cycle. The fluctuations in economic conditions over time. Prosperity turns to recession, recession may turn to depression, depression may turn to recovery, and recovery may again change to prosperity. The four phases in this phenomenon tends to recur at unpredictable intervals.

Economic history. The progress of economic events over a long period of time.

Economic obsolescence. The loss in market value of a real property which is derived from external sources. Examples: Access to the site is cut off by the construction of a new freeway or a polluting industrial plant is opened nearby. The property owner can do nothing to reduce the loss in property value because he or she has no control over the outside, detrimental sources.

Effective gross income. The revenue remaining after vacancy, rent, and bad debt or rent losses are subtracted from total gross revenue. The operating expense ratio is usually calculated on the base of effective gross income.

Ellwood formula and tables. An analytical formula and associated tables devised by L. W. Ellwood, who was employed by a major New York life insurance company, for the derivation of the appropriate capitalization rate for appraisal of income properties which takes into account their typical financing, the typical investor's equity yield requirement, and expected capital appreciation or depreciation.

Equity. The difference between total value and the monies borrowed, or the difference between total cost and the monies borrowed. The amount of money in dollars which represents the ownership interests in a property.

Equity buildup. The increased amount of the equity the mortgagor has in a financed property because a number of loan payments containing repayments of principal have been paid previously to the mortgagee.

Equity dividend. The cash flow dividend realized on the cash investment.

Equity participation. Additional investment return which comes from the sharing of the gross storeroom rental receipts, the net cash flow before taxes, the refinancing proceeds, and/or the net sale proceeds with the owner-mortgagor of the property.

Equity position. An ownership interest.

Equity yield. The total investment return from all sources including the periodic cash flows, the capital appreciation, the equity buildup from the mortgage repayment, and the tax shelter benefits.

Excess depreciation. The depreciation for federal income tax purposes which exceeds that which would be taken if straight-line depreciation methods were used. Excess depreciation results from the taxpayer use of accelerated depreciation methods for tax purposes.

Feasibility study. A study in advance of commencement of a real estate project which summarizes the income potential of the proposed investment. The "bottom line" for each projected operating period shows the expected net cash flow before federal income taxes are paid by the owner. The expected internal rate of return on the project can be calculated and compared to the expected returns from other proposed investments.

Federal Deposit Insurance Corporation. The federal agency of the executive branch of the government that insures the deposits of member institutions. Usually they insure the deposits of commercial banks, but mutual savings banks may request FDIC insurance of their deposits, also. Currently each depository account of the bank is insured up to $100,000.

Federal Home Loan Bank System. The federal agency whose board charters, regulates and controls its member savings and loan associations. The national headquarters are located in Washington, D. C. The agency is part of the executive branch of the federal government.

Federal Housing Administration. Once an independent federal agency which provided mortgage insurance for qualified mortgagors and their qualified properties. There is no longer an independent federal agency by this name. The functions of the earlier agency are now performed within the various divisions and departments of the U.S. Department of Housing and Urban Development which is a cabinet department of the executive branch of the federal government.

Federal Reserve System. The central banking system of the United States which formulates and implements the monetary policy of the federal government. Since the financial reform of 1980, the Federal Reserve Board of Governors in cooperation with other federal government agencies and offices carry out monetary policies by regulation of all financial institutions. Reserves of all depository financial institutions of the United States are controlled by a financial committee of which the Federal Reserve Board, the

Federal Deposit Insurance Corporation, the Federal Home Loan Bank Board, the Federal Savings and Loan Insurance Corporation, the Comptroller, and the U.S. Treasury are members. The Federal Reserve Board is headquartered in Washington, D. C. and is a part of the executive branch of the federal government.

Federal Savings and Loan Insurance Corporation. The subsidiary of the Federal Home Loan Bank System that insures the deposits of member savings and loan associations. Currently each deposit of insured savings and loan associations is insured up to $100,000.

FHA mortgage insurance. Mortgage insurance provided by the U.S. Department of Housing and Urban Development (HUD) for qualified mortgagors and properties where the mortgagor pays each year to HUD one-half of one percent of the average outstanding mortgage balance for the insurance protection for the private mortgage lender.

Financial features. The financial characteristics of an asset, for example, the amount of mortgage debt outstanding, the amount of equity invested by one or more classes of investors, the operating expense ratio, the debt coverage ratio, the loan-to-value ratio used for the first mortgage, and the total construction cost per square foot.

Financing. Finding monies to purchase and maintain an asset. For example, locating ownership monies and loanable funds for the purchase and operation of a property.

Financing patterns. Systems of financing for land acquisition, land development, building construction, and long-term building operation. The systems involve such methods of financing as sale-leasebacks, convertible mortgage and straight mortgage financing, all-equity financing, and land contracts.

First mortgage. The mortgage whose lender has first priority on the cash flows generated by the income property.

Fiscal policy. The financial policies related to the financing of government through taxation and sale of government securities.

Fixed-rate mortgage. A mortgage loan with a fixed contract rate of interest.

Floating rate. An interest rate that changes with the changes in a base or index rate.

Fully amortized. The principal of the loan is repaid and the interest is paid gradually in total over the life of the loan through the numerous loan payments.

Functional obsolescence. The loss in market value of a real property which may come from obsolete room arrangement, obsolete room size, insufficient parking under roof, inadequate electrical wiring for the currently used appliances, ceilings too high for energy conservation, and other such features of a property.

General partnership. Two or more investors become partners of a single class in order to purchase and operate an income property. The partnership income itself is not subject to federal income taxation, but the distributions over time to the partners are taxed along with the rest of their personal taxable incomes.

Glut of space on the market. Excess space for which there is insufficient current demand.

Gross leasable area. All space available in a shopping center including the mall or common areas used by the public.

Hedge against inflation. An investment return with increases or decreases with the path of inflation.

High leverage. A relatively high portion of the value of the property is financed with borrowed money.

Hybrid debt-equity instrument. A security like a convertible mortgage or a convertible bond that is a debt obligation until it is converted into an equity interest at the option of the security holder. The issuer has given the holder the right of conversion in return for investment funds.

Income approach to value. The present value of the property is found by discounting the anticipated future net cash flows or by capitalizing a stabilized net operating income into value with the use of an appropriate capitalization rate.

Income property. A real property that generates income for its owner(s).

Indexation. The change of rents or costs based on the changes of an index.

Inflation protection. The protection of the value of the dollar from devaluation through investment in assets whose value rises with inflation or whose investment income rises with inflation.

Inflation rate. The rate at which the value of the dollar declines over the given period of time. The rate is usually based on the period of one year. More and more dollars chase a given amount of goods. Prices rise more than the volume of goods and services do.

Initial lease. The first lease term which may be followed by additional lease terms as the tenant renews the lease with the landlord.

Institutional decision making. Decisions made by businesses and financial institutions.

Intermediation. The investment of funds by individuals and businesses with financial intermediaries who accomplish the investment.

Internal rate of return. The rate of return earned by an investment which equates the amount of the initial investment with the future cash flows from that investment.

Internal Revenue Service. The federal agency charged with the collection of federal income taxes.

International Council of Shopping Centers. The trade association comprising the majority of the shopping center developers whose activities are headquartered in New York City. The organization was founded in 1957.

Investment. The release of money by its owner to attain the ownership of an asset or to lend temporarily to another party.

Investment climate. The relative investment opportunities available at a given time. The investment opportunities usually depend partly upon the current state of the economy and its position in the economic cycle.

Joint venture. A partnership arrangement for a single real estate venture. The partners may be corporations, proprietorships, or partnerships themselves. Typical joint venture partners for a shopping center are the developer and one or more financial sources. A pension fund and a commercial bank may be the joint venture partners of the developer, for example.

Junior mortgage. A mortgage subordinate to the preceding mortgage placed on the property.

Kicker. A potential source of income to the mortgage lender, also called an "equity kicker." The mortgage lender receives debt service from the borrower on a scheduled basis and then expects to participate in the growth in net operating income or gross sales from the financed property. The growth in net operating income or gross sales usually accrues to the equity investor, but the equity investor may let the lender participate in this normal flow to the investor in return for mortgage money. When a kicker is part of the lending agreement, the scheduled mortgage debt service is usually lower than it otherwise would have to be in order for the lender to derive the required yield from the mortgage.

Kiosk. A selling booth or sales vehicle in the middle of a shopping center mall from which goods and services are dispensed to paying customers.

Landlord. The individual or business who owns the real property rights. The landlord is often called the lessor in lease contracts.

Lease. A contract between landlord and tenant or between sublessee and prime lessee. The individual or business with the ownership right or the right of possession gives the right of possession to another individual or business in return for the payment of the return by the new lessee.

Legal list. A list of the investments approved for investment of institutional funds. Legal lists usually restrict somewhat the investment of life insurance company money.

Lender. A person, business, or institution who lends money to another in return for interest and other forms of compensation.

Lessee. The individual or business renting space from another individual or business.

Level-annuity recapture rate. A present value interest factor that represents the recapture of the invested capital over the investment holding period when the amounts set aside for capital recapture each operating period are reinvested at the market rate of interest. The market rate of interest is usually equated with the current overall yield from the income property being appraised.

Leverage. The use of borrowed money to supplement equity.

Lien theory state. A state that operates under the legal theory that the borrower gives a mortgage or deed of trust to the lender or trustee and keeps the title to the property pledged as collateral. A lien is placed on the title. The borrower retains possession until a default on the mortgage or note occurs.

Life insurance company. The financial intermediary that sells four general types of life insurance policies: ordinary life, group, industrial, and annuity. Life insurance companies' investments are regulated by the legal lists of the pertinent state insurance commissions and tend to invest in most types of capital market securities. They have recently turned to construction lending and real property development.

Limited partnership. Two or more partners are separated into two classes, general and limited partners. The general partner(s) actively manage the business or income property while the limited partners merely contribute the funds for the investment and do not take an active management role. The partnership income is not usually subject to income taxation, but the cash distributions to the individual partners are.

Liquidity. The ability to turn an asset into cash within a period of time. A low degree of liquidity means that conversion of the asset into cash takes a relatively long period of time. A high degree of liquidity means that the conversion into cash takes a relatively short period of time.

Loan constant. The percentage of the original loan amount that is used to find the level mortage payments due over the term of the mortgage. The loan constant may be found in pertinent tables when the contract rate and the term of the loan are known.

Loan package. The combination of loan terms which make up a mortgage financing deal.

Loan prospectus. The accumulated, organized information underlying a loan application which is presented in order to persuade the lender to make the loan on the desired terms.

Loan-to-value ratio. The ratio composed of the loan amount divided by the appraised value of the real property. The ratio is often used by mortgage lenders to decide how many dollars they will loan. They multiply the appropriate ratio times the appraised value of the property to find the loan amount.

Long-term capital gain. A capital gain incurred after the holding of the capital asset more than 12 months.

Market comparison approach. The value of the subject is found by comparing to it similar properties which have sold recently. By looking at each component of difference between the subject and each of the comparables, the value of the subject may be estimated out of current market conditions.

Market rate. The interest set by market forces for the particular type of security.

Market study. An analysis of the demand for a proposed real estate project. The analysis takes into account the current and the proposed competition, their rate structures, operating costs, and vacancy and absorption rates.

Market value. The estimated amount of dollars which would be paid for a property if a reasonable sales period were permitted and if the buyers and sellers were well acquainted with the possible legal and feasible uses for the property and given no coercion or undue influence over the sale or purchase in an arm's length transaction.

Maturity of the mortgage. The due date of the mortgage loan. All principal must be repaid and interest paid to the mortgagee on that date.

Monetary policy. The financial policies related to the furtherance of economic development, the increase of employment with the increase in population, the minimization of unemployment, the stabilization of the value of the dollar, and the stability and profitability of the private financial institutions.

Money market. The market for short-term securities with high credit ratings which are usually issued by commercial banks, the thrift institutions, money market mutual funds, finance companies, and the U.S. Treasury.

Mortgage. The pledge of real estate collateral in return for a loan of money. The two-part financing arrangement involves a mortgagor and a mortgagee.

Mortgagee. Lender.

Mortgage-backed security. A pass-through type indenture agreement backed by a pool of mortgages of similar type and duration. The repayment of principal and payment of interest to the investor may be guaranteed by the Government National Mortgage Association or by the issuer of the security.

Mortgage banker. A person who originates a mortgage loan, sells it to an investor, and retains the servicing for a fee.

Mortgage broker. A person who originates a mortgage loan and places it with an investor without retaining the mortgage servicing.

Mortgage-equity techniques. Appraisal techniques used in deriving the current value of a property based on the typical financing methods, expected depreciation or appreciation, and typical equity yield requirements.

Mortgage financing. The financing of the purchase and operation of real properties with loans which are secured by real estate collateral. Usually the real estate collateral is the real property being financed.

Mortgage Guaranty Insurance Corporation. A private corporation based in Milwaukee, Wisconsin that insures mortgage loans.

Mortgage market. The market for the trading of existing mortgages and the underwriting and financing of new mortgages.

Mortgage note. A promissory note attached to the mortgage document.

Mortgage out. The permanent loan amount equals or exceeds the construction and development costs.

Mortgage rate. The nominal or contract rate on the mortgage.

Mortgagor. Borrower.

Municipal financing. The financing by means of the sale of debt obligations by local governments and their constituent agencies.

Mutual savings bank. Thrift institutions concentrated in the Northeast, Middle Atlantic, and Northwest states which invest primarily in mortgages and industrial bonds. The savings banks' deposits may be insured by either the Federal Deposit Insurance Corporation or state insurance companies designed for savings bank service.

National Credit Union Administration. The federally sponsored agency for the regulation and supervision of federally chartered credit unions.

Neighborhood shopping center. The small retail complex of six to ten stores which serves the ultimate consumers in the near vicinity. The average driving time may be five minutes or less. Mainly convenience goods and services are offered for sale. The anchor tenant is usually a supermarket.

Net cash flow. The balance of the cash revenue after the cash operating and financial expenses are deducted.

Net cash proceeds from sale. The net cash proceeds remaining after the sales commission and the remaining mortgage obligation are subtracted from the sale price of the property.

Net leasable area. The area left when common areas are subtracted from gross leasable area. Usually square footage rents are calculated on the basis of net leasable area, not gross leasable area.

Net lease. A lease which provides for tenant payment of all or part of the traditional landlord expenses associated with the leased space. For example, the tenant may agree to pay the energy costs, property tax expense, hazard insurance premiums, and other maintenance costs beyond the landlord's original costs when the lease was negotiated.

Net operating income. Often called "net income" by real estate industry people. The amount left when operating expenses and estimated vacancy and bad debt or rent loss are subtracted from gross revenues.

Net present value. The positive or negative residual value of the investment when the initial investment is subtracted from the present value of the expected future net cash flows.

Nondurable good. An asset with a relatively short useful economic life. Such an asset might be personal clothing, restaurant food, or toys.

Nonnegotiable instrument. A security that cannot be traded from person to person. It is designed for assignment to other investors.

Obsolescence. Loss in value from functional or environmental causes.

Offshore investor. An investor whose investment organization is chartered in a foreign country and subject to its tax rules and regulations.

Operating expense. A fixed or variable expense associated with the daily operation and maintenance of an income property. Fixed operating expenses are payable regardless of the occupancy level of the property. Variable operating expenses vary in amount with the occupancy level.

Operating expense ratio. Operating expenses divided by effective gross income.

Option. An agreement between the optionor and the optionee that causes the optionee to withhold from the market the sale or lease of an asset in exchange for option money or other consideration from the optionor. The optionor may exercise the option, renew the option, or let it lapse. With the exercise of the option, the option money will probably apply toward the purchase or lease of the desired asset.

Overage payment. A payment over and above a base amount. The payment may be a percentage of the tenant's gross revenue above a base amount. The basic rent which is periodically payable to the landlord may be rent per square foot of gross or net space leased.

Overall ordinary tax rate. When the taxes paid are related to the taxable income, the ratio may be called the taxpayer's overall ordinary tax rate.

Overbuilding. Constructing space beyond the current demand for that type of space.

Ownership entity. The form of business ownership adopted for the ownership of an asset.

Participation. Sharing of revenues and expenses with one or more other parties. The storeroom lessee often shares revenues and expenses with the lessor.

Partnership. Two or more investors joined together for an investment when the individual investment returns are taxed at the individual's tax rates based on the consolidated income. The joint ownership may be a general or limited partnership.

Peak. The uppermost point of a fluctuating phenomenon. The maximum prosperity reached in the recurrent economic and business cycle.

Pension fund. The financial institution that derives its funds from the contributions from private business or government employers and private business or government employees. The employees await cash distributions from the fund upon their retirement from the government or business. The fund administrators invest the accumulated sums as well as the new contributions for the future financial security of the employees involved.

Percentage net lease. A lease that provides for tenant assumption of all or a part of the landlord's traditional operating expenses a payment based on the square footage utilized, plus a percentage of the tenant's gross revenue beyond a base amount.

Point. One percent. One percent of the original mortgage amount.

Portfolio. The mixture of various types and varieties of investments held by a single investor at the current time.

Preferred stock. A preferred ownership interest of a corporation whose dividends are payable before the common stockholders receive dividends but whose ownership rights usually do not include voting.

Prepayment provisions. The lender's provisions for penalties for the mortgagor's early payment of the loan. "Early payment" means payment before the maturity of the loan or payments earlier than the lender's scheduled payments.

Pro forma statement. An estimated balance sheet and profit and loss statement for a future operating period of a business or income property.

Property tax. The *ad valorem* tax on real property. The tax amount depends on the value of the property. The tax amount is calculated by multiplying the tax rate times the assessed value of the taxable property.

Qualified pension fund. A pension fund that is registered with the Internal Revenue Service as a tax-exempt financial institution.

Real estate investment. The purchase of an ownership interest in real property by the possessor of money or the loan of money to another party for the financing by that party of a real property's purchase and operation.

Real estate investment trust. A tax-exempt business trust for the investment of shareholder monies in real estate and mortgages. The tax-exempt real estate mutual fund which was established by Congress in 1960 through revision of the Internal Revenue Code. The financial intermediary was designed to permit the smaller investor to invest monies with others to participate in the financial rewards from real estate and mortgage ownership. Three general types of REITs developed: the equity, the mortgage, and the hybrid REITs.

Recapture rate. The percentage portion of the investment amount which will be returned to the investor every year of its economic life. The portion may be reinvested or not. The rate may be lower per year if the monies are to be reinvested as they are returned to the investor. The lowest recapture rate may be attained if the assumption is made that reinvestment will take place at current market yields. A rate lower than a straight-line rate but higher than an annuity rate may be attained with the assumption that reinvestment will take place at a conservative rate of interest rather than at a higher market rate of interest. The highest rate, the straight-line rate, may be found by dividing the economic life of the asset into 100 percent.

Refinancing. The restructuring of the original loan by the original lender or the replacement of the original loan with a new loan with different terms. The restructuring of the original loan may mean change in the loan term to maturity, the contract interest rate, the loan constant, the loan amount outstanding, and the call option or the prepayment penalty.

Refinancing, advantageous. The restructuring of an original loan with longer term to maturity, lower loan constant, lower contract interest rate, or higher loan amount. These changes would be considered favorable to most borrowers.

Regional shopping center. One to three full-line, major department stores along with many other smaller tenants, usually attracting shoppers from a driving radius of 15 to 30 minutes. Specialty, shopping, and convenience goods and services appeal to these potential consumers with adequate buying power.

Regulation Q. The Federal Reserve regulation which permits the establishment of maximum interest rates on various types of institutional deposits less than $100,000 in denomination. It is often nicknamed "Reg Q."

Residential mortgages. Mortgages placed on any residential property which includes single-family traditionally built houses, mobile homes, duplexes, triplexes, and other multifamily apartment buildings and their individual units.

Residual. Remaining portion. The surplus after another amount is taken away from the whole amount.

Restructuring a loan. Change of the terms of the original loan involving such terms as the contract interest rate, term to maturity, loan constant, the loan amount outstanding, the call option, or the prepayment penalty.

Return of investment. The return over time of the monies invested or loaned by the original party. Recapture of the original capital invested.

Return on investment. The interest and dividend income to the person investing money in an asset in addition to the return to the original owner of the original sum of money.

Risk/return relationship. The relationship between the amount of risk and the amount of investment return. Usually the preferred relationship is a relatively high investment return for the assumption of a relatively high degree of risk. In like manner, a relatively low investment return is usually associated with a relatively low degree of investment risk.

Savings and loan associations. One of the two thrift institutions that serve the consumer, business and government with depository income and residential mortgage loan primarily. The S&L is chartered either by the Federal Home Loan Bank Board or the appropriate state department of financial institutions. The vast majority of its deposits are insured up to $100,000 by the Federal Savings and Loan Insurance Corporation.

Secondary mortgage market. The mortgage market in which existing mortgages are traded among individuals, primary mortgage lenders, and secondary mortgage market institutions.

Secondary mortgage market institutions. The specially designed financial institutions which do mortgage business in the secondary mortgage market include the Federal National Mortgage Association, the Federal Home Loan Mortgage Corporation, and the Government National Mortgage Association. At times privately owned secondary mortgage market institutions, such as MGIC Investment Corporation, also trade mortgages in the secondary market.

Seller-financed loans. Loans which are financed by the seller of the asset. The buyer of the asset gives a mortgage or an unsecured promissory note with a cash down payment to the seller in return for the title to the seller's property.

Shared equity mortgages. The lender shares with the mortgagor the increased value of the financed property.

Shopping center. The planned and integrated retail center usually created by a real estate developer and financed by mortgages and equity contributions from long-term investors.

Shopping goods and services. The goods and services for which the consumer shops. Time is taken for comparison of price, quality, quantity, color, style, and manufacturer guarantees. The consumer will travel some distance in order to do comparison shopping among alternative goods and services.

Sinking fund. A fund or reserve established by the addition of cash periodically to the existing accumulated amount. From the amounts set aside and the interest received from their investment at a conservative rate of interest, usually below the market yield from the property, the capital originally invested in the asset is recouped or recaptured.

Sinking fund recapture rate. The conservative rate of interest that is assumed for the investment of amounts periodically set aside to recapture the original capital investment. This rate of interest may be the regular savings rate of the local financial institutions or a Treasury security rate. The rate of interest represents a high degree of liquidity, a low degree of financial risk, and a low degree of interest rate risk. This rate may be added to the investor's required rate of return in order to arrive at an appropriate capitalization rate.

Socialism. A form of government characterized by numerous government programs for the social welfare of its citizens. Most industries are owned and operated by the government in order to serve the collective needs of its citizens. Private enterprise represents a low portion of personal and business enterprise.

Specialty goods and services. The consumer seeks special qualities and manufacturer's labels in these goods and services which deserve perhaps extended search and considerable travel time. Very few substitutable goods and services are acceptable to the particular buyer. Camera equipment, antique furniture, and expensive foreign car repair are examples of specialty goods and services.

Specialty shopping center. A complex of independent, nonchain retail stores that offer to shoppers primarily specialty goods and services. It may be a retail complex of small boutiques of relatively high-priced lines which draws consumers from a substantial distance.

Speculation. Investment when little is known about the dimensions of the investment risk. There is a great amount of uncertainty. The future consequences may range over a wide span of risk and dollar profits and losses.

Square foot. Two-dimensional space one foot wide and one foot deep.

Stock. The common and preferred shares that show ownership interest in a corporation.

Sum-of-the-years-digits method of depreciation calculation. The remaining economic life in years is divided by the sum of the digits in the original economic life to find the current year's allowable depreciation deduction.

Superregional shopping center. A retail complex which was planned and developed under the control of a single developer which has four or more major department stores. It may be located in the central business district of an urban area or in a suburban area of substantial consumer population and overall retail buying power.

Syndicate. A business organization where a syndicate manager makes an offering and sells syndicate shares to an investor clientele which hope to gain reasonable yields from joint real estate ownership with professional management.

Syndicate share. A portion of the ownership of syndicated property.

Tax-deductible expenses. Business or personal expenses which may be deducted for federal income tax purposes by the taxpayer.

Tax exempt. Not subject to federal income taxation. Perhaps also not subject to income taxation of certain states of the nation.

Tax-free proceeds from refinancing. When the original loan that has been paid down some is refinanced, often the borrower asks the lender to increase the amount of the loan perhaps up to or exceeding its original amount. The other terms of the loan may also be changed such as the required debt service; the loan constant may be changed, for example. The Internal Revenue regulations permit the borrower to take away from the transaction monies which are tax free for federal income tax purposes. The refinancing may take place because the financed property has increased in value while the outstanding loan amount has been reduced substantially.

Tax laws. The tax laws and regulations of the Internal Revenue Service and the revenue departments and agencies of the state and local governments.

Tax shelter. The deductibility of expenses which leads to a reduction of the taxable income and, therefore, to the reduction of payment of federal income taxes.

Tenant. The individual or business who holds the right of possession to the leased space. For the right of possession this individual or business must usually pay rent to the individual or business with the original right of possession.

Termination. Conclusion. Sale. End of investment holding period.

Title theory state. A state that operates under the legal theory that, when a mortgage or deed of trust is given by the borrower to the lender or trustee, the title to the property is transferred by the borrower to that party. The lender permits the borrower to occupy the mortgaged property until a default on the mortgage or note occurs.

Traditional mortgage lenders. The traditional mortgage lenders include commercial banks, savings and loan associations, mutual savings banks, life insurance companies, and pension funds.

Treasury Department. The financial department of the executive branch of the United States government that prints currency, mints coins, and finances the federal government expenditures with sales and purchases of various forms of securities guaranteed by the full faith and credit of the federal government and with the collection of federal income taxes. The Treasury Department carries out the fiscal policies of the government by trading in Treasury securities and by collecting taxes.

Treasury, Secretary of. A cabinet officer of the executive branch of the federal government who represents the Treasury Department.

Treasury securities. Financial contracts, not secured by collateral, which are sold by the federal government of the United States to finance its operations and to stabilize the economy. The agreements of indebtedness are sold in various terms to maturity and in various amounts. The repayment of the principal and interest is guaranteed by the good faith and credit of the United States government.

Trough. The lowest point of a fluctuating phenomenon. The lowest economic condition with the greatest unemployment rate and the lowest levels of personal and business incomes of the economic and business cycle.

Trust deed. A pledge of real estate collateral in return for money where there is a three-party financing agreement. The trustor is the borrower, the trustee holds the title to the collateral, and the beneficiary loans the money.

Trustee. The middleman or fiduciary agent in a trust deed who holds the title to the pledge property.

Trustor. The borrower on the basis of a trust deed.

Usury rate. A maximum rate of investment yield which may be received by a mortgage lender from the nominal rate of interest and the prepaid interest. If the lender's yield from these sources surpasses the usury rate, the borrower may be refunded the usurious interest or the lender may forfeit the loan principal and previously accepted interest.

Variable-rate mortgage. A mortgage whose interest rates for debt service purposes change with a selected money and capital market index or a selected, basic interest rate, such as the commercial paper rate or the bank prime rate. Periodic mortgage payments may change as the effective rate changes. The lender, otherwise, may change the term of the loan as the rate changes rather than change the established mortgage payment.

INDEX